The Great War and Medieval Memory

This is a genuinely comparative study of the cultural impact of the Great War on British and German societies in the first half of the twentieth century. Taking public commemorations as its focus, this book unravels the search of Britons and Germans for historical continuity and meaning in the shadow of an unprecedented human catastrophe. In both countries, the survivors of the Great War pictured the conflict as the 'Last Crusade' and sought consolation in imagery that connected the soldiers of the age of total war with the knights of the Middle Ages. Stefan Goebel shows that medievalism as a mode of war commemoration transcended national and cultural boundaries. This is an invaluable contribution to the burgeoning study of cultural memory and collective remembrance which will appeal to researchers and students in the history of the First World War, social and cultural history of warfare and medieval studies.

STEFAN GOEBEL is Lecturer in Modern British History at the University of Kent at Canterbury and Visiting Fellow at the Institute of Historical Research, London.

D1351230

Studies in the Social and Cultural History of Modern Warfare

General Editor

Jay Winter *Yale University*

Advisory Editors

Omer Bartov *Brown University*
Carol Gluck *Columbia University*
David M. Kennedy *Stanford University*
Paul Kennedy *Yale University*
Antoine Prost *Université de Paris-Sorbonne*
Emmanuel Sivan *Hebrew University of Jerusalem*
Robert Wohl *University of California, Los Angeles*

In recent years the field of modern history has been enriched by the exploration of two parallel histories. These are the social and cultural history of armed conflict, and the impact of military events on social and cultural history.

Studies in the Social and Cultural History of Modern Warfare presents the fruits of this growing area of research, reflecting both the colonisation of military history by cultural historians and the reciprocal interest of military historians in social and cultural history, to the benefit of both. The series offers the latest scholarship in European and non-European events from the 1850s to the present day.

For a list of titles in the series, please see end of book.

The Great War and Medieval Memory

War, Remembrance and Medievalism in Britain and Germany, 1914–1940

Stefan Goebel

University of Kent at Canterbury

CAMBRIDGE UNIVERSITY PRESS
Cambridge, New York, Melbourne, Madrid, Cape Town, Singapore,
São Paulo, Delhi, Dubai, Tokyo

Cambridge University Press
The Edinburgh Building, Cambridge CB2 8RU, UK

Published in the United States of America by Cambridge University Press, New York

www.cambridge.org
Information on this title: www.cambridge.org/9780521123068

First published 2007
Reprinted 2008
This digitally printed version 2009

A catalogue record for this publication is available from the British Library

ISBN 978-0-521-85415-3 Hardback
ISBN 978-0-521-12306-8 Paperback

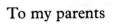
To my parents

Contents

Illustrations

Acknowledgments

Many scholars have helped me in numerous ways since I started working on the remembrance of the Great War almost ten years ago, and to all of them I would like to express my gratitude. Special thanks are due to Jay Winter for his encouragement and help at all phases of this project. Malcolm Gaskill gave crucial advice on how to turn a thesis into a book. For comments on the text as a whole I am also grateful to Alexander Baer, Richard Bessel, Ana Carden-Coyne, Richard J. Evans, Adrian Gregory, and Gerhard Schneider. For comments on specific points and chapters, I wish to thank Marcus Clausius, Santanu Das, Cian Duffy, Helen Evans, Stefan Haas, Hubertus Jahn, Derek Keene, Reinhart Koselleck, Peter Martland, Aribert Reimann, and Bernhard Rieger. I am also obliged to my editor at Cambridge University Press, Isabelle Dambricourt.

I have benefited from generous financial support from the following organisations, to which I am indebted: the Arts and Humanities Research Board (now Council); the University of Cambridge and the Cambridge History Faculty; Churchill College, Cambridge; Magdalene College, Cambridge; the Leverhulme Trust, London; the Centre de Recherche de l'Historial de la Grande Guerre, Péronne; and the Sir John Plumb Charitable Trust, Cambridge. Post-doctoral Research Fellowships at Churchill College, Cambridge, and at the Centre for Metropolitan History at the Institute of Historical Research, London, provided congenial communities for the discussion of ideas explored in this book.

I should like to record my warm appreciation to the staff in the following archives and libraries in Britain and Germany: Bedford Central Library; Cambridge University Library; County Record Office, Cambridge; King's College Modern Archives Centre, Cambridge; Essex Record Office, Colchester; Cathedral Archives, Coventry; Herefordshire Record Office, Hereford; Suffolk Record Office, Bury St Edmunds and Ipswich; Stewartry Museum, Kirkcudbright; Leeds Central Library; West Yorkshire Archive Service, Leeds; British Library, London;

Guildhall Library, London; Imperial War Museum, London; National Inventory of War Memorials, London; Public Record Office at the National Archives, Kew; St Paul's Cathedral Library, London; Westminster Abbey Muniment Room and Library, London; Commonwealth War Graves Commission, Records Section, Maidenhead; Norfolk Record Office, Norwich; Christ Church Archive, Oxford; Keble College Archive, Oxford; St Helens Local History and Archives Library; Eton College Archives, Windsor; York Minster Library and Archives; Niedersächsisches Staatsarchiv Aurich; Bundesarchiv, Berlin; Geheimes Staatsarchiv Preußischer Kulturbesitz, Berlin; Landesarchiv Berlin; Hochschularchiv of the Technische Universität Berlin; Staatsarchiv Bremen; Stadtarchiv Dorsten; Stadtarchiv Dortmund; Stadtarchiv Düsseldorf; Stadtarchiv Essen; Stadtarchiv Hagen; Warburg-Haus, Hamburg; Volksbund Deutsche Kriegsgräberfürsorge e.V., Kassel; Stadtarchiv Leer; Staatsarchiv Munich; Stadtarchiv Munich; Nordrhein-Westfälisches Staatsarchiv Münster; Universitäts- und Landesbibliothek Münster; Bibliothek für Zeitgeschichte, Stuttgart; Hauptstaatsarchiv Stuttgart; Stadtarchiv Stuttgart; and Stadtarchiv Ulm. Unless I indicate otherwise, all translations of German sources are my own.

Every effort has been made to secure necessary permissions to reproduce copyright material in this book, though in some cases it has proved impossible to trace copyright holders. If any omissions are brought to my notice, I shall be happy to include appropriate acknowledgements on reprinting. For permission to cite from copyright material, I should like to thank the Provost and Scholars of King's College, Cambridge (unpublished writings of Eric Milner-White copyright the Provost and Scholars of King's College, Cambridge); the Keeper of the Ely Diocesan Records and Dean and Chapter Archives at Cambridge University Library; the Provost and Fellows of Eton College, Windsor; the Dean and Chapter of Westminster Abbey; and the Guildhall Library, Corporation of London. Parts of chapters 3 and 4 were first published in different form in Pearl James (ed.), *Picture This! Reading World War I Posters* (Lincoln, NE, University of Nebraska Press, 2006). Portions of chapter 5 first appeared in the *Journal of Contemporary History* and are reprinted here by kind permission of Sage Publications.

Many institutions and individuals provided me with illustrations of war memorials and wartime artworks. For permission to reproduce images in this volume I am grateful to the Courtauld Institute of Art, London; Commonwealth War Graves Commission, Maidenhead; Norfolk Record Office, Norwich; Eton College, Windsor; Geheimes

Staatsarchiv Preußischer Kulturbesitz, Berlin; Staatsarchiv Bremen; Stadtarchiv Dorsten; Stadtarchiv Dortmund; Museum Folkwang, Essen; Gerhard Schneider, Freiburg; Stadtarchiv Hagen; Stadtarchiv Kaiserslautern; Volksbund Deutsche Kriegsgräberfürsorge e.V., Kassel; Stiebner Verlag, Munich; Gymnasium Dionysianum, Rheine; Bibliothek für Zeitgeschichte, Stuttgart; Matthaes Verlag, Stuttgart; Stadtarchiv Stuttgart; Stadtarchiv Ulm; and Ingeborg and Dr Wolfgang Henze-Ketterer, Witrach/Bern. The photographs of the Unknown Warrior and the Oddington war memorial published in this book are courtesy of the Imperial War Museum, London. The image of the Scottish National War Memorial is courtesy of the Trustees of the Scottish National War Memorial. The sketch of a memorial cross by Ninian (later Sir Ninian) Comper is reproduced by kind permission of the Warden and Fellows of Keble College, Oxford. Jonathan Black lent me the photograph of the T. E. Lawrence effigy by Eric Kennington, which is reproduced here by permission of the family of the artist. The Photographic Unit of the Templeman Library, University of Kent provided technical assistance with the photos and digital images.

Most of all, I have to thank my wife Irini and my parents for their unfailing encouragement and support (and my father, in particular, for running our private *Fernleihe* service between Münster and Cambridge/London). This book is dedicated to Heinz and Renate Goebel.

Abbreviations

BArch	Bundesarchiv, Berlin
BfZ	Bibliothek für Zeitgeschichte, Stuttgart
CAC	Cathedral Archives, Coventry
CROC	County Record Office, Cambridge
CUL	Cambridge University Library
CWGC	Commonwealth War Graves Commission, Maidenhead
EROC	Essex Record Office, Colchester
GStAPK	Geheimes Staatsarchiv Preußischer Kulturbesitz, Berlin
HStAS	Hauptstaatsarchiv Stuttgart
IWM	Imperial War Museum, London
KCMAC	King's College Modern Archives Centre, Cambridge
LCL	Leeds Central Library
NIWM	National Inventory of War Memorials at the Imperial War Museum, London
NRO	Norfolk Record Office, Norwich
PRO	Public Record Office, The National Archives, Kew
SROI	Suffolk Record Office, Ipswich
StA	Staatsarchiv
StAA	Niedersächsisches Staatsarchiv Aurich
StAB	Staatsarchiv Bremen
StAMS	Nordrhein-Westfälisches Staatsarchiv Münster
StdA	Stadtarchiv
StdAD	Stadtarchiv Düsseldorf
StdADO	Stadtarchiv Dortmund
StdAE	Stadtarchiv Essen
StdAH	Stadtarchiv Hagen
StdAL	Stadtarchiv Leer
StdAM	Stadtarchiv Munich
StdAU	Stadtarchiv Ulm

TUB	Hochschularchiv, Technische Universität Berlin
WAML	Westminster Abbey Muniment Room and Library, London
Warburg-Haus, Bildindex	Warburg-Haus, Hamburg, Bildindex zur politischen Ikonographie
WYASL	West Yorkshire Archive Service, Leeds

Introduction

In the aftermath of the first global and mass-industrialised war, contemporary observers coined the terms 'the Great War' and 'der große Krieg' to suggest a temporal watershed, a departure from the conditions of warfare as they had been known before. The Great War of 1914–18 and its attendant emotional shocks and socio-political upheavals rocked the foundations of all belligerent European societies. Some survivors, though, set out to heal the fractures of war by asserting historical continuity through memorials and acts of remembrance. The aim of war commemoration should be, the architect Herbert (later Sir Herbert) Baker suggested shortly after the Armistice, 'to express the heritage of unbroken history and beauty of England which the sacrifices of our soldiers have kept inviolate'.[1]

This book explores the kind of temporal anchoring in the wake of the Great War envisaged by Baker, but from a comparative, Anglo-German perspective (excluding Ireland).[2] In both Great Britain and Germany, there were people whose epochal consciousness was premised on continuity, people who refused to see history as irretrievably past. Looking to a misty past in order to understand the war-torn present, they enveloped recollections of the First World War in an imagery derived from interpretations of native, pre-industrial history, particularly the Middle Ages. The 'medievalising' of the memory of the Great War is the subject-matter of this study. It argues that the Middle Ages figured centrally in the remembrance of the First World War in both Britain and Germany between 1914 and 1940. The Crusades, chivalry and medieval spirituality and mythology provided rich, protean sources of images, tropes and narrative motifs for people to give meaning to the legacy of the Great War.

---

[1] Herbert Baker, 'War Memorials: The Ideal of Beauty', *The Times*, 41993, 9 January 1919, p. 9.

[2] For a discussion of war and remembrance in Ireland, see Keith Jeffery, *Ireland and the Great War* (Cambridge, Cambridge University Press, 2000), ch. 4; Anne Dolan, *Commemorating the Irish Civil War: History and Memory, 1923–2000* (Cambridge, Cambridge University Press, 2003).

Sites of mourning, sites of mobilisation

Scholars have interpreted war commemorations in general, and war memorials in particular, as either sites of personal mourning or as sites of political (re)mobilisation. Grief was ubiquitous by the end of the First World War, but arguably, so were anger and resentment at the unfulfilled expectations of August 1914. In terms of casualties, the war's toll was appallingly high; in the military service of Britain and Germany roughly one in eight/six men died.[3] Politically, Britain had not been transformed into the promised 'land fit for heroes', while Germany was burdened with the twin problems of defeat and revolution.[4] The rituals and rhetoric of war commemoration have thus been read as attempts to console the bereaved or soothe the frustrated.

In an influential article published in 1981, David Cannadine draws attention to the existential character of commemorative activities. British war memorials, he argues, 'were in large part spontaneously generated by the bereaved for their own comfort [. . .] this "cult of the dead" was not so much "an expression of patriotism" as a display of bereavement'.[5] Jay Winter, taking his cue from Cannadine, is the most eloquent and decided representative of what might be called the grief school, a historiographical school which assesses the cost of war at much more intimate levels than historians interested in nationalism and identity politics. Winter's main contribution to the debate, which appeared in 1995 under the programmatic title *Sites of Memory, Sites of Mourning*, surveys the cultural history of the war in western Europe with the politics left out.[6] The proliferation of commemorative artefacts and signifying practices (both public and private), he suggests, were above all

[3] J[ay] M. Winter, *The Great War and the British People* (Basingstoke and London, Macmillan, 1986), provides full casualty figures.
[4] For an introduction, see Richard Bessel, *Germany after the First World War* (Oxford, Clarendon, 1993); Gerard J. DeGroot, *Blighty: British Society in the Era of the Great War* (London and New York, Longman, 1996).
[5] David Cannadine, 'War and Death, Grief and Mourning in Modern Britain', in Joachim Whaley (ed.), *Mirrors of Mortality: Studies in the Social History of Death* (London, Europa, 1981), p. 219.
[6] Jay Winter, *Sites of Memory, Sites of Mourning: The Great War in European Cultural History* (Cambridge, Cambridge University Press, 1995). This book has inspired many titles in the *Studies in the Social and Cultural History of Modern Warfare* (Cambridge, Cambridge University Press) and *The Legacy of the Great War* (Berg) series, both edited by Jay Winter. See, for example, David W. Lloyd, *Battlefield Tourism: Pilgrimage and the Commemoration of the Great War in Great Britain, Australia and Canada, 1919–1939* (Oxford and New York, Berg, 1998); Joy Damousi, *The Labour of Loss: Mourning, Memory and Wartime Bereavement in Australia* (Cambridge, Cambridge University Press, 1999).

reflections of the depth of the trauma of 1914–18, understood as a sustained mass experience leaving particularly dense memory traces.[7]

This is not to say that one huge community of suffering was created by the losses of the Great War; what mattered was the accumulated presence of death in society, and it is through this fog that individual emotions were mediated. War memorials providing symbolic foci of bereavement functioned as substitutes for the graves of the missing and the absent dead (soldiers and sailors).[8] Notably, in Britain and Germany, the two major belligerents which, generally speaking, did not repatriate their fallen soldiers, monuments helped to trigger memory in the absence of bodies. Originally advanced by historians of Britain, the grief theory has recently been endorsed by works on the German memory landscape. A thorough case study of the Rhenish district of Viersen stresses the sombre, existential purpose of war memorials and – despite French occupation – their relative freedom from expressions of bitterness and revanchism.[9]

In placing emphasis on the personal instead of the political, these authors react against an older strain of historiography which has neglected to take seriously contemporaries' need to mourn the dead. The functionalist school conceptualises memory as a resource of symbolic power which can be marshalled just like material power. In a groundbreaking article published as early as 1978, Reinhart Koselleck traces the evolution of the cult of the fallen soldier in Europe since the late eighteenth century. In the modern age, Koselleck maintains, the meaning of death is no longer attached to references to the hereafter. Instead, political meanings of this world are invented. The war memorial as a political tool, Koselleck writes, 'gives the remembering of the soldiers'

[7] Jay Winter and Emmanuel Sivan, 'Setting the Framework', in Jay Winter and Emmanuel Sivan (eds.), *War and Remembrance in the Twentieth Century* (Cambridge, Cambridge University Press, 1999), pp. 6–39. See also Paul Lerner and Mark S. Micale, 'Trauma, Psychiatry, and History: A Conceptual and Historiographical Introduction', in Mark S. Micale and Paul Lerner (eds.), *Traumatic Pasts: History, Psychiatry, and Trauma in the Modern Age, 1870–1930* (Cambridge, Cambridge University Press, 2001), pp. 20–1.

[8] K[en] S. Inglis, 'War Memorials: Ten Questions for Historians', *Guerres Mondiales et Conflits Contemporains*, 167 (1992), p. 9.

[9] Arie Nabrings, '. . . eine immerfort während Mahnung . . .': Denkmäler für die Gefallenen des 1. Weltkriegs im Kreis Viersen* (Viersen, Kreis Viersen, 1996), pp. 125, 141. On nearby Düsseldorf, see Susanne Brandt, 'Trauer und fortgesetzter Krieg: Totengedenken zwischen Trauer und Kriegsverherrlichung in Düsseldorf nach dem Ersten Weltkrieg', in Jost Dülffer and Gerd Krumeich (eds.), *Der verlorene Frieden: Politik und Kriegskultur nach 1918* (Essen, Klartext, 2002), p. 260. On rural Bavaria, see Benjamin Ziemann, *Front und Heimat: Ländliche Kriegserfahrungen im südlichen Bayern 1914–1923* (Essen, Klartext, 1997), p. 460.

4   The Great War and Medieval Memory

death an earthly function directed only towards the future of those still living. This disappearance of the Christian interpretation of death creates a vacuum for the establishment of purely political and social meanings.'[10] In subsequent publications, Koselleck and his pupils have refined the argument, but the late Professor Koselleck's definitive work on European war memorials was still unpublished at his death. Meanwhile, George L. Mosse has written a stimulating account of Great War remembrance and its nineteenth-century precursors, extending the work of Koselleck. In his book *Fallen Soldiers*, Mosse shows how the dual impulses of trivialisation and sacralisation played into the hands of extremist forces who thus managed to instrumentalise the memory of the world war.[11] A congenial discourse to right-wing politics, war commemoration, especially in Germany, became eventually subsumed in rehearsals for fascism.

The functionalist position taken by Koselleck and Mosse reflects two general features of the German historiographical agenda: its political focus and its preoccupation with National Socialism. Mosse's *ideologiekritisch* stance on inter-war commemoration, in particular, has been moulded by the Nazi cult of the dead. With the wisdom of hindsight, he conflates the phenomenon of war memory with its fascist incarnations. Unsurprisingly, British research into the political implications of war remembrance has, by and large, followed a different trajectory, emphasising negotiation rather than manipulation. Nevertheless the work of Bob Bushaway departs from this interpretative pattern. Like Mosse, he assumes that commemorations reinforced a kind of false consciousness. But unlike Mosse, Bushaway construes the British cult of the fallen soldier as a force of social integration and moderate conservatism instead of political polarisation and extreme nationalism. The elevation of the dead, Bushaway points out, inhibited criticism of Britain's social and political constitution.[12] By contrast, other scholars

---

[10] Reinhart Koselleck, 'Kriegerdenkmale als Identitätsstiftungen der Überlebenden', in Odo Marquard and Karlheinz Stierle (eds.), *Identität* (Munich, Wilhelm Fink, 1979), p. 259. More recently, Koselleck has developed his ideas in *Zur politischen Ikonologie des gewaltsamen Todes: Ein deutsch–französischer Vergleich* (Basle, Schwabe, 1998). See also Reinhart Koselleck and Michael Jeismann (eds.), *Der politische Totenkult: Kriegerdenkmäler in der Moderne* (Munich, Wilhelm Fink, 1994). Two important works inspired by Koselleck are Meinhold Lurz, *Kriegerdenkmäler in Deutschland*, 6 vols. (Heidelberg, Esprint, 1985–7); Gerhard Schneider, '. . . nicht umsonst gefallen'? *Kriegerdenkmäler and Kriegstotenkult in Hannover* (Hanover, Hahn, 1991).

[11] George L. Mosse, *Fallen Soldiers: Reshaping the Memory of the World Wars* (New York and Oxford, Oxford University Press, 1990).

[12] Bob Bushaway, 'Name upon Name: The Great War and Remembrance', in Roy Porter (ed.), *Myths of the English* (Cambridge, Polity, 1992), pp. 136–67. See also his more

have revealed the multivocality of commemorative discourses. Alex King, in his exhaustive study *Memorials of the Great War in Britain*, finds that the dead were invoked in both conservative and radical causes. Moreover, he allows that bereavement remained a decisive factor: 'Personal feelings and needs were deeply involved in the practice of commemoration; but it was the organisation of public action which gave it form. At the same time, commemoration raised political issues which participants had to address.'[13]

This study aims to synthesise the two schools of thought outlined above. The commemorations I analyse colonised the grey area between the personal and the political. The survivors' decision to remember collectively, to act in public, originated in the overwhelming experience of war as trauma. While remembrance activities could not cure sadness, they helped with the management of bereavement. Narrowly political readings of war commemorations, treating them as monumental mani-festos, have overlooked this aspect of their significance. Yet if mourning was profoundly personal, remembrance – through the establishment of social networks and the formulation of languages of commemoration – was a socially framed, value-laden practice and thus inherently political (in the broadest sense). The challenge is, however, to avoid the pitfall of equating political with politicised. To remember meant to affirm or reassemble community, to aver its legitimacy and morality, but not necessarily to engage in the partisan politics of the day. To be sure, the need of the bereaved for solemn, public acknowledgment of personal grief, on the one hand, and the interest of the state or its subsidiary

---

recent statement, 'The Obligation of Remembrance or the Remembrance of Obligation: Society and Memory of World War', in Peter Liddle, John Bourne and Ian Whitehead (eds.), *The Great World War 1914–45*, vol. II, *The Peoples' Experience* (London, Harper Collins, 2001), pp. 489–508. See also Nick Mansfield, 'Class Conflict and Village War Memorials, 1914–24', *Rural History*, 6 (1995), p. 84.

[13] Alex King, *Memorials of the Great War in Britain: The Symbolism and Politics of Remembrance* (Oxford and New York, Berg, 1998), p. 6. British war memorials have been thoroughly explored in recent years; see especially Mark Connelly, *The Great War, Memory and Ritual: Commemoration in the City and East London, 1916–1939* (Woodbridge and Rochester, NY, Boydell, 2002); Angela Gaffney, *Aftermath: Remembering the Great War in Wales* (Cardiff, University of Wales Press, 1998); Catherine Moriarty, 'Narrative and the Absent Body: Mechanisms of Meaning in First World War Memorials', D.Phil. dissertation, University of Sussex, 1995; Keith Grieves, 'Investigating Local War Memorial Committees: Demobilised Soldiers, the Bereaved and Expressions of Local Pride in Sussex Villages, 1918–1921', *Local Historian*, 30 (2000), pp. 39–58. For the purpose of comparison, see K[en] S. Inglis, *Sacred Places: War Memorials in the Australian Landscape* (Melbourne, Melbourne University Press, 1998); Chris Maclean and Jock Phillips, *The Sorrow and the Pride: New Zealand War Memorials* (Wellington, GP, 1990).

organisations in giving this some concrete political meaning, on the other, have frequently proved compatible.[14]

European convergences, national peculiarities, and sectional diversities

This book ventures into a significantly underdeveloped field of historical enquiry: empirical comparative history. Notwithstanding decades of European integration and burgeoning globalisation, the overwhelming majority of historians today are still imprisoned in the national framework firmly established by the founding fathers of our subject in the nineteenth century. The shortcomings and distorting effects of a narrowly national approach are particularly apparent in the field of cultural history, for its categories have never been national in scope or content. Still, those who have embarked on comparative cultural history in search of a panacea have found themselves opening up Pandora's box. The archival holdings are vast, the secondary literatures rarely congruent, and languages unevenly mastered. Cross-national approaches involve a radically selective treatment of the past and its documentation. But language poses probably the greatest obstacle of all. Salman Rushdie's dictum that a culture is defined by its untranslatable words highlights the problematical situation facing comparative cultural historians who presume a primacy of texts and languages.[15] In particular, the evocative rhetoric of medievalism tends to defy translation. I have attempted to

---

[14] See Peter Fritzsche, 'The Case of Modern Memory', *Journal of Modern History*, 73 (2001), pp. 107–8; T[imothy] G. Ashplant, Graham Dawson and Michael Roper, 'The Politics of War Memory and Commemoration: Contexts, Structures and Dynamics', in T[imothy] G. Ashplant, Graham Dawson and Michael Roper (eds.), *The Politics of War Memory and Commemoration* (London and New York, Routledge, 2000), pp. 3–85.

[15] Jay Winter, 'Shell-Shock and the Cultural History of the Great War', *Journal of Contemporary History*, 35 (2000), p. 8. See also Pierre Bourdieu, 'Die Besonderheiten der Nationalgeschichten: Vergleichende Geschichte relevanter Unterschiede zwischen den Nationen', in Pierre Bourdieu, *Schwierige Interdisziplinarität: Zum Verhältnis von Soziologie und Geschichtswissenschaft*, ed. Elke Ohnacker and Franz Schultheis (Münster, Westfälisches Dampfboot, 2004), p. 160. For a discussion of definitions and methodology, see Hartmut Kaelble, *Der historische Vergleich: Eine Einführung zum 19. and 20. Jahrhundert* (Frankfurt am Main and New York, Campus, 1999); Heinz-Gerhard Haupt and Jürgen Kocka, 'Historischer Vergleich: Methoden, Aufgaben, Probleme: Eine Einleitung', in Heinz-Gerhard Haupt and Jürgen Kocka (eds.), *Geschichte und Vergleich: Ansätze und Ergebnisse international vergleichender Geschichtsschreibung* (Frankfurt am Main and New York, Campus, 1996), pp. 9–45; Deborah Cohen and Maura O'Connor, 'Introduction: Comparative History, Cross-National History, Transnational History – Definitions', in Deborah Cohen and Maura O'Connor (eds.), *Comparison and History: Europe in Cross-National Perspective* (New York and London, Routledge, 2004), pp. ix–xxiv.

render quotations from German sources into English, but the polyglot reader should consult the German originals provided in the notes.

The marginality of comparative research contrasts with the prominence of comparative assumptions and statements. A whole generation of critical German social historians has claimed that the German way of modernisation represented a *Sonderweg*, a 'special path', which diverged from the western democracies, notably Britain and France, and ultimately led to the Nazi dictatorship. Today, many historians believe the *Sonderweg* thesis to be dead, buried in the 1980s by British historians working on modern German history and its peculiarities.[16] Yet Heinrich August Winkler has recently revived the idea in his magisterial *Der lange Weg nach Westen*, a history of Germany from the end of the Holy Roman Empire to the reunification. 'There *was* a German *Sonderweg*', he concludes, 'It was the long path towards modernity taken by a country shaped and moulded by the Middle Ages.'[17] Such a sweeping comparative conclusion to a mono-national study – quite illustrative of a number of works on the German *Sonderweg* – is both theoretically and methodologically problematic.[18] First, it makes a normative presupposition, setting the exceptional (German) against the normal (western) model. Second, it is not the result of a thorough exploration of the comparative method, but of selective readings of Anglo-American and French secondary works.

The notion of a German special path of commemoration is also established in the corpus of the historiography of the First World War, although most authors eschew the *Sonderweg* terminology. George L. Mosse contends that the cult of the fallen soldier, while non-poisonous in the victorious countries, namely Britain and France, had not only greater urgency in defeated Germany, reinforcing fascism, but also a brutal edge, legitimising violence.[19] While Mosse in his broad survey of four nations necessarily paints with bold strokes, narrower approaches singling out one specific feature for comparison have the advantage of drawing a more

---

[16] David Blackbourn and Geoff Eley, *The Peculiarities of German History: Bourgeois Society and Politics in Nineteenth-Century Germany* (Oxford, Oxford University Press, 1984); Richard J. Evans, *Rethinking German History: Nineteenth-Century Germany and the Origins of the Third Reich* (London, Unwin Hyman, 1987).

[17] Heinrich August Winkler, *The Long Shadow of the Reich: Weighing up German History* (London, German Historical Institute, 2002), p. 20, author's italics; and his *Der lange Weg nach Westen*, vol. II, *Deutsche Geschichte vom 'Dritten Reich' bis zur Wiedervereinigung* (Munich, C. H. Beck, 2000), p. 648.

[18] John Breuilly, 'Introduction: Making Comparisons in History', in John Breuilly, *Labour and Liberalism in Nineteenth-Century Europe: Essays in Comparative History* (Manchester and New York, Manchester University Press, 1992), pp. 6–7.

[19] Mosse, *Fallen Soldiers*, pp. 106, 124.

nuanced, and perhaps balanced, picture. Nevertheless, a recent comparative study of French and German war memorials basically confirms Mosse's thesis. German memorials after 1918, this study concludes, were monumental manifestations of dull heroism, overt revanchism and martial manliness, whereas their French equivalents conveyed a broad spectrum of messages ranging from pacifism to patriotism. What is more, *monuments aux morts* were generally places where people assembled to grieve in public.[20] In a nutshell, it seems that the Germans mobilised and the French mourned. While victory meant cultural closure, defeat left a symbolic vacuum that the nationalists attempted to fill. The French side of this analysis owes much to the pioneering work of Antoine Prost.[21] War memorials in France, Prost tells us, evolved into sites where the veterans could teach their children that war was an abomination, never to be re-enacted – in stark contrast, it seems, to their bellicose German counterparts, unwilling to accept defeat.

Historical comparisons, Hartmut Kaelble has noted, tend to concentrate on national idiosyncrasies and to overlook cultural convergences.[22] Scholars disclosing the commonality of cultural history, however, often receive vicious criticism from their peers. Jay Winter has controversially drawn attention to the traditional overemphasis of the facts of victory and defeat. 'They mattered; but all too often victory had a taste of ashes.' He adds that 'all major combatants went through a "special" path, the path of collective slaughter'.[23] Victory was cool consolation for those who were in mourning. Among the major belligerents, Winter estimates, virtually every family had lost a father, a husband, a son, a brother or a friend. In fact, people were also shocked or sentimental about deaths of men they knew only slightly, or even not at all. The cultural history of the war is inseparable from its demographic history.[24] Death and

---

[20] Michael Jeismann and Rolf Westheider, 'Wofür stirbt der Bürger? Nationaler Totenkult und Staatsbürgertum in Deutschland und Frankreich seit der Französischen Revolution', in Reinhart Koselleck and Michael Jeismann (eds.), *Der politische Totenkult: Kriegerdenkmäler in der Moderne* (Munich, Wilhelm Fink, 1994), pp. 29–30. See also Omer Bartov, 'Trauma and Absence: France and Germany, 1914–1945', in Paul Addison and Angus Calder (eds.), *Time to Kill: The Soldier's Experience of War in the West 1939–1945* (London, Pimlico, 1997), pp. 353–4.

[21] Antoine Prost, 'Monuments to the Dead', in Pierre Nora (ed.), *Realms of Memory: The Reconstruction of the French Past*, vol. II, *Traditions* (New York, Columbia University Press, 1997), pp. 307–30. See also Antoine Prost, 'The Impact of War on French and German Political Cultures', *Historical Journal*, 37 (1994), pp. 209–17.

[22] Kaelble, *Der historische Vergleich*, p. 22.

[23] Winter, *Sites of Memory*, p. 227.

[24] Winter, *Great War*, ch. 9. See also Jay Winter, 'Forms of Kinship and Remembrance in the Aftermath of the Great War', in Jay Winter and Emmanuel Sivan (eds.), *War and*

bereavement became the salient signatures of the then bloodiest war in modern history and its cultural repercussions. The exploration of mourning uncovers fully the European dimension of the Great War. Nonetheless, the codes of mourning can differ between nations since they are drawn from the respective national repertoires of cultural forms and practices. At the same time, national styles of commemoration were not independent of one another, and the historian has to consider the importance of intersecting memories originating in mutual observation and – positive as well as negative – inter-cultural transfer.[25] For example, the meteoric rise of the institution of the unknown soldier throughout (and beyond) Europe – with the notable exception of Germany – illuminates the high degree of cultural exchange in the inter-war period.[26]

Even though the First World War was, by definition, a transnational event, commemoration was, on the whole, cast within the confines of national culture. The nation state has, therefore, remained the preferred analytical unit of cultural history. But increasingly, mono-national works employ an implicit or reflective comparative method, presenting national evidence in the light of international findings.[27] Adrian Gregory's powerful *The Silence of Memory*, an exploration of the British Armistice Day ritual between 1919 and 1946, uses comparison as a heuristic tool. It

Remembrance in the Twentieth Century (Cambridge, Cambridge University Press, 1999), pp. 40–60. A provocative reappraisal is offered by Adrian Gregory, 'Demobilizing the Nation: Remobilizing the Dead: The Persistent Mythologies of British Commemoration', paper presented at the conference on 'Demobilizing the Mind: Culture, Politics and the Legacy of the Great War, 1919–1933', Trinity College, Dublin, 26 August–8 September 2001.

[25] Stefan Goebel, 'Intersecting Memories: War and Remembrance in Twentieth-Century Europe', *Historical Journal*, 44 (2001), pp. 853–8. On the concepts of cultural transfers and entangled history, see Michel Espagne, 'Sur les limites du comparatisme en histoire culturelle', *Genèses*, 17 (1994), pp. 112–21; Michael Werner and Bénédicte Zimmermann, 'Vergleich, Transfer, Verflechtung: Der Ansatz der *Histoire croisée* und die Herausforderung des Transnationalen', *Geschichte und Gesellschaft*, 28 (2002), pp. 607–36. On cultural exchanges between Britain and Germany in particular, see Rudolf Muhs, Johannes Paulmann and Willibald Steinmetz (eds.), *Aneignung und Abwehr: Interkultureller Transfer zwischen Deutschland und Großbritannien im 19. Jahrhundert* (Bodenheim, Philo, 1998).

[26] K[en] S. Inglis, 'Entombing Unknown Soldiers: From London and Paris to Baghdad', *History and Memory*, 5, 2 (1993), pp. 7–31; Volker Ackermann, 'La vision allemande du soldat inconnu: débats politiques, réflexion philosophique et artistique', in Jean-Jacques Becker *et al.* (eds.), *Guerres et cultures, 1914–1918: Vers une histoire comparée de la Grande Guerre* (Paris, Armand Colin, 1994), pp. 385–96.

[27] Rudy Koshar, *From Monuments to Traces: Artifacts of German Memory, 1870–1990* (Berkeley, Los Angeles and London, University of California Press, 2000) is a good example.

seeks to answer the question why war remembrance in Britain was markedly different from the French and German models described by Prost and Mosse respectively. In the end, Gregory rejects the idea of a unitary national version of Great War remembrance but underlines the plurality of British memories of war. Instead of presenting a state-bounded narrative, he highlights sectional diversities (such as class, denomination, gender and region) within the national community of inter-war Britain.[28]

In sum, the comparative historian of the First World War seems to tread a tightrope between emphasising European convergences, national peculiarities, or sectional diversities within nations. However, the authors of *Capital Cites at War* conclude their collective research into the microcosms of wartime Paris, London and Berlin by reasserting that the 'analytical force of the comparison is [. . .] to revise and rejuvenate, rather than to reject, national histories. For only after discovering convergences [. . .] can true national distinctions be made.'[29]

Medievalism and the modern

Much recent writing of the Great War discusses to what extent the years 1914–18 marked a cultural disjuncture in contemporary history. What is at issue here is the significance of the war as the incubator of 'modernism', often understood as a new, iconoclastic language of truth-telling about war in art and literature. The controversy has been sparked off in 1975 by Paul Fussell's classic *The Great War and Modern Memory*. Analysing the writings of (ex-)servicemen like Wilfred Owen and Siegfried Sassoon and other, non-combatant writers like T. S. Eliot and Ezra Pound, Fussell comes to the conclusion that the war gave way to an attitude of ironic scepticism and bitter disillusionment.[30] Fussell's contention that there was a fundamental link between the

---

[28] Adrian Gregory, *The Silence of Memory: Armistice Day 1919–1946* (Oxford and Providence, Berg, 1994), p. 6. On regional peculiarities and comparative history, see Deborah Cohen, 'Comparative History: Buyer Beware', *Bulletin of the German Historical Institute, Washington, D.C.*, 29 (2001), p. 26.

[29] Jean-Louis Robert and Jay Winter, 'Conclusions: Towards a Social History of Capital Cities at War', in Jay Winter, Jean-Louis Robert [*et al.*], *Capital Cities at War: Paris, London, Berlin 1914–1919*, vol. I (Cambridge, Cambridge University Press, 1997), p. 553. See also the forthcoming second volume.

[30] Paul Fussell, *The Great War and Modern Memory* (London and Oxford, Oxford University Press, 1975), p. 35. See Leonard V. Smith, 'Paul Fussell's *The Great War and Modern Memory*: Twenty-Five Years Later', *History and Theory*, 40 (2001), pp. 241–60.

war and modernism has been echoed many times.[31] A more recent, stimulating contribution to the modernist interpretation is Samuel Hynes's examination of what he has dubbed the 'myth of the war' in British culture. The myth, defined as a narrative about the war, was generated by the clash of 'big words' like honour and glory with the terrors of combat. Those who experienced the ugliness of war identified the 'big words' with the elder generation who had sent them into battle. As a result, the young 'rejected the values of the society that had sent them to war, and in doing so separated their own generation from the past and from their cultural inheritance'.[32]

The issue of modernism represents primarily a preoccupation of Anglo-American scholars of the Great War, who have also exported the debate to German historiography. Modris Eksteins's *Rites of Spring* proposes an alternative concept of cultural modernity, revealing its Janus face. He argues that the First World War fostered and furthered a peculiar, misanthropic version of modernism, celebrating the beauty of violence and the power of the irrational, a development which culminated in the aestheticisation of Nazi politics. Germany, characterised by Eksteins as the quintessential dynamic nation, was in the vanguard of the modernist struggle for liberation through destruction whereas 'conservative' Britain upheld the traditional. Hence, European modernism bore the unmistakable stamp of apocalyptic German art (notably expressionism) and ethics. Reading European cultural history through German eyes, Eksteins states that the 'Great War was the psychological turning point, for Germany and for modernism as a whole. The urge to create and the urge to destroy changed places. The urge to destroy was intensified; the urge to create became increasingly abstract.'[33]

A second school of thought reads the war as a retarding rather than a progressive moment in cultural history. The upheaval of war led thus not to a rejection, but to a reiteration or even deepening of well-established

[31] Arthur Marwick, 'Painting and Music during and after the Great War: The Art of Total War', in Roger Chickering and Stig Förster (eds.), *Great War, Total War: Combat and Mobilization on the Western Front, 1914–1918* (Cambridge, Cambridge University Press, 2000), pp. 501–17; Allyson Booth, *Postcards from the Trenches: Negotiating the Space between Modernism and the First World War* (New York and Oxford, Oxford University Press, 1996); Douglas Mackaman and Michael Mays (eds.), *World War I and the Cultures of Modernity* (Jackson, University Press of Mississippi, 2000).

[32] Samuel Hynes, *A War Imagined: The First World War and English Culture* (London, Bodley Head, 1990), p. x.

[33] Modris Eksteins, *Rites of Spring: The Great War and the Birth of the Modern Age* (London, Bantam, 1989), p. 328. There are some overlaps between the interpretations of Eksteins and Herf. See Jeffrey Herf, *Reactionary Modernism: Technology, Culture, and Politics in Weimar and the Third Reich* (Cambridge, Cambridge University Press, 1984).

Victorian sentiments and the euphemisms of wartime propaganda. The war put the clock back from the modern in favour of the traditional. High diction providing the contemporaries with 'a "gold standard" of meaning' set the tone in the aftermath of the shocking experience of mass-industrialised warfare.[34]

To some degree, the scholarly dispute over traditionalism and modernism arises from the type of primary source material considered representative of the period. While the modernist school cites principally the works of intellectual writers and artists, traditionalists tend to rely on lowbrow and middlebrow accounts of the war. In recent years, historians have endeavoured to go beyond this divide between 'high' and 'low', arguing that the Great War blurred the boundaries between elite and popular culture. In both the expressionist painting by an acclaimed artist and the village war memorial by an undistinguished mason, they discern a tendency to hark back to earlier forms and notations. In contrast to acid irony, a traditional vocabulary of remembrance offered some consolation and allowed the bereaved to cope with their grief.[35]

The modernism debate is linked to the broader issue of fundamental caesuras in twentieth-century history. It has been suggested that Fussell's *The Great War and Modern Memory* is really about the author's own trial by fire as a combatant in the Second World War. Significantly, Fussell dedicated the book to a comrade 'Killed beside me in France March 15, 1945' (incidentally, Hynes, too, is a veteran of the Second World War).[36] In other words, 'modern memory' was the product of the Second World War rather than the First. While the horrors and losses of 1914–18 could still be encoded in coherent, meaningful, and time-honoured cultural forms, the experiences of 1939–45 ultimately shattered that possibility. After Auschwitz and Hiroshima, meaning and symbolism, intrinsic to the repercussions of Verdun and the Somme, became questionable concepts. The limits of representation have been reached, and yet artists are trying hard to give this state some form. Holocaust memorials, expressing speechlessness or enshrining voids, use the grammar of abstraction and deconstruction. Again, intellectuals

---

[34] Rosa Maria Bracco, *Merchants of Hope: British Middlebrow Writers and the First World War, 1919–1939* (Providence and Oxford, Berg, 1993), p. 220. See also Ted Bogacz, '"A Tyranny of Words": Language, Poetry, and Antimodernism in England in the First World War', *Journal of Modern History*, 58 (1986), pp. 643–68.
[35] See, especially, Winter, *Sites of Memory*, pp. 2–5, 225–8.
[36] J[ay] M. Winter, 'Catastrophe and Culture: Recent Trends in the Historiography of the First World War', *Journal of Modern History*, 64 (1992), p. 531. Compare Paul Fussell, *Wartime: Understanding and Behavior in the Second World War* (New York and Oxford, Oxford University Press, 1989).

have been ahead of their time and detached from a mass audience often puzzled by the paradox of post-war commemoration. Moreover, some echoes of older languages could be heard after 1945. In general, however, no recourse to the 'high diction' that had helped to accommodate the experience of the Great War took place in the long process of representing (or rather deconstructing) the 1939–45 conflict.[37]

Medievalism was the ultimate casualty of the Second World War. Inappropriate if not obscene after 1939–45, medievalist diction providing solace through the historical continuum of the wars and warriors of yore flourished after 1914–18. An accessible mode of war commemoration that ennobled the fallen and gave comfort to the bereaved, its building blocks had been assembled during the nineteenth century (c. 1800–1914): the Gothic revival in architecture; Romanticism in literature; the cult of chivalry in popular culture; the Arthurian revival and the Arts and Crafts movement in British art and design; Germanicism in German art and music. The very term 'medievalism', apparently coined by John Ruskin in the 1850s, is indicative of the historical consciousness of the nineteenth century. In the period between the Napoleonic wars and the outbreak of the Great War, the idealisation of the Middle Ages had pointed to dissatisfaction with the aesthetic, moral and social condition of contemporary society and a desire to return to (or at least to remember) the imagined harmony or purposefulness of the remote past.[38]

---

[37] For an introduction into the literature of Holocaust remembrance, see James E. Young, *The Texture of Memory: Holocaust Memorials and Meaning* (New Haven and London, Yale University Press, 1993). On cultural caesuras and the two world wars, see also Winter, *Sites of Memory*, pp. 9, 228–9.

[38] The literature on nineteenth-century medievalism is vast. Particularly important is the journal *Studies in Medievalism*, ed. Leslie J. Workman, first issue 1979. For an introduction, see also Florence S. Boos (ed.), *History and Community: Essays in Victorian Medievalism* (New York and London, Garland, 1992); Debra N. Mancoff (ed.), *The Arthurian Revival: Essays on Form, Tradition, Transformation* (New York and London, Garland, 1992); Gerd Althoff (ed.), *Die Deutschen and ihr Mittelalter: Themen and Funktionen moderner Geschichtsbilder vom Mittelalter* (Darmstadt, Wissenschaftliche Buchgesellschaft, 1992); Reinhard Elze and Pierangelo Schiera (eds.), *Italia e Germania: Immagini, modelli, miti fra due popoli nell'Ottocento: il Medioevo* (Berlin and Bologna, Duncker & Humblot, 1988). Medievalism in the first half of the twentieth century has received less attention. For some exceptions, see Otto Gerhard Oexle, 'Das Mittelalter und das Unbehagen an der Moderne: Mittelalterbeschwörungen in der Weimarer Republik and danach', in Susanna Burghartz et al. (eds.), *Spannungen und Widersprüche* (Sigmaringen, Jan Thorbecke, 1992), pp. 125–53; Hans Wisskirchen, 'Mittelalterrezeption um 1920: Ein Beitrag zur Wirklichkeitsbewältigung der bürgerlich-konservativen Intelligenz nach dem 1. Weltkrieg', in Rüdiger Krohn (ed.), *Forum: Materialien und Beiträge zur Mittelalter-Rezeption*, vol. I (Göppingen, Kümmerle, 1986), pp. 257–75.

The medieval past was a prism through which the contemporaries viewed the present. Medievalism is defined, according to its pre-eminent scholar, Leslie Workman, as 'the continuing process of creating the Middle Ages'.[39] This process had peaked during the nineteenth century; after 1914–18, medievalism entered into a new, distinctive phase. My study will show how pre-existing medievalist idioms took on new meanings from the context in which they were newly imbricated after the war. Prior to the 1914–18 conflict, medievalism had essentially been a discourse of identity, fuelled by cultural despair in the era of industrialisation. In the commemoration of the Great War, medievalism was transmuted into a discourse of mourning in an age of industrialised carnage, a discourse recovering the individual soldier who had perished in the anonymous battles of *matériel* of the machine age. Medievalism as a mode of war commemoration is best understood as a state of mind rather than a state of history, an amalgam of temporal notions rather than a coherent set of intellectual propositions. In fact, medievalist narratives incorporated a set of notations which the historian of today might classify as Germanic, Celtic or classical – notations which were, however, elaborations on the central theme.

Memory and remembrance

Memory has been on everyone's lips over the last decade, but the memory boom has particularly gripped the historical profession. Memory, some researchers claim, is now *the* new paradigm of historical study, overshadowing and reconfiguring established organising concepts such as class or gender.[40] Even so, communication in academia about memory has become increasingly difficult because the central term has different meanings to different authors. As a consequence, we are confronted with a multitude of memories: collective memory, communicative memory, cultural memory, public memory and social memory, to name but the most widespread examples. The common ground seems to be the assumption that memory constitutes a discursive construct or a cultural representation rather than a mirror or storehouse of past 'reality'. Such 'representations of the social world themselves are the constituents of social reality', as Roger Chartier reminds us, and there are no 'facts' separate from the language in which they are

[39] Leslie J. Workman, 'Preface', *Studies in Medievalism*, 8 (1996), p. 1.
[40] Jay Winter, 'The Generation of Memory: Reflections on the "Memory Boom" in Contemporary Historical Studies', *Bulletin of the German Historical Institute, Washington, D.C.*, 27 (2000), pp. 69–92.

encoded.[41] Discourse – practice – representation: Daniel J. Sherman summarises succinctly the key terminology used for analysing the construction of memory:

> *commemoration* mobilizes a variety of discourses and practices into a representation of an event or epoch; this representation contains within it a social and cultural vision it casts as inherent in the 'memory' of the commemorated event. *Discourse* may be defined, summarily, as a group of statements linked by their object; *representation* [. . .] is an operation, and the artifacts of that operation, that causes signs to stand for an absent referent. Representation constitutes a potentially endless process of the production of meaning.[42]

The term *memory* deserves further scrutiny. The observations of Jan Assmann about the workings of commemoration in antiquity have informed a general discussion, notably in German historiography.[43] Jan Assmann's theory (formulated in co-operation with Aleida Assmann) combines, in essence, the works of two pioneers of the study of memory, the sociologist Maurice Halbwachs and the art historian Aby Warburg. Assmann draws a distinction between two types, communicative and cultural memory. The concept of communicative memory, which follows Halbwachs's work on *mémoire collective*, is defined as the memory of everyday life. It is informal, amorphous, barely shaped, and based on interaction within social groups. 'Every individual memory constitutes itself in communication with others.'[44] Consequently, the duration of communicative memory is the duration of the group

[41] Roger Chartier, 'Intellectual History or Sociocultural History? The French Trajectories', in Dominick LaCapra and Steven L. Kaplan (eds.), *Modern European Intellectual History: Reappraisals and New Perspectives* (Ithaca and London, Cornell University Press, 1982), p. 41.

[42] Daniel J. Sherman, *The Construction of Memory in Interwar France* (Chicago and London, University of Chicago Press, 1999), p. 6, author's italics.

[43] Jan Assmann, *Das kulturelle Gedächtnis: Schrift, Erinnerung and politische Identität in frühen Hochkulturen* (Munich, C. H. Beck, 2nd edn 1997); Aleida Assmann, *Arbeit am nationalen Gedächtnis: Eine kurze Geschichte der deutschen Bildungsidee* (Frankfurt am Main and New York, Campus, 1993). For a reappraisal of these works, see Clemens Wischermann (ed.), *Die Legitimität der Erinnerung und die Geschichtswissenschaft* (Stuttgart, Franz Steiner, 1996). In subsequent publications, Jan and Aleida Assmann have refined their definition of collective and cultural memory. See Jan Assmann, 'Einführung: Was ist das "kulturelle Gedächtnis"?', in Jan Assmann, *Religion und kulturelles Gedächtnis: Zehn Studien* (Munich, C. H. Beck, 2000), pp. 11–44; Aleida Assmann, *Erinnerungsräume: Formen and Wandlungen des kulturellen Gedächtnisses* (Munich, C. H. Beck, 1999).

[44] Jan Assmann, 'Collective Memory and Cultural Identity', *New German Critique*, 65 (1995), p. 127. See Maurice Halbwachs, *The Collective Memory* (New York, Harper & Row, 1980).

producing it. It is bound to die out after three generations – if not transformed into cultural memory.

Cultural memory, this second type, constitutes a community's collective memory materialised in forms and practices and referring to a distant past. Cultural memory has, therefore, to rely on a system of memory aids like rites, myths or monuments supervised by specialists. At this point, Assmann reintroduces Warburg's idea of the enduring mnemonic power of cultural artefacts, an aspect which has been neglected by Halbwachs. However, the notion of a nexus between cultural memory and social framework is Halbwachsian. It is noteworthy that, according to Assmann, the commemoration of the dead represents a special case. The memory of death occupies an intermediate position between spontaneous communicative memory and elaborate cultural memory. 'The commemoration of the dead', Assmann writes, 'is "communicative" in as much as it is a universal human form and it is "cultural" to the extent to which it generates its specific agents, rites and institutions'.[45]

What are the implications of Assmann's theory for the subject of medievalism in the commemoration of the Great War? This study follows Assmann in distinguishing between two intermingled yet distinct layers of memory: first, the *cultural memory* of an idealised medieval past, a configuration dating back to the medievalism of the nineteenth century; and secondly, the commemoration of the fallen soldiers themselves. The latter I call the *existential memory* of the Great War, a recollection of the human toll of war. In this second point I differ from Assmann, who considers the commemoration of the dead, and particularly the war dead, as a means of identity politics, that is 'memory "which establishes community"'.[46] While Assmann's general treatment of the commemoration of death is not suitable for categorising the emotional impact of modern warfare, it rightly highlights its transitory character. In the era of the Great War, the remembrance of the dead soldiers was more sophisticated than communicative memory, but had not yet reached the state of firm cultural memory with an existence of its own. Existential memory was a transitory phenomenon that bridged the gap between lived memory and institutionalised remembrance. It originated in experience but relied on sophisticated memory aids. Furthermore, existential memory belonged neither exclusively to the family nor to the public realm, but penetrated both spheres.

[45] Assmann, *Das kulturelle Gedächtnis*, p. 61.
[46] Ibid., p. 63.

Categories like collective memory provide historians interested in overarching social and cultural phenomena with a convenient tool. Yet one has to bear in mind that the term *memory* is borrowed from cognitive psychology and that is only the intermeshing of individual – albeit socially mediated – recollections of experience which engenders a 'collective' representation of the past. Collective memory is mediated or 'collected' memory. It requires organisation, guidance and direction. It does not have an autonomous existence, but embodies a social intentionality. Activity, agency and creativity are the keys to unlock collective remembrance. In short, remembrance is a process; memory, the product (though memory is often invoked as a shorthand for remembrance). One can speak of collective memory only when groups of people act in public together. But the product of collective action is not identical with the aggregate collection of individual memories. In the act of joining individual components together a new, collective pattern emerges, embraced by individuals as their own. 'The "collective memory" of war is not what everybody thinks about war; it is a phrase without purchase when we try to disentangle the behaviour of different groups within the collective. Some act; others – most others – do not.'[47]

Collective remembrance meant mediation and negotiation between a multiplicity of agents (operating from both above and below) as different memories struggled to find space in which they could coexist. Obviously, the weight of various partners in this process was by no means equal. Sometimes, a dominant agent repressed or displaced individual recollections, but counter-voices usually managed to carve a niche for themselves in a pluralistic society.[48] The relationship between memory and power has inspired much research unravelling the complexities of that rich field of social action. Scholars adopting a Foucauldian framework tend to interpret commemoration as an attempt to conceal the contestatory elements of the appropriation of individual memories in the course of public remembrance.[49] However, commemoration was an exercise in both politics and business, instrument and bargain. The analogy of a

---

[47] Winter and Sivan, 'Setting the Framework', p. 9. On memory as symbolic representation and social action, see Alon Confino and Peter Fritzsche, 'Introduction: Noises of the Past', in Alon Confino and Peter Fritzsche (eds.), *The Work of Memory: New Directions in the Study of German Society and Culture* (Urbana and Chicago, University of Illinois Press, 2002), pp. 4–7. On agency generally, see David Gary Shaw (ed.), 'Agency after Postmodernism', theme issue of *History and Theory*, 40 (2001).

[48] Winter and Sivan, 'Setting the Framework', p. 30. See also Ashplant, Dawson and Roper, 'Politics of War Memory'.

[49] See, for example, Sherman, *Construction of Memory*, p. 6, who frames his study in Foucauldian terms.

market illustrates the dynamics of war remembrance best. The sources testify to a situation of give-and-take between agents and audiences, between the suppliers and the consumers of the business of commemoration. The producers had to meet people's existential needs – meaning and symbolism – and they did so by reproducing a well-established brand: medievalism.

It may be helpful at this point to examine briefly the market forces at work in inter-war Britain and Germany. There were commemorative networks linking five main players: memorial committees, veterans, families, artists and the state. Generally speaking, second- and third-order elites within civil society in collaboration with artists played the most active and creative part in launching commemorative forms and practices in Britain as well as in Germany.[50] Despite a 'huge paper plebiscite', the writer G. K. Chesterton observed with amusement, the war memorial in his home town 'was decided at the private discretion of the Squire and Parson, as it was in the days of old'.[51] Chesterton exaggerates two features of the decision-making process on the local level. The general public, especially the bereaved families, had a certain input into memorial projects by means of open meetings, letters to the editor of the local newspaper and voluntary donations (or, alternatively, refusal to contribute gifts of money), but in some cases consultation was a mere formality. The memorial committees were normally the driving force behind the memorialisation of the war. Their composition was intended to make them representative of the local community as a whole, although 'representative' was often taken to mean local worthies and public-spirited individuals who were seen (or saw themselves) as representing communal interests.[52] But in any case, the committees remained answerable to the public whose support was vital to sustain the original impulse of commemorative acts: the 'virtual consensus of need'.[53]

---

[50] Winter and Sivan, 'Setting the Framework', pp. 10, 38–9.
[51] G[ilbert] K. Chesterton, *Autobiography* (London, Hutchinson, 1936), pp. 241–2.
[52] King, *Memorials of the Great War*, pp. 26–36, 94–101; Peter McIntosh Donaldson, 'The Memorialisation of the Great War in Folkestone, Canterbury and Dover, 1918–24', Ph.D. dissertation, University of Kent, 2005. For the German case I rely on my own archival research.
[53] Moriarty, 'Narrative and the Absent Body', p. 71. See also Gaffney, *Aftermath*, pp. 112–13; Nabrings, '. . . *eine immerfort währende Mahnung . . .*', pp. 135–6. In contrast, other historians emphasise class conflict and social control. See, for instance, Gilbert Torrance Bell, 'Monuments to the Fallen: Scottish War Memorials of the Great War', Ph.D. dissertation, University of Strathclyde, 1994, pp. 184–5, 335; Mansfield, 'Class Conflict', p. 84.

What distinguished British from German memorial committees was essentially the role assigned to veterans. Condemned to a marginal existence in Britain, veterans had a critical say in communal commemorations in Germany where they regularly sat on memorial committees. Furthermore, German veterans were equally prepared to seize the initiative in building local war monuments.[54] Yet the veterans rarely spoke with one voice. There was a division between the traditional *Kriegervereine*, warriors' societies, predominantly dating from the late nineteenth century, and the *Kampfbünde* or *Wehrverbände*, newly founded paramilitary associations, which were themselves split along the borders of different socio-political milieux.[55] The two leading *Kampfbünde* were the Social Democratic Reichsbanner Schwarz-Rot-Gold (founded in 1924; a maximum of 2,000,000 members) and the nationalist Stahlhelm, Bund der Frontsoldaten (founded in 1918; a maximum of 400,000 members). The officially non-partisan, but de facto staunchly conservative Kyffhäuserbund (established between 1892 and 1900), the national umbrella organisation of some thirty thousand local *Kriegervereine*, numbered around 2,200,000 members when at a low ebb in 1921. In addition, separate organisations catered for officers and disabled veterans.[56]

In Germany, war commemoration was built into the associational life of war veterans. To be sure, the majority of those who came home from the trenches and managed to pick up the pieces of their civilian lives remained aloof from the veterans' movement.[57] And yet the membership

---

[54] Martin Bach, *Studien zur Geschichte des deutschen Kriegerdenkmals in Westfalen and Lippe* (Frankfurt am Main, Peter Lang, 1985), p. 268; Jeismann and Westheider, 'Wofür stirbt der Bürger?', pp. 35–6. However, both studies overestimate the importance of veterans' initiatives. See, by contrast, Nabrings, '. . . *eine immerfort währende Mahnung* . . .', p. 122; Bernd Schmid-Kemmer, '". . . leuchtest mir zum frühen Tod": Kriegsdenkmäler im Landkreis Ludwigsburg als Geschichtsquellen', *Ludwigsburger Geschichtsblätter*, 46 (1992), pp. 84–160.

[55] Benjamin Ziemann, 'Die Erinnerung an den Ersten Weltkrieg in den Milieukulturen der Weimarer Republik', *Krieg und Literatur*, 3–4 (1997–8), pp. 249–70.

[56] Benjamin Ziemann, 'Republikanische Kriegserinnerung in einer polarisierten Öffentlichkeit: Das Reichsbanner Schwarz-Rot-Gold als Veteranenverband der sozialistischen Arbeiterschaft', *Historische Zeitschrift*, 267 (1998), pp. 362–70; James M. Diehl, *Paramilitary Politics in Weimar Germany* (Bloomington and London, Indiana University Press, 1977), pp. 293–7; Robert Weldon Whalen, *Bitter Wounds: German Victims of the Great War, 1914–1939* (Ithaca and London, Cornell University Press, 1984), pp. 117–27; C. J. Elliot, 'The Kriegervereine and the Weimar Republic', *Journal of Contemporary History*, 10 (1975), pp. 118–19. On warriors' societies before the Great War, see Thomas Rohkrämer, *Der Militarismus der 'kleinen Leute': Die Kriegervereine im Deutschen Kaiserreich 1871–1914* (Munich, R. Oldenbourg, 1990).

[57] Ziemann, *Front und Heimat*, pp. 419–20, 437.

figures of the German associations are impressive compared to the lack of appeal of the British Legion (founded in 1921; a maximum of 400,000 members) and its precursors.[58] Keen to return to their pre-war lives, fewer than ten per cent of British ex-servicemen joined the British Legion, 'precisely *because* it was too reminiscent of the army'.[59] The numerical weakness of their national association does not, however, fully account for the marginality of ex-servicemen in local commemoration. They commanded moral authority in society, and their disapproval could seriously hamper the making of a war memorial, but direct involvement in communal commemorations was, compared to the German case, minimal.[60] British ex-servicemen played the role of guardians rather than agents of public remembrance; when they became active they set up regimental memorials separate from the civic ones.

The social and political space occupied by German veterans did not exist in Britain for two reasons. First, the war had not bridged the gap between military virtues and civic values. The cult of the *Kriegserlebnis*, the 'war experience', and the importance attached to its 'eyewitnesses' in Germany, was an anathema to the unmilitary British nation. Second, nineteenth-century Britain had largely been untouched by what Koselleck calls the 'democratisation' of war remembrance.[61] On the Continent, the Revolutionary and Napoleonic wars had transformed the character of commemoration and the status of the soldier. Since then, the ordinary and individual citizen-soldier, the celebrated war volunteer, had been increasingly deemed worthy of public remembrance, and veterans had attained a prominence unknown in Britain. In nineteenth-century Britain, with its small professional army, ordinary soldiers tended to be vagrants who could find no better job. Thus, the ordinary dead soldier, that is the regular, had been principally commemorated within a regimental rather than a civic context. Community ties did not play a significant part in war commemoration until the mass death of

---

[58] N[iall] Barr, 'The British Legion after the Great War: Its Identity and Character', in Bertrand Taithe and Tim Thornton (eds.), *War: Identities in Conflict 1300–2000* (Stroud, Sutton, 1998), p. 217. See also Charles Kimball, 'The Ex-Service Movement in England and Wales, 1916–1930', Ph.D. dissertation, Stanford University, 1990, p. 12.

[59] Adrian Gregory, 'Peculiarities of the British? War, Violence and Politics: 1900–1939', *Journal of Modern European History*, 1 (2003), p. 52, author's italics.

[60] Gaffney, *Aftermath*, pp. 26–33; Connelly, *Great War, Memory and Ritual*, p. 190; Gregory, *Silence of Memory*, ch. 2. For a contrary opinion on the role played by British ex-servicemen, see King, *Memorials of the Great War*, pp. 79–80, 90, 209; Keith Grieves, 'Common Meeting Places and the Brightening of Rural Life: Local Debates on Village Halls in Sussex after the First World War', *Rural History*, 10 (1999), pp. 171–92.

[61] Koselleck, 'Kriegerdenkmale als Identitätsstiftungen', pp. 259–60. See also Mosse, *Fallen Soldiers*, pp. 15–50, and chapter 3 below.

volunteers in South Africa at the turn of the century. Although of limited scale, the building of Boer War memorials in Britain after 1902 resembled the Continental model of commemorating the citizen-soldier and foreshadowed the massive proliferation of war memorials after 1914–18.[62]

Everywhere memorial committees worked closely together with architects or sculptors who had either won public competitions or been directly invited to create Great War memorials. Most designers were prepared to conform to the expectations of their clients, but still managed to retain their artistic independence within the limits set by the popular taste. Medievalism proved to be a safe bet, generally satisfying all parties alike. However, the issue of good taste brought further agents into the commemorative arena. Artistic institutions issued advisory circulars urging local committees to consult a competent artist instead of a monumental mason or, in Germany, a landscape gardener. In Germany, the state, too, saw the need to ensure some basic aesthetic standards for commemorative monuments. The *Reichskunstwart* (Reich Art Custodian), a senior civil servant attached to the Ministry of the Interior, made generic recommendations, and state and provincial governments set up special advisory strata for war commemorations (*Beratungsstellen für Kriegerehrungen*) in 1916. In Prussia, for instance, consultation was in theory mandatory – refractory communities were liable to a stiff fine (a so-called 'luxury tax') – but in reality rarely enforced. The advice centres, composed largely of civil servants, church officials, art historians and artists, preferred co-operation to confrontation in order to maintain the consensus built up around a design.

Strong voluntary initiative and a reluctant state were the basic ingredients of war remembrance in Germany. The British state (except for the Established Church) took an even less interventionist approach in commemorative affairs, at least on the local level. The burial and commemoration of Britain's fallen soldiers in military cemeteries, however, was the responsibility of an official commission formed in 1917 by a resolution of the heads of government of the United Kingdom, the Dominions and India.[63] The Imperial War Graves Commission (renamed Commonwealth War Graves Commission in 1960) operated as a civilian, inter-governmental body, which, although not part of the British civil service, followed civil-service practice. In contrast, the impetus to

---

[62] King, *Memorials of the Great War*, pp. 42–4, 68–70, 185–6.
[63] Philip Longworth, *The Unending Vigil: A History of the Commonwealth War Graves Commission 1917–1984* (London, Leo Cooper, [2nd] edn 1985).

the establishment of German war cemeteries, in particular at the Western Front, reflects the profound force of civil society (understood here as the network of voluntary institutions and organisations that mediated between the individual and the state).[64] Founded by bereaved and veterans from a middle-class background in 1919–20, the Volksbund Deutsche Kriegsgräberfürsorge (with about 150,000 members in 1932, including 5,000 corporate members, especially warriors' societies) was, however, run on authoritarian lines by the national board in Berlin. Towns, regiments, companies, schools, societies and individuals were encouraged to support the Volksbund's work by joining the *Patenschaft* scheme whereby they would sponsor a particular war cemetery abroad. Private but not autonomous, the Volksbund had to co-operate fully with the Reich government (which provided crucial financial support) and its subsidiary organisations.[65]

In the context of war commemoration it is often not possible to draw a hard and fast line between voluntary association and the state. Still, the state as the carrier of the brunt of total war regarded it as its duty to initiate and choreograph national commemorations. In Britain, central government had played a minimal role in the organisation of commemoration prior to the Great War. Yet in 1919, David Lloyd George's coalition government commissioned a temporary Cenotaph for a victory parade in Whitehall which, in the event, resembled a funeral march. Moreover, the Cenotaph (flanked by the Unknown Warrior in Westminster Abbey) was later transformed by popular demand into the permanent locus of national grief.[66] Weimar's politicians did not try to impose a national monument from above. In 1924, Reich President Friedrich Ebert announced the state's wish to see a Reich memorial

---

[64] On civil society, see Frank Trentmann, 'Introduction: Paradoxes of Civil Society', in Frank Trentmann (ed.), *Paradoxes of Civil Society: New Perspectives on Modern German and British History* (New York and Oxford, Berghahn, 2000), pp. 3–46; José Harris, 'Introduction: Civil Society in British History: Paradigm or Peculiarity', in José Harris (ed.), *Civil Society in British History: Ideas, Identities, Institutions* (Oxford, Oxford University Press, 2003), pp. 1–12.

[65] Johann Zilien, 'Der "Volksbund Deutsche Kriegsgräberfürsorge e.V." in der Weimarer Republik: Ein Beitrag zum politischen Denkmalkult zwischen Kaiserreich und Nationalsozialismus', *Archiv für Kulturgeschichte*, 75 (1993), pp. 445–78. See also Susanne Brandt, *Vom Kriegsschauplatz zum Gedächtnisraum: Die Westfront 1914–1940* (Baden-Baden, Nomos, 2000), pp. 127–69, who emphasises the tension between the Volksbund and the Reich government.

[66] Penelope Curtis, 'The Whitehall Cenotaph: An Accidental Monument', *Imperial War Museum Review*, 9 (1994), pp. 33, 37–8; Allan Greenberg, 'Lutyens's Cenotaph', *Journal of the Society of Architectural Historians*, 48 (1989), pp. 5–23. On the role of the government in commemoration before 1914, see Max Jones, *The Last Great Quest: Captain Scott's Antarctic Sacrifice* (Oxford, Oxford University Press, 2003), p. 137.

(*Reichsehrenmal*) erected and thus unleashed a prolonged, highly local-
ised debate about its form and location.[67] Ebert's vision never materialised during the Weimar Republic, but the public discussion between
1924 and 1933 shows that the social organisation of Great War remembrance was decentralised. Although the Reich Art Custodian acted as
the governmental co-ordinator and spokesmen, the vast majority of the
roughly three hundred proposals that reached him originated from civil
society, its local communities and voluntary associations. However, the
nationwide discussion, recorded and reported by the Reich Art Custodian, in its turn, influenced local discourses of commemoration. Hence,
German and British collective memories arose out of a dialogue between
high politics and vernacular culture, from a dialogue between agents
working within state institutions and civil society.

Archival sources and time-span

The book that follows is a study of medievalism in *public* war remembrance. Private mementos and recollections such as memoirs, letters and
poems have not been considered, except for instances where they were
brought into the public domain by means of publication and citation.
I focus principally on the most visible and, arguably, the most significant
manifestation of collective remembrance: war memorials or *Kriegerdenkmäler*, literally 'warrior memorials' (also referred to as *Ehrenmäler*,
'honour memorials', in order to distinguish them from earlier war memorials). Omnipresent in both Britain and Germany after the First
World War, war memorials of various forms (sculptural, architectural,
horticultural, paper and utilitarian) and origins (governmental, parochial, regimental and institutional) are an ideal *tertium comparationis* for
a cross-national analysis of commemorative styles and languages in the
early twentieth century.

There are three dimensions to the study of war memorials: their
iconography, epigraphy and ceremonial role. War memorials combined
visual with discursive and performative modes of representation.
Much research into (German) war memorials has limited itself to readily

---

[67] Peter Bucher, 'Die Errichtung des Reichsehrenmals nach dem ersten [*sic*] Weltkrieg',
Jahrbuch für westdeutsche Landesgeschichte, 7 (1981), pp. 359–86; Benjamin Ziemann,
'Die deutsche Nation und ihr zentraler Erinnerungsort: Das "Nationaldenkmal für die
Gefallenen im Weltkriege" und die Idee des "Unbekannten Soldaten" 1914–1935', in
Helmut Berding, Klaus Heller and Winfried Speitkamp (eds.), *Krieg und Erinnerung:
Fallstudien zum 19. und 20. Jahrhundert* (Göttingen, Vandenhoeck & Ruprecht, 2000),
pp. 67–91.

available iconographic evidence, evidence which does not require digging in archives. This book pays particular attention to the contexts and processes which connected objects to words. Memorial designs and inscriptions needed interpretation, and agents of remembrance were anxious to clear up any ambiguities in the preliminary discussions, fund-raising campaigns, unveiling and dedication addresses and newspaper articles. Moreover, some committees published souvenir programmes and memorial volumes containing photographs, descriptions or speeches, and, in doing so, created 'secondary memorials'. Such representations of war were, of course, embedded in a longer tradition. Apart from sources relating directly to the construction, inauguration and reception of war memorials, I also read memorials in relation to other visual objects that shaped post-war commemorations, notably wartime picture postcards and poster art (both bearing the stamp of nineteenth-century medievalism), which function as what Daniel Sherman calls 'registers of experience'.[68] The imagery of visual propaganda, once freed from its wartime aggressiveness, offered a template or repository of images for the construction of memorials and memory after the catastrophe of 1914–18.

The specific discourse surrounding a concrete war memorial can only be illuminated through archival investigation. For official commemorations on the national level, the documentation is abundant. An extensive range of materials concerning the national memorials of Britain and Germany has been preserved in the Public Record Office and the Bundesarchiv respectively. Thanks to Weimar Germany's federal structure, further papers have been deposited in the state archives, especially the Prussian Geheimes Staatsarchiv in Berlin. However, many German archives, notably those in the capital, suffered badly from Allied bombing during the Second World War. As a consequence, there are hardly any manuscript records of the German war graves association to match the rich holdings of the archives of the Commonwealth War Graves Commission. Unfortunately, the papers of the Volksbund's architectural office in Munich were destroyed around 1960.[69] Such a disparity potentially poses a cardinal problem to comparative research,

---

[68] Sherman, *Construction of Memory*, pp. 15, 59. See also Arnold Vogt, *Den Lebenden zur Mahnung: Denkmäler and Gedenktstätten: Zur Traditionspflege und historischen Identität vom 19. Jahrhundert bis zur Gegenwart* (Hanover, Lutherisches Verlagshaus, 1993), pp. 115–20.

[69] However, the papers of the legal service of the Foreign Office (kept at the Politisches Archiv des Auswärtigen Amts, Berlin) shed some light on the maintenance of German war cemeteries abroad.

but fortunately in this case the researcher can at least fall back on the Volksbund's periodical entitled *Kriegsgräberfürsorge*. The Imperial War Graves Commission, in contrast, had no reason to publish a glossy magazine, because, as an inter-governmental institution, it was neither dependent on subscriptions nor directly accountable to members. This example demonstrates how two factors – chance and agency – have influenced the state of archival documentation.

The comparative historian of localities faces considerably greater obstacles. In Britain, the source materials for local war memorials in parochial records often offer fragmentary clues. Incomplete or lost papers reflect the nature of British commemorations, that is the laissez-faire policy of the state and the unofficial character of local committees, specifically in rural areas. In urban communities, however, the mayor would typically serve ex officio as chairman of the war-memorial committee, and the administrative co-ordination would normally be entrusted to the town clerk's department.[70] The involvement of local officials increases the likelihood of papers surviving in county record offices. By comparison, German laws and bureaucratic spirit have guaranteed better archival documentation. Although they had no obligation to do so, even some *Kriegervereine* deposited their files in the city and district archives. In addition, legal provisions for official supervision through advice centres generated further paperwork. Yet researchers are frustrated by the absence of a full inventory for war memorials in Germany. (A contemporary inventory of the war memorials of Württemberg is kept at the Hauptstaatsarchiv in Stuttgart.)[71] While any survey of the German memorial scene is necessarily provisional, the National Inventory of War Memorials at the Imperial War Museum, initiated in 1989, will, once completed, provide a data bank of the estimated 54,000 war memorials (from the Crimean War to the Gulf War) throughout the United Kingdom.[72]

[70] King, *Memorials of the Great War*, pp. 34–5.
[71] HStAS, M 746, Denkmäler und Ehrentafeln für die Gefallenen des Ersten Weltkrieges, 1923–31. Karl von Seeger, director of the Bibliothek für Technik, Kunst und Wirtschaft (Württembergisches Landesgewerbeamt) in Stuttgart, also collected photographs of Great War memorials. It seems that this important collection was destroyed in the Second World War. However, Seeger published a valuable selection of his photographs under the title *Das Denkmal des Weltkriegs* (Stuttgart, Hugo Matthaes, [1930]). Equally useful is the catalogue of German war memorials entitled *Deutscher Ehrenhain für die Helden von 1914/18*, intro. Ernst Bergmann (Leipzig, Dehain, 1931).
[72] For an illustrated catalogue of British war memorials, see the two volumes by Derek Boorman, *At the Going Down of the Sun: British First World War Memorials* (York, Ebor, 1988); and *For Your Tomorrow: British Second World War Memorials* (York, Boorman, 1995).

This book covers roughly the period from 1914 to 1940, that is from the earliest attempts to represent and remember the First World War to the outbreak of the Second World War in western Europe, but the bulk of the material presented here concerns the 1920s. It is hardly surprising that the business of commemoration peaked in the decade after 1918. The mass of British memorials was put up during the early 1920s. In many German communities, there was a time-lag of five to ten years between the ceasefire and the unveiling of the war memorial. Political conflict may have been one reason, certainly in the case of the Reich memorial. Yet a great many projects were simply delayed due to the inflation between 1918 and 1924 which ate up memorial funds and put financial constraints on the contributors. Monuments that had still not been completed by 1928 had to be put on ice again because of the economic slump. After 1933, the new Nazi rulers invested a lot of energy in erecting Great War memorials (often reviving already existing plans) or, sometimes, demolishing inopportune ones.[73] Nonetheless, 1933 marked not a radical turning-point, but the beginning of a period of transition.[74] The fade-out of Weimar was marked by ambiguities and inconsistencies. For this reason, my discussion of medievalism, although not intended to give a full account of Nazi commemoration, does not stop in 1933 – which is, in any case, a meaningless date in British history.

A few words may be useful to indicate the structure of this book. It is organised thematically and divided into five chapters. Each chapter explores a theme of medievalism in war remembrance based on evidence drawn from both countries' histories. Chapter 1, 'Catastrophe and continuity: the place of the war dead in history', sets the framework of the entire volume. It examines the dialectic of lamenting catastrophe and describing continuity. First, it considers the significance of medievalism as a mode of recovering – identifying and historicising – the war dead. Second, it analyses the composition of medievalist war remembrance, its dimensions, techniques and narratives.

Chapters 2 to 5 explore significant medievalist themes in war remembrance. Chapter 2, 'Mission and defence: the nature of the conflict',

---

[73] For a discussion of Nazi commemorations, see Sabine Behrenbeck, *Der Kult um die toten Helden: Nationalsozialistische Mythen, Rituale and Symbole 1923–1945* (Vierow, SH, 1996); Jay W. Baird, *To Die for Germany: Heroes in the Nazi Pantheon* (Bloomington and Indianapolis, Indiana University Press, 1990); Hans-Ulrich Thamer, 'Von der Monumentalisierung zur Verdrängung der Geschichte: Nationalsozialistische Denkmal-politik and die Entnazifizierung von Denkmälern nach 1945', in Winfried Speitkamp (ed.), *Denkmalsturz: Zur Konfliktgeschichte politischer Symbolik* (Göttingen, Vandenhoeck & Ruprecht, 1997), pp. 109–36.

[74] Brandt, *Vom Kriegsschauplatz zum Gedächtnisraum*, p. 14.

looks at representations of the nature of the First World War ranging from notions of national defence to the idea of a new Crusade. The nature of the war mattered to the memorial makers, for it legitimised the cause for which the soldiers fought. I begin with representations of the war in general and then turn to narratives about particular theatres of military operation, namely the Far East, eastern Europe, and the Western Front. Chapter 3, 'Destruction and endurance: the war experience', and chapter 4, 'Chivalry and cruelty: the soldiers' character and conduct', form a unit. While the former provides a study of encodings of the combatants' 'war experience', the latter shows how (civilian) memory agents reconfigured the soldiers' murderous deeds in terms of chivalrous warfare. However, the ultimate challenge facing war remembrance was not to sanctify the collective slaughter, but to assign meaning to mass death. Finally, chapter 5, 'Regeneration and salvation: the prospects for the living and the dead', charts how medievalism responded to a popular need to give transcendental meaning to these human losses. I conclude my study of medievalism as a commemorative mode with a discussion of the demise of older languages of remembrance in the aftermath of the Second World War.

1   Catastrophe and continuity: the place of the war dead in history

The Great War was murderous without precedent. Some of those living in the shadow of the great slaughter recognised 1914–18 as a historical turning-point, representing a rupture not only with the conditions of the Edwardian or Wilhelmine era but with the past as such. A sense of a radical discontinuity between the present and the past is the prevailing mood in certain writing about the period of the Great War. 'It must be all lies and of no account when the culture of a thousand years could not prevent this stream of blood being poured out', reads a passage from Erich Maria Remarque's novel *All Quiet on the Western Front*, published in 1929.[1] The contemporary British writer Siegfried Sassoon described his personal disillusionment with the war in his poem 'The Poet as Hero' of 1916:

> You are aware that once I sought the Grail
> Riding in armour bright, serene and strong;

and Sassoon added:

> But now I've said good-bye to Galahad,
> And am no more the knight of dreams and show
> For lust and senseless hatred make me glad,
> And my killed friends are with me where I go.[2]

The carnage of the First World War gave rise to the notion of 'a gap in history'.[3] This feeling of discontinuity with the past, of historical dislocation and impoverishment, is at the core of what Samuel Hynes calls the 'myth of the war'. *Pace* Hynes's seminal study, in the course of this chapter I want to argue that remembrance activities taking place in the public domain were creative efforts to affirm rather than reject

---

[1] Erich Maria Remarque, *All Quiet on the Western Front* (London, G. P. Putnam, 1929), p. 287.
[2] Siegfried Sassoon, 'The Poet as Hero', in *The War Poems of Siegfried Sassoon*, ed. Rupert Hart-Davis (London, Faber and Faber, 1983), p. 61.
[3] Hynes, *War Imagined*, p. xi.

historical continuity: continuity with a remote, pre-industrial past, in particular the Middle Ages. The language of medievalism in war commemoration presented an alternative vision of time which turned the trauma of war into a coherent narrative. The fallen combatants were meaningfully relocated in medieval history, thereby making the victim visible within a traditional framework. This discourse restored the individual soldier who had perished in the anonymous *Materialschlacht*, battle of *matériel*, of the first mass-industrialised war the world had seen. The recovery of the victims through commemorative practice is the subject-matter of the first part of this chapter. I explore its dual components: identifying and historicising the fallen. In part two, I systematise my findings and I analyse how continuity was conceptualised and constructed. This chapter focuses on the composition of medievalism in war commemoration and on overlaps with parallel narratives; the contents of medievalist representations will be discussed in later chapters.

Recovering the dead

The 1914–18 war triggered off an explosion of naming in memorialisation. The practice of naming recalled each individual victim and returned to him an individuated existence against the oblivion to which he had been consigned on the battlefield. Even if the soldiers did not return physically, commemorations gave the pledge that 'Their Name Liveth for Evermore'.[4] At the suggestion of Rudyard Kipling – a man shaken by the fate of his only son who was lost, presumably killed, at Loos – this motto, borrowed from Ecclesiasticus (Sirach) 44:14, was adopted by the Imperial War Graves Commission. The Commission's Menin Gate memorial to the missing of the Ypres Salient, designed by Sir Reginald Blomfield, is a most powerful monument to the eternal perpetuation of soldiers' names – 'intolerably nameless names' for Sassoon.[5] The memorial takes the form of an arch on which the names of 54,896 missing soldiers who have no known grave are recorded. Though a British-Imperial monument, it did not fail to impress German

---

[4] Mosse, *Fallen Soldiers*, p. 83. See also Thomas W. Laqueur, 'Memory and Naming in the Great War', in John R. Gillis (ed.), *Commemorations: The Politics of National Identity* (Princeton, Princeton University Press, 1994), p. 153.

[5] Siegfried Sassoon, 'On Passing the New Menin Gate', in *War Poems*, p. 153. On the making of the Menin Gate, see Longworth, *Unending Vigil*, pp. 86–93; Michael Heffernan, 'For Ever England: The Western Front and the Politics of Remembrance in Britain', *Ecumene*, 2 (1995), p. 308.

visitors who did not share Sassoon's bitterness. A journalist from Berlin remarked approvingly: 'It is integrated into the city's former ramparts. In the course of time, the English Gate will grow completely into the surrounding city of Ypres. It will record the names of the Anglo-Saxon [*sic*] auxiliary troops till the far-off days in history.'[6]

The attempt to embed the Menin Gate in history should not be dismissed as journalistic embellishment. Agents of remembrance endeavoured to tie commemoration to history. The names of the fallen soldiers were sacred as such, but history placed the names under eternal guarantee and invested them with meaning. In Halberstadt, in the Prussian Province of Saxony, the fourteenth-century chancel of a church founded in the eleventh century was converted into a hall of remembrance. The names of those who had died in the war were listed on the panelling. The plan met with the approval of the local press, which emphasised the time-honoured stateliness of the 'hundreds-of-years old' building.[7] Similarly, commemoration of Cambridgeshire's casualties was amalgamated into the fabric of Ely Cathedral, that 'matchless monument of eight hundred years of history'.[8] A side chapel was fitted up as a memorial, decorated with oak panels like shutters on which nearly six thousand names were inscribed (arranged alphabetically by parish, without rank). A regional newspaper concluded that 'these men who made the greatest sacrifice are part of England, their names, unknown outside their own country are woven into the texture of her history as the chapel is part of the fabric of the Cathedral'.[9]

In Ely and elsewhere, the designers faced the challenge of devising memorials to accommodate hundreds or even thousands of legible names. Books of remembrance, often as a supplement to artistic memorials, offered a pragmatic (and less expensive) solution to the task of comprehensive naming. A book recording the names of Norfolk's fallen

[6] BArch, R 8034 II/7692, folio 172, Kurt Bährens, 'Endlich deutsches Heldendenkmal von Langemarck', *Berliner Illustrierte Nachtausgabe*, 9 July 1932: 'Es ist den einstigen Festungswällen der Stadt eingereiht. Das englische Tor wird mit der Zeit völlig mit der umliegenden Stadt Ypern verwachsen. Es wird die Namen der angelsächsischen Hilfstruppen bis in die fernsten Tage der Geschichte festhalten.'
[7] 'Eine Gedenkhalle in der Paulskirche', *Halberstädter Zeitung und Intelligenzblatt*, 99, 27 April 1924, p. 5. A photograph of the memorial is published in Siegfried Scharfe (ed.), *Deutschland über alles: Ehrenmale des Weltkrieges* (Königstein and Leipzig, Karl Robert Langewiesche, 1938), p. 39.
[8] 'They Died that We Might Live: Cambridgeshire Honours Its Dead', *Cambridge Chronicle and University Journal*, 9041, 17 May 1922, p. 8.
[9] Ibid. See also K[en] S. Inglis, 'The Homecoming: The War Memorial Movement in Cambridge, England', *Journal of Contemporary History*, 27 (1992), pp. 592–3.

Figure 1. Book of Remembrance. Illuminated page featuring General Allenby's entry into Jerusalem in 1917. Norwich Cathedral, 1932.

servicemen was placed in the county war memorial chapel in Norwich Cathedral (see figure 1). Today, the book is locked away in a showcase, but from the committee papers we learn that 'All the pages contain illuminated borders of varied mediaeval designs, illustrated with about 30 miniatures of Churches & other local views, Army and Navy scenes.'[10] The return to medieval art at Norwich may have been inspired by an exhibition organised by the Medici Society in London early in the war. The rolls of honour which were on show (for instance, an illuminated sheet for 'The Holy Grail') attempted to revive a 'beautiful mediaeval art' for modern commemorative purposes.[11] In Germany, too, books of remembrance were widespread.[12] In the Hanover suburb of Linden, the war's death toll was made an integral part of local history: the town compiled a chronicle recording both events since the year 1115 and the names of all citizens killed in the Great War.[13]

The invocation of soldiers' names offered an effective antidote to the 'powerful anxiety of erasure, a distinctly modern sensibility of the absolute pastness of the past', as Thomas Laqueur has pointed out.[14] Naming was crucial to the act of remembrance; precisely this, however, was beyond the bounds of practicality on the level of national commemorations. How could one possibly find space for the plethora of names? Instead, a symbolic language representing more than 720,000 British and two million German losses had to be invented. The authorities in charge of the Armistice Day celebrations in London in 1920 formulated an ingenious scheme for recovering the dead: the tomb of the Unknown Warrior (see figure 2). The government entrusted the practical arrangements for the burial to a cabinet committee chaired by Lord Curzon, the unrivalled ceremonial impresario of the age. To Curzon, David Cannadine writes, 'history was a pageant, and pageantry was history'.[15] The making of the Unknown Warrior is a case in point. Following a complicated process of selection, one unidentified corpse, exhumed from one of the major battlefields of the Western Front, was repatriated to Britain

[10] NRO, DCN 106/25, 'Descriptions of the Book of Remembrance', n.d.

[11] 'Rolls of Honour: Mediaeval Art Revived', *Pall Mall Gazette*, 15438, 24 October 1914, p. 4. See Adrian Gregory, 'Lost Generations: the Impact of Military Casualties on Paris, London, and Berlin', in Jay Winter, Jean-Louis Robert [*et al.*], *Capital Cities at War: Paris, London, Berlin 1914–1919* (Cambridge, Cambridge University Press, 1997), p. 88.

[12] Meinhold Lurz, *Kriegerdenkmäler in Deutschland*, vol. IV, *Weimarer Republik* (Heidelberg, Esprint, 1985), pp. 277, 407, 410; Bach, *Studien zur Geschichte*, pp. 5–6.

[13] Schneider, '. . .*nicht umsonst gefallen*'?, p. 159. For a similar case, see StAMS, OP 5556, folio 222, 'Zur Einweihung des Ehrenmales der Landgemeinde Lüdenscheid', 16 October 1929.

[14] Thomas W. Laqueur, 'Names, Bodies, and the Anxiety of Erasure', in Theodore R. Schatzki and Wolfgang Natter (eds.), *The Social and Political Body* (New York and London, Guilford, 1996), p. 133. See also Sherman, *Construction of Memory*, ch. 2.

[15] David Cannadine, 'Lord Curzon as Ceremonial Impresario', in David Cannadine, *Aspects of Aristocracy: Grandeur and Decline in Modern Britain* (New Haven and London, Yale University Press, 1994), p. 78.

Figure 2. The Unknown Warrior. Westminster Abbey, London, 11 November 1920 (photograph courtesy of the Imperial War Museum, London).

where he received a state funeral in Westminster Abbey on 11 November 1920. The ritual of his selection and the choreography of his inauguration guaranteed that the soldier would remain unidentifiable. Hence the Unknown could act as a universal surrogate body. This is a striking case of fictive kinship; the bereaved could imagine him as a lost son, brother, or friend.[16]

Even though the French buried a *soldat inconnu* on the same day and other countries followed suit, the semantics of 'Unknown Warrior' are peculiar to the British case. The term both identified ('Unknown') and historicised ('Warrior') the dead. The wording was carefully chosen, partly because it was 'neutral' so as to include army, air force and navy.[17] The titles 'Unknown Combatant', 'Unknown Comrade' or 'Unknown Fighting Man' were options, but, as the *British Legion Journal* noted, the 'name Warrior of itself stands for something more than the word Soldier'.[18] By means of 'high diction', the authorities drafted the 'Warrior' posthumously into the armed force of an heroic age. One newspaper even outdid the official rhetoric by dubbing him the 'Unknown Arthur'.[19]

The cabinet committee emphasised historical continuity rather than human catastrophe; it hoped to transform private grief into a public ritual. The committee felt that 'as Armistice Day is not a day of National grief, but rather a commemoration of a great occasion in the National history, it is undesirable to lay stress upon the idea of mourning'.[20] Yet the Armistice Day ritual was dominated by the millions of mourners who paid homage at the tomb in Westminster Abbey during the inter-war years. The Unknown Warrior, that symbolic gesture of the return of the absent dead granted 'from above', elicited an overwhelming response 'from below'. Ultimately, it was the presence of ordinary people

---

[16] Inglis, 'Entombing Unknown Soldiers', pp. 7–31; Michael Gavaghan, *The Story of the Unknown Warrior: 11 November 1920* (Preston, M and L, 1995); John Wolffe, *Great Deaths: Grieving, Religion, and Nationhood in Victorian and Edwardian Britain* (Oxford, Oxford University Press, 2000), pp. 260–4; Cannadine, 'War and Death', pp. 219–26. On recovering the dead, see Joanna Bourke, *Dismembering the Male: Men's Bodies, Britain and the Great War* (London, Reaktion, 1996), ch. 5.

[17] PRO, CAB 27/99, p. 57, 'Memorandum Summarising the Dean of Westminster's Suggestion', 15 October 1920. See also ibid., p. 35, 'Secretary's Notes of a Meeting of the Committee', 19 October 1920. On the French *soldat inconnu*, see Avner Ben-Amos, *Funerals, Politics, and Memory in Modern France, 1789–1996* (Oxford, Oxford University Press, 2000), pp. 215–24.

[18] Herbert Jeans, 'In Death's Cathedral Palace: The Story of the Unknown Warrior', *British Legion Journal*, 9, 5 (1929), p. 118. Internal documents of the cabinet committee in charge of the burial refer to 'an unknown British Fighting man'. See BL, IOR, MSS Eur F 112/318, 'Memorial Services (November 11th) Committee: Recommendations of the Committee', 5 November 1920, p. 2; and similarly ibid., 19 October 1920, p. 2.

[19] As cited in Lloyd, *Battlefield Tourism*, p. 89. See also Fussell, *Great War*, p. 175.

[20] BL, IOR, MSS Eur F 112/318, 'Observation of Armistice Day (November 11th): Note by the Secretary, Cabinet', 17 October 1921, p. 2.

which infused the static signifier with meaning. High politics could prepare the ground for the memorial rite, but it could not endow it with meaning and purpose. Individual and collective pilgrimages to the Unknown Warrior merged public ceremony with private experience, and national (or imperial) history with family history.[21] This link became visible in the creation of the Empire Field of Remembrance on the old graveyard of St Margaret's Church opposite the abbey.[22] In November 1928 and in subsequent years, the bereaved were invited to plant little crosses or poppies, provided by the British Legion's poppy factory, in remembrance of lost relatives and friends. Like the common act of touching a war memorial, and especially touching names inscribed on it (as can be seen on photographs of the period), putting tokens in the ground of St Margaret's constituted a ritual of mourning and separation.[23] These crosses and poppies were public markers of private loss in a historic setting. A British Legion pamphlet noted: 'It is moving and inspiring to see men, women and children planting their Crosses or Poppies in this hallowed lawn nestling in the shadow of the historic Abbey.'[24]

The imperial war memorials in Westminster and Whitehall entwined intimate responses with cultural ones. Together they marked out a commemorative landscape transforming 'all of "official" London into an imagined cemetery'.[25] Some local projects aimed to duplicate this ensemble. Leeds examined the possibility of the burial of a local Unknown Warrior in addition to a cenotaph. Also at Gloucester the idea of a grave of an Unknown Warrior was taken into consideration.[26] Germans, too, felt the need to bring their dead home and put them to rest, at least symbolically.[27] Edwin Redslob, the Reichskunstwart (Reich Art Custodian), brought the idea of an unknown soldier prominently under discussion. In his capacity as a governmental 'spin doctor' of

[21] Gregory, *Silence of Memory*, pp. 24–8; Lloyd, *Battlefield Tourism*, pp. 49–93. In general, see Jay Winter, 'Forms of Kinship', pp. 42, 46.
[22] WAML, Newspaper Cuttings, vol. 1a, British Legion Poppy Factory, *The Story of the Empire Field of Remembrance* (Richmond, British Legion Poppy Factory Press, n.d.), n.p.
[23] Winter, *Sites of Memory*, p. 113.
[24] IWM, Eph. Mem., K 94/113, British Legion Poppy Factory, 'The Empire Field of Remembrance', n.d. On the symbolism of poppies, see Gregory, *Silence of Memory*, pp. 99–104.
[25] Winter, *Sites of Memory*, p. 104. See also Jay Winter, Jean-Louis Robert et al., *Capital Cities at War: Paris, London, Berlin 1914–1919*, vol. II, *A Cultural History* (Cambridge, Cambridge University Press, forthcoming).
[26] LCL, LQ 940.465 L 517, 'Leeds War Memorial Problem: Position of Subscribers to Original Scheme', *Yorkshire Evening News*, 24 January 1921; King, *Memorials of the Great War*, pp. 139, 169 n. 25.
[27] Ackermann, 'La vision allemande', pp. 385–96; Ziemann, 'Deutsche Nation', pp. 78–88.

cultural policies and political aesthetics, Redslob proposed, in an article published in the left-liberal *Berliner Tageblatt* in summer 1925, to inter an 'unknown dead man' in the River Rhine as a memorial to all Germany's fallen. Redslob, himself a supporter of the avant-garde, found his inspiration in a festival production by the pacifist author Fritz von Unruh performed as part of the Rhineland's millennium celebrations of 1925. In his article, Redslob suggests historical continuity in the shadow of catastrophe. He makes allusions to Germanic saga: the 'unknown dead man' in the River Rhine, he writes, 'fulfils a fantasy of our people which lives in the legend of the sunken golden treasure of the Nibelungen, and in the funeral of Alaric, King of the Goths'.[28] At the same time, Konrad Adenauer of the Catholic Centre Party, then mayor of Cologne, was campaigning for the burial of an unknown soldier in the city's cathedral. In response to these initiatives, the Reich Art Custodian received an anonymous letter which vetoed the 'French' expression 'unknown' and propounded the supposedly Germanic term 'Nameless Soldier'. He suggested 'that our mother tongue has [. . .] the marvellous old word Nameless – already frequently and solemnly used in the *Niebelungenlied* [sic]'.[29] Ironically, the letter is signed 'An unknown volunteer'.

Neither idea was pursued any further. In fact, the entire project of a German national or Reich memorial (*Reichsehrenmal*) never got off the ground until after the Nazis' accession to power. On 2 October 1935, Adolf Hitler personally proclaimed the Tannenberg memorial in East Prussia a Reich memorial (see figures 3–4 and 30).[30] The foundation stone, however, had been laid by ultra-conservative groups as early as 1924. Built in a style reminiscent of a medieval castle, the memorial's

[28] BArch, R 43 I/713, folio 58, Edwin Redslob, 'Das Soldatengrab im Rhein', *Berliner Tageblatt*, 362, 28 June 1925: the unknown dead 'erfüllt ein Stück Phantasie unseres Volkes, die in der Sage vom versenkten Nibelungengold wie in der Bestattung des Gotenkönigs Alarich lebt'. On the Reich art custodian, see Annegret Heffen, *Der Reichskunstwart – Kunstpolitik in den Jahren 1920–1933: Zu den Bemühungen um eine offizielle Reichskunstpolitik in der Weimarer Republik* (Essen, Blaue Eule, 1986), pp. 231–56; Winfried Speitkamp, '"Erziehung zur Nation": Reichskunstwart, Kulturpolitik und Identitätsstiftung im Staat von Weimar', in Helmut Berding (ed.), *Nationales Bewußtsein und kollektive Identität: Studien zur Entwicklung des kollektiven Bewußtseins in der Neuzeit*, vol. II (Frankfurt am Main, Suhrkamp, 1994), pp. 541–80.
[29] BArch, R 32/361, folio 23, Unbekannter Kriegsfreiwilliger to Reichskunstwart, 3 October 1925: 'der unbekannte Soldat erscheint mir als eine zu enge Übersetzung der französischen Prägung des Gedankens zu sein, während unsere Muttersprache in diesem Fall noch über das herrliche alte Wort Namenlos [sic], schon im Niebelungenlied [sic] häufig & feierlich in Gebrauch, verfügt'.
[30] Jürgen Tietz, *Das Tannenberg-Nationaldenkmal: Architektur, Geschichte, Kontext* (Berlin, Bauwesen, 1999), provides a detailed history of the Tannenberg memorial. See also chapter 2.

Figure 3. The Tannenberg memorial with the grave of twenty unknown soldiers by Walter and Johannes Krüger. Tannenberg, 1927.

Figure 4. The Tannenberg memorial redesigned under the Nazis by Walter and Johannes Krüger. Tannenberg, 1935.

architecture seemed to protect the grave erected in its centre. Under-
neath a huge metal cross, the bodies of twenty unidentified German
soldiers from the Russian front had been entombed. Tannenberg
illustrates a German transformation of the Anglo-French tradition.
The unknown soldier, who originally represented the recovery and restoration of the individual, had been turned into a symbol of the *völkisch*
community. In doing so, the designers anticipated the concept of *Totenburgen*, 'fortresses of the dead' (see figures 20–1) housing mass graves of
soldiers, an idea developed in the 1920s and 1930s which will be discussed in chapter 2. A commentary of 1935 explained the ideology
behind the construction of mass graves: 'the individual grave has been
subordinated to the idea of community, which is greater and more
lasting. Seen over decades and centuries – when the name has blown
and faded away – it will merely be crucial to know that those who have
been laid to eternal rest here were Germans and soldiers.'[31]

The inventors of the mass grave at Tannenberg imagined therein a
new world of their creation, a new, *völkisch* community of the dead. Yet
the twenty unknown German soldiers did not rest in peace. Under the
regime of Adolf Hitler, who fancied himself the embodiment of the
unknown soldier, all twenty were reburied according to a scheme for
redesigning the memorial.[32] In 1935, Tannenberg was re-launched as
the mausoleum of that recently deceased hero of the battle of 1914, Field
Marshal Paul von Beneckendorff und von Hindenburg. The dead were
subsumed into the cult of military leadership. Already deprived of their
individuality, they were now subjected to the oligarchy of commemoration. At Tannenberg, the notion of elite heroism superseded the idea of
equality of sacrifice which had been intrinsic to the genuine Unknown
Warrior in London. The Tannenberg memorial was reconstructed to
eternalise just one single name: Hindenburg.[33]

[31] 'Die Bauten des Volksbundes in ihrer geschichtlichen und kulturellen Bedeutung',
Kriegsgräberfürsorge, 15, 2 (1935), p. 20: 'ist das Einzelgrab der Idee der Gemeinschaft
untergeordnet. Sie ist das Größere, Dauernde. Über Jahrzehnte und Jahrhunderte
gesehen – wenn einmal der Name verweht und verklungen sein wird – ist es nur
wesentlich zu wissen, daß die, die hier zu ewiger Ruhe gebettet sind, Deutsche und
Soldaten waren.'
[32] Lurz, *Kriegerdenkmäler*, vol. IV, p. 206; Meinhold Lurz, *Kriegerdenkmäler in Deutschland*,
vol. V, *Drittes Reich* (Heidelberg, Esprint, 1986), p. 46. On Hitler and the idea of the
unknown soldier, see Behrenbeck, *Der Kult um die toten Helden*, pp. 153–4; Bartov,
'Trauma and Absence', p. 354; Volker Ackermann, *Nationale Totenfeiern in Deutschland:
Von Wilhelm I. bis Franz Josef Strauß: Eine Studie zur politischen Semiotik* (Stuttgart,
Klett-Cotta, 1990), pp. 106–7.
[33] Gert Buchheit, *Das Reichsehrenmal Tannenberg: Seine Entstehung, seine endgültige Gestaltung und seine Einzelkunstwerke* (Munich, Knorr & Hirth, 1936), p. 9.

Constructing continuity

In Ely or Halberstadt, Norwich or Linden, Westminster or Tannenberg, war commemorations established a striking nexus between the immediate and the remote past, between catastrophe and history. The experience of loss became encoded in a language of historical continuity. In the second part of this chapter, I explore the composition of this language. I examine its dimensions, techniques and narratives.

Dimensions

Why did people embark on historicising or medievalising the fallen soldiers of 1914–18? Medievalism had both a retrospective and a prospective dimension. First of all, it meant a retreat from the uncertainties of the war into the mythologies of an immutable past. In medievalist narratives, the cohesive force of history overshadowed the traumatic watershed for kith and kin of the deceased: whatever the circumstances of the soldiers' deaths, the mourners could feel assured that the fallen had their place in history. This assertion of continuity materialised in the war monument of Royston, Hertfordshire. It features the bronze figure of a British soldier of the First World War (see figure 5). He is surrounded by a group of pale marble sculptures representing his military predecessors since the Hundred Years War. A journalist reported: 'In the centre is a typical "Tommy" who "did his bit" in the mud of Flanders, accompanied by the shades of those ancestors of Royston, who, in the past, have on the battlefield and elsewhere done their bit.' At the unveiling ceremony the hope was expressed that the memorial will still 'be looked upon reverently by our children and their children's children'.[34]

Like all war memorials, Royston's was designed to mediate between past (both immediate and remote), present and future. But how could this linkage be maintained? The bereaved sought assurance of the eternal validity of their commemorative efforts. In both Britain and Germany, artistic institutions worked out blueprints for ideal, everlasting memorials. The Royal Academy of Arts regarded the following principle as vital:

It is essential that memorials within our Churches and Cathedrals, in the close, the public park, or the village green should not clash with the spirit of the past;

[34] 'Royston War Memorial: Unveiling and Dedication Ceremony', *Herts and Cambs Reporter and Royston Crow*, 2376, 31 March 1922, p. 4. Compare J. Bartlett and K. M. Ellis, 'Remembering the Dead in Northop: First World War Memorials in a Welsh Parish', *Journal of Contemporary History*, 34 (1999), p. 232.

Figure 5. British soldier of the First World War and his military ancestors by Mr Clemons. Royston, 1922.

that, however simple, they should express the emotion of the present and hope of the future without losing touch with the past, and that instead of being a rock of offence to future generations, they should be objects of veneration to those who follow us.[35]

Experts were alarmed by the example of the monumental legacy of the nineteenth century. Built for eternity, by 1918 these works were predominantly deemed to be tasteless and outdated. In Britain, self-appointed arbiters of taste like Lawrence Weaver criticised the 'exceeding poverty of memorial design' after the Boer War and urged his contemporaries to focus attention to 'sound traditions' in monumental art.[36] Similarly, in Germany, plastered with hideous monuments to the Bismarckian wars, many were embarrassed to witness the 'shelf-life' of memory. As a consequence, German central and provincial governments set up special advice centres during the war in an effort to improve the artistic quality of future memorial projects.[37] The Prussian centre, the Staatliche Beratungsstelle für Kriegerehrungen, published in connection with an arts pressure group, the Vaterländische Bauhütte, the 'Ten Commandments' of memorial art, as they were entitled. This guideline for memorial committees, drafted by Hermann Hosaeus, was circulated widely in the 1920s. The author, a professor in Berlin and one of the foremost sculptors of the Weimar Republic, recommended that war monuments should be adapted to their environment and be based on 'the artistic traditions of our *Altvorderen* [forebears]', while avoiding slavish copies thereof.[38] The Prussian Beratungsstelle as well as Britain's Royal Academy of Arts argued in favour of what might

---

[35] Royal Academy of Arts, *Annual Report 1918* (London, Royal Academy of Arts, 1918), p. 2; 'The Royal Academy War Memorials Committee', *Architectural Review*, 45 (1919), p. 20. On artistic institutions as agents of remembrance, see Moriarty, 'Narrative and the Absent Body', pp. 111–18; King, *Memorials of the Great War*, pp. 71, 109. Some memorial committees sought aesthetic autonomy and were therefore resistant to guidelines issued by the Royal Academy and other institutions, according to Keith Grieves, 'Investigating Local War Memorial Committees', p. 53.

[36] Lawrence Weaver, *Memorials & Monuments: Old and New: Two Hundred Subjects Chosen from Seven Centuries* (London, Country Life, 1915), pp. 1–2.

[37] Nabrings, '. . . *eine immerfort während Mahnung* . . .', pp. 14–25; Meinhold Lurz, *Kriegerdenkmäler in Deutschland*, vol. III, *1. Weltkrieg* (Heidelberg, Esprint, 1985), pp. 38–9, 46, 64–7; Bach, *Studien zur Geschichte*, pp. 237–9; Schneider, '. . . *nicht umsonst gefallen*'?, pp. 141, 184–8; Ziemann, *Front und Heimat*, pp. 443–4, 448 n. 409; Jeismann and Westheider, 'Wofür stirbt der Bürger?', pp. 35–6.

[38] StAMS, OP 5556, folio 28, Hermann Hosaeus, 'Das Denkmal', in Vaterländische Bauhütte, *Gedenktafeln und andere Kriegerehrenmale: Grundsätze und Ratschläge*, ed. im Auftrage der Staatlichen Beratungsstelle für Kriegerehrungen (Berlin, Deutscher Bund Heimatschutz, 1920), p. 8. On Hosaeus, see Martina Weinland, *Kriegerdenkmäler in Berlin 1870–1930* (Frankfurt am Main, Peter Lang, 1990), ch. 4.

be called contextual memorials. The underlying assumption was that commemorations of the fallen soldiers linked to either history or art history or both would perpetuate memory down through the ages. To put it in the terminology of recent scholarship, the architects of remembrance intended to contain oblivion by fusing two layers of memory. The elision of the existential memory of death in war with the cultural memory of the distant past was meant to accommodate the human toll of the war in a vision of historical continuity – continuity between the past, present and future.

Even though there was little or no compulsion for local committees to follow such guidance, particular schemes adopted the suggested commemorative strategy. It is often hard to judge whether or not this was done deliberately. Even in Prussia, where consultation with the Beratungsstellen was in theory mandatory (but in reality rarely enforced), it is difficult to produce evidence of direct influence on this matter. Nevertheless, the frequent inclusion of copies of the 'Ten Commandments' and comparable publications by other centres and pressure groups in the surviving records of memorial committees may well be indicative of their impact. However that may be, the manuals were inherently abstract and the final decision rested with the committees who were for their part accountable to the subscribers and mourners. In the following section I shall, therefore, turn to the prime movers of memorial making. More precisely, I want to introduce some techniques employed by these agents of memory to convey historical continuity. I shall focus on the resonances of historic settings, the role of historical preservation, the symbolic force of commemorative ceremonies, the tradition of institutions, and, lastly, memorial designs and the process of designing as vectors for the transmission of memory.

Techniques

Collective memory, Maurice Halbwachs has suggested, 'unfolds within a spatial framework. [. . .] space is a reality that endures'.[39] Numerous post-1914–18 commemorations invoked the tradition of suitably historic settings. A perfect illustration of this can be found in a memorial chapel in Bremen. During the war, the distinguished Bremen-born architect and co-founder of the Deutscher Werkbund, Fritz Schumacher, put forward a plan for incorporating the remembrance of the war into the cultural memory of the city. He envisaged the installation of a memorial

---

[39] Halbwachs, *Collective Memory*, p. 140.

in Bremen's ancient cathedral.[40] The actual project was stillborn, yet
Schumacher's principal idea finally took shape. In 1924, the Tresekammer, the treasure-house situated in the annex to one of the oldest inner-
city churches, was turned into the joint memorial chapel of the parochial
parish and Bremen's infantry regiment. At the dedication ceremony,
the parish priest pronounced that in future this 'site of memory [. . .]
shall remain a "Tresekammer", a treasure-house'.[41] From the thirteenth
to the early twentieth century the Tresekammer had functioned as a
depository for the official records of the free and Hanseatic city. Today's
state archive, which indeed preserves some of the source material for this
study, traces its origins to the medieval institution of the Tresekammer.
A more literal blend of different layers of memory, of existential memory
with cultural memory, would be hard to find. When dedicating the
chapel, the pastor could claim with some confidence that the names of
the fallen had been logged indelibly in history and memory.[42]

'The undying memory of an unknown British Warrior', as Sir Henry
Wilson, the chief of the Imperial General Staff, wanted to phrase the
inscription, was integrated into a treasure-house of memory too.[43] While
a powerful icon of remembrance in its own right, its meaning is partly
defined by its location in Westminster Abbey. Human remains rather
than historical documents form a bond between the generations in the
abbey. In the words of the Dean of Westminster, the abbey represents
'a spot where historic treasures are preserved, and where all people are
free to come and gaze. Saxon and Norman, Plantagenet and Tudor,
are lying there at the east end of this building and are visited by thousands of your countrymen from year to year.'[44] The abbey, Britain's

---

[40] StAB, 3–B.13. Nr. 126, folio 10, Fritz Schumacher, 'Kriegsgedächtnis-Stätten: Anre-
gung für Bremen', *Weser-Zeitung*, 25009, 21 May 1916; ibid., folio 26, Fritz Schumacher, 'Der Kreuzgang des Bremer Domes als Kriegsgedächtnis-Stätte', 6 July 1926.

[41] StAB, Ag–9993–11, 'Weihe der Ehrentafeln für die aus der Gemeinde von Unser Lieben
Frauen Gefallenen in der Gedächtniskapelle', 1924, p. 7, my italics: 'soll die Gedächtnis-
stätte [. . .] eine "Tresekammer" bleiben, eine Schatzkammer'. See also StAB, 3–B. 13.
Nr. 92, folio 8, Pastor Groscurth, 'Das Heldenmal in der Liebfrauenkirche', *Bremer
Nachrichten*, 261, 19 September 1924; *Die Krieger-Gedächtniskapelle (Tresekammer) in
Unser Lieben Frauen-Kirche zu Bremen* (Bremen, G.A. Dörrbecker, n.d).

[42] StAB, Ag–9993–11, 'Weihe der Ehrentafeln für die aus der Gemeinde von Unser
Lieben Frauen Gefallenen in der Gedächtniskapelle', 1924, p. 9. See also StAB, 13–
G.7. Nr. 140 (16), 'Aufbewahrung Gedenkbuch zu Ehren der gefallenen Angehörigen
des früheren Infanterie-Regiments Bremen im Gobelinzimmer des Rathauses', 1925–6;
StAB, Ab–53a, 'Gedenkbuch Inf. Rgt. Bremen (I. Hanseat.) No. 75', 2 vols., 1925.

[43] WAML, 58672 B, Henry Wilson to the Dean of Westminster, 7 October 1920.

[44] *The Decoration by General Pershing of the Grave of the Unknown British Warrior in
Westminster Abbey and the Award of the Victoria Cross to the American Unknown: London
October 17, 1921* (New York, Bankers Trust, 1921), p. 8.

national 'Valhalla' of great names, saw the apotheosis of a nameless, ordinary soldier.[45] The Unknown was not only ennobled as a 'Warrior', but also placed in a coffin in form of a sixteenth-century chest made of wood from Hampton Court Palace, and decorated with a 'Crusader's sword' (see figure 2). High diction came full circle in 1921 when the original tomb-slab bearing the simple inscription 'A BRITISH WARRIOR WHO FELL IN THE GREAT WAR' was replaced by an elaborate gravestone crowded with texts. One sentence was borrowed from the tomb of a bishop who had been laid to rest in the abbey in 1395: 'THEY BURIED HIM AMONG THE KINGS BECAUSE HE / HAD DONE GOOD TOWARD GOD AND TOWARD / HIS HOUSE'.[46]

Effectively, the Anglican establishment created a deferential Christian courtier – in stark contrast to Paris's *soldat inconnu* associated with French republicanism. (On his journey through Paris, the unknown soldier was accompanied by the heart of Léon Gambetta, hero of French republicanism at the time of the Franco-Prussian war.[47]) Prior to the ceremony in London, the socialist *Daily Herald* exposed the cult of the Unknown Warrior as a political conjuring trick. 'Who have [*sic*] organised the pageant?', the former editor asked in a published letter. He accused clergy, politicians, press and war profiteers of using the Unknown Warrior as 'emotional doping' in order to distract people from the fate of the survivors.[48] On the following day, the same newspaper made a remarkable volte-face and reported favourably on the return of 'this representative of the Common People; the Man Who Won the War; this Unknown British Warrior – to his last resting place among the captains and the kings of long ago'.[49] The burial also had democratic connotations for the liberal *Manchester Guardian*: 'The nave from ancient times was the people's part of a great church.'[50] The left-wing and liberal press was prepared to join in the official rhetoric of historical continuity. More grandiloquent were, of course, accounts printed in the more conservative newspapers. The *Daily Telegraph* suggested that

[45] P. O'Donovan 'Mothers and Wives: Queens in Tears', *Daily Express*, 6423, 12 November 1920, p. 7.

[46] Inglis, 'Entombing Unknown Soliders', p. 15.

[47] Ibid., pp. 13–14.

[48] Francis Meynell, 'The Unknown Warrior', *Daily Herald*, 1497, 11 November 1920, p. 4. See Gregory, *Silence of Memory*, p. 26.

[49] 'England Honours Its Unknown Dead: The Warrior Laid to Rest', *Daily Herald*, 1498, 12 November 1920, p. 1.

[50] 'A Nation's Remembrance and Devotion: The Nameless Warrior's Abbey Burial', *Manchester Guardian*, 23168, 12 November 1920, p. 9.

he [the Unknown Warrior] stands for all the long centuries of our national life and loyalty, purpose, strength, and faith. He is no product of the last six years. He has always lived in our midst, and please God, he is not dead to-day. He – just he, and no other – fought with Clive and Wellington; he died with Nelson and with Wolfe: Marlborough knew him well – and far away beyond the high altar, beyond the Chapel of the Confessor, Henry the Fifth hails him as one of his grim and indomitable company to whom the honour he promised them on the morning of his great fight has at last been rendered, 'For he to-day that sheds his blood with me, shall be my brother.' And as a brother of Kings he was given a place in our Abbey yesterday.[51]

It is noteworthy that the Unknown Warrior was interred in Westminster Abbey rather than St Paul's Cathedral. The cathedral, the final resting-place for naval and military heroes like Nelson and Wellington, was particularly associated with the armed forces. A memorial chapel holding the graves of Field Marshal Earl Kitchener of Khartoum, Secretary of State for War until he was drowned in 1916, and other outstanding generals had been suggested for St Paul's as early as 1915.[52] Eventually, a Kitchener memorial chapel with an empty tomb was consecrated in 1925 (see figure 56). St Paul's, it seems, was intended to be reserved for high-ranking officers. Yet, more importantly, the cathedral lacked the abbey's symbolic force. Westminster Abbey established a relationship between the absent dead of 1914–18 and the army of the first battle of the Somme, the men of Agincourt under Henry V. *The Times* saw the historic parallels:

Fitly is the 'Unknown Warrior' buried in the soil of France [this soil was brought to Britain together with the corpse], the soil of France henceforth sacred to us as to her own sons, and consecrated for ever by the heroic sacrifices of both in common warfare against the over-weening insolence of armed lawlessness and wrong. Fitly will he rest in French soil, the gift of French hands, beneath the chapel where hang the helmet and the sword of the conqueror of Agincourt. His blood and the blood of his great company, now sleeping in that same soil across the Channel, has washed away, we trust for ever, the memories of old enmity from the bosoms of the two peoples, and has cemented between them an amity that will know no end.[53]

---

[51] Perceval Landon, 'Brother of Kings: Unknown Buried in the Abbey', *Daily Telegraph*, 20460, 12 November 1920, p. 13. The quotation is from William Shakespeare, *King Henry V*, IV, iii, 61–2.

[52] Guildhall Library, London, Ms 24.468/3, Lord Knutsford to Canon Alexander, 8 March 1915.

[53] 'Armistice Day', *The Times*, 42565, 11 November 1920, p. 15. Compare 'The Living and the Dead', *The Times*, 42875, 11 November 1921, p. 11.

The way the Unknown Warrior was absorbed into the history of the setting also fascinated German observers. A member of the national parliament, Walther Lambach of the right-wing German National People's Party (DNVP), was thrilled that the unknown man

> places the dead in the long procession of the makers of English history. Through this grave of the Unknown Soldier, the Great War with all its pain and pride is fitted into history. The lessons he teaches are rooted in the ages which have generated this war, and in even older ones. Nothing is an isolated event in this place. Everything becomes a living link in the making of English greatness.[54]

In the public discussion on the Reich memorial issue, demands were made for a German version of Westminster Abbey, either with or without the tomb of an unknown soldier. Candidates nominated for this purpose included Mainz Cathedral and Ulm Minster.[55] However, given the denominational split within German society, the most likely candidate was Cologne Cathedral. Despite its Roman Catholic character, the building had gained iconic status for the nationalist movement in the early nineteenth century. Later in the same century, the cathedral was appropriated by the Prussian Crown to turn nationalist longings to Prussia's advantage. Under royal patronage, building work on the unfinished cathedral resumed in 1842 and was completed with a pompous ceremony in 1880. The project had owed much to the example of Westminster Abbey, or to its imaginative construction in Germany as a shrine of nationalism and religion.[56] After the Great War, Konrad Adenauer set out to return to the nineteenth-century tradition. He approached the Reich Art Custodian in writing in order to win support for the burial of an unknown soldier in Cologne Cathedral. With his letter he enclosed a photograph of the tomb of the Unknown Warrior in London as well as six lengthy extracts from speeches made at the cathedral over the previous hundred years. What Adenauer had in mind was the rebirth of the cathedral as a symbol of the 'unity of all German tribes' that would obliterate the memory of past conflicts between Protestants and Catholics – with the unknown soldier added as a mere

---

[54] BArch, R 43 I/714, folio 196, Walther Lambach, 'Die andere Seite des Reichsehrenmals', *Politische Wochenschrift für Volkstum und Staat*, 32, 12 Aug. 1926, p. 770: 'Es reiht den Toten ein in die lange Reihe der Träger englischer Geschichte. Durch dieses Grab des Unbekannten Soldaten ist der große Krieg mit all seinem Schmerz und seinem Stolz eingereiht in die Geschichte. Lehren, die er gibt, sind verwurzelt in den Zeiten, die diesen Krieg geboren haben und in noch älteren. Nichts ist an dieser Stelle Einzelereignis. Alles wird zum lebendigen Gliede des Werdens englischer Größe.'
[55] BArch, R 32/361a, folio 21, Ein Rheinländer to Reichskunstwart, n.d.
[56] Thomas Nipperdey, 'Der Kölner Dom als Nationaldenkmal', *Historische Zeitschrift*, 233 (1981), pp. 549–50, 556, 601–2. See also Ludger Kerssen, *Das Interesse am Mittelalter im deutschen Nationaldenkmal* (Berlin and New York, Walter de Gruyter, 1975), pp. 16–48.

afterthought.[57] Adenauer's initiative failed, not least because it was an unbalanced blend of cultural and existential memory, of identity politics and the encoding of trauma.

In nineteenth-century Cologne, a building site had acquired the status of a memorial. The search for a national symbol had translated into an effort to complete and secure the country's architectural remains. Historic preservation as a type of memorial and technique of (re)constructing continuity flourished after 1918. It was a memorial type which became very congenial to people with a preference for amenity over imagery.[58] For a commemoration to endure it had to yield service to the survivors, reasoned the war memorial committee of Christ Church, Oxford, which planned a memorial that was 'useful to the College rather than pure ornament'. They meant to restore the old library 'to some former condition'.[59] Until the dissolution of the priory, which antedated the foundation of the college in the reign of Henry VIII, the upper storey had served as a refectory. This part of the building was to be fitted up as a combined memorial and exhibition hall containing a list of names of fallen members and the college art collection. The idea of reconstructing the refectory or the old library was not altogether new. A thorough restoration had been recommended by a historian of the college in 1900. He was appalled at the 'serious mutilation of an ancient and beautiful building, the former monastic refectory' which since the late eighteenth century had provided students' accommodation.[60] The memorial hall was never built, but during the 1920s the fellows and old members of Christ Church discussed a number of alternatives. Interestingly, the working party's original concern for beauty versus utility resurfaced and proved a bone of contention.[61]

The British taste for utilitarian memorials stemmed largely from Protestant 'iconophobia'.[62] For die-hard Protestants, restorations of relics of the past were sufficiently useful ventures. But they were problematic if those relics were opulent, Catholic religious art. In Norfolk, it

---

[57] BArch, R 43 I/713, folio 29, Konrad Adenauer to Reichskunstwart, 2 June 1925: 'Sinnbild der Einigkeit aller deutschen Stämme'. The extracts are on fos. 28–33. See also ibid., fos. 49–50, Reichskunstwart to Konrad Adenauer, 9 June 1925.

[58] See, for instance, IWM, Eph. Mem., K 4086, 'Perthshire War Memorial: Restoration of the Church of St John, Perth', 1923, pp. 1–2.

[59] Christ Church Archives, Oxford, GB xv.c.3, 'Memorandum by Committee on War Memorial', 12 May 1919.

[60] Henry L. Thompson, Christ Church (London, F. E. Robinson, 1900), pp. 161–2.

[61] Christ Church Archives, GB xv.c.3, H. J. White, 'Christ Church War Memorial Fund', December 1926, and letters by old members.

[62] Inglis, 'The Homecoming', pp. 585–6, 595. On 'iconophobia', see chapter 5.

Figure 6. Medieval tower with Roland-style statues by Wilhelm Kreis and Josef Buerbaum. Dorsten, 1925.

was decided to rebuild the eastern chapel of Norwich Cathedral, a medium-sized room, to 'serve a useful purpose', as the dean stressed.[63] The ancient chapel had either collapsed or been demolished by iconoclasts in Elizabethan times. The architect, the external consultants, and the dean and chapter were divided over the issue of the new chapel's design. After all, there were three historic forerunners: an early Saxon church, the Norman chapel of the Holy Saviour of the eleventh century, and the thirteenth-century Gothic-style Lady Chapel. The commissioned architect, Sir Charles Nicholson, imagined a Gothic structure resembling the Lady Chapel of St Germain at Auxerre.[64] His proposal clashed with the chapter's demands for the reconstruction of a more functional chapel less dependent on stained glass. Nicholson suspected that his critics were actuated by 'Puritan motives'.[65] Eventually, they reached a compromise: the chapel's architecture was neo-Gothic, its name was taken from the Norman chapel, and the lines of all foundations were marked on the pavement.[66]

[63] 'In the Cathedral: Book of Remembrance Unveiled by Prince', *Eastern Daily Press*, 19136, 4 May 1932, p. 13.
[64] NRO, DCN 106/2, Charles Nicholson to Dean Crang, [c. 1929].
[65] Ibid., 106/7, Charles Nicholson to William Hope, 30 March 1919.
[66] Ibid., 106/12, 'Points of Agreement', 19 December 1929.

Figure 6. (*cont.*).

Restorations and reconstructions enjoyed popularity with Britons and Germans alike. In Dorsten, Westphalia, the ruined tower of the former city wall underwent a process of restyling (see figure 6). The memorial makers showed themselves pleased with the outcome: 'In itself a venerable memorial of past centuries, it [the tower] has willingly and intimately wedded a site of memory for times to come.'[67] Similarly, in Dülken, Rhine Province, the conservation of the town's medieval ramparts was made part of the war memorial.[68] In both cases, the provincial advice centres, the Westphalian and the Rhenish Beratungsstellen für Kriegerehrungen

---

[67] Joseph Wiedenhöfer, *Die Kriegergedächtnisstätte der Stadt Dorsten: Zum Weihetag 4. Oktober 1925* (Dorsten, Hermann Majert, 1925), p. 13: 'Selbst ein ehrwürdiges Denkmal vergangener Jahrhunderte, hat er sich willig und innig mit einem Gedächtnismal für die kommenden Zeiten vermählt.'
[68] Nabrings, '. . . *eine immerfort währende Mahnung* . . .', pp. 19, 46–8.

respectively, acted in an advisory capacity to the committees. In general, the Beratungsstellen welcomed the incorporation of historic preservation into the grammar of war remembrance. But restorations brought further agents into the commemorative arena. Curators of monuments intervened when they felt that war memorials would not enhance but endanger the cultural heritage. In the East Friesian town of Norden, Hanover, the provincial curator was dissatisfied with some details of the redecoration of the tower of a late-Gothic church to accommodate a 'Hall of Fame'. Yet the town council, the instigator of the memorial, commissioned an independent (and more favourable) report by a professor of art history from the Technical University of Berlin.[69]

On the whole, consultative arrangements in Britain were less formalised and state-centred. Private and semi-official pressure groups played a critical role. The Dean and Chapter of Ely Cathedral, for instance, engaged the services of the Royal Academy of Arts to reconcile the adornment of the memorial chapel with the architecture of the cathedral.[70] The memorial's equivalent at Norwich Cathedral attracted heavy criticism from the Society for the Protection of Ancient Buildings (SPAB). The Society, founded by William Morris in 1877, objected in principle to the falsification of ancient monuments through drastic methods of restoration. The SPAB aimed to preserve – rather than restore – the integrity of the architectural inheritance from further decay.[71] Two other bodies were officially called in by the Norfolk committee. Neither of them shared the SPAB's minimalism. The Royal Fine Arts Commission endorsed the plan for a Norman building whereas the Gothic chapel found favour with the Central Council for Care of Churches.[72]

---

[69] StAA, Dep. 60, Acc. 1993/13, Statement by Stadtbauamt Norden, 1 February 1933; ibid., Provinzial-Konservator to Magistrat Norden, 7 February 1933; ibid., Professor Bock to Bürgermeister Norden, 4 December 1931. On networks of historic preservation generally, see Winfried Speitkamp, *Die Verwaltung der Geschichte: Denkmalpflege und Staat in Deutschland 1871–1933* (Göttingen, Vandenhoeck & Ruprecht, 1996), esp. pp. 395–6; Rudy Koshar, *Germany's Transient Pasts: Preservation and National Memory in the Twentieth Century* (Chapel Hill and London, University of North Carolina Press, 1998), ch. 2.

[70] CUL, EDC 2/1/10, p. 77, 'Architect for the War Memorial', 4 November 1919; ibid., p. 81, 'Site of War Memorial', 25 November 1919. On the Royal Academy's attitude towards historic preservation, see Royal Academy of Arts, *Annual Report 1918*, p. 67.

[71] Charles Dellheim, *The Face of the Past: The Preservation of the Medieval Inheritance in Victorian England* (Cambridge, Cambridge University Press, 1982), pp. 85–92.

[72] NRO, DCN 106/1, 'Minute Book of Cathedral War Memorial Chapel Committee', 9 November 1929; ibid., 106/14, 'Report of Central Council for Care of Churches', 28 March 1929; ibid., 106/7, Charles Nicholson to William Hope, 30 March 1919; ibid., 106/39, SPAB to Dean of Norwich, 30 April 1927.

In 1920, the Dean of Norwich launched a public appeal to raise money for the rebuilding of the Norman chapel. He suggested that 'we of the 20th century shall be linked up with our fellow Churchmen of 820 years ago'.[73] After ten years of discussion and planning that moment had finally arrived. The foundation stone was laid in November 1930 at a spectacular service, which the dean's successor explained as follows:

The ceremony at two o'clock to-day will be a wonderful echo of that which took place in 1096 under the guidance of Herbert de Losinga. Our present Bishop is the 64th since the founder, and in laying the central stone he will use the identical words pronounced in 1096, substituting only 'Bertrandus' for 'Herbertus': *In nomine Patris et Filii et Spiritus Sancti. Amen. Ego Bertrandus Episcopus opposui istum lapidem.* A second stone was laid in 1096 by a prominent nobleman, Hubert de Ry; and a second stone to-day will be placed in memory of Dr. Beeching [dean, 1911–1919] by Canon Allen Bell, Vice-Dean, who has been honorary secretary all through of the War Memorial Committee.[74]

The spirit of reconstruction, which in spite of all the disagreement over details had pervaded the project from the outset, climaxed in the pageantry of the inauguration. The ceremony was a powerful display of the Church of England's special status, its historical legitimacy and its ability to rejuvenate liturgy.

The Anglican clergy were all too aware of the threat the upheaval of war had posed to institutionalised religion in general and the Established Church in particular – a threat potentially more dangerous than the disestablishment question of the nineteenth century. The war fostered the existing trend towards the diversification and privatisation of religion.[75] Soldiers and mourners were driven by their spiritual needs to embrace unconventional forms of contact with the supernatural, notably spiritualist seances.[76] Alert theologians voiced their concerns. In 1918, the newly elected Dean of King's College, Cambridge, and erstwhile army chaplain, Eric Milner-White, concluded that Britain was on the threshold of 'a second Reformation'.[77] From his High Church point of view, Milner-White saw liturgical reform as a suitable antidote, and King's College Chapel as the optimal centre of this reform movement.

---

[73] Ibid., 106/28, 'Proposed War Memorial Chapel: Statement by the Dean and Appeal for Further Support', July 1920.

[74] Dean of Norwich, 'Cathedral War Memorial Chapel', *Eastern Daily Press*, 18468, 29 November 1930, p. 6, italics in the original.

[75] On the nineteenth century, see José Harris, *Private Lives, Public Spirit: Britain 1870–1914* (Oxford, Oxford University Press, 1993), p. 179.

[76] Winter, *Sites of Memory*, ch. 3.

[77] KCMAC, EM-W, 2/4, 'Memorandum "The Chapel" Presented to King's College Council', 1918, [p. 1].

Later in the same year, the dean introduced on Christmas Eve the 'Festival of Nine Lessons and Carols', which since 1928 has been broadcast on radio every year (except in 1930). The actual invention of this form dates back to 1880 when Bishop E. W. Benson composed a carol service for his new Cathedral of Truro. Benson drew on examples from the Middle Ages, when great feasts were marked by a series of nine Lessons.[78]

A peculiar blend of Christian and pagan, medieval and Germanic traditions is characteristic of rites of remembrance in Germany. The Austro-German wartime phenomenon of iron-nail war landmarks or *Kriegswahrzeichen zum Benageln* is illustrative of the significance of ceremony in the construction of continuity. Throughout the German and Austro-Hungarian empires local communities erected wooden objects which, in the course of month-long and sometimes year-long celebrations, were described or outlined by a series of nails. The nailing ceremonial was conceived as a community event. All citizens, both young and old, male and female, rich and poor, were called on to hammer iron, copper, silver and golden nails, or metal plaques, into war landmarks. The participants had to pay for the privilege by contributing to war charities, mostly in aid of war widows and orphans.

The meteoric career of iron-nail objects in 1915–16 started in Vienna in March 1915. Although the very first war landmark had been unveiled in Villingen, Baden, earlier in the same year, the one at Vienna became paradigmatic.[79] It denoted a medieval knight in a suit of armour carrying a sword. The iconography of iron-nail objects will be dealt with in the following chapters. At this point, the symbolism of nailing is of interest. The commemorative ritual was a practical recourse to myths surrounding the *Stock im Eisen*, a time-honoured tree stump studded with nails and enclosed by a metal ring, situated in the historic part of Vienna.[80]

[78] KCMAC, Coll., 21/1, Eric Milner-White, 'The Origin of the Carol Service', 1952. The service was adopted at Great Wilbraham, Cambs. See CROC, P 174/1/23, 'A Festival of Nine Lessons and Carols in King's College Chapel upon Christmas Eve 1930: Order of Service', 1930. See also Mark Connelly, *Christmas: A Social History* (London and New York, I. B. Tauris, 1999), pp. 140–5.

[79] Gerhard Schneider, 'Zur Mobilisierung der "Heimatfront": Das Nageln sogenannter Kriegswahrzeichen im Ersten Weltkrieg', *Zeitschrift für Volkskunde*, 95 (1999), pp. 36–7. See also Gerhard Schneider, 'Über hannoversche Nagelfiguren im Ersten Weltkrieg', *Hannoversche Geschichtsblätter*, new ser., 50 (1996), p. 213–15; Stefan Goebel, '"Kohle und Schwert": Zur Konstruktion der Heimatfront in Kriegswahrzeichen des Ruhrgebietes im Ersten Weltkrieg', *Westfälische Forschungen*, 51 (2001), pp. 257–81.

[80] Michael Diers, 'Nagelmänner: Propaganda mit ephemeren Denkmälern im Ersten Weltkrieg', in Michael Diers, *Schlagbilder: Zur politischen Ikonographie der Gegenwart* (Frankfurt am Main, Fischer, 1997), pp. 78–84.

Legend had it that for centuries passing craftsmen had followed the superstitious custom of hitting nails into the stump. The Viennese practice provided a model for war landmarks everywhere. Reporting on the inauguration of Stuttgart's iron-nail figure – also a knight (see figure 34) – a local newspaper recalled the story of Vienna's *Stock im Eisen*:

An apprentice locksmith [. . .], with the assistance of the Devil, made the iron ring which surrounds the trunk, and the allegedly un-openable lock on it; later, however, when he missed Mass once on a Sunday, he became, according to the pact he had made, the Devil's, and since then every apprentice locksmith departing from Vienna has been obliged to hit a nail into the trunk and to say a brief prayer for his accursed fellow craftsman. Yet recent research claims to have found out that the nailing of the larch trunk goes back to an age-old heathen custom.[81]

Iron-nail war landmarks contributed to the cultural and financial mobilisation of the population. The aspect of commemoration was built into the propaganda (generated from below).[82] Nailing ceremonies sometimes marked private moments of grief and contemplation in the public arena. 'We are nailing for the dead a statue of their ancestors', informs a postcard depicting the iron-nail monument of Cologne (again, a warrior in armour).[83] In Hagen, Westphalia, death in war was linked to Christ's sacrifice. On Good Friday 1916, the bereaved were invited to hammer special memorial nails into the city's war landmark (see figure 9). In return, the participants received a certificate as a private memento. A memorial volume celebrating the first anniversary of Hagen's war landmark 'quotes' the wooden figure: 'Their names, their

---

[81] 'Im Zeichen des Sedantages: Genagelte Kriegswahrzeichen', *Stuttgarter Neues Tagblatt*, 443, 2 September 1915, p. 5: 'Ein Schlosserlehrling habe [. . .] mit Hilfe des Teufels das eiserne Band, das den Stamm umschließt und das angeblich unaufsperrbare Schloß daran angefertigt; später aber sei er, als er eines Sonntags die Messe versäumte, dem abgeschlossenen Pakt gemäß vom Teufel geholt worden, und seitdem sei jeder aus Wien abreisende Schlosserlehrling verpflichtet gewesen, einen Nagel in den Stamm zu schlagen und für seinen unseligen Berufsgenossen ein kurzes Gebet zu sprechen. Neuere Forschungen wollen jedoch herausgebracht haben, daß die Nagelung des Lärchenstocks auf einen uralten heidnischen Gebrauch zurückgehe.' See also Julius Lasius, 'Kriegswahrzeichen in rheinisch-westfälischen Industriestädten', *Stahl und Eisen*, 36,6 (1916), pp. 133–4; 'Kriegsnagelungen', in *Illustrierte Geschichte des Weltkrieges 1914/16*, vol. IV (Stuttgart, Union Deutsche Verlagsgesellschaft, [1916]), p. 334; Maximilian Rapsilber, *Der Eiserne Hindenburg von Berlin: Ein Gedenkblatt* (Berlin, Hermann Bartdorff, 1918), p. 42.

[82] By contrast, Schneider, 'Mobilisierung der "Heimatfront"', pp. 52–3, holds that the commemoration of the war dead was merely a secondary aspect which only came to the fore from 1917 onwards. See also Schneider, 'Hannoversche Nagelfiguren', pp. 220, 251.

[83] Warburg-Haus, Bildindex, 100/10, Postcard, Cologne, 1915: 'Wir nageln den Toten ein Standbild der Ahnen'.

commemoration must be affixed to my war sign for centuries [to come].'[84] Bremen's iron-nail figure bore a shield, the edges of which were reserved for nails in remembrance of fallen citizens (see figure 22).[85] For the time after the expected military victory, it was planned to exhibit the object permanently in Bremen's local history museum. Indeed, most communities drew up schemes for transforming ephemeral war landmarks into enduring memorials.

Pre-existing memorials could also provide the foci of new rituals of war remembrance. A local branch of the conservative veterans' association, Kyffhäuserbund (officially, since 1921, called Deutscher Reichskriegerbund Kyffhäuser), organised a ceremony in the spirit of the ancient Teutons which took place at a Bismarck column outside Hanover.[86] Bismarck columns had been the foremost articulation of the cult of the ex-chancellor in Wilhelmine Germany. Hundreds of simple, solid towers, usually between ten and twenty metres in height, topped with a fire bowl, crown the hills of the German countryside to this day. Contemporaries were reminded of sepulchral monuments for Saxon and Norman warriors. A streak of para-religion runs through the memorial movement. *Götterdämmerung*, the 'Twilight of the Gods', was, after all, the motto of Wilhelm Kreis's epoch-making design for the ideal Bismarck column. Kreis had won the first prize in a national competition initiated by the German students' union in 1898.[87] The columns, based on Kreis's model and raised locally in the following years, became instrumental in exalting Otto von Bismarck as a German superman and students' hero. Yearly on 1 April, Bismarck's birthday, and on 21 June, the summer solstice, students built bonfires on top of the columns. After the war, the Bismarck craze and midsummer festival became fused with war remembrance at the University of Tübingen. From 1922 onwards, midsummer night was reserved for homage to fellow students killed in the war. Ceremonies were either held at the war memorial (inaugurated on 21 June 1922) or the Bismarck column.[88]

[84] *Der Eiserne Schmied von Hagen: Das Erste Jahr seiner Geschichte* (Hagen, Verlag des Eisernen Schmiedes, 1916), p. 68. On Vienna's *Stock im Eisen*, see ibid., p. 5. See also StdAH, 809/0, 'Der Eiserne Schmied von Hagen an seine lieben Mitbürger', 1915; Goebel, 'Kohle und Schwert', pp. 275–80.
[85] StAB, 7,60/2–9.b.1, 'Der Eiserne Roland in Bremen: Die Einweihungsfeier', *Bremer Nachrichten*, 195, 16 July 1915.
[86] Schneider, '. . . *nicht umsonst gefallen*'?, p. 175.
[87] Reinhard Alings, *Monument und Nation: Das Bild vom Nationalstaat im Medium Denkmal – zum Verhältnis von Nation und Staat im Deutschen Kaiserreich 1871–1918* (Berlin and New York, Walter de Gruyter, 1996), pp. 128–42, 235–45.
[88] Mathias Kotowski, ' "Noch ist ja der Krieg gar nicht zu Ende": Weltkriegsgedenken der Universität Tübingen in der Weimarer Republik', in Gerhard Hirschfeld *et al.* (eds.),

Music is an important element in church liturgy. At the Klosterschule
in Magdeburg, a secularised convent school, the singing of hymns
bridged the gap between the modern *Gymnasium* – the German equivalent of the British grammar and public schools – and the monastic
community from which it originated: 'Ancient medleys of tunes fill the
church of the monastery, link centuries with each other. This memorial,
too, shall now stand amidst the sound of those holy chants.'[89] Ignoring
the impact of the Reformation and modern curricula, the school nur-
tured the vision of institutional continuity in the aftermath of the war.
Similarly, the Master of Magdalene College, Cambridge, A. C. Benson
(son of Bishop E. W. Benson), suggested institutional continuity between
the Benedictine students' hostel of the fifteenth century and its twentieth-
century successor. At the dedication of the memorial tablet in 1923, A. C.
Benson – actually a great moderniser of the college – associated the 'battle
of life' fought by the medieval monk-scholars with the task faced by
modern soldiers.[90]

The affirmation of continuity contrasted with a parallel discourse: the
myth of 'the lost generation'. The notion of the Great War as a demographic disaster exercised a firm hold on British imagination in the inter-
war period. The nation, noticeably the upper classes, lamented over a
whole generation of young men wiped out in the trenches of the Western
Front. The belief in a generational rupture was all-pervasive in the
context of Oxford and Cambridge colleges and the public schools.[91]
Large plaques listing name upon name, put up prominently in chapels
and elsewhere, are the still visible signs of the grief over 'the lost generation'. At the same time, 'Oxbridge' and public school war memorials
reasserted older lines of continuity which were rooted in the history
of the institutions. Alongside the names of the fallen, memorials
recall the debt to founders, patrons and benefactors. Ethelfreda (an early

Kriegserfahrungen: Studien zur Sozial- und Mentalitätsgeschichte des Ersten Weltkriegs
(Essen, Klartext, 1997), pp. 427–8, 437.
[89] Albrecht Kaiser, *Das Denkmal der Gefallenen Lehrer und Schüler des Klosters Unserer Lieben Frauen zu Magdeburg* (Magdeburg, Haenel, 1920), p. 14: 'Uralte Melodien gehen durch die Klosterkirche, verbinden Jahrhunderte miteinander. Unter den Klängen dieser heiligen Choräle soll nun auch dieses Denkmal stehen.'
[90] *Magdalene College War Memorial: Dedication by the Bishop of Ely: November 11th 1923* (Cambridge, Magdalene College, 1923), p. 12.
[91] Catherine Jamet-Bellier de la Duboisière, 'Commemorating "the Lost Generation": First World War Memorials in Cambridge, Oxford and Some English Public Schools', M.Litt. dissertation, University of Cambridge, 1995, pp. 7–10, 252; Jay M. Winter, 'Die Legende der "verlorenen Generation" in Großbritannien', in Klaus Vondung (ed.), *Kriegserlebnis: Der Erste Weltkrieg in der literarischen Gestaltung und symbolischen Deutung der Nationen* (Göttingen, Vandenhoeck & Ruprecht, 1980), esp. p. 138.

foundress and daughter of King Alfred), Edward the Confessor (a founder and patron saint) and Henry VIII (chief patron) appear in the memorial window of Warwick School.[92] Rugby School, founded 'only' in 1567, added imagined ancestors to its genealogical tree: the memorial window depicts the founder side by side with King Arthur and King Alfred, Saint Edmund and Saint Oswald.[93] Eton College wanted to honour its dead by fulfilling the founder's will of 1444. Henry VI's decree contained a provision for the building of a great square tower at the angle of the intersection of Upper and Lower School. A letter to the college magazine was full of praise for the idea:

> The building of such a tower would be an act of faith – faith in the Founder's judgment, which has been so wonderfully vindicated down the ages, faith in this our own generation as capable of producing something worthy of the sacrifice made in this War, a humble faith in the greatness of our destiny and of our opportunities in the training of future generations. The tower would be an outward and visible symbol of faith, and a glorious memorial of those who have gone from us.[94]

Eton's architect had sketched out a design for the Henry VI tower and also produced a miniature model by the time the college authorities resolved to drop the project. Several smaller memorials were realised instead. Four memorial tapestries, in the style of the Arts and Crafts movement – the tapestries were made by Morris & Company at Merton Abbey – narrating the story of the boyhood of St George embellish the walls of the Lower Chapel where the younger Etonians attend services (see figure 7). Remarkably, the artist used the faces of young pupils as models for images of the saint.[95] The same technique of blending past with present, legend with actuality, was employed in the design of the war landmark at Havelberg, Brandenburg. It showed a triumphant knight standing on a slain beast. The iconography is reminiscent of representations of St George, yet the knight's face has the unmistakable features of Hindenburg and the dragon is replaced by the Russian bear.[96]

---

[92] C[harles] F. Kernot, *British Public Schools War Memorials* (London, Roberts & Newton, 1927), p. 166.

[93] Ibid., p. 60.

[94] E. W. Stone, 'Etona Non Immemor', *Eton College Chronicle*, 1669, 31 October 1918, p. 508; also cited in Eton College Archives, Windsor, ED 53/2, 'A Plan for a Tower at Eton as a Memorial of the Great War', n.d. The file ED 53/2 contains, in addition, drawings and photographs of the model by the architect Thomas Carter. See also the booklet ibid., COLL/P6/12/21, 'Letter to the Provost of King's College, Cambridge, Commending the Drawings for the King's Tower at Eton', 1918.

[95] Kernot, *Public Schools War Memorials*, p. 44.

[96] Warburg-Haus, Bildindex 100/10, Postcard Havelberg, n.d. See also ibid., 100/10, Postcard Graudenz, n.d.; Schneider, 'Mobilisierung der "Heimatfront"', fig. 8.

Figure 7. St George fighting the dragon. Tapestry designed by Mrs Akers-Douglas and manufactured by Morris & Co. Eton College, Windsor, 1923.

Projecting features of modern soldiers on to historic or legendary characters was a mnemonic strategy commonly applied by families to commemorations in stained glass of fallen individuals. A number of British memorial windows portray the deceased person as St George clad in armour.[97] Windows dedicated to a larger group of people achieve a similar effect by attributing emblems of modernity to medieval warriors. At Chatteris, Cambridgeshire, unnamed knights display the symbols of modern nationalism, viz. the American Stars and Stripes and the French Tricolour, among others.[98]

Stained glass was an effective medium for constructing narratives of continuity (see figures 27 and 33). What is more, stained glass was by its very nature evocative of the aura of medieval churches and cathedrals. Its whole development took place during the Middle Ages, and it was an art form that was peculiar to western Christianity. The catalogue of a war memorial exhibition organised by the Victoria and Albert Museum in

[97] NIWM, 4558, Kentford, W. Suff.; NIWM, 5572, Theberton, E. Suff.; NIWM, 16045, Ladybarn, Lancs.
[98] County Record Office, Cambridge, P 38/6/6, Statements by Thomas F. Curtis, 1921–5; NIWM, 3515, Chatteris, Cambs.

Figure 7 (*detail*).

co-operation with the Royal Academy War Memorials Committee
states: 'Stained glass windows, by origin an ecclesiastical form of art,
were employed at first mainly as an embellishment for the churches in
which they were set, with the ulterior object of teaching Bible history,

theology, and the lives of the saints by means of pictorial representation to an unlettered congregation.'[99] Stained-glass windows proved indeed a popular alternative to figurative monuments in Britain after 1918, often featuring medieval knights, with images of modern weaponry adding to the time-honoured lexicon of warfare in art.

The Victoria and Albert Museum promoted tried and tested forms – such as stained-glass windows – rather than transitory artistic fashions. Memorial windows gained currency during the inter-war years. Many examples bear the distinct stamp of the Arts and Crafts movement or the Gothic revivalists and thus stand in the tradition of the style of Boer War windows. In fact, Morris & Company and its leading competitor, C. E. Kempe of London, continued to produce memorial windows after 1918.[100] In Germany, on the other hand, windows were but a negligible segment of war memorials. Stained glass was conspicuously absent from a selection of historic memorials since the Stone Age presented jointly by progressive artistic institutions, amongst others the Deutscher Werkbund, in 1917.[101] Both the Victoria and Albert Museum and the Werkbund advocated ancient formulae as a source of inspiration, not imitation. In practice, German artists proved freer than their British peers in adapting historic forms to modernist developments. The contrast between the simplicity of the design of the castle-style memorial of Tannenberg with its expressionist façades and the opulence of the neo-Baronial Scottish memorial hall in Edinburgh Castle may serve as an example (see figures 3 and 36).[102] In Britain, borrowings from art history tended to follow nineteenth-century revival styles or Arts and

[99] Victoria and Albert Museum, *Catalogue of the War Memorials Exhibition 1919* (London, HMSO, 1919), p. 20.

[100] See, for instance, two East Anglian examples. NIWM, 3508, Wisbech, Cambs., was designed by Morris & Co.; NIWM, 288, Huntingdon, was produced by C. E. Kempe. In general, see Martin Harrison, 'Church Decoration and Stained Glass', in Linda Parry (ed.), *William Morris* (London, Victoria & Albert Museum, 1996), pp. 106–7; Joanna Banham and Jennifer Harris (eds.), *William Morris and the Middle Ages* (Manchester and Dover, N.H., Manchester University Press, 1984). To see the similarity in design between Boer War and Great War memorial windows, visit the memorials in Norwich Cathedral. An inventory of Boer War memorials is provided by James Gildea, *For Remembrance and in Honour of Those Who Lost Their Lives in the South African War 1899–1902* (London, Eyre and Spottiswoode, 1911).

[101] Peter Jessen *et al.*, *Kriegergräber im Felde und daheim*, ed. im Einvernehmen mit der Heeresverwaltung (Munich, F. Bruckmann, 1917). On the Deutscher Werkbund in general, see Frederic J. Schwartz, *The Werkbund: Design Theory and Mass Culture before the First World War* (New Haven and London, Yale University Press, 1996).

[102] The 'expressionism' of the façades is captured in a photograph published in Buchheit, *Reichsehrenmal Tannenberg*, p. 50.

Crafts aesthetics. To be sure, there were notable exceptions like the work of the sculptor Eric Gill.

Gill belonged to a generation of avant-garde artists which one scholar has called 'medieval modernists'. Gill's 'medieval modernism' is rooted in a specific understanding of the act of designing and its purpose. Like William Morris and John Ruskin before him, Gill repudiated the separation between art and design, or art and life, since the Renaissance and sought to restore the pre-modern definition of art as both aesthetic and functional. Unlike his nineteenth-century predecessors, Gill renounced medievalism, especially the Gothic revival, as a stylistic fashion.[103] He received a number of commissions to design war monuments which allowed him to translate his ideas into reality. Simplified, archaising forms, carved directly in stone, are the signature of Gill's memorial art.

For Trumpington, Cambridgeshire, he created a plain 'cross of vaguely medieval form' adorned with four small reliefs (see figure 8).[104] One of the reliefs was based on a design by the author David Jones (like Gill a convert to Roman Catholicism), who had joined Gill's radical 'guild [. . .] of craftsmen' which sought to revive the communal spirit of medieval society.[105] Guild craftsmanship, underpinned by religious and socialist fervour, provided the frame of Gill's colony of artists at Ditchling, Sussex. The concept of a guild emulated the medieval workshop tradition, linking arts and crafts and fostering a community of creators – in contrast, so it seemed, to the modern worker and his apparent alienation from the products of his labour. A German parallel was the radical, but reactionary *Bauhütten* principle of the German war graves association (Volksbund Deutsche Kriegsgräberfürsorge). Here the individual artist was absorbed by the designers' collective, the *Bauhütte*. The way in which the Volksbund's workshops at Munich were organised derived from medieval craft lodges for artisans working on cathedrals. The

[103] Michael T. Saler, *The Avant-Garde in Interwar England: Medieval Modernism and the London Underground* (New York, Oxford University Press, 1999). On Morris, see Peter Stansky, *Redesigning the World: William Morris, the 1880s, and the Arts and Crafts* (Princeton, Princeton University Press, 1985), pp. 30–2.

[104] Alan Borg, *War Memorials: From Antiquity to the Present* (London, Leo Cooper, 1991), p. 94.

[105] Eric Gill, *Autobiography* (London, Jonathan Cape, 1940), p. 206. On the wider context of 'guild socialism', see J[ay] M. Winter, *Socialism and the Challenge of War: Ideas and Politics in Britain 1912–18* (London and Boston, Routledge & Kegan Paul, 1974), pp. 121–49, 281. Regarding the Trumpington cross, see Judith Collins, *Eric Gill: The Sculpture: A Catalogue Raisonné* (London, Herbert, 1998), pp. 43, 121–2.

Figure 8. Cross by Eric Gill. Trumpington, 1921.

design of German war graves aspired, after all, to eternal fame matching that of medieval cathedrals.[106]

---

[106] Willi F. Könitzer, 'Besuch in den Münchener Werkstätten des Volksbundes', *Kriegsgräberfürsorge*, 16,5 (1936), pp. 71, 77. On *Bauhütten* and modernism, see Magdalena Bushart, *Der Geist der Gotik und die expressionistische Kunst: Kunstgeschichte und Kunsttheorie 1911–1925* (Munich, Silke Schreiber, 1990), pp. 183–8.

In sum, memorial makers in Britain and Germany developed similar mnemonic techniques for constructing a sense of historical continuity that overshadowed the material and emotional immensity of the industrialised conflict. They chose loci, devised practices, and created icons of commemoration that linked past traditions with the impact of modern warfare. So far, I have concentrated on the significance or dimensions and the technical aspects but neglected the narrative structures of languages of continuity. In the following section, I analyse overlapping themes or narratives of war remembrance, showing that British and German agents tended to hark back to or reconfigure parallel bodies of reference. In both countries, medievalist commemorations sometimes incorporated classical, Germanic or Celtic notations, notations that were elaborations on the central theme of historical continuity.

Narratives

The war memorials of Leeds (see figure 40), Burton-upon-Trent, and Colchester – all by the sculptor H. C. Fehr – denote St George as a knight in a naturalistic manner. Fehr's naturalism, however, fell short of contemporary demands for historical exactitude. A Leeds citizen pointed out 'that it is important to have the historical details of such a Memorial as reasonably accurate as may be':

I noticed that the figure of St. George on the model of the Memorial exhibited in the Art Gallery was shown without Spurs. Am I not right in thinking that it was an unheard of thing for a Knight in full armour to appear without his Spurs?, and that the Spurs were regarded symbolically as one of the most important appanages of the Noble Order of Knighthood? I think that I remember reading that they were hacked off on the rare occasion when a Knight was degraded! It seems to me that the omission of the Spurs must probably be an accidental oversight on part of the Designer or the Sculptor.[107]

Historical authenticity was too important an issue to be trusted to the designers alone. The Empire cavalry war memorial in London shows a mounted St George, holding up his lance after triumphing over the dragon. The memorial committee made sure that the statue, which was cast from metal obtained from captured enemy guns, bore an exact copy of late medieval armour by seeking advice from an authority on armour.[108] Historical expertise was even more respected in Germany. Professional historians had their say in the competition for the Reich

---

[107] WYASL, LC/TC/R 18, Charles C. Frank to Robert Fox, 24 August 1921.
[108] 'The Unveiling and Dedication of the Cavalry War Memorial', *Cavalry Journal*, 14 (1924), p. 267.

memorial which was to be placed at Germany's most central (historically or geographically) spot. Thus historical scholarship fed into popular representations of the past. Academics from the University of Bonn and a professor from Würzburg acted as experts on behalf of the Rhineland ('a focal point during the Middle Ages') and Mount Dolmar in Thuringia ('arch-Germanic') respectively.[109] Historians helped to reinvent the Middle Ages in the early twentieth century, and their scholarship carried weight in an age of scientific 'rationalism'. Scholars involved in commemorative activities managed to create an air of academic credibility or modern *Wissenschaftlichkeit* about narratives of continuity – narratives which were in the main eclectic, speculative and ambiguous, for they represented a state of mind rather than a state of history. In the final section of this chapter, I deal with this conglomerate of historical associations in British and German commemorations. I focus particularly on overlaps between and syntheses of co-existing historical narratives.

Commemorative forms were retrieved from epochs other than the Middle Ages as well. The nineteenth century had seen the emergence not only of medievalism, but also of classicism.[110] Sir Edwin Lutyens, the architect of over ninety war memorials including the Cenotaph in London, drew on classical examples, but reduced them to simpler, minimalist outlines. Lutyens's monument for Leicester takes the form of a triumphal arch, a recurring motif in his *œuvre*. Contemporary viewers compared Leicester's Arch of Remembrance to Roman and Byzantine edifices, the Arc de Triomphe in Paris and Marble Arch in London.[111] Nonetheless, the memorial committee was anxious to link the arch to the history of Leicester Castle, particularly its connections with Simon de Montfort and John of Gaunt. Thus they medievalised the neo-classical design. In so doing the committee hoped to please supporters of the initial idea to utilise land adjoining the castle as a setting. The unveiling programme suggested

---

[109] GStAPK, I. HA Rep. 77, Tit. 1215 Nr. 3c Bd. 1, fos. 148–9, C. Burger, 'Das Reichsehrenmal auf der Insel Hammerstein im Rhein', n.d.; GStAPK, I. HA Rep. 77, Tit. 1215 Nr. 3c Beiheft 'Pressestimmen', 'Das Reichsehrenmal gehört an den Rhein: Eine Einspruchskundgebung in Koblenz', *Kölnische Volkszeitung*, 531, 21 July 1926; BArch, R 32/365a, folio 14, 'Das Reichs-Ehrenmal auf dem Dolmar: Der heilige Berg der Deutschen', n.d. On the historical imagination of medievalists generally, see Norman F. Cantor, *Inventing the Middle Ages: The Lives, Works and Ideas of the Great Medievalists of the Twentieth Century* (New York, William Morrow, 1991).

[110] Richard Jenkyns, *The Victorians and Ancient Greece* (Oxford, Blackwell, 1980); John Pemble, *The Mediterranean Passion: Victorians and Edwardians in the South* (Oxford, Clarendon, 1987), pp. 60–84.

[111] IWM, Eph. Mem., K 3819, 'The Form and Order of the Unveiling Ceremony of the Arch of Remembrance: The Memorial to the City and County of Leicester', 1925, p. 5; 'Leicester Memorial Arch', *The Times*, 44066, 6 July 1925, p. 11.

that in the position finally selected it will still have associations with both these Patriots, Soldiers, Statesmen, friends of Freedom and outstanding figures in Leicester's and in England's story. Simon de Montfort was assuredly in some way connected with the land on which the Memorial stands, and in the names 'Lancaster Road' – and 'Lancaster Gate', which we understand is to be in the name of the new approach to the Arch – we are helping to commemorate one whom Shakespeare speaks of as 'Old John of Gaunt, time-honoured Lancaster.'[112]

The same discrepancy between iconographical evidence and contemporary discourse is noticeable with regard to German monuments featuring nude warriors. From an aesthetic point of view, these objects reveal the formative influence of Johann Joachim Winckelmann's teaching on the Greek ideal of male beauty. Even though the iconography may seem unambiguously classical, figures of nude soldiers frequently carried multiple meanings. A memorial in Dortmund, Westphalia, represented a naked rider armed with a spear. In a poem the horseman was celebrated as a *deutscher Ritter*, a 'German knight'.[113] A *Gymnasium* in Zwickau, Kingdom of Saxony, chose a nude warrior as a timeless and 'eternally valid embodiment of the German fighter spirit'. The warrior was identified as St George, 'a favourite theme of medieval German art up to Dürer', regardless of his nudity.[114] These two examples show that iconographic evidence examined in isolation can be misleading.

Classical figures of heroic youth were used for commemorative purposes, albeit not as universally as George L. Mosse has claimed.[115] However, Mosse observes correctly that in Germany such figures were concentrated in the universities. It is hardly surprising that the principal institutions of the *Bildungsbürgertum* (that is the educated middle classes with particularly close ties to the state), the *Gymnasium* and the university, the upholders of Latin and Greek, would fall back on classical images. The University of Berlin honoured its fallen students, the *Kommilitonen* (from the Latin *commilites*), appropriately with a sculpture of a naked warrior designed by Hugo Lederer, the well-known creator of Hamburg's medievalist Bismarck memorial. Notwithstanding the style, at the unveiling the figure was described as a Dürer-like *Ritter*,

---

[112] IWM, Eph. Mem., K 3819, p. 4.
[113] StdADO, 502, Postcard 'Ehrenmal Reiter', n.d.
[114] BArch, R 32/352, folio 214, *Zwickauer Zeitung*, May 1923: 'ein Lieblingsmotiv der mittelalterlichen deutschen Kunst bis zu Dürer', and 'eine ewig gültige Verkörperung deutschen Kämpfergeistes'.
[115] Mosse, *Fallen Soldiers*, p. 102. See also his study *The Image of Man: The Creation of Modern Masculinity* (New York, Oxford University Press, 1996). In Berlin, however, figures of nude warriors were exceptionally popular; see Weinland, *Kriegerdenkmäler in Berlin*, p. 108. On Hanover, see Schneider, '. . . nicht umsonst gefallen'?, pp. 201–3.

'knight'.[116] Berlin's nude knight has no equivalent in British commemorations. The naked warrior is practically absent from British memorial
art, although educated Britons shared the German *Bildungsbürger*'s adoration of the classics. Inscriptions in Greek or Latin, rather than the
iconography of public school and 'Oxbridge' war memorials, taught
British youth a lesson in antique feats of valour.[117] Take the memorial
of the Leys School, Cambridge, a Methodist public school. Horace's
motto, 'DULCE ET DECORUM EST PRO PATRIA MORI', is engraved on the
monument. This dictum was a popular choice among British elites
despite Wilfred Owen's satirical poem. At the Leys School, the ancient
inscription clashes with the medievalist design, for the memorial shows
St George as a knight in full armour (see figure 51).[118]

There were educated men who objected to this kind of eclecticism.
They drew a clear distinction between native and classical, Christian and
pagan traditions. The nation's central war monument of 1920, the
Cenotaph (a temporary structure had been erected in July 1919),
was a thorn in the Anglican side. The Cenotaph, literally an 'empty
tomb', recalled Greek commemorative forms, without the slightest hint
of Christian symbolism.[119] Britain's precariously Established Church
responded with the burial of the Unknown Warrior (see figure 2). It

---

[116] GStAPK, I. HA Rep. 76 Va, Sekt. 2 Tit. X Nr. 27 Bd. 6, folio 151, p. 17, Friedrich-
Wilhelms-Universität zu Berlin, 'Feier bei der Enthüllung des Denkmals für die
im Weltkriege gefallenen Studierenden, Dozenten und Beamten der Universität am
10. Juli 1926', 1926; 'Weihe des Ehrenmals der Universität: In Anwesenheit des
Reichspräsidenten', *Berliner Lokal-Anzeiger*, 322, 10 July 1926. On the making of the
memorial, see Kathrin Hoffmann-Curtius, 'Das Kriegerdenkmal der Berliner Friedrich-Wilhelms-Universität 1919–1926: Siegexegese der Niederlage', *Jahrbuch für
Universitätsgeschichte*, 5 (2002), pp. 87–116; Christian Saehrendt, *Der Stellungskrieg
der Denkmäler: Kriegerdenkmäler im Berlin der Zwischenkriegszeit (1919 – 1939)* (Bonn,
J. H. W. Dietz Nachf., 2004), pp. 116–27.

[117] See the inventories of Oxford and public school memorials in Patricia Utechin, *Sons of
This Place: Commemoration of the War Dead in Oxford's Colleges and Institutions* (Oxford,
Robert Dugdale, 1998); Kernot, *Public Schools War Memorials*. In addition, see Jamet-
Bellier de la Duboisière, 'Commemorating "the Lost Generation"', pp. 3–4, 140, 146.
For the purpose of comparison, see Reinhard Ilg, 'Katholische Bildungsbürger und die
bedrohte Nation: Das katholische Gymnasium Ehingen (Donau) im Kaiserreich und
während des Ersten Weltkriegs', in Gerhard Hirschfeld *et al.* (eds.), *Kriegserfahrungen:
Studien zur Sozial- und Mentalitätsgeschichte des Ersten Weltkriegs* (Essen, Klartext,
1997), pp. 345, 365.

[118] George Hayter Chubb, *The Memorial Chapel of the Leys School Cambridge: Its Structure,
Windows, Carvings and Memorials* (London, Herbert Jenkins, 1925), pp. 32–3; Borg,
War Memorials, p. 100. On the quotation from Horace, see Koselleck, *Zur politischen
Ikonologie*, pp. 34–6.

[119] Lloyd, *Battlefield Tourism*, pp. 87–92; Winter, *Sites of Memory*, pp. 102–5. See also
Greenberg, 'Lutyens's Cenotaph', pp. 12–20; Eric Homberger, 'The Story of the
Cenotaph', *The Times Literary Supplement*, 3896, 12 November 1976, pp. 1429–30.

was the Dean of Westminster who pushed through the tomb in the abbey as a counter-memorial to the Greek 'empty tomb' in Whitehall.

In Germany, too, some people rejected Greek paganism. In the discussion about the iron-nail landmark of Hagen, Karl Ernst Osthaus tried to exploit popular prejudice to the advantage of his preferred design. Osthaus, a chief patron of modern art in Germany, agitated against the naturalistic figure of a blacksmith by the sculptor Friedrich Bagdons (see figure 9). He denounced the artwork as 'Zeus disguised as a smith' and as a 'showy muscular demigod'.[120] On the other hand, Osthaus endorsed an expressionist design by his friend and protégé, Ernst Ludwig Kirchner of the Brücke group (see figure 10). He put Kirchner's rough-hewn figure on par with one of Germany's finest pieces of medieval sculpture, the statue of Roland in Bremen dated 1404. Osthaus received support from Botho Graef, professor of archaeology and art history at the University of Jena. Graef characterised medieval art as the prime expression of the Nordic-German spirit. The expert certified that the intense artistic quality of medieval German sculpture also pervaded Kirchner's works. Furthermore, Graef echoed Osthaus's disparagement of antiquity (and the Renaissance). He concluded that Greek gods were alien to German culture: 'We are not Greeks; we do not wish to be and cannot be Greeks.'[121]

Today's reader may be puzzled by tendencies to blur distinctions between *nordische* (Nordic) and *germanische* (Germanic) or medieval traditions. By the 1920s, 'Germanic' had evolved into a widely accepted collective term encompassing roughly the period of German (including Scandinavian) history between Neanderthal Man and Charlemagne. Germanicism in war remembrance goes back to the signifying practices of nationalist *Bürger* following the liberation from Napoleonic occupation. After the Bismarckian wars, Germanophilia entered the vocabulary of monarchist and conservative circles. Finally, in the wake

[120] Karl Ernst Osthaus, 'Die Kunst und der Eiserne Schmied in Hagen', *Westfälisches Tageblatt*, 214, 13 September 1915: 'als Schmied verkleidete Zeus'; Karl Ernst Osthaus, 'Offener Brief an den Ausschuß zur Errichtung des Eisernen Schmiedes in Hagen', *Westfälisches Tageblatt*, 217, 16 September 1915. On Kirchner's design, see Michael Diers, 'Ernst Ludwig Kirchner und Friedrich Bagdons: Der Hagener Wettbewerb um den "Eisernen Schmied" – eine "Kunst im Krieg"-Episode des Jahres 1915', in Uwe Fleckner and Jürgen Zänker (eds.), *Friedrich Bagdons (1878–1937): Eine Bildhauerkarriere vom Kaiserreich zum Nationalsozialismus* (Stuttgart, Gerd Hatje, 1993), pp. 21–31.
[121] StdAH, 809/1, Botho Graef, 'Der Eiserne Schmied von Hagen', *Hagener Zeitung*, 461, 2 October 1915: 'Wir sind keine Griechen, wir wollen und können auch keine Griechen sein.'

Figure 9. 'Iron Blacksmith' by Friedrich Bagdons. Hagen, 1915.

Figure 10. 'Iron Blacksmith'. Model of a proposed iron-nail statue by Ernst Ludwig Kirchner. Hagen, 1915.

of the world war, Germanicism became fully entrenched in popular culture.[122] Stone circles, erratic boulders, dolmens and groves were tangible manifestations of the reorientation towards the native, idealised Germanic past.

British war propaganda had declared 'Germanic' culture anathema. War remembrance cultivated instead Britain's 'Celtic' inheritance. Celtic crosses in the style of the seventh and eighth centuries, and modern, simplified adaptations, sprang up all over the British Isles. In England, agents of remembrance conceived and advertised them 'as a distinctively British type'.[123] At Wisbech, Cambridgeshire, a Celtic cross 'of runic design' was erected (see figure 11).[124] The Celtic cross of the Dragon School, Oxford, was prepared by one C. Lynam, an antiquarian who was acclaimed as an 'author of many works on archaeology, and an expert student of old crosses'.[125] On the Celtic fringe, it seems, such crosses constitute the favourite memorial type; in Scotland, Celtic crosses were the most common form.

Scotland possesses a memorial which is unique in Britain. A temple-like structure open to the sky and supported by eight pillars is dedicated to the dead of Stonehaven near Aberdeen.[126] The architecture resembles contemporaneous German attempts to revive stone circles à la 'Germanic' Stonehenge.[127] The city of Marienburg (Malbork), West Prussia, set up a highly abstract *altgermanisches*, 'old-Germanic', or 'Nordic' memorial on the model of surviving circular rings of primeval standing stone.[128] A striking minimalism is also evident in the red-brick 'stone circle' of Leer, Hanover (East Friesland) (see figure 12). Before its completion in 1926, Leer's town council had entered into

[122] Lurz, *Kriegerdenkmäler*, vol. IV, p. 343. On pre-war Germanicism, see Rainer Kipper, *Der Germanenmythos im Deutschen Kaiserreich: Formen und Funktionen historischer Selbstthematisierung* (Göttingen, Vandenhoeck & Ruprecht, 2002).

[123] Borg, *War Memorials*, p. 8. On Celtic crosses in Scotland, see Bell, 'Monuments to the Fallen', pp. 225, 420, 431, 436–7.

[124] NIWM, 3473, Wisbech, Cambs.

[125] As cited in Boorman, *At the Going Down of the Sun*, p. 17. See also 'The War Memorial', *Draconian*, 92, December 1918, p. 5117.

[126] Martin Sim, 'A Memorable Memorial . . .', *Leopard*, 258, December 1999, pp. 34–5. Neither the minutes of the Stonehaven Town Council, kept at the Aberdeen City Archives, nor the records of the Stonehaven Heritage Society give information as to why this particular style was chosen.

[127] One of the grandest circle-style memorials was the navy monument at Laboe near Kiel, Schleswig-Holstein. See Lurz, *Kriegerdenkmäler*, vol. IV, p. 199; Thorsten Prange, *Das Marine-Ehrenmal in Laboe: Geschichte eines deutschen Nationalsymbols* (Wilhelmshaven, Deutscher Marinebund, [1996]).

[128] StdAL, 1631, folio 210, Erster Bürgermeister Marienburg to Magistrat Leer, 24 August 1925.

Figure 11. Celtic cross by W. Davis. Wisbech, 1921.

Figure 12. Stone circle with a cross by Walter and Johannes Krüger. Lutheran cemetery, Leer, 1926.

correspondence with their colleagues at Marienburg. Unlike them, the Leer authorities showed neither awareness of nor interest in the memorial's Germanic quality. Nor did the local press. The newspapers referred merely to an 'open temple rotunda' or an *Ehrenring*, a 'ring of honour'.[129] Nevertheless, its architects, Walter and Johannes Krüger, saw Leer's monument as the prototypical modern stone circle. In an essay published in 1939, they outlined a progression from the Leer to the Tannenberg memorial with its eight towers arranged in a circle symbolising erect monoliths (rather than a castle). The Krügers underpinned their designs for Leer and Tannenberg by a pseudo-historical theory about the prehistoric use of stone circles as Germanic assembly grounds where a *Führer* would address his entourage.[130]

The Krügers' account shows that by the late 1930s, a discursive shift had occurred in the commemoration of Tannenberg. In the course of the remodelling of the site as a Nazi place of worship in 1935, the Germanic past became the primary point of reference. The legacy of Stonehenge began to overshadow that of the first battle of Tannenberg (between the Teutonic Order and a Slavic army) in 1410.[131] The cornerstone of the Nazi memorial, the Hindenburg vault, illustrates this transition. Traditionally, war landmarks and memorials had presented the legendary general as a Teutonic knight, and the vault in the Tannenberg memorial also conjured up images of the resting-places of medieval rulers. Yet the impressive entrance to the tomb was importantly constructed like a *Hünengrab*, literally 'giants' grave', crowned with a huge monolith or *Findling*.[132]

Both *Hünengrab* and *Findling* were established forms in the commemorative lexicon of Weimar Germany (see figure 13). They were

---

[129] 'Die Weihe des Gedächtnismals der Kriegsopfer', *Volksbote: Wochenblatt für Ostfriesland und Papenburg*, 47, 26 November 1926; 'Einweihung des Ehrenmals der Stadt Leer', *Leerer Anzeigeblatt*, 273, 22 November 1926. By contrast, the architectural press was more explicit about the Germanic connotations. See 'Kriegerdenkmal zu Leer in Ostfriesland', *Bauwelt*, 16 (1925), p. 236.

[130] Walter Krüger and Johannes Krüger, 'Bauliche Gedanken um das Reichsehrenmal Tannenberg und seine Einfügung in die Landschaft', in Kuratorium für das Reichsehrenmal Tannenberg (ed.), *Tannenberg: Deutsches Schicksal – Deutsche Aufgabe* (Oldenburg and Berlin, Gerhard Stalling, [1939]), esp. pp. 227–8.

[131] Hans Kahns, *Das Reichsehrenmal Tannenberg* (Königsberg, Gräfe und Unzer, [1937]), pp. 9–11; Erich Maschke, 'Deutsche Wacht im Osten durch die Jahrhunderte', in Kuratorium für das Reichsehrenmal Tannenberg (ed.), *Tannenberg: Deutsches Schicksal – Deutsche Aufgabe*, pp. 167–9; Buchheit, *Reichsehrenmal Tannenberg*, p. 10; *Reichsehrenmal Tannenberg: [Seine Geschichte: Der Weg durch das Ehrenmal]* (Hohenstein, Verkehrsverein, [1936]), p. 3. On the Tannenberg myth, see chapter 2.

[132] Krüger and Krüger, 'Bauliche Gedanken', pp. 235, 238.

Figure 13. 'Giant's grave' (*Hünengrab*)-style memorial. Trittau, 1920s.

confined neither to the right-wing milieu – although they were preferred by conservative veterans' associations – nor to any region, although they were relatively rare in southern Germany.[133] *Findlinge* retaining their natural contours were particularly widespread, not least for financial and pragmatic reasons. Simple rocks reduced expenditure and planning to a bare minimum. This memorial type came thus into conflict with vested interests. Boulders provoked outcry from the architectural profession as 'Primitive art of the Teutons *anno domini* 1926. Sentimental expression of immature aesthetics'.[134] The Prussian advice centres for war commemoration, staffed with architects and artists, were in disagreement over the artistic merits of boulders. In 1917, the Berlin headquarters intervened on behalf of a family which was refused

[133] Lurz, *Kriegerdenkmäler*, vol. IV, pp. 194–7; Schneider, '. . . *nicht umsonst gefallen*'?, pp. 105, 203–4; Ziemann, *Front und Heimat*, p. 443. Commemorative boulders were virtually non-existent in Britain, but for some exceptions see NIWM, 5808, Callander, Stirling; NIWM, 8634, Torphins, Aberdeen; NIWM, 14276, Harpur Hill, Derbys.

[134] GStAPK, I. HA Rep. 77, Tit. 1215 Nr. 3c Beiheft 'Pressestimmen', E. Lyonel Wehner, 'Reichsehrenmal – Schlageterdenkmal: Gedanken über Denkmalskunst', *Kölnische Zeitung*, 465, 25 June 1926: 'Primitive Kunst der Teutonen im Jahre des Herrn 1926. Sentimentaler Ausdruck eines unreifen Formwillens'.

permission to set up a boulder (with an Iron Cross and other insignia in relief) in memory of a lost son in a public cemetery. The negative decision was taken by the cemetery manager who belonged to the provincial advice centre of Pomerania. He held that boulders came close to the cultural sophistication of cavemen.[135]

Yet more interests were at stake. The cemetery manager was confirmed in his attitude by the local pastor. Religious-minded men were capable of offering stiff resistance to Germanicism. Designers who were aware of this obstacle modified their sketches accordingly. Dominikus Böhm, a pioneer of modernism in church architecture, proposed a harmonious blend of Germanic and Christian-medieval motifs. He explained his entry for the memorial competition in Benrath, Rhine Province, near Düsseldorf in the following words: 'no ideology, neither left-wing nor right-wing, can feel discriminated against, because the national idea is visible in the Germanic concept of runic stones [. . .]; the religious ethos is discreetly given expression in the central pillar, the form of which is reminiscent of the cross.'[136]

I want to argue that, in spite of nationalist and racial connotations, Germanic designs appealed to agents of memory principally on the grounds of their eternal character. Their 'timeless' aesthetics and indestructible material contrasted with 'our modern, ephemeral times'.[137] Monoliths were perceived as monuments of historical continuity par excellence. 'Documents decompose, pictures go blind and fall apart, buildings decay', whereas erratic blocks represented 'immortal signs'.[138] Moreover, 'giants' graves' composed of boulders and soil offered an exemplary burial custom. Professor Dethlefsen set out the meaning of

---

[135] Lurz, *Kriegerdenkmäler*, vol. III, pp. 48–9.

[136] StdAD, XX 120, Dominikus Böhm to Memorial Committee, 12 November 1927: 'dass sich keine Gedankenrichtung weder links noch rechts benachteiligt fühlen kann; denn der nationale Gedanke ist durch die germanische Idee der Runensteine erkenntlich [. . .]; die religiöse Gesinnung ist im dezent an das Kreuz erinnernden Form des Mittelpfeilers zum Ausdruck gebracht'. Böhm's proposal was rejected; the committee decided on the *Hünengrab*-style memorial by Hubert Netzer. See ibid., Report by Provinzialkonservator der Rheinprovinz, 23 October 1926; StdAD, XX 122, Hubert Netzer to the Memorial Committee, 7 Nov. 1925.

[137] StAMS, OP 5556, folio 174, Wilhelm Kreis, 'Der Künstler über sein Werk', in Walther Etterich [ed.], *Das Kriegerdenkmal der Stadt Hattingen a.d. Ruhr für ihre im Weltkriege gefallenen Söhne: Zur Denkmalsweihe am 25. September 1927* (Hattingen, Hundt, 1927), p. 52.

[138] BArch, R 1501/113066, folio 38, Max Hasse, 'Heldenverehrung: Ein Aufruf!', *Magdeburgische Zeitung*, Sonderdruck, 229, 26 March 1916: 'Das Schriftwerk zermürbt, Bildwerk erblindet und zerfällt, Bauwerke stürzen zusammen.' See also Christian Fuhrmeister, *Beton, Klinker, Granit: Material, Macht, Politik: Eine Materialikonographie* (Berlin, Bauwesen, 2001), pp. 250–1.

funeral mounds in a book edited by the provincial advice centre of East Prussia:

It has been said that the concept of immortality is an innate idea of human beings. Indeed, something in them has always resisted the notion that death is the end of everything. For them, death has always been merely a kind of sleep; for this reason, the deceased body was preserved as well as possible for resurrection, and this depository itself became a permanently visible memorial perpetuating fame and names in the environment of descendants; or the resting-place was at least marked by a special, visible sign. The most original form of funeral monuments promising permanence has been preserved in the Germanic north. [. . .] Burial chambers were made of large granite stones, and high mounds were piled up on top of these *Totenwohnungen* [dwellings of the dead]. Monuments like the mound of the three kings near Old Uppsala or the two mounds of King Gorm the Elder and Queen Thyre near Jelling are impressive achievements in respect of permanence and monumental effect.[139]

Boulders were recommended for use as headstones in a *Heldenhain*, 'heroes' grove', sometimes called *Ehrenhain*, 'grove of honour' (see figures 14–15). The *Heldenhain* caught the German imagination like no other form of war memorial. According to its inventor, the Berlin landscape architect Willy Lange, the ideal heroes' grove consisted of four basic elements: 'Germanic' oak trees planted for every fallen soldier (the names could be inscribed on boulders); a raised central point with a linden tree symbolising either peace or the Kaiser; a round festival ground; and embankments and trenches enclosing and separating the grove from its surroundings. Lange's horticultural vision of late 1914 became a reality in his four-hectare large surrogate military cemetery for Soltau, Hanover in 1922. There, on the Lüneburg Heath, 271 oak trees

---

[139] [Richard] Dethlefsen, 'Das Kriegergrab im Wandel der Zeiten', in Provinzialberatungsstelle für Kriegerehrungen in Ostpreußen [ed.], *Kriegergrabmale und Heldenhaine* (Munich, Georg D. W. Callwey, [1917]), p. 5: 'Man nennt den Begriff der Unsterblichkeit eine eingeborene Idee der Menschen. Und in der Tat hat sich wohl in ihnen stets etwas gegen die Vorstellung gesträubt, daß mit dem Tode nun alles zu Ende sein solle. Der Tod war ihnen immer nur ein Schlaf; für die Wiederauferstehung ward deshalb der abgeschiedene Leib möglichst gut verwahrt, und dieser Aufbewahrungsort selbst wurde dann zum dauernd sichtbaren, Ruhm und Namen auch in der Umwelt der Nachkommen erhaltenden Denkmale ausgestaltet, oder es wurde die Ruhestätte wenigstens durch ein beigesetztes, sichtbares Merkmal gekennzeichnet. Die ursprünglichste Form Dauer versprechender Totenmäler ist im germanischen Norden erhalten. [. . .] Aus großen Graniten wurden die Grabkammern aufgerichtet, und hohe Hügel über diesen Totenwohnungen gehäuft. Mäler wie die der drei Königshügel bei Alt-Uppsala oder die beiden Hügel König Gorms des Alten und der Königin Thyra Dannebod bei Jellinge können sich nach Leistung wie nach Dauer und monumentaler Wirkung sehen lassen.' The burial mounds of Old Uppsala and Jelling date from the sixth and tenth centuries A.D. respectively.

Figure 14. Heroes' grove by Willy Lange. Soltau, 1922.

Figure 15. Heroes' grove. Neumünster, 1920s.

were planted, one for each absent dead man (see figure 14).[140] Throughout Germany, the *Heldenhain* concept was enthusiastically received by

[140] Willy Lange, 'Die leitenden Gestaltungsgedanken für Heldenhaine', in Willy Lange (ed.), *Deutsche Heldenhaine*, ed. im Auftrage der Arbeitsgemeinschaft für Deutschlands Heldenhaine (Leipzig, J. J. Weber, 1915), p. 12. See also Gerhard Schneider, 'Heldenhaine als Visualisierung der Volksgemeinschaft im Ersten Weltkrieg', in Gerhard

landscape gardeners and memorial committees. The Volksbund Deutsche Kriegsgräberfürsorge adopted the idea for military cemeteries abroad. However, derivative designs tended to dilute Lange's strict standards. In fact, many *Heldenhaine* had little but the name in common with the master scheme. Often memorial makers dispensed with a core idea – the symbolism of individualised trees – for practical, financial or ideological reasons.[141] Notably, the Volksbund laid out groves where the commemoration of the individual dead was swallowed up in the celebration of community and camaraderie.

A feature which all groves shared was their prospective dimension; they were conceptualised as memorials in progress.[142] The oak is a massive and long-lived tree but slow growing. The preference for this particular tree underlined confidence in the continuity of things. Once planted, the trees and bushes would ideally grow for ever and ever. The beautification society of Dortmund envisaged in 1916 a heroes' grove 'growing out of the German cast of mind through the centuries'.[143] Lange himself dreamt of 'centuries of Germanic ages looking into the future'.[144] He and his disciples traced the German adoration of nature back to *Alt-Germanien*, 'old Germania', quoting Tacitus' observation about ancient Germans worshipping in 'holy groves'.[145] In his essays, Lange set the German *Waldseele*, 'forest soul', off against *südische*, 'southern', civilisation, in particular urban society and Renaissance culture.[146] Other authors linked *Heldenhaine* to medieval history,

---

Schneider (ed.), *Die visuelle Dimension des Historischen* (Schwalbach, Wochenschau, 2002), pp. 49–71; Uwe Schneider and Gert Gröning, 'Nature Mystification and the Example of the Heroes [sic] Groves', *Environments by Design*, 2 (1998), pp. 205–28; George L. Mosse, 'Soldatenfriedhöfe und nationale Wiedergeburt: Der Gefallenenkult in Deutschland', in Klaus Vondung (ed.), *Kriegserlebnis: Der Erste Weltkrieg in der literarischen Gestaltung und symbolischen Deutung der Nationen* (Göttingen, Vandenhoeck & Ruprecht, 1980), pp. 254–6. On Soltau's heroes' grove, see Seeger, *Denkmal des Weltkriegs*, pp. 28–9, 130.

[141] See, for example, [Karl] Elkart, 'Der Ideenwettbewerb für die Gestaltung des Reichsehrenmals', *Deutsche Bauzeitung*, 66 (1932), 441–50.

[142] BArch, R 32/355, fos. 102–5, 'Vom Reichsehrenmal: Leitgedanken für die im Verlag G.D.W. Callway erschienende Schrift von Karl August Walther', 4 January 1926.

[143] StdADO, 3–2026, Verschönerungsverein to Vereine, 30 April 1916: 'wachsend aus deutscher Gesinnung in die Jahrhunderte'.

[144] GStAPK, I. HA Rep. 77, Tit. 1215 Nr. 3d Bd. 1 (M), folio 40, Willy Lange, 'Heldeneichen und Friedenslinden: Ein Ruf und Widerhall', n.d., p. 7: 'Seit die "Idee" als eine Vision mir vor Augen trat, lebendig, Jahrhunderte Germanenzeit der Zukunft schauend, erfüllte sie mich'. See also GStAPK, I. HA Rep. 77, Tit. 1215 Nr. 3c Beiheft 'Pressestimmen', Willy Lange, 'Um das Reichsehrenmal', *Tägliche Rundschau*, 188, 13 August 1926.

[145] Willy Lange, 'Heldeneichen und Friedenslinden', in Lange, *Deutsche Heldenhaine*, pp. 78–81. See also Johannes Speck, 'Heldenhaine und Jugendpflege', ibid., p. 27; Möller, 'Forstliche Bemerkungen zur Pflanzung von Eiche und Linde', ibid., p. 52.

[146] BArch, R 32/354, fos. 124–5, Willy Lange, 'Um das Reichsehrenmal', [c. 1926].

which Lange only mentioned in parenthesis. Gothic architecture in Germany was allegedly rooted in the experience of the forest. Coniferous forests had supposedly inspired the shape of pointed arches and the refraction of light in Gothic cathedrals.[147]

The Working Group for Germany's Heroes' Groves (Arbeitsgemeinschaft für Deutschlands Heldenhaine), an association under the direction of Willy Lange, received prominent backing. The Prussian Ministry of War welcomed the 'resumption of a holy, age-old custom of our people'.[148] The Ministry of the Interior, too, approved of the idea and distributed copies of Lange's publications to local administrations. In addition, Lange's initiative enjoyed the patronage of Hindenburg, a cult figure during and after the war. Still, the *Heldenhain* was not universally accepted. The sculptor Hermann Hosaeus protested emphatically against the idea. The first of his 'Ten Commandments' of memorial art stated 'You shall not plant *Heldenhaine*.' As a sculptor, he considered heroes' groves an uncultivated and potentially short-lived memorial form, since 'caterpillars and droughts can eat them up'.[149] Hosaeus indicated a nightmare scenario of commemoration: a heroes' grove slowly dying instead of growing for all eternity. This pessimism was not without foundation. Crooked and underdeveloped *Bismarckeichen* and *Kaisereichen*, oaks dedicated to the ex-chancellor or the Kaiser in the late nineteenth century, stood as a precedent. A dying oak tree planted in remembrance of an individual fallen hero would have seriously undermined the *Heldenhain* concept.[150] After all, the heroes' grove was a surrogate war cemetery where each tree stood for an individual, absent dead man.

The *Heldenhain* was a space within nature designed for contemplation and self-communion. Such a 'place of silent reflection' was proposed for Mount Donnershaugk in the Thuringian forest.[151] The proposal

[147] GStAPK, I. HA Rep. 77, Tit. 1215 Nr. 3c Beiheft 'Pressestimmen', 'Goslar und der Ehrenhain', *Berliner Börsen-Courier*, 307, 6 July 1926; E[mil] Schindhelm, *Reichsehrenmal im heiligen Hain bei Bad Berka-Weimar* (Weimar, Fritz Fink, [1933]), p. 8.
[148] GStAPK, I. HA Rep. 77, Tit. 1215 Nr. 3d Bd. 2, folio 94, Kriegsministerium to Arbeitsgemeinschaft für Deutschlands Heldenhaine, 6 Jan. 1917: 'ich begrüße sie als Wiederaufnahme eines geheiligten uralten Brauches unseres Volkes'; GStAPK, I. HA Rep. 77, Tit. 1215 Nr. 3d Bd. 1 (M), fos. 25–8, Minister des Innern to Königliche Landräte in Preußen, [c. 1915].
[149] As cited in Nabrings, '. . . *eine immerfort währende Mahnung . . .*', p. 24.
[150] GStAPK, I. HA Rep. 77, Tit. 1215 Nr. 3d Bd. 2, folio 41, 'Heldenhaine', *Die Gartenkunst*, 9, September 1916, p. 119.
[151] GStAPK, I. HA Rep. 77, Tit. 1215 Nr. 3c Beiheft 'Pressestimmen', 'Der Platz für das Reichsehrenmal: Der Reichskunstwart auf der Suche im Thüringer Wald', *Leipziger Tageblatt*, 100, 11 April 1926.

coupled the *Heldenhain* idea with Germanic mythology, for Mount Donnershaugk belonged to the realm of Donar (Thor), the god of thunder. At this point we enter a new discursive field. Apart from conveying a sense of eternity, Germanicisms were instrumental in the reconfiguration of the war as a national epic. 'We hope that some day an epic will grow out of this war, a new *Song of the Nibelungen*', suggested the *Berliner Tageblatt* in 1915.[152] The saga's protagonist, Siegfried, became indeed a pre-eminent representation of the war (see figure 58). The hero turned out to be a chameleon-like figure. In some places he appeared as a nude warrior in the tradition of 'Nordic-Greek ideal figures'.[153] Elsewhere, features of Wotan (Odin), Balder, Arminius (Hermann the German), St Michael and St George blended into images of Siegfried.[154]

To a certain extent, the visual grammar for the war epic had been created during the previous century. The decoration of the royal residence in Munich exemplifies the nineteenth-century vogue for all things Germanic. At Munich, during the years 1827 to 1867, Julius Schnorr von Carolsfeld painted episodes of the *Song of the Nibelungen* in fresco. At the time, the murals caused an international sensation. Prince Albert, an arbiter of taste in Britain, set out to rival Continental achievements and to establish the Arthurian legend as an English equivalent of the *Song of the Nibelungen*. In 1841, the Prince Consort was appointed chairman of the commission which supervised the embellishment of the Houses of Parliament. For the Queen's robing room they commissioned a series of frescoes telling the story of King Arthur and the knights of the Round Table by William Dyce.[155] Albert and his adherents were successful in setting the artistic agenda. Arthurian themes flourished in the following decades, culminating in memorial art after 1914. Numerous war memorials, particularly windows, depict King Arthur and his knights Sir Galahad, Sir Lancelot and Sir Tristram. In contrast to Siegfried, Dietrich or Hagen, the English heroes were represented in a distinctly Christian-chivalric manner – a theme I will return to in depth in subsequent chapters.

---

[152] BArch, R 8034 II/7690, folio 2, Gottfried Traub, 'Heldenehrung', *Berliner Tageblatt*, 217, 21 April 1915. See also David Midgley, *Writing Weimar: Critical Realism in German Literature 1918–1933* (Oxford, Oxford University Press, 2000), p. 229; Elizabeth A. Marsland, *The Nation's Cause: French, German and English Poetry of the First World War* (London and New York, Routledge, 1991), p. 82.

[153] Seeger, *Denkmal des Weltkriegs*, p. 23: 'diese nordisch-griechischen Idealgestalten'.

[154] Lurz, *Kriegerdenkmäler*, vol. III, pp. 67, 104; Andreas Dörner, *Politischer Mythos und symbolische Politik: Sinnstiftung durch symbolische Formen am Beispiel des Hermannsmythos* (Opladen, Westdeutscher Verlag, 1995), pp. 314–22.

[155] Debra N. Mancoff, *The Arthurian Revival in Victorian Art* (New York and London, Garland, 1990), pp. 100–35. Generally, see Maike Oergel, *The Return of King Arthur and the Nibelungen: National Myth in Nineteenth-Century English and German Literature* (Berlin and New York, Walter de Gruyter, 1998).

Tombs for Unknown Warriors' surrogate bodies, endless lists of names, memorial trees and other commemorative tokens remind us to this day of the key signature of the Great War: more than nine million men were killed, that is roughly one in eight of those who served in the war. For the bereaved the war meant an unprecedented and unbearable human catastrophe. The instigators and commentators of war memorials countered the fractures of war by constructing historical continua that mediated between the past, present and future. The maintenance of a sense of connection with the distant, native (or national) past was one means by which the survivors came to terms with the experience of loss. Memory, Thomas Laqueur has suggested, 'is not about actual communication with the dead but with keeping them alive in the ongoing historical narratives of the living'.[156] The act of joining the existential memory of death in war and the cultural memory of the remote past together served to incorporate the recent trauma into historical narratives. Such narratives were not a coherent set of ideas, but (often eclectic) amalgams of temporal notions.

The dialectic of lamenting human catastrophe and describing historical continuity was at the core of the commemorative practices I analyse in this study. War remembrance created a paradoxical situation which the Bishop of Norwich tried to solve as follows: 'it [Norwich's restored memorial chapel] will not be an effort to recall or reproduce the past, as if the war had come and gone and made no new and lasting mark upon us and upon all. For the world has changed [. . .]. We build upon the old, but we do not wish to hide the scars of the past; even they are part of our heritage'.[157] Yet the *longue durée* of the past, especially the medieval past, tended to smooth away the gap the war had caused in family history. The names of the individual fallen were embedded in historical narratives, narratives which denied the pastness of the past and stretched easily into time without end.

---

[156] Laqueur, Thomas, 'Cemeteries and the Decline of the Occult: From Ghosts to Memory in the Modern Age', *Österreichische Zeitschrift für Geschichtswissenschaften*, 14,4 (2003), p. 40.
[157] 'The War Memorial Chapel: Norwich Cathedral's Eastward Extension', *Eastern Daily Press*, 18469, 1 December 1930, p. 8.

2　Mission and defence: the nature of the conflict

At the peak of the crisis of July 1914, the Kaiser, who during his reign had never been at a loss for 'big words', publicly washed his hands of political responsibility. He told the crowd that had gathered outside the royal palace in Berlin on the evening of 31 July that the enemy challenge forced him to 'draw the sword'. Wilhelm II continued by expressing his conviction that God would help his victimised German nation to carry the 'sword'.[1] This sentiment was echoed in a book on heroes' groves published in 1916: 'when the Kaiser faithfully drew the sword it glowed like the spear of the Holy Grail [. . .]: the German war became the will of God'.[2] Germany's wartime enemy on the other side of the North Sea employed a very similar language of propaganda. In a speech delivered in London on 9 November 1914, the Liberal prime minister, Herbert Henry Asquith, insisted that 'We shall not sheathe the sword until Belgium recovers all, and more than all, she has sacrificed.'[3] This same passage from his London address was later quoted in a poster issued by the Parliamentary Recruiting Committee appealing for voluntary enlistment. Purely textual posters like this one, however, fell behind the aesthetic standards of the burgeoning advertising industry.[4] Another, more sophisticated placard, which urged the viewers to

---

[1] As cited in Helmut Fries, *Die große Katharsis: Der Erste Weltkrieg in der Sicht deutscher Dichter und Gelehrter*, vol. I, *Die Kriegsbegeisterung von 1914: Ursprünge – Denkweisen – Auflösung* (Constance, Hockgraben, 1994), p. 239.

[2] Willy Lange, 'Die leitenden Gestaltungsgedanken für Heldenhaine', in Lange, *Deutsche Heldenhaine*, p. 79: 'als der Kaiser im Treu-Geloben das Schwert zog, da erglühte es wie der Gralsspeer [. . .]: da ward der deutsche Krieg ein Gottgewollter'.

[3] IWM, PST 5033, PRC 110, 'A Long Drawn-Out Struggle', [*c.* 1915]. On British Liberals and the rhetoric of sacred strife in 1914, see the contemporary analysis by Irene Cooper Willis, *England's Holy War: A Study of English Liberal Idealism during the Great War* (New York, Alfred A. Knopf, 1928).

[4] In general, see Stefan Haas, 'Die neue Welt der Bilder: Werbung und visuelle Kultur der Moderne', in Peter Borscheid and Clemens Wischermann (eds.), *Bilderwelt des Alltags: Werbung in der Konsumgesellschaft des 19. und 20. Jahrhunderts* (Stuttgart, Franz Steiner, 1995), pp. 64–77.

'TAKE UP THE / SWORD OF JUSTICE', also visualised the metaphor.[5] The poster features a large sword held aloft by a woman, and, in the background, the sinking of the *Lusitania* ocean liner by a German submarine. A Scottish war monument demonstrates the lasting impact of this diction almost three years after the Armistice. The memorial figures a warrior holding 'The sword of Justice in his hand, / To shield and guard his native land.'[6]

Both nations presented themselves as having been dragged into a war which was defensive in nature and yet pursued with a messianic zeal. The ambivalence which shines through the use of the sword metaphor in early works of propaganda is also characteristic of medievalist war commemorations. The conflict was represented as either a sacred mission or a war of defence or both; and the agents of remembrance, regardless of their nationality, sometimes switched freely from one pole to the other. The nature of the war mattered to the survivors, for it determined the righteousness and significance of the cause for which the soldiers had died. Whether the emphasis was put on mission or defence depended on the theatre of military operation which was commemorated.[7] The geography of war opened up spaces of thinking, and this chapter will therefore focus on the remembrance of different battlefields: firstly, Palestine, Arabia and Gallipoli; secondly, Tannenberg and eastern Europe; and thirdly, the war in the west. These case studies are preceded by an analysis of allegories of the nature of the First World War in general, with respect to either missionary or defensive warfare.

The world war

Shining armour held a peculiar fascination for the contemporaries of Wilhelm II and Asquith. A war memorial window in an Anglican church in Wisbech, Cambridgeshire, depicts a group of knights clad, as the inscription explains, in the 'ARMOUR OF GOD'.[8] Similarly, the memorial of a Roman Catholic parish in Münster, Westphalia, refers to the 'Armour of

---

[5] IWM, PST 409, PRC 111, 'Sword of Justice', June 1915. See also PST 5065, PRC 123, 'Sword of Justice', [*c.* 1915].

[6] Stewartry Museum, Kirkcudbright, Acc. 7216, vol. 3, pp. 13–17, 'Kirkcudbright War Memorial: Unveiled by Lord-Lieutenant', unspecified newspaper cutting, 14 April 1921. For a Roman Catholic example, see 'Northampton: A War Memorial', *Tablet*, 131 (1918), p. 92.

[7] Generally, see Bernd Hüppauf, 'Das Schlachtfeld als Raum im Kopf: Mit einem Postscriptum nach dem 11. September 2001', in Steffen Martus, Marina Münkler and Werner Röcke (eds.), *Schlachtfelder: Codierung von Gewalt im medialen Wandel* (Berlin, Akademie, 2003), pp. 207–33.

[8] NIWM, 3465, Wisbech, Cambs.

Righteousness', the 'Shield of Faith', the 'Helmet of Salvation' and the 'Sword of the Spirit'.[9] These inscriptions, all taken from Ephesians 6:13–17, served to point up the legitimacy of military action and give spiritual significance to individual self-sacrifice and the war effort as a whole.

A holy war

The language of sanctity originated in wartime images of the Great War as a transcendental strife against evil. The conflict was pronounced a holy war, and German and British propagandists alike claimed to be fighting shoulder to shoulder with the Lord. Many a patriotic Christian chose to believe that soldiers who were fighting a holy war would naturally go to heaven if they were killed in combat. Most notorious, in Britain, was the Bishop of London, Arthur Winnington-Ingram. In 1915, Winnington-Ingram defined the Church of England's task as to 'MOBILISE THE NATION FOR A HOLY WAR'.[10] For bellicose members of the clergy the war provided a splendid opportunity to relocate religion at the centre of national life. In fact, to a certain degree Winnington-Ingram and his disciples succeeded in shaping the discourse. The rhetoric of the street-shrine movement indicates the influence of the bishop's following, at least in High Church circles. During the war, neighbourhoods, initially in the East End of London, constructed temporary war shrines recording the names of inhabitants who had joined up. Prayers for the safety of the living incorporated the commemoration of the dead. When intercessions were made at the shrines, the congregation was frequently reminded that the soldiers were fighting a holy war on behalf of the British people.[11]

This Catholic practice had little appeal to Protestants within and outside the Established Church, but they were not entirely resistant to

---

[9] Martin Papenheim, '"Trauer und Propaganda" – eine Fallstudie zu Aussagen und Funktionen von Kriegerdenkmälern', in Franz-Josef Jakobi (ed.), *Stadtgesellschaft im Wandel: Untersuchungen zur Sozialgeschichte Münsters* (Münster, Regensberg, 1995), pp. 452–7. The memorial at Liebfrauen-Überwasser, Münster, depicts the Saints Michael ('Harnisch der Gerechtigkeit'), Sebastian ('Schild des Glaubens'), Barbara ('Helm des Heiles') and Theodore ('Schwert des Geistes').

[10] 'The Church and the Great War: A Call to Prayer and Service', *Guardian*, 70 (1915), p. 539, italics in the original. See Alan Wilkinson, *The Church of England and the First World War* (London, SCM, 2nd edn 1996), p. 253; Albert Marrin, *The Last Crusade: The Church of England in the First World War* (Durham, NC, Duke University Press, 1974), pp. 125, 140, 142; Bogacz, '"A Tyranny of Words"', pp. 657–60; Niall Ferguson, *The Pity of War* (London, Allen Lane, 1998), pp. 208–11.

[11] Connelly, *Great War, Memory and Ritual*, p. 28; King, *Memorials of the Great War*, pp. 55–6. See also Wilkinson, *Church of England*, pp. 67, 170–1, 300.

the idea of sacred strife.[12] Robert Graves noted after the war that, when the nonconformist David Lloyd George was appointed Minister of Munitions in 1915, he 'persuaded the chapels that the war was a crusade'. As a consequence, Graves's regiment, the Royal Welch Fusiliers, had 'a sudden tremendous influx of Welshman from North Wales'.[13] Nevertheless, not all churchmen embraced the holy war propaganda and critical voices were heard. Henry Scott Holland, Regius Professor of Divinity at the University of Oxford, was outraged that fellow clergymen acted like 'Mad Mullahs preaching a Jehad'.[14]

Germans, too, were prepared to buy such religious militaristic verbiage. A commercial publishing house brought out a do-it-yourself manual for patriotic evenings and celebrations of remembrance in wartime. The booklet assembled a number of exemplary, edifying plays and poems on the theme of 'The Holy War'.[15] Humble publications such as this were intended to disseminate the intelligentsia's wartime discourse. Among members of the *Bildungsbürgertum*, the educated middle classes, especially its Protestant faction, the notion of a holy war enjoyed great popularity.[16] For them, holy warfare had distinct apocalyptic connotations. What they envisaged was a Germanic apocalypse, a notion which fused Biblical stories with Nordic mythology and nineteenth-century German thought.[17] According to this idea, the German nation was

[12] Stuart Paul Mews, 'Religion and English Society in the First World War', Ph.D. dissertation, University of Cambridge, 1974, pp. 8–9. Compare Marrin, *Last Crusade*, p. 135, who holds that Protestants and Roman Catholics did not subscribe to the idea of holy war. On the Church of Scotland, see Fiona Carol Douglas, 'Ritual and Remembrance: The Church of Scotland and National Services of Thanksgiving and Remembrance after Four Wars in the Twentieth Century', Ph.D. dissertation, University of Edinburgh, 1996, pp. 47–9. For comparison, see Laurent Gambarrotto, 'Guerre sainte et juste paix', *14–18: Aujourd'hui – Today – Heute*, 1 (1998), pp. 27–38.

[13] Robert Graves, *Good-Bye to All That: An Autobiography* (London, Jonathan Cape, 1929), p. 115.

[14] As cited in Wilkinson, *Church of England*, p. 253.

[15] Ernst Heinrich Bethge (ed.), *Der heilige Krieg: Kriegsabende und Gedächtnisfeiern*, vol. I, *Kriegruf – Schwertweihe – Ausmarsch* (Leipzig, Arwed Strauch, [1915]), esp. pp. 17, 40. On propaganda of private enterprise, see J[ay] M. Winter, 'Nationalism, the Visual Arts, and the Myth of War Enthusiasm in 1914', *History of European Ideas*, 15 (1992), pp. 359–61. On patriotic plays in particular, see Jeffrey Verhey, *The Spirit of 1914: Militarism, Myth, and Mobilization in Germany* (Cambridge, Cambridge University Press, 2000), pp. 121–5; Martin Baumeister, *Kriegstheater: Großstadt, Front und Massenkultur* (Essen, Klartext, 2005), pp. 33–42.

[16] Klaus Vondung, 'Deutsche Apokalypse 1914', in Klaus Vondung (ed.), *Das Wilhelminische Bürgertum: Zur Sozialgeschichte seiner Ideen* (Göttingen, Vandenhoeck & Ruprecht, 1976), pp. 157, 160. On Roman Catholics, see the case study by Ilg, 'Katholische Bildungsbürger', pp. 353–54.

[17] Klaus Vondung, 'Geschichte als Weltgericht: Genesis und Degradation einer Symbolik', in Klaus Vondung (ed.), *Kriegserlebnis: Der Erste Weltkrieg in der literarischen Gestaltung und symbolischen Deutung der Nationen* (Göttingen, Vandenhoeck & Ruprecht, 1980),

presiding over or executing the *Weltgericht*, the world judgment, which was followed by the redemption of the world through German *Kultur*, culture – a term which comprised Germany's achievements in art, music, literature and science as well as national virtues such as order and thoroughness. In August 1914, at a service held at the monumental Völkerschlacht memorial in Leipzig, Kingdom of Saxony, unveiled in 1913 (see figure 35), the pastor – who happened to be a professor – preached to the congregation: 'But who does not sense that in the world storm [*Weltensturm*] of our age God himself is speaking to our people, and that this gigantic episode in world history [*Weltgeschichte*] we are living through is an act of the divine world judgment [*Weltgericht*]? We, however, salute the world judge [*Weltenrichter*] as our nation's saviour.'[18]

Here the apocalypse is conceived as God's Last Judgment. At the same time, the terms 'world storm' and 'world history' conjure up notions of the mythical Ragnarök (the final battle between the gods and the monstrous forces hostile to them) and Friedrich Schiller's dictum 'Die Weltgeschichte ist das Weltgericht', 'world history is the Last [World] Judgment'.[19] This mélange of religious, mythological and secular ideas is typical of wartime apocalyptic imagery. To be sure, the German quest was not generally derived from the Judaeo-Christian tradition. Emphasis was placed rather on the Germanic element: the 'world storm' or 'world fire'. The war landmark in Hagen, Westphalia, is a case in point (see figure 9). It was celebrated in a poem as the embodiment of 'The will: to carry proudly the *Weltenbrandes* [world fire's] curse'.[20]

However, one should not exaggerate the prevalence of such orgiastic language of destruction, language which Modris Eksteins regards as German intellectual property *par excellence*.[21] Aggressive and apocalyptic notations, while widespread during the initial phase of the war, were by and large confined to nationalist *Bildungsbürger*. Moreover, the less

pp. 62–84. See also Michael Jeismann, *Das Vaterland der Feinde: Studien zum nationalen Feindbegriff und Selbstverständnis in Deutschland und Frankreich 1792–1918* (Stuttgart, Klett-Cotta, 1992), p. 301.

[18] F[ranz] Rendtorff, *Bittgottesdienst am Völkerschlachtdenkmal in Leipzig am 26. August 1914* (Leipzig, Krüger, 1914), p. 5: 'Doch wer spürt es nicht, daß im Weltensturm dieser Zeiten Gott selbst mit unserm Volk zu reden begonnen hat, daß dies gewaltige Stück Weltgeschichte, das wir durchleben, ein Akte ist im göttlichen Weltgericht? Wir aber grüßen im Weltenrichter unseren Volksretter.'

[19] As cited in Vondung, 'Geschichte als Weltgericht', p. 70.

[20] Warburg-Haus, Bildindex 100/10, Postcard Hagen, [c. 1915]: 'Der Wille: stolz zu tragen des Weltenbrandes Fluch'.

[21] Eksteins, *Rites of Spring*, esp. pp. 92, 284.

specific idea of 'holy war' was reduced to a mere ornament as time marched on. For instance, at the inauguration ceremonies of the monuments to fallen members of the Universities of Berlin and Göttingen in 1925 and 1926 respectively, both rectors made a passing reference to the holy war of 1914–18, but did not pursue this motif any further.[22] On the whole, the concept of pure holy warfare proved of marginal interest in the post-1918 era. First, it clashed with the dominant narrative of the Great War as a defensive struggle, which I explore later on in this chapter. Secondly, it was too highbrow and metaphysical to be exploited as a popular motive.

In Britain, the term 'holy war', widely employed during the actual conflict, again disappeared from the commemorative scene in the 1920s. Instead, the related concept of a crusade came to the fore. From the outset, Lloyd George, to name but one example, liked to apply this label to the war. Indeed, a published collection of his wartime speeches was entitled *The Great Crusade*.[23] Yet only in the aftermath of the British victories in Palestine in 1917–18 (a theme to which I shall return later in this chapter) did the term 'crusade' gradually become the shorthand for the First World War. Instrumental in this process were two national memorial projects: the establishment of the tomb of the Unknown Warrior in Westminster Abbey and the adornment of British-Imperial war cemeteries with the 'Cross of Sacrifice'.

When the Dean of Westminster Abbey approached the king to gain support for the burial of an unknown soldier in the abbey, the monarch at first shrank from the novel idea. Eventually, he became enthusiastic about the scheme and donated an antique but otherwise undefined sword he himself had selected from his private collection. This sword was to be placed on the soldier's chest-style coffin.[24] The history of the sword's reception is instructive. Virtually all journalists writing for national newspapers dubbed it 'the Crusader's sword'. The *Scotsman* wrote: 'Completely enveloped in a Union Jack on the top could be seen

[22] GStAPK, I. HA Rep. 76 Va, Sekt. 2 Tit. X Nr. 27 Bd. 6, folio 149, Friedrich-Wilhelms-Universität zu Berlin, 'Feier bei der Enthüllung des Denkmals für die im Weltkriege gefallenen Studierenden, Dozenten und Beamten der Universität am 10. Juli 1926', 1926, p. 13; *Dem Andenken ihrer im Weltkriege Gefallenen: Gewidmet zum 1. März 1925 von der Georg-August-Universität Göttingen* (Munich, C. Wolf, 1925), p. 26.

[23] David Lloyd George, *The Great Crusade: Extracts from Speeches Delivered during the War*, ed. F[rances] L. Stevenson (London, New York and Toronto, Hodder and Stoughton, 1918), e.g. p. 11. On the notion of Crusade during the Great War, see Alphonse Dupront, *Le mythe de croisade*, vol. II (Paris, Gallimard, 1997), pp. 1184–8, 1195.

[24] WAML, Newspaper Cuttings, vol. 1, p. 30, 'Moving Funeral Scenes at Boulogne: How Our Unknown Warrior Left France', *Evening News*, 10 November 1920.

the Crusader's sword, presented by the king, a relic of long ago, together with, in sharp contrast, the webbing belt and trench helmet that we have associated with modern warfare'.[25]

It is not clear who exactly invented the term. The working papers of the committee in charge of the funeral in the abbey neither identify it as a 'Crusader's sword' nor specify its age or origin. Although the chairman of one of the sub-committees realised the symbolic potential of the king's gift, he recommended against fuelling the popular imagination. He observed that 'Both the sword [. . .] and the bands make [. . .] the sign of the Cross on the coffin, although this need not be in any way advertised. The sword itself is merely emblematic of a warrior.'[26] The arrangement of the sword on the coffin and, in addition, the setting as such stimulated the imagination; after all, 'There are so many knights of the old Crusaders in the Abbey', as the *Daily Telegraph* remarked.[27] Moreover, an impressive statue of a powerfully muscular Richard Cœur de Lion, which was first displayed at the Great Exhibition in 1851, dominates the space between Westminster Abbey and the Houses of Parliament. Thus it was the interplay between the instigators and interpreters on the one hand, and the signifier and site on the other, which created the image of the 'Crusader's sword'.

In subsequent years, memorial services in the abbey rehearsed the theme. In 1923, the Order of Crusaders, a brotherhood of right-wing patriots modelled on the military orders of the Middle Ages, but founded only in 1921, held a service in the abbey. They tried to enhance and, at the same time, to capitalise on the crusading pathos surrounding the Unknown Warrior. Brothers of the order laid a wreath on the Unknown's tomb and honoured him as 'the Principal Knight and Supreme Head of the Order'.[28] To round off the ceremony, the music for the procession in the church was carefully chosen from a setting of one of the most popular tales of crusader knights: Sir Walter Scott's historical novel *Ivanhoe*.[29]

Whoever introduced the term 'Crusader's sword' for the king's gift certainly did not invent it, however. A 'Cross of Sacrifice' bearing a

---

[25] 'Nation's Tribute to the "Unknown Warrior": Burial in Westminster Abbey', *Scotsman*, 24168, 12 November 1920, p. 7.

[26] PRO, CAB 27/99, p. 60, Memorandum by Lionel Farle, 23 October 1920.

[27] 'The Day of Remembrance', *Daily Telegraph*, 20459, 11 November 1920, p. 12.

[28] 'Crusaders at the Abbey: Duke of York Present', *The Times*, 43511, 29 November 1923, p. 10. See also Lloyd, *Battlefield Tourism*, p. 90.

[29] Ibid. On settings of Scott's works, see Elizabeth Siberry, *The New Crusaders: Images of the Crusades in the Nineteenth and Early Twentieth Centuries* (Aldershot, Ashgate, 2000), p. 124.

'Crusaders' Sword' was already part of the uniform style of war cemeteries under the auspices of the Imperial War Graves Commission (with notable exceptions, such as Turkish Gallipoli where the cross was tactfully carved in stone).[30] The shape of the 'Cross of Sacrifice' by Sir Reginald Blomfield was often imitated for local war memorials.[31] The original plans for the cross, which the Commission's architects regarded 'as a mark of the symbolism of the present crusade', date back to the time when the war was still in progress, but were finalised in the post-war period.[32] Of the Commission's principal architects, Herbert (later Sir Herbert) Baker was most obsessed with the idea of a 'modern Crusade'.[33] Baker submitted an alternative design for a cross, named the 'Ypres Cross' (see figure 16). His proposal, which eventually was not accepted, denoted a ship in addition to the sword. The architect himself explained: 'If you have the crusade symbol of the *Sword* [. . .] why not the Henry the Navigator *ship*, which really won the old Crusades – as an emblem of our Sea Power, which helped the army to win this new Crusade.'[34]

It is difficult to estimate the impact of the national crusading discourse at the level of parochial and institutional war commemorations. In both contexts references to the new crusade made up a significant, but not predominant feature of remembrance activities (except for those focusing on the Palestine campaign). Moreover, the crusade symbolism departed from the national models in so far as it lacked their subtlety. In England, allusions to the Crusades usually drew on unequivocal images of either St George or Richard I or both (see figure 27). In the parish church of Hadlow, Kent, the memorial window depicts, as the unveiling programme revealed, 'the figure of St. George, or of a Knight Crusader'.[35] The Roman Catholic Church of Our Lady and the English Martyrs in Cambridge put up a memorial plaque surmounted by a figure of St George and the dragon. The local newspaper reported on the

[30] CWGC, SDC 61, Herbert Baker to Frederic Kenyon, 16 December 1918. In addition, see CWGC, WG 358, 'War Crosses: General File', 1921–9; Sidney C. Hurst, *The Silent Cities: An Illustrated Guide to the War Cemeteries and Memorials to the 'Missing' in France and Flanders: 1914–1918* (London, Methuen, 1929); Inglis, *Sacred Places*, p. 255.

[31] WYASL, LC/TC/R 17, Becket & Sons, 'The National War Cross', [c. 1919]. See also King, *Memorials of the Great War*, pp. 150–5. Compare also Mansfield, 'Class Conflict', p. 80; Grieves, 'Investigating Local War Memorial Committees', pp. 47, 51, 55.

[32] CWGC, WG 18, Minutes of the Meeting at DGRE, 14 July 1917.

[33] CWGC, WG 18, Herbert Baker to Fabian Ware, 27 July 1917.

[34] CWGC, SDC 61, Herbert Baker to Frederic Kenyon incl. sketch of the 'Ypres Cross', n.d., italics in the original.

[35] IWM, Eph. Mem., K 3874, 'Hadlow Church, Kent: Unveiling and Dedication of the Memorial Window', 1920, p. 10.

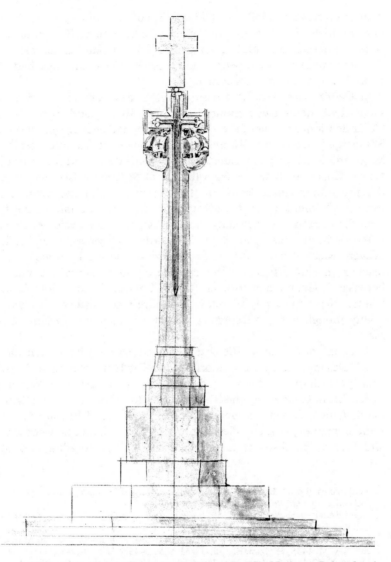

Figure 16. 'Ypres Cross' by Herbert (later Sir Herbert) Baker for the Imperial War Graves Commission. The design is based on the 'Cross of Sacrifice' by Sir Reginald Blomfield. Drawing, c. 1918.

dedication service as follows: 'Old families of this land were proud to go into a parish church to see the effigy of a Crusader. For centuries to come the descendants of the men who died for England in the war would repeat the names of their people, and they would feel the stock had been ennobled by the glorious sacrifice.'[36]

St George was associated with the Crusades, for the historical crusaders had themselves honoured the saint. In England, King Richard Cœur de Lion, a leader of the Third Crusade, had encouraged the cult of St George.[37] Consequently, memorials to the Great War often depict the king and his saint side by side.[38] Eton College decorated the walls of its Lower Chapel with scenes from the life of St George (see figure 7). In the preliminary discussions on the construction of the memorial, a former schoolmaster proposed omitting the fantastic tale of the fight with the dragon and including the 'real' story of the rescue of Richard Cœur de Lion's fleet from a storm. In order to express his gratitude to heaven, Richard gave relics of St George to the local church. For the teacher, the importance of this episode lay in the proved connection between St George and 'British' (that is English) history, notably naval history: 'It seems a pity therefore to ignore what history does give us, scanty though it be, yet connected at two vital points *Palestine* & the *Fleet*.'[39]

The romantic image of Richard I, beloved hero of Victorian medievalism,[40] was invoked by the memorial of the Toc H movement, a Christian charity which during the war had cared for Allied servicemen fighting at Ypres. In All Hallows-by-the-Tower in London, Toc H placed a 'lamp of maintenance ... near the burial place of the heart of Richard Cœur de Lion' in memory of their fallen comrades.[41] The alliance between Britain and France lent itself to an enlargement of the crusading ensemble.

---

[36] 'Catholic Memorial: Bishop's Clarion Call to Lovers of England', *Cambridge Chronicle and University Gazette*, 9066, 8 December 1920, p. 7.

[37] Sigrid Braunfels-Esche, *Sankt Georg: Legende, Verehrung, Symbol* (Munich, Georg D. W. Callwey, 1976), p. 94.

[38] SROI, FB 74, E 3/4, Faculty for a Memorial Window, Higham St Mary, 30 April 1920, and NIWM, 4438, Higham, E. Suff.; IWM, WM 2945, box 15, Leasingham, Kesteven, Lincs.; NIWM, 396, Brampton, Hunts. For further examples of Richard I in war memorials but without St George, see IWM, WM 2614, box 15, Lower Beeding, E. Susx; IWM, WM 2919, box 11, Highworth, Wilts.; NIWM, 9930, Nantwich, Ches.

[39] Eton College Archives, COLL/P6/17, Henry Elford Luxmoore to the Lower Master, January 1921, italics in the original.

[40] To be sure, nineteenth-century anti-imperialists criticised Richard I for abandoning England for the Crusades; see Stephanie L. Barczewski, *Myth and National Identity in Nineteenth-Century Britain: The Legends of King Arthur and Robin Hood* (Oxford, Oxford University Press, 2000), pp. 224, 242.

[41] '"Toc H" Lamps: To be Lit by the Prince', *The Times*, 43202, 30 November 1922, p. 9.

Richard Cœur de Lion's mythic counterpart, Louis IX, saint and king, appeared occasionally in British war memorials. St Louis stands for the solidarity between Britain and France in a righteous struggle, the new crusade. At Bathford, Somerset, as well as at Oddington, Louis IX was depicted together with the British patron saint, St George (see figure 17).[42] The unifying effect of the crusading spirit was also prominently emphasised at Winchester College. Writing about the memorial cloister, the school magazine coupled old and new crusaders as follows:

And all about the walls are the symbols of great countries which for the England of King Richard and the France of Saint Louis did not exist: countries which came crusading side by side with our own Crusaders against the Paynim [sic] of our modern age; countries which must play a great part in any scheme of life offered to modern youth and undertaken by modern youth.[43]

If the war was a new crusade, for what and against whom was the nation waging war? The dead Wykehamists were held up as fighters against paganism. Commonly, however, post-war commemorations celebrated the new crusaders on the grounds that they had struggled *for* specific objects rather than *against* an enemy. In contrast to a holy war, the crusading effort was above all directed towards profane ideals. A publication of 1918 distinguished old from new crusaders: the first were defenders of faith; the second 'Defenders of Truth, Manhood and Democracy'.[44] The Paisley war memorial, entitled 'The Spirit of the Crusaders', also conveyed the impression that 'our men in the Great War in their splendid determination were animated by the same spirit as the Crusaders, and were striving towards an ideal similar to that which stimulated them'.[45] This ideal was defined as 'freedom', 'mercy', 'right-eousness', and 'truth'.[46] Britain's prime crusader, the Unknown Warrior, had allegedly set out to uphold 'the cause of human liberty'.[47] He was pictured as standing firmly in the tradition of Magna Carta, and of 'that heritage of which the ancient Abbey was a shrine – the heritage of the ideals of freedom, of order, of self-discipline, of self-respect'.[48]

[42] NIWM, 7523, Bathford, Somer.; IWM, WM 2627, box 19, Oddington, Oxon.
[43] 'The War Cloister', *Wykehamist*, 648, suppl., 16 June 1924, p. 504. The memorial was designed by Alfred Turner. See *Alfred and Winifred Turner: The Sculpture of Alfred Turner and his Daughter Winifred Turner* (Oxford, Ashmolean Museum, 1988), p. 26.
[44] Bennet A. Molter, *Knights of the Air* (New York and London, D. Appelton, 1918), p. 13.
[45] 'To Memory Dear', *Paisley and Renfrewshire Gazette*, 2958, 21 January 1922, p. 2. See Bell, 'Monuments to the Fallen', pp. 444, 512.
[46] 'The Immortal Memory: Paisley's Tribute to the Fallen', *Paisley and Renfrewshire Gazette*, 3091, 2 August 1924, p. 5.
[47] WAML, Newspaper Cuttings, vol. 1, p. 42, 'A Pledge to the Dead', *Daily Telegraph*, 20748, 18 October 1921, p. 10.
[48] *The Decoration by General Pershing*, p. 12. See also ibid., p. 6.

Figure 17. St George and St Louis. Stained-glass window. Oddington, 1920s (photograph courtesy of the Imperial War Museum, London).

Liberal instincts remained deeply ingrained across British society (despite the weakness of the Liberal Party) and are much in evidence in commemorative discourses. The language of British liberalism in commemorations of the 1920s stands in sharp contrast to the first uses of crusading metaphors in war propaganda. The Dean of Norwich proclaimed in 1914: 'It is a holy war in which we have taken our part; a war of Christ against anti-Christ. Our young men [. . .] must come in the spirit of crusaders.'[49] The dean elaborated on the point that the battle 'is God's, it is indeed Armageddon. Ranged against us are the Dragon and the False Prophet.'[50] As the subject of the dean's sermon – 'Armageddon' – indicated, his crusade had a manifestly apocalyptic quality which was not dissimilar to contemporaneous German concepts of an apocalyptic holy war.

Revelation, from which the Dean of Norwich drew his lessons, was not unknown to agents of remembrance after 1918. On the contrary, St Michael became one of the most common motifs in war memorials, especially in stained-glass windows. A sculpture of the archangel in armour slaying the dragon adorns the interior of the shrine of the Scottish National War Memorial in Edinburgh (see figure 18). He, the conqueror of the powers of hell and captain of heavenly hosts fighting in a just cause, was chosen because he was symbolic of right overcoming wrong. The official guidebook to the memorial cited a suitable passage from Revelation 12:7–9: 'Michael and his angels fought against the dragon . . . and the great dragon was cast out'.[51] The Allied war effort was theologically sanctioned by identifying it with Michael's cause; the stress was placed on the righteousness of military action instead of the arrival of a new millennium.

The figure of St Michael in Ulm Minster, Württemberg, is the equivalent of the Scottish memorial in iconography and prominence (see figure 19). Already contemporaries recognised the parallels. Dr von Seeger, author of a book on war memorials who had a predilection for all things modern and German, compared the 'impressive memorial' of Ulm with the 'expressionless figure' at Edinburgh.[52] He rejected the latter because of its theatrical and uninspired borrowings from Gothic sculpture; the

[49] H[enry] C. Beeching, *Armageddon: A Sermon Upon the War Preached in Norwich Cathedral* (London and Brighton, SPCK, 1914), pp. 13–14.

[50] Ibid., p. 14. See Marrin, *Last Crusade*, p. 137.

[51] As cited in F. W. Deas, *The Scottish National War Memorial: Official Guide* (Edinburgh, David Macdonald, [1928]), p. 27, ellipsis in the original. See also Lawrence Weaver, *The Scottish National War Memorial: The Castle, Edinburgh* (London, Country Life, [1927]), p. 13.

[52] Seeger, *Denkmal des Weltkriegs*, pp. 43–4.

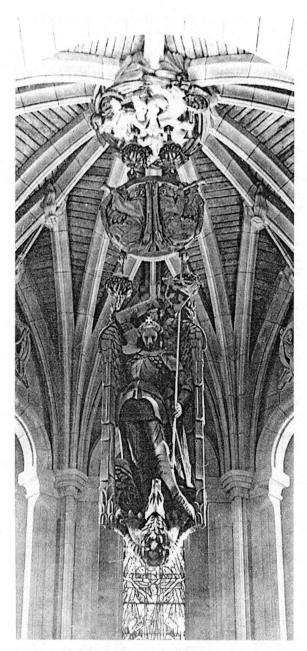

Figure 18. St Michael by Alice Meredith-Williams. Scottish National War Memorial, Edinburgh Castle, 1927.

Figure 19. St Michael by Heinz Wetzel and Ulfert Janssen. Ulm
Minster, 1934.

former he praised for its original and unpretentious style. The memorial in Ulm Minster represents, by means of formal abstraction, the archangel wearing armour, spreading his wings and surmounting a miniature globe which is threatened by two snakes. With his right arm he is brandishing a sword and his left arm is holding a shield.

At the time, not everybody was satisfied with the executed design.[53] The artists' original proposal comprised a figure folding his hands and leaning on a sword, but omitted the globe. Heinz Wetzel, who designed the memorial in conjunction with Ulfert Janssen, declared himself pleased with the final alterations. 'I am glad that we have abandoned the former pose of mourning', he wrote in a letter.[54] However, Wetzel's principal concern was not content but form; he regarded the sword primarily as a 'secant to a tangent' (the figure is placed in an arch separating nave and vestibule). Furthermore, for Wetzel the statue of the archangel simply fulfilled the function of an ornament.[55] Public reaction to the memorial did not mirror the artist's formalistic view of his work. Committee members and journalists gave free play to their imagination when they explained the symbolism to Ulm's citizens. Two themes prevailed: apocalypse and protection.

According to a statement issued by the memorial committee, the monument was based on the angel of Daniel 22:1.[56] The committee recalled the deeds of St Michael, who protects and delivers the chosen people. By contrast, von Seeger felt reminded of the sinister doomsday scenario described by Walter Flex, who was then a famous war poet:

> Archangel Michael summons to court,
> His face flames with world fire's [*Weltbrand's*] glow,
> To God's judgment with gleaming steel
> He embraces mountains and valley as the battlefield [*Walstatt*].[57]

The blending of the story of St Michael with a Germanic saga was not new. For centuries, St Michael had been associated with Wotan (Odin)

---

[53] StdAU, E 603/6, 'Auszug aus dem Verhandlungsbuch des Gesamtkirchenrats und Münsterbaukomitees', 10 June 1929; StdAU, E 603/11, 'Das Gefallenendenkmal im Münster', *Ulmer Tageblatt*, 38, 15 February 1928.

[54] StdAU, E 603/13, Heinz Wetzel to Oberst Port, 16 February. 1928: 'ich [bin] froh, daß die frühere Trauerpose überwunden ist'.

[55] Ibid.

[56] StdAU, E 603/4, 'Das Gefallenen-Denkmal im Ulmer Münster', n.d. This statement was reprinted in the local press. See StdAU, E 603/11, 'Das Gefallenen-Denkmal im Ulmer Münster', *Ulmer Tageblatt*, 272, 18 November 1924.

[57] Seeger, *Denkmal des Weltkriegs*, p. 43: 'Erzengel Michael lädt zum Gericht, / Weltbrands Glut überflammt sein Gesicht, / Zum Gottesurteil mit lohendem Stahl / Umhegt er als Walstatt Berge und Tal.'

since their legends shared many features such as the fight against fabulous beasts.[58] Ulm's Society for Art and Antiquity praised the symbiosis of Christian and Germanic motifs. But contrary to Flex's aggressive diction, the society focused on the sculpture's defensive pose: 'his sword is raised to repel the enemy's attack'.[59] Similarly, a press statement by the committee referred to 'an arch-German figure of Michael in armour and arms [*Wehr und Waffen*]'.[60] Hence St Michael, guardian angel of Germany, stands for the archetypal German, ready for defence. The local paper took up this interpretation: the statue could be understood 'as a symbol of the effort made by the German people in the struggle for the protection of their native soil or as [a symbol] of the protective divine powers'.[61]

Wilhelmines would hardly have believed their eyes. In 1902, the Kaiser had granted permission for the erection of a monument in Münster to the diplomat Baron von Ketteler, who had been killed during the Boxer Rising in Peking in 1900, and a figure of the archangel was selected to epitomise the claims of Christian imperialism.[62] Rabble-rousing propaganda after 1914 operated along the same lines. Picture postcards denoted St Michael with the flaming sword, his foremost attribute, assuming a pugnacious posture.[63] In March 1918, the saint

---

[58] Bernd Grote, *Der deutsche Michel: Ein Beitrag zur publizistischen Bedeutung der Nationalfiguren* (Dortmund, Ruhfus, 1967), pp. 14–15, 68.

[59] StdAU, E 603/11, Verein für Kunst und Altertum, 'Das Kriegsmal im Münster: Zur Wahl des Aufstellungplatzes', *Ulmer Tageblatt*, 109, 10 May 1928: 'daß die christlich-germanische Symbolisierung dieses Gedankens in dem sein Schwert zur Abwehr der Feinde erhebenden Erzengel Michael einen glücklichen und starken Ausdruck gefunden hat'. However, there is no direct reference to Wotan (Odin).

[60] StdAU, E 603/4, 'Kriegerdenkmal im Ulmer Münster', 1 July 1923: 'Eine urdeutsche Michaelsfigur in Wehr und Waffen'.

[61] StdAU, E 603/11, 'Das Gefallenendenkmal im Münster', *Ulmer Tageblatt*, 38, 15 February 1928: 'als Sinnbild der Kraft betrachten, die das deutsche Volk im Ringen um den Schutz des heimischen Bodens aufgewandt hat, oder ihn als die abwehrende und schützende göttliche Macht deuten'.

[62] Birgit Langenscheid and Victoria von Schönfeldt, '"Märtyrer" des deutschen Imperialismus: Das Ketteler-Denkmal im Schloßgarten in Münster', in Heinrich Avenwedde and Heinz-Ulrich Eggert (eds.), *Denkmäler in Münster: Auf Entdeckungsreise in die Vergangenheit* (Münster, Schriftproben, 1996), pp. 281–5.

[63] Private Collection, Hanover, Postcard 'Im Kampf für Recht und Freiheit', n.d. I am grateful to Gerhard Schneider for drawing this collection to my attention. On picture postcards of the First World War, see Gerhard Schneider, 'Kriegspostkarten des Ersten Weltkrieges als Geschichtsquellen', in Udo Arnold, Peter Meyers and Uta C. Schmidt (eds.), *Stationen einer Hochschullaufbahn* (Dortmund, Ebersbach, 1999), pp. 148–96. See also Hans-Dieter Mück, 'Popularisierung des Mittelalters auf Propaganda-Postkarten der Gründerzeit (1870–1918)', in Jürgen Kühnel *et al.* (eds.), *Mittelalter-Rezeption*, vol. III, *Gesammelte Vorträge des 3. Salzburger Symposions: 'Mittelalter, Massenmedien, Neue Mythen'* (Göppingen, Kümmerle, 1988), pp. 231–47.

had to lend his name to 'Operation Michael', one of the four consecutive assaults on the enemy lines on the Western Front in spring 1918. The Ulm memorial, however, represents a departure from pre-war and war-time medievalism. At Ulm, St Michael was stripped of imperialistic militarism. Instead, accounts of the Ulm memorial were couched in defensive terminology. As the Munich architect Fritz Behn pointed out, Michael represented 'the successful repulsing of all enemies during the world war'.[64] Nonetheless, Behn also celebrated him as 'the heavenly warrior against all things base'.[65]

St Michael epitomised the *Gottesstreiter*, the 'divine warrior'[66] combatting wickedness, at both Ulm and Edinburgh.[67] The German memorial, however, marks the intersection of two narratives: St Michael's mission and the German war of defence. It is worth noting that an alternative design for the Ulm memorial, submitted by the sculptor Fritz von Graevenitz, was similarly equivocal. Although entitled 'Flaming Sword' it actually represented Roland, the guardian of civic freedom – a recurring motif in the tale of defensive warfare, as we shall see in the following section.[68]

On the defensive

Images of defensive warfare in commemorative culture betray the continuing influence of war propaganda. German official propaganda successfully coined a phrase when it declared that the fatherland, encircled by hostile powers, was struggling against 'Eine Welt von Feinden', 'a world full of enemies'. War remembrance in Hagen was in line with the official reading of the conflict. A book published on the first anniversary of Hagen's iron-nail monument in 1916 drew a picture of Germany

---

[64] StdAU, E 603/11, 'Das Gefallenendenkmal im Münster', *Ulmer Tageblatt*, 66, 19 March 1928: 'Er ist für uns als das Symbol des himmlischen Kämpfers gegen alles Niedere fest eingewurzelt, ein Symbol auch gerade für diesen Zweck als sieghafte Abwehr aller Feinde im Weltkrieg.'

[65] Ibid.

[66] StdAU, E 603/17, 'Totengedenken und alter Frontgeist in Ulm: Denkmalsweihe im Münster', *Ulmer Tageblatt*, 180, 6 August 1934.

[67] Ibid. On the symbolism of the archangel generally, see Siegmar Holsten, *Allegorische Darstellungen des Krieges 1870–1918: Ikonologische und ideologiekritische Studien* (Munich, Prestel, 1976), pp. 34–6.

[68] StdAU, E 603/2, 'Ideenwettbewerb für eine Münsterdenkmal: Sitzungsbericht des Preisgerichtes', 14 March 1923. For an example from Göttingen, see Albrecht Saathoff (ed.), *Göttinger Kriegsgedenkbuch 1914–1918* (Göttingen, Vandenhoeck & Ruprecht, 1935), p. 213.

maintaining her position '*reckenstark* [strong like a warrior] in a gigantic defence against a world full of enemies' (see figure 9).[69]

The actual geopolitical isolation of the country at the outbreak of war seemed to confirm this vision of international conspiracy. Moreover, for years political thinkers in Imperial Germany had been troubled by fears of encirclement. After 1914, the paranoia about *Einkreisung*, the systematic isolation of Germany by her neighbours, entered the curriculum. School textbooks brought out during and after the war traced the origins of the First World War to the Allies' foreign policy prior to 1914.[70] Children were also mobilised in the context of celebrations at iron-nail memorials. In Münster, Westphalia, twelve thousand pupils from local schools hammered iron nails into the wooden statue of a Germanic warrior armed with a primitive cudgel. The war landmark was appropriately named *Junggermane*, the 'Young Teuton'. The owner of a factory made a donation of two thousand iron nails costing one mark each to enable poor children to do their bit.[71] Naturally, all participants took up the cudgel for the defence of the realm of which the *Junggermane* was a symbol. The inscription enhanced this notion:

> You want to exterminate us?
> You believe we're in distress?
> Come on, go to it! – You're on!
> Victory or death![72]

To be sure, the emergence of pro-annexation agitation during the war compromised the legend of defence. Soldiers' letters of 1916–17 reveal that servicemen and their relatives no longer perceived the German military effort as a defensive measure.[73] In spite of the change in attitudes towards the end of the war, however, the pendulum swung back to the defensive narrative in the 1920s. After all, the territorial losses stipulated in the peace settlement of Versailles appeared to underpin this view. Therefore it is not surprising that the protection of the *Heimat*,

---

[69] *Der Eiserne Schmied von Hagen*, p. 7: 'das sich in diesem riesenhaften Verteidigungskampfe reckenstark gegen eine Welt von Feinden wehrt'.

[70] Rainer Bendick, 'Zur Wirkung und Verarbeitung nationaler Kriegskulturen: Die Darstellung des Ersten Weltkriegs in deutschen und französischen Schulbüchern', in Gerhard Hirschfeld *et al.* (eds.), *Kriegserfahrungen: Studien zur Sozial- und Mentalitätsgeschichte des Ersten Weltkriegs* (Essen, Klartext, 1997), pp. 410–12.

[71] Eduard Schulte, *Kriegschronik der Stadt Münster 1914/18* (Münster, Aschendorff, 1930), p. 181. On the subject of mobilisation of children, see Schneider, 'Hannoversche Nagelfiguren', pp. 228–9, 247–53.

[72] Schulte, *Kriegschronik*, p. 135: 'Ihr wollt uns vernichten? / Ihr glaubt uns in Not? / Nur ran' denn! – Es gilt! / Sieg oder Tod!'.

[73] Ziemann, *Front und Heimat*, p. 466.

the homeland, and the fatherland, figure most prominently in German commemorative culture. In addition, commemorations highlighted the defence of freedom and liberty. This section will largely deal with the German case. In Britain, the concept of defensive warfare was peripheral compared to invocations of the Crusades.

Franz Seldte, leader of the Stahlhelm, Bund der Frontsoldaten, the association of nationalist-minded 'front-line soldiers', rejected the belief that fallen comrades had given their lives for idealistic motives. He reduced the war to a 'holy fight' to preserve the nation's territorial integrity.[74] The Stahlhelm league's Social-Democratic counterpart, the Reichsbanner Schwarz-Rot-Gold, took a very similar stance.[75] For Germans, whether sympathising with the political Right or the moderate Left, the efficacious defence of the fatherland or the home lent validity to the lost war. *Vaterland* and *Heimat* – both words occurred frequently in inscriptions. A study of German war memorials argues that urban communities favoured the fatherland whereas rural society put the emphasis on *Heimat*.[76] While both terms describe an unchanging sense of community and place, they also signify different hierarchies and iconographies of belonging. *Heimat* was typically identified with the region, its nature and landscape, rather than the nation state and its institutions. But there was more to the *Heimat* idea as it had emerged in the nineteenth century than mere provincialism. *Heimat* as the federal incarnation of the nation could potentially embrace all of Germany and thus serve as a mediator between the familar local realm and the impersonal national one.[77]

After the war, castles became major icons of the protection of the national or regional community and territory. A substantial number of memorials were placed in or outside medieval fortresses, such as one Austro-German memorial dedicated to all fallen soldiers of 'German tongue',[78] which was situated in Feste Geroldseck in Kufstein, Tyrol: a

---

[74] GStAPK, I. HA Rep. 77, Tit. 1215 Nr. 3c Bd. 1, folio 40, Franz Seldte, 'Volk ehre Deine Toten!', *Der Stahlhelm*, 30, 26 July 1925, p. 1.

[75] Ziemann, 'Republikanische Kriegserinnerung', pp. 376–7.

[76] Jeismann and Westheider, 'Wofür stirbt der Bürger?', p. 33. See also Ziemann, *Front und Heimat*, p. 455.

[77] Lurz, *Kriegerdenkmäler*, vol. III, p. 24, and vol. IV, pp. 163, 322–4. See also Aribert Reimann, 'Die heile Welt im Stahlgewitter: Deutsche und englische Feldpost aus dem Ersten Weltkrieg', in Gerhard Hirschfeld *et al.* (eds.), *Kriegserfahrungen: Studien zur Sozial- und Mentalitätsgeschichte des Ersten Weltkriegs* (Essen, Klartext, 1997), p. 140; Celia Applegate, *A Nation of Provincials: The German Idea of Heimat* (Berkeley, Los Angeles and Oxford, University of California Press, 1990), pp. 115–19.

[78] BArch, R 43 I/712, folio 87, Gesandschaft der Republik Österreich to Reichsminister des Inneren, 10 February 1928.

'1000-year-old *Trutzburg* [stronghold]'.[79] In England, castles similarly provided a setting for war memorials, but here the architecture accentuated continuity with 'struggles of ages agone' – as in the case of Colchester, Essex – rather than explicitly defence.[80] In Scotland, on the other hand, there were attempts to revive a defensive Celtic tradition in the aftermath of the Great War. The Scottish National War Memorial by Robert (later Sir Robert) Lorimer, which was integrated into the time-honoured castle of Edinburgh, bore a resemblance to 'some feudal keep crowning a lonely Scottish hill-top' (see figure 36).[81] It was built in the fashion of late-medieval Scottish Baronial architecture, a style which was adopted for war-memorial towers throughout Scotland.[82] A commentary on the Edinburgh monument dwelt on the martial legacy of Scottish (architectural) history:

Scottish Baronial is a tower architecture, an expression of methods of living which were crude to the point of being barbarous. In England the type of house which grew round the central hall and developed horizontally was always growing in the amenities of civilisation. The early manor house of the south marked the security of English life. The Scottish tower was no less an expression of the long-continuing element of private warfare which seethed through Scottish life until a far later period. It was not so much a question of the education of the individual who built those stark comfortless homes, but of a defensive tradition which had a practical and continuing significance. [. . .] The instinct for defence remained vivid when the need was less, but by no means wholly past.[83]

While British fortress-style memorials were mainly restricted to Scotland,[84] they constituted an almost universal feature of German commemorations, particularly war cemeteries. From 1930 onwards, the Volksbund Deutsche Kriegsgräberfürsorge discussed plans for so-called

---

[79] StAMS, OP 5510, folio 285, 'Tönendes Denkmal: Zur Einweihung der Kufsteiner Heldenorgel am 3. Mai', unspecified newspaper cutting, 1931. For a similar description, see Seeger, *Denkmal des Weltkriegs*, p. 27. On the project in general, see Joachim Giller, Hubert Mader and Christina Seidl, *Wo sind sie geblieben..? Kriegerdenkmäler und Gefallenenehrung in Österreich* (Vienna, Österreichischer Bundesverlag, 1992), pp. 77–8.
[80] EROC, Acc. C 3, vol. 17, p. 358, 'The Colchester War Memorial', *Essex County Telegraph*, 26 May 1923, p. 6.
[81] Ian Hay, *Their Name Liveth: The Book of the Scottish National War Memorial* (London, Bodley Head, 1931), p. 35.
[82] For examples of Scottish Baronial towers, see NIWM, 5696, Forfar, Angus; NIWM, 8626, Rosehearty, Aberd.; NIWM, 8845, Stornoway, Isle of Lewis, Ross and Cromarty; IWM, WM 3055, box 34, Thiepval, Somme, France. See also Borg, *War Memorials*, p. 133. The Ulster Tower on the Somme is one of the few non-Scottish memorials in Baronial style. See Jeffery, *Ireland and the Great War*, pp. 108–9.
[83] Weaver, *Scottish National War Memorial*, p. 16.
[84] See NIWM, 27979, Stocksbridge, W. Yorks., and NIWM 555, Heapey and Wheelton, Lancs., for clock-towers with battlements in England.

Totenburgen, 'fortresses of the dead', as burial places.[85] Stark fortresses reminiscent of medieval fortifications, consisting of thick walls surrounding an open space, replaced the original concept of Germanic-style heroes' groves. Draft schemes for *Totenburgen* in Yugoslavia and Palestine were made public in 1932, but the fortresses of Bitola (Bitolj) and Nazareth were not completed until after the Nazis had come to power (see figures 20–21 and 29).[86] When the *Totenburg* of Bitola was opened in 1936, the Volksbund's magazine praised the self-contained and defensive appearance of the *Festung*, the 'fortress', which typified the struggle of the German *Volk* against 'a world full of enemies'.[87] This vocabulary is Wilhelmine rather than fascist. In addition, the bulwark style for memorials derived from the period before 1933.

Numerous commemorations in the era of the Weimar Republic represented fortified towers, citadels or castles, often built of coarse bricks offering imaginary refuges. The central cemetery in Vienna houses a striking but unusual example. This modernist octagonal building, resembling a castle with battlements, was set up in 1929 to commemorate the fallen Jewish soldiers of the city. The inscription in both German and Hebrew, taken from Isaiah 2:4, gave the memorial a distinct pacifist aura: 'nation shall not lift up sword against nation, neither shall they learn war any more'.[88] Clemens Holzmeister, the architect who had presided over the jury in Vienna, was, ironically, also the designer of the memorial to Albert Leo Schlageter – the 'martyr' of the *Freikorps*, Free Corps – in Düsseldorf, a meeting ground for nationalistic celebrations which was made a German national memorial in May 1933.[89]

[85] Monika Kuberek, 'Die Kriegsgräberstätten des Volksbundes Deutsche Kriegsgräberfürsorge', in Michael Hütt et al. (eds.), *Unglücklich das Land, das Helden nötig hat: Leiden und Sterben in den Kriegsdenkmälern des Ersten und Zweiten Weltkrieges* (Marburg, Jonas, 1990), pp. 79, 82–5; Mosse, *Fallen Soldiers*, pp. 85–6. It seems that the term *Totenburg* was invented around 1935. See Tietz, *Tannenberg-Nationaldenkmal*, p. 168.
[86] 'Neue Baupläne des Volksbundes', *Kriegsgräberfürsorge*, 12,6 (1932), pp. 83–5; Hans Gstettner, *Deutsche Soldatenmale: Erbaut vom Volksbund Deutsche Kriegsgräberfürsorge e.V.* (Berlin, Volksbund Deutsche Kriegsgräberfürsorge, [1940]).
[87] Franz Hallbauer, 'Die Totenburg deutscher Helden in Bitolj, Jugoslawien', *Kriegsgräberfürsorge*, 16,1 (1936), p. 12: 'das gegen eine Welt von Feinden sich verteidigte'. See Christian Fuhrmeister, 'Die "unsterbliche Landschaft", der Raum des Reiches und die Toten der Nation: Die Totenburgen Bitoli (1936) und Quero (1939) als strategische Nationalarchitektur', *kritische berichte*, 29,2 (2001), pp. 61–4.
[88] Martin Senekowitsch, *Ein ungewöhnliches Kriegerdenkmal: Das jüdische Heldendenkmal auf dem Wiener Zentralfriedhof* (Vienna, Militärkommando Wien, 1994), [p. 2].
[89] Lothar Schiefer, 'Das Schlageter-Denkmal: Vom Soldatengrab zum Forum', in Hütt et al., *Unglücklich das Land, das Helden nötig hat*, pp. 50–5; Michael Knauff, 'Das Schlageter-Nationaldenkmal auf der Golzheimer Heide in Düsseldorf', *Geschichte im Westen*, 10 (1995), pp. 168–91; Fuhrmeister, *Beton, Klinker, Granit*, pp. 191–258.

Figure 20. 'Fortress of the Dead' (*Totenburg*) from outside. Built by Volksbund Deutsche Kriegsgräberfürsorge. Bitola, Yugoslavia, 1936.

Figure 21. 'Fortress of the Dead' (*Totenburg*) from inside. Built by Volksbund Deutsche Kriegsgräberfürsorge. Bitola, Yugoslavia, 1936.

A variation on the fortress theme represented the use of remains of medieval city walls and citadels for commemorative purposes. Dorsten, Westphalia, transformed the tower of the city's former ramparts into a site of war remembrance (see figure 6).[90] Historic towers and protective walls invoked stories of medieval cities besieged by hostile armies, a situation which seemed to be analogous to Germany's alleged isolation in 'a world full of enemies'.

Two *Torwächter*, gate-keepers – figures of nude warriors – guard the gate of Dorsten's memorial tower.[91] Their hands are clasped on the pommels of their swords which are held point downward. Despite their nudity, the combination of their deportment and setting calls up the image of Roland, the legendary paladin of Charlemagne and guardian of municipal sovereignty. In the later Middle Ages, columns depicting the knight were placed in market squares of cities in the north German states, Thuringia and Saxony. To historians in the early twentieth century, the origin and significance of these columns was still obscure, but popular myth assigned multiple meanings to them. They were believed to symbolise either a city's rights, especially its privilege of holding markets; royal jurisdiction; or Donar (Thor), the god of thunder.[92] Germany's most famous Roland column survived in Bremen in front of the city hall. In 1915, this Roland, dated 1404, was joined by a doppelgänger, a wooden statue which was to be marked by a series of nails over a period of four years (see figure 22). At the inauguration of the wooden 'Iron Roland', Bremen's mayor, Dr Buff, explained the connection between the duplicate and the historic monument:

For centuries Roland the Giant has faithfully kept watch in front of our city hall, the Roland of stone, he the keeper of civic liberty. [. . .] A doppelgänger to the *Recke* [warrior] of stone has arisen, the wooden Roland [. . .] Dark times have descended on German lands. Soon it will be a year ago to the day that the commander-in-chief called us to the colours to fight for the German people's freedom. Enemies filled with envy have arisen against us with the intention of striking down our treasured fatherland and her allied powers.[93]

---

[90] *Deutscher Ehrenhain*, p. 36; Seeger, *Denkmal des Weltkriegs*, p. 93.

[91] Joseph Wiedenhöfer, *Die Kriegergedächtnisstätte der Stadt Dorsten: Zum Weihetag 4. Oktober 1925* (Dorsten, Hermann Majert, 1925), p. 22, also in StAMS, OP 5556, folio 155. See also Lurz, *Kriegerdenkmäler*, vol. IV, pp. 138–9, 319–20.

[92] StAB, 7,60/2–9.b.1, 'Eine neue Lösung des Roland-Rätsels', *Bremer Nachrichten*, [*c.* 1917]. See also Rapsilber, *Der Eiserne Hindenburg von Berlin*, p. 42.

[93] StAB, 7,60/2–9.b.1, 'Der Eiserne Roland in Bremen: Die Einweihungsfeier', *Bremer Nachrichten*, 195, 16 July 1915: 'Treue Wacht hält durch die Jahrhunderte Roland der Riese vor dem Rathaus unserer Stadt, der Roland aus Stein, er der Hüter bürgerlicher Freiheit. [. . .] Ein Doppelgänger ist dem steinernen Recken erstanden, der Roland aus Holz [. . .] Dunkle Zeiten sind über deutsche Lande hereingebrochen. Bald jährt sich der Tag, an dem der oberste Kriegsherr Deutschlands Wehrkraft zu den

Figure 22. 'Iron Roland'. Wartime postcard depicting the iron-nail statue by H. Schubert. Bremen, 1915.

The Roland 'brothers', as the local newspaper dubbed them, bridged the gap between past and present as well as between the locality and the nation state. Roland, the traditional guardian of *Stadtfreiheit*, civic liberty, metamorphosed during the war into a fighter for the freedom of the German *Volk*.

Although the organisers took care not to mention it, the colossal Roland statue of Bremen's arch-rival had certainly impressed them: Hamburg's Bismarck memorial of 1906, which was then widely regarded as a paradigm for modern memorial art, had put the Roland motif back on the artistic agenda. Unlike Bremen's naturalistic 'Iron Roland', the Hamburg memorial was stylised. The twenty-metre-tall granite monument by Hugo Lederer and Emil Schaudt shows Bismarck stiffly erect, clad in armour, resting on a huge sword. The memorial committee understood the Bismarck-Roland as the 'embodiment of heroic greatness and symbol of fortified watchfulness'.[94] For Hamburg's patrician classes, the instigators of the memorial, the project was a way of asserting Hamburg's independence and cultural aspirations vis-à-vis the aesthetics of the Berlin monarchy.[95] This 'German Statue of Liberty', as it was known, achieved enduring national fame, as reflected in the discussion on the design of war memorials after 1914.[96] Moreover, an iron-nail landmark of 1916 in the town of Rheydt, Rhine Province, boldly plagiarised from Lederer and Schaudt's work (see figure 23).[97]

Prominent examples such as Hamburg's statue (or Bernhard Hoetger's 1915 Roland for Hanover) provided stimuli for the use of the motif in Great War monuments.[98] There were also variants on the Roland theme such as the 'Iron Blacksmith' in Essen or the 'Iron St Reinoldus' of

flatternden Fahnen rief, zum Kampf für des Deutschen Volkes Freiheit. Neidvolle Feinde in mächtiger Zahl sind uns erstanden, bestrebt, unser teures Vaterland und die verbündeten Mächte zu Boden zu ringen.' For a reference to Bremen's Roland in the discourse on war memorials, see e.g. Schindhelm, *Reichsehrenmal im heiligen Hain*, p. 12.

[94] As cited in Mark A. Russell, 'The Building of Hamburg's Bismarck Memorial, 1898–1906', *Historical Journal*, 43 (2000), p. 153. On the history and iconography of the monument, see Alings, *Monument und Nation*, pp. 134, 247–54. In 1931, a modern Roland-style memorial to Bismarck designed by Fritz Behn was unveiled in Munich. See StdAM, ZA Denkmäler/Bismarckdenkmal, 'Der Bismarck-Roland', *Bayerische Staatszeitung*, 247, 26 October 1931; 'Erstes Bismarck-Denkmal für München: Eine Stiftung Kommerzienrats Dr. Reusch', *München-Augsburger Abendzeitung*, 57, 26 February 1931; 'Armer Bismarck!', *Münchener Post*, 212, 15 September 1931.

[95] Russell, 'Hamburg's Bismarck Memorial', p. 139.

[96] BArch, R 32/359, folio 1, 'Ehrenmal auf dem Brocken?', *Braunschweiger Neueste Nachrichten*, 238, 11 October 1930; BArch, R 32/362, folio 96v, Citizens of Hacklberg to Reichskunstwart, 20 September 1929; Deutscher Bund Heimatschutz (ed.), *Kriegergräber und Denkmäler: Unsere Wünsche und Pflichten* (Munich, Georg D. W. Callwey, [1918]), p. 6.

[97] Bibliothek für Zeitgeschichte, Stuttgart, Feldpostsammlung Schüling, vol. 76, Postcard Rheydt, 1916.

[98] Dietrich Schubert, 'Hoetgers Waldersee-Denkmal von 1915 in Hannover', *Wallraf-Richartz-Jahrbuch*, 43 (1982), esp. pp. 240–1; Schneider, '. . .nicht umsonst gefallen'?, pp. 124–5. On the Roland motif in wartime advertisements, see Harriet Rudolph, 'Männerikonographie: Dimensionen von Männlichkeit in der Wirtschaftswerbung während des Ersten Weltkrieges in Deutschland und England', *Archiv für Sozialgeschichte*, 36 (1996), p. 271.

Figure 23. 'Iron Bismarck'. Wartime postcard depicting the iron-nail statue by Franz Bürgerling. The design is plagiarised from the Bismarck memorial by Hugo Lederer and Emil Schaudt unveiled in Hamburg in 1906. Rheydt, 1916.

Dortmund (both of 1915).[99] The latter depicted Dortmund's legendary watchman, a mystical paladin of Charlemagne.[100] Although figures called the 'Iron Roland' sprang up throughout Germany – even Mannheim, in Baden, had one – the symbol was most popular in the urban areas of northern Germany.[101] This concentration is understandable given the actual presence of medieval models in the cities of this region. The idea of an unbroken tradition of Roland columns built in token of civic liberty was, of course, a myth, but it offered a starting point nonetheless. A factor which might have supported the dissemination of the Roland symbol in the north of Germany is Protestant iconophobia. A leaflet issued by the Westphalian Bauberatungsstelle, an advisory bureau for building work, suggested that Roland would be an alternative to the warrior saints and thus be an appropriate symbol for the non-Roman Catholic districts of the province. Whether German saga, fairy tale, folk song or Christian legend, according to the advisory body, they were all 'nothing but a song of the fight against a world full of craftiness and deception'.[102]

East Friesland, on the German North Sea coast, was a bastion of – both Lutheran and Calvinist – Protestantism. The war memorial in the East Friesian town of Norden is a stylised bronze figure of a grim-faced watchman who appears to deter potential intruders (see figure 24). The monumental guard is posted at the tower of the Lutheran parish church, a massive building which heightened the impression of *Wehrhaftigkeit*, 'defensiveness'.[103] Even though the figure is located in a provincial town, it attracted considerable attention, for it is a work by Hermann Hosaeus, one of the outstanding sculptors of Weimar Germany.[104] Edwin Redslob, the official Reich Art Custodian, showed an interest in the statue, which he identified as an image of Roland.[105] Redslob's

---

[99] 'Der Zweck des "Eisernen Mannes" in Essen', *Rheinisch-Westfälischer Anzeiger*, 160, 11 June 1915, p. 7.

[100] 'Die Weihe des Eisernen Reinoldus von Dortmund', *Tremonia*, 268, 27 September 1915. The imagery dates back to 1913, when the city council considered the erection of a figure of St Reinoldus. See StdADO, 3–3086, Minutes of the Baukommission, 12 February 1920.

[101] 'Schlagt euren Nagel in den Eisernen Roland, 1914/18', in Deutsches Historisches Museum (ed.), *Plakate des Ersten Weltkrieges 1914–1918*, CD-ROM (Munich, K. G. Saur, 1996), P 57/1385.

[102] StAMS, OP 5603, folio 15, Westfälische Bauberatungsstelle *et al.*, 'Ehret die Krieger! Merkblatt für Kriegerehrungen', 1915, p. 5: 'Sind doch alle Sagen im Grunde nichts weiter als ein Lied vom Kampf gegen eine Welt von Hinterlist und Trug.'

[103] StAA, Dep. 60, Acc. 1993/13, Statement by Stadtbauamt Norden, 1 February 1933.

[104] Seeger, *Denkmal des Weltkriegs*, pp. 148–9; *Deutscher Ehrenhain*, p. 58.

[105] BArch, R 32/350, folio 211, Reichskunstwart to Edgar C. Kiesel, 2 May 1930.

Figure 24. Steel-helmeted German soldier by Hermann Hosaeus. Norden, 1920s.

finding is revealing. The memorial clearly features a *Feldgrauer,* a German soldier of the First World War clothed in a 'field-grey' uniform.[106] A steel helmet crowns his head. The accessories are distinctly modern. His posture, on the other hand, is evocative of representations of Roland; the soldier stands erect with his legs apart, his hands clasp the barrel of a long rifle.

The borrowings from Roland columns were deliberate. The sculptor himself labelled his private photographs of the Norden memorial 'The "Roland" of Norden'.[107] Modernised Rolands were a common motif after the Great War; indeed Hosaeus himself designed similar figures for the city of Osnabrück, Hanover, and the town of Bleicherode in the Prussian Province of Saxony.[108] Still, Norden's Roland is unique to East Friesland. The inscription in Low German dialect reads 'Leewer dod as Slaw – 'Rather dead than a slave'. At first glance the monument seems to encapsulate the type of misanthropic modernism which – as maintained by Eksteins – overshadowed Germany's post-1914 art, ethics and politics.[109] 'Leewer dod as Slav' [*sic*] was, in fact, the motto of a bellicose nationalistic remembrance ceremony which took place on the East Friesian isle of Borkum.[110]

However, I want to suggest that the saying 'Rather dead than a slave' testifies to a commemorative 'special path' of a different sort, a path which is peculiar to Friesian folklore. On the eve of the First World War, in late May 1914, the Friesian memorial was opened in Hartwarden, Oldenburg (Rüstringen). It denoted a Friesian peasant warrior armed with a cudgel and a round shield.[111] The plinth bore the inscription 'Rather dead than a slave'. Iconography and inscription were embedded in the cultural memory of Friesian liberty and defensiveness – a tradition

---

[106] StAA, Dep. 60, Acc. 1993/13, Memorandum by Stadtbaumeister Dorner, 20 October 1932.
[107] TUB, Nachlaß Hermann Hosaeus, Ho 854, Photographs 'Der "Roland" von Norden', n.d.
[108] Lurz, *Kriegerdenkmäler,* vol. IV, p. 163. See BArch, R 32/350, folio 211, Reichskunstwart to Edgar C. Kiesel, 2 May 1930; Ilona Brumme, 'Das Kriegerdenkmal des Infanterie-Regiments Herzog Friedrich Wilhelm von Braunschweig (Ostfr.) Nr. 78 und seiner Töchterregimenter am Bocksturms', in Jutta Held (ed.), *Symbole des Friedens und des Krieges im öffentlichen Raum: Osnabrück, die 'Stadt des Westfälischen Friedens'* (Weimar, VDG, 1998), pp. 145–71.
[109] Eksteins, *Rites of Spring.*
[110] BArch, R 8034 II/7691, folio 82, 'Die Brigade Ehrhard. . . [*sic*]: Einweihung des Borkumer Denkmals für die Gefallenen der II. Marine-Brigade', *Deutsche Zeitung,* 326, 28 July 1921.
[111] See also O[tto] Weltzien, 'Kriegsnagelungen in Niederdeutschland', *Niedersachsen,* 22,3 (1916), p. 39; BfZ, Feldpostsammlung Schüling, vol. 95, Postcard Rüstringen, 1915.

which was not invented, but revived during the nineteenth century (see figure 25). In early medieval times, Friesian peasants had been granted a royal charter guaranteeing them personal freedom. In exchange it was the peasants' responsibility to protect the land against military invaders and the flood tide. Pride in the absence of serfdom from Friesian history found expression in the East Friesian watchword 'Eala frea Fresena', 'Stand up, you free Friesians'. When the city of Leer invited artists to submit proposals for the city war memorial in 1924 (see figure 12), one design was actually entitled 'Eala frea Fresena'. Other entries also dwelt on the lore of Friesian liberty; two entries recalled the saying 'Rather dead than a slave'.[112]

A legendary, albeit somewhat anarchical, defender of freedom from the coastal area who would have fitted ideally into the defensive narrative is Klaus Störtebeker. In the late thirteenth century, Störtebeker and his gang of pirates had seized merchant ships sailing in the Baltic and North Seas. In 1401, the pirates were executed after they had been taken prisoner by the Hanseatic League. Folk tale and nineteenth-century literature elevated Störtebeker to a noble outlaw, a Robin-Hood-like character who robbed the rich to help the poor. Although a folk hero, he does not appear in war commemorations. From the outset, contemporary observers of the vogue for iron-nail heroes were dismayed at the disregard of Störtebeker.[113] Both Störtebeker and Roland are, on the one hand, upholders of freedom, yet on the other hand they form an antithetical pair: action versus reaction, liberation versus protection, rebellion versus order.

A vigorous freedom fighter other than Störtebeker who arrested national imagination was the Swiss warrior Arnold Winkelried. His deeds have been evoked time and again since the nineteenth century. He had a place in the German pantheon, the *Walhalla* opened in 1842 near Regensburg, Bavaria, as well as in propaganda posters and war memorials.[114] At the battle of Sempach between the Swiss confederates and

---

[112] StdAL, 1631, fos. 49–51, 'Niederschrift über die Verhandlungen des Preisgerichts zum Wettbewerb "Kriegerehrung" der Stadt Leer', 1 October 1924.

[113] Weltzien, 'Kriegsnagelungen in Niederdeutschland', p. 39. Generally, see Karin Cieslik, 'Der Mythos vom Außenseiter: Klaus Störtebeker, Pirat und Volksheld des Nordens', in Ulrich Müller and Werner Wunderlich (eds.), *Mittelaltermythen*, vol. I, *Herrscher, Helden, Heilige* (St Gallen, UVK, 1996), pp. 451–66.

[114] Paul Herre, *Deutsche Walhall: Eine Auseinandersetzung und ein Programm zu einem Ehrenmal des Deutschen Volkes* (Potsdam, Athenaion, [1930]), p. 31; StAMS, OP 5510, folio 79, Adolf Reuter, 'Das Reichsehrenmal und die Oberweser', n.d.; BfZ, Dokumentesammlung 1914–1918, 7. Kriegsanleihe, Poster, no. 12, 'Der Freiheit eine Gasse!', 1917. On the *Walhalla* memorial in the nineteenth century, see Kerssen, *Interesse am Mittelalter*, ch. 5.

Figure 25. Friesian warrior. Wartime postcard depicting the iron-nail statue. Rüstringen, 1915.

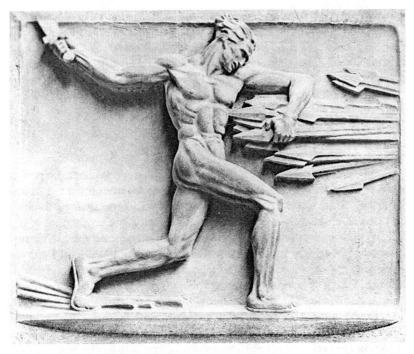

Figure 26. Winkelried by Hermann Hosaeus. Kaiser Wilhelm Memorial
Church, Berlin, 1928.

Austrian troops in 1386, Winkelried had purportedly stormed into a
phalanx of lance-bearers. His self-sacrifice had proverbially paved the
way to Swiss independence: 'Der Freiheit eine Gasse!' – 'A path for
freedom!' The fabled battle-cry materialised in Hosaeus' relief for the
Kaiser Wilhelm Memorial Church in Berlin (see figure 26).[115] The
moment of Winkelried's kamikaze attack is the subject of the memorial.
For the church council, Winkelried – depicted as a nude warrior – was
iconic of the brave *Vaterlandsverteidiger*, the 'defender of the fatherland',
facing a superior foe.[116] German war remembrance cultivated a
number of archetypal freedom fighters like Winkelried or Arminius the
Cheruscan, 'who for the first time [in history] formed a path for German

---

[115] TUB, Ho 842, Photographs 'Winkelried', n.d. See Seeger, *Denkmal des Weltkriegs*, p.
169; Weinland, *Kriegerdenkmäler in Berlin*, pp. 121–2.
[116] TUB, Ho 112, Gemeindekirchenrat Kaiser-Wilhelm-Gedächtniskirche to Hermann
Hosaeus, 14 November 1928.

freedom'.[117] In Britain, commemorations of the 1914–18 conflict offered no match for them, in spite of the fact that figures such as Robin Hood or Owen Glendower (Owain Glyndŵr) were ingrained cultural memory.[118] To be sure, a small number of Scottish war memorials resurrected 'defenders of Scottish freedom', notably two champions of the Scottish War of Independence, Robert the Bruce and William Wallace.[119]

The battlefields

References to legendary heroes like Winkelried or Wallace helped to reassert the role of the individual in shaping and determining the course of history. Sometimes, the personalisation of war through the invocation of historic characters went hand in hand with the exaltation of the military leaders of the Great War. Generals Edmund Allenby (Viscount Allenby of Megiddo and Felixstowe since October 1919) and Paul von Hindenburg – imagined as the descendants of King Richard I and Grand Master Ulrich von Jungingen respectively – personified particular theatres of battle. The names Allenby and Jerusalem, and Hindenburg and Tannenberg, became to some extent interchangeable. War remembrance linked the nature of these campaigns to the person of the commanding general. The commemoration of the war in the east – in the Middle East and eastern Europe – is the subject of the first two parts of this section. The image of a war of movement and great men in the east clashed with the stalemate and anonymity of the Western Front. The final part centres the discussion on the imagined nature of the war in the west.

Palestine, Arabia and Gallipoli

Allenby died in 1936. He was laid to rest in the Warriors' Chapel in Westminster Abbey near the tomb of the Unknown Warrior. Consecrated in 1932, the Warriors' Chapel (formerly the Chapel of the Holy

[117] Wilhelm Müller-Loebnitz (ed.), *Das Ehrenbuch der Westfalen: Die Westfalen im Weltkrieg* (Stuttgart, Oskar Hinderer, [1931]), p. 3: 'der deutschen Freiheit erstmals eine Gasse bahnte'. On the evolution of the cult of Arminius, see Dörner, *Politischer Mythos*; Charlotte Tacke, *Denkmal im sozialen Raum: Nationale Symbole in Deutschland und Frankreich im 19. Jahrhundert* (Göttingen, Vandenhoeck & Ruprecht, 1995).
[118] Hereward the Wake, however, appears in a memorial window in Ely Cathedral; see the discussion of representations of the war in the west in this chapter.
[119] Hay, *Their Name Liveth*, p. 139. See Deas, *Scottish National War Memorial*, pp. 26–7; 'Scottish Memorials in Jerusalem', *The Times*, 46169, 25 June 1932, p. 11; IWM, WM 1022, box 1, Ardrossan, Ayr.

Cross; rededicated as St George's Chapel in 1944) functioned as a final resting-place for deceased generals of the Great War. Field Marshal Herbert Plumer was the first to be buried in the chapel built by Ninian (later Sir Ninian) Comper. When the ashes of Allenby, who had been promoted to the rank of field marshal, were placed in the Warriors' Chapel, the *Daily Sketch* lamented the death of the 'conqueror of Palestine, leader of the last and greatest Crusade'. 'Farewell to the Last Crusader' was the headline.[120] The newspaper renewed a form of notation – the 'last crusade' – which had been promulgated by publishers in the early 1920s. Books with titles such as *Khaki Crusaders* (1918), *The Last Crusade* (1920), *With Allenby's Crusaders* (1923) and *The Romance of the Last Crusade* (1923) appeared within a few years of Allenby's capture of the Holy City in December 1917.[121] The December 1917 issue of *Punch* probably set the trend. A cartoon entitled 'The Last Crusade' depicted Richard Cœur de Lion looking down on Jerusalem and saying 'My dream comes true!'[122]

The attempt to draw a direct parallel between the medieval king and the modern general is evident in war memorials too. At Brampton, Huntingdonshire, a stained-glass window, designed by the firm of C. E. Kempe, features Richard I (see figure 27) and, below him, Allenby entering the capital of Palestine through the Jaffa Gate. The inscription reads:

> Here General Allenby entereth
> Jerusalem on December 11th
> Ao Dni 1917 and initiates
> under Christian Government
> a rule of justice and freedom
> for the Holy City.[123]

Allenby's was a crusade in pursuit of liberal values: 'justice and freedom'. The humility of the British liberator stood out against the imperialistic arrogance of an earlier German visitor. In 1898, Wilhelm II had undertaken a tour of the Middle East, ironically arranged by the

---

[120] WAML, Newspaper Cuttings, vol. 2, p. 113, 'Farewell to the Last Crusader', *Daily Sketch*, 8442, 20 May 1936, p. 6.

[121] Jonathan Newell, 'Allenby and the Palestine Campaign', in Brian Bond (ed.), *The First World War and British Military History* (Oxford, Clarendon, 1991), p. 191; Eitan Bar-Yosef, 'The Last Crusade? British Propaganda and the Palestine Campaign, 1917–18', *Journal of Contemporary History*, 36 (2001), pp. 87, 94; Luke McKernan, '"The Supreme Moment of the War": "General Allenby's Entry into Jerusalem"', *Historical Journal of Film, Radio and Television*, 13 (1993), pp. 170–1.

[122] 'The Last Crusade', *Punch*, 153 (1917), p. 415.

[123] NIWM, 396, Brampton, Hunts.

Figure 27. Richard I. Stained-glass window by C. E. Kempe. Church of St Mary Magdalene, Brampton, 1919.

British travel agent Thomas Cook. Like a conqueror, the Kaiser had entered Jerusalem on horseback wearing a field marshal's white uniform. Allenby's ceremonial entry into the Holy City had been carefully stage-managed in order to distinguish him from his German predecessor. The Englishman arrived in the city as a pedestrian rather than a rider. The deliberate humility of Allenby's walk into Jerusalem contrasted with all the pomp of the Kaiser's visit.[124] The scene of Allenby's entry into the city has been captured in Norfolk's book of remembrance in Norwich Cathedral (see figure 1). The volume also contains a miniature of Jerusalem and a tiny map of Palestine: 'This view is inscribed with the opening verses of Psalm 122 ["Our feete shall stand within thy gate, O Ierusalem"] & the prophetic words of Isaiah 31:5 ["As birds flying, so will the Lord of hostes defend Ierusalem, defending also hee will deliver it, and passing ouer, he will preserve it."], so literally fulfilled in the War.'[125]

Journeys to the Holy Land had come back into vogue in the nineteenth century.[126] The travellers set out for different reasons; some went on a pilgrimage, others carried out academic fieldwork, or pursued an imperialistic adventure. The Kaiser regarded himself as a pilgrim. The official purpose of his trip in 1898 was to dedicate the Erlöserkirche, the Church of the Redeemer, in his capacity as *summus episcopus* of the largest Protestant church of Germany.[127] The fact that the church building represented a reconstruction of the church of Santa Maria Latina, founded by the Order of St John in the thirteenth century, gave the ceremony a crusading undertone. Indeed, the Kaiser himself held the title of Grand Master of the Order of St John (Johanniter-Orden) which had been revived in Prussia in 1852.[128]

By the late nineteenth century, Palestine and Jerusalem had become contested sites of memory. The Roman Catholic, Anglican, Orthodox

---

[124] Bar-Yosef, 'Last Crusade?', pp. 100–1; Newell, 'Allenby', pp. 189–90.

[125] NRO, DCN 106/25, Descriptions of the Book of Remembrance, n.d.; NRO, DCN 106/31, Photographs of the Book of Remembrance, n.d.

[126] Heinz Gollwitzer, 'Deutsche Palästinafahrten des 19. Jahrhunderts als Glaubens- und Bildungserlebnis', in Wolfgang Stammler (ed.), *Lebenskräfte in der abendländischen Geistesgeschichte* (Marburg, Simons, 1948), pp. 286–324; Pemble, *Mediterranean Passion*, pp. 57–9.

[127] Gollwitzer, 'Deutsche Palästinafahrten', p. 319. See also Thomas Benner, *Die Strahlen der Krone: Die religiöse Dimension des Kaisertums unter Wilhelm II. vor dem Hintergrund der Orientreise 1898* (Marburg, Tectum, 2001).

[128] Jürgen Krüger, *Rom und Jerusalem: Kirchenbauvorstellungen der Hohenzollern im 19. Jahrhundert* (Berlin, Akademie, 1995), pp. 56–123. On the revival of military orders in the nineteenth century, see Jonathan Riley-Smith, 'The Order of St John in England, 1827–1858', in Malcolm Barber (ed.), *The Military Orders: Fighting for Faith and Caring for the Sick* (Aldershot and Brookfield, Ashgate, 1994), pp. 121–38.

and Lutheran churches established missions and other institutions in the Holy Land. Furthermore, the Zionist movement sought to recover for the Jewish people its historic Palestinian homeland after centuries of dispersion. The Kaiser trod a fine line between competing claims and memories. He had come to the Middle East, after all, as the official guest of the Turkish sultan. Placing a bronze laurel wreath with the inscription 'From one great emperor to another' on the tomb of Sultan Saladin in Damascus was Wilhelm's gesture towards Muslim supremacy over the region.[129] A *Punch* cartoon, reprinted on propaganda postcards during the war, highlighted the absurdity of the situation. It depicted the Kaiser as a Knight Templar in conversation with Saladin: '*WHAT*!! / THE CHRISTIAN POWERS PUTTING PRESSURE UPON *YOU*, / MY DEAR FRIEND!! HORRIBLE! I CAN'T THINK HOW / PEOPLE CAN DO SUCH THINGS!'[130]

Today, Saladin's laurel wreath is on display in the Imperial War Museum in London. It was taken to Britain as a war trophy by T. E. Lawrence, known to posterity as Lawrence of Arabia.[131] Lawrence ventured in his own way into the Holy Land. A British intelligence officer who lived among Bedouin Arabs and planned their revolt against Turkish rule in 1916–18, he became a media celebrity in the inter-war years. Journalists, rather than historians or participants in the revolt, fashioned the cult of Lawrence.[132] Lawrence's fame even overshadowed the reputation of his superior, General Allenby. Like Allenby, Lawrence was associated with the crusaders, an association he himself encouraged. E. M. Forster wrote after his death: 'the notion of a crusade, of a body of men leaving one country to do noble deeds in another, now possessed him, and I think never left him'.[133] Lawrence's gravestone in a small church in Wareham, Devon, tries to recapture this facet of his life (a cast of the original was later acquired by the Tate Gallery). The tomb shows a crusader knight, recumbent, with crossed legs (see figure 57).[134] It was carved by one of his friends, the former official war artist

---

[129] Siberry, *New Crusaders*, pp. 67–8.

[130] IWM, Postcard Collection, British Artists World War I, 'Cook's Crusader', n.d., italics in the original.

[131] Siberry, *New Crusaders*, p. 68.

[132] Brian Holden Reid, 'T. E. Lawrence and his Biographers', in Bond, *The First World War and British Military History*, p. 228; Graham Dawson, *Soldier Heroes: British Adventure, Empire and the Imagination of Masculinities* (London and New York, Routledge, 1994), ch. 6; Jay Winter and Blaine Baggett, *1914–18: The Great War and the Shaping of the 20th Century* (London, BBC Books, 1996), pp. 376–9.

[133] As cited in Siberry, *New Crusaders*, p. 95. See also ibid., p. 51; Bar-Yosef, 'Last Crusade?', p. 95.

[134] Richard Knowles, 'Tale of an "Arabian Knight": The T. E. Lawrence Effigy', *Church Monuments*, 6 (1991), pp. 67–76.

Eric Kennington, a man who believed in the individuality and heroism of modern soldiers.[135] At Lawrence's feet there is a pile of books – among them *Morte d'Arthur* – which he had by all accounts carried with him during the Arab revolt.

Kennington's effigy ennobled Lawrence as a knight, a knight of the desert. Lawrence, the Arabist with a penchant for the art and history of the Middle Ages, is clothed in an Arab robe resembling a medieval gown. Lawrence himself held that the ideal of chivalry was, in the modern world, essentially practised by the Arabs.[136] Lloyd George and Georges Clemenceau's betrayal of the Arab cause at the peace conference of 1919 confirmed Lawrence in his attitude. Western politicians had broken the knight's integrity. He had crusaded to no avail for the liberation of Arabia; western imperialism seemed to take the place of Turkish suppression. The inconsistencies underlying the story of Lawrence, the fantasy of a crusader bestowing freedom on oppressed Muslims, either did not strike or did not matter to the British audience.

The German public witnessed a similar intellectual balancing act between the invocation of a Germanic holy war and the promotion of an Islamic jihad. In an effort to undermine the existing colonial order and force the enemy to the peace table, Germany and Turkey issued calls for a jihad against the Entente powers. German war propaganda attempted to arouse revolutionary tendencies among the Moslem members of the Allied armies. While the German military circulated propaganda leaflets at the front, academics and journalists justified the jihad at home. One writer pictured 'the holy German war, shoulder to shoulder with the jihad'.[137] A professor at the University of Berlin stressed that the current jihad was a genuine war of defence against British, French and Russian colonialism free of any anti-Christian feelings.[138]

---

[135] Maria Tippett, *Art at the Service of War: Canada, Art, and the Great War* (Toronto, Buffalo and London, University of Toronto Press, 1984), pp. 67–9.

[136] M[alcolm] D. Allen, *The Medievalism of Lawrence of Arabia* (University Park, Pennsylvania State University Press, 1991), p. 194.

[137] Gottfried Galli, *Dschihad: Der Heilige Krieg des Islams und seine Bedeutung im Weltkrieg unter besonderer Berücksichtigung der Interessen Deutschlands: Vortrag gehalten in Freiburg i.B. und Cassel* (Freiburg, Br., C. Troemer, 1915), p. 4: 'Der Heilige Deutsche Krieg, Schulter and Schulter mit dem Dschihad'. See also Herbert Landolin Müller, *Islam, gihad ('Heiliger Krieg') und Deutsches Reich: Ein Nachspiel zur wilhelminischen Weltpolitik im Maghreb 1914– 1918* (Frankfurt am Main, Peter Lang, 1991), pp. 173–7; Hew Strachan, *The First World War*, vol. I, *To Arms* (Oxford, Oxford University Press, 2001), pp. 694–712; Jeismann, *Vaterland der Feinde*, pp. 325–6.

[138] Josef Kohler, *Der heilige Krieg: Rede am 19. Februar 1915* (Berlin, Carl Heymann, 1915), pp. 11–12. On German academics and jihad propaganda, see Wolfgang G. Schwanitz, 'Djihad "Made in Germany": Der Streit um den Heiligen Krieg 1914–1915', *Sozial.Geschichte*, 18,2 (2003), pp. 7–34.

The jihad idea was contrary to the British frame of mind. The notion of oriental wickedness had been a prominent strand of nineteenth-century thought.[139] War propagandists identified the Turks as the incarnation of evil orientalism. The Englishman's burden lay in the deliverance of the city of Constantinople, and particularly the Hagia Sophia Basilica, from paganism. 'It is, in a very real sense, the last of the Crusades. Should Constantinople fall it will be the greatest Christian victory that has occurred for hundreds of years', claimed the Anglican clergyman Basil Bourchier in 1915.[140] The disastrous attack against the Turkish defences on the Gallipoli peninsula in 1915–16 was not only a military humiliation, but also a shattering blow to the crusading fervour. The Gallipoli crusade had to be rewritten as the story of a heroic failure. John Masefield, during the war a government propagandist and later named Poet Laureate, set himself the task of reconfiguring the Dardanelles campaign as a new *Song of Roland*. In *Gallipoli*, Masefield's brief account of the operation published in 1916, the British and Anzac forces blend with the Christian Franks and their Turkish opponents with the heathen Saracens:

The cry for 'fifty thousand more men and plenty of high explosive' went up daily from every trench in Gallipoli, and we lost the campaign through not sending them in time. On the spot, of course, our Generals knew that war (like life) consists of a struggle with disadvantages, and their struggle with these was a memorable one. Only, when all was done, their situation remained that of the Frank rearguard in the 'Song of Roland'. In that poem the Franks could and did beat the Saracens, but the Saracens brought up another army before the Franks were reinforced. The Franks could and did beat that army, too, but the Saracens brought up another army before the Franks were reinforced. The Franks could and did beat that army, too, but then they were spent, and Roland had to sound his horn, and Charlemagne would not come to the summons of the horn, and the heroes were abandoned in the dolorous pass.[141]

An official commission, Masefield's *Gallipoli* was, however, commercially distributed by the publisher W. Heinemann. It went through several editions, sold in Britain and the Commonwealth. In Ontario,

---

[139] On orientalism, see the classic study by Edward W. Said, *Orientalism* (Harmondsworth, Penguin, 1995).

[140] B[asil] G. Bourchier, *'For All We Have and Are': Being Ten Addresses during the Year 1915* (London, Skeffington, [1915]), pp. 76–7. See also Wilkinson, *Church of England*, pp. 149, 255.

[141] John Masefield, *Gallipoli* (London, William Heinemann, [2nd edn] 1923), pp. 95–6. See Paul Fussell, 'The Fate of Chivalry and the Assault upon Mother', in Paul Fussell, *Killing, in Verse and Prose and Other Essays* (London, Bellew, 1990), pp. 224–5. On the memory of Gallipoli, see Jenny Macleod, *Reconsidering Gallipoli* (Manchester and New York, Manchester University Press, 2004).

Canada, the department of education included the monograph in a list of recommended literature for school libraries.[142]

The drama of Gallipoli would have been incomplete without a proper tragic hero. War commemoration assigned this role to Rupert Brooke, the poet of Edwardian England. Brooke volunteered in order to fight against the Turks. In letters to his friends he described himself as a crusader driven by the desire to take Constantinople.[143] His dream remained unfulfilled. While en route to Gallipoli, Brooke fell terminally ill – a striking parallel to the fate of another war volunteer and freedom fighter, Lord Byron, who had died of fever in 1824 during the Greek War of Independence.[144] Brooke was buried on the Greek island of Skyros on St George's Day 1915. The wooden cross which originally marked his grave was brought to Britain and placed in a cemetery at Rugby in the 1930s. The epitaph reads: 'Here lies the servant of God / Sub-Lieutenant in the English Navy, who died for the / Deliverance of Constantinople from the Turks.'

The images of the Dardanelles, Arabian and Palestine campaigns intermingled with the identity of their respective exponents. Brooke, Lawrence and Allenby represented 'the face of battle'. The personalisation of war should not be confused with blind hero worship. The lionisation of some individuals was a by-product of the construction of a larger narrative which reduced the complex nature of the conflict to statements comprehensible to a mass audience: Palestine campaign = Allenby = Richard I = crusade. The elevation of certain individuals was by no means contrary to the restoration of the ordinary soldier, as described in chapter 1. The paradox of the leadership cult on the one hand, and the democratisation of commemoration on the other, are to some degree typical of war remembrance in the modern age.[145] Having focused on remarkable personalities, I will now turn to the commemoration of ordinary soldiers at home and abroad.

St Albans Abbey houses a painting entitled 'The Passing of Queen Eleanor' which was presented to the church as a memorial to the men of Hertfordshire who died in the Great War. A contemporary picture postcard explains how the theme of the artwork relates to the war:

---

[142] Jonathan F. Vance, *Death So Noble: Memory, Meaning, and the First World War* (Vancouver, University of British Columbia Press, 1997), p. 237.

[143] Siberry, *New Crusaders*, p. 92; Winter, 'Legende der "verlorenen Generation"', p. 116; Michael Paris, *Warrior Nation: Images of War in British Popular Culture, 1850–2000* (London, Reaktion, 2000), pp. 117–20.

[144] On Byron and the construction of the 'Myth of War Experience', see Mosse, *Fallen Soldiers*, pp. 29–31.

[145] Koselleck, 'Kriegerdenkmale als Identitätsstiftung', p. 269.

'The Hertfordshire Regiment's part in the liberation of Jerusalem by Allenby in 1917 forms a link with Edward I, who was a last crusader in 1272.'[146] Army units which had been stationed in Palestine during the war tended to attach special importance to this episode, even if they had been deployed at other fronts too. Take the memorial window to the non-commissioned officers and privates of the Queen's Westminster Rifles in Westminster Abbey. In the unveiling programme, references to the services of the regiment in the capture and defence of Jerusalem abound. 'The main figures are St. George, the Patron Saint of England and of the Army, and King Richard I., the great crusader. Below the Figure of St. George is a view of the ruins of the Cathedral of Ypres, and below that of King Richard I. a view of the Church of the Holy Sepulchre at Jerusalem.'[147]

The Church of the Holy Sepulchre, Northampton, is one of the only four remaining round churches built in Britain by returning crusaders on the model of Jerusalem's Holy Sepulchre Church. After the First World War, a side chapel was fitted up as a combined regimental and parochial memorial. The subjects of the stained-glass windows are in perfect keeping with the history of the church. Simon de Senlis, who built the church as an offering of thanks for his safe return from the Holy Land in 1099, Godfrey de Bouillon, the conqueror of Jerusalem in 1099, and Louis IX of France are represented in this 'Heroes' Valhalla'.[148] Richard I appears twice, in both a Boer War and a Great War window. When the memorial of the Fourth Battalion of the Northamptonshire Regiment was unveiled, the local newspaper heralded the rebirth of the Crusades:

After the lapse of 800 years the Church of the Holy Sepulchre, Northampton, our soldiers' church, built by the Crusaders on their return from the Holy Land, was on Sunday afternoon again the scene of a gathering in honour of warriors who fought and died in overthrowing the infidel in far off Palestine. [. . .] What a contrast those two widely divided spectacles afford. In those distant days the metallic music of knightly armour and the jingle of spurs. On Sunday, drab khaki and a solemn silence, thrillingly pierced by the bugles sounding 'The Last Post' and 'The Reveille'. One point of similarity there was, the display of the colours of the Regiment in place of the shields and banners of the victorious knights.[149]

[146] NIWM, 14682, St Albans, Herts.
[147] IWM, Eph. Mem., K 74907–1, 'Westminster Abbey: Dedication of a Window in Memory of the Officers, Non-Commissioned Officers and Private Riflemen of the Queen's Westminster Rifles', 1923.
[148] 'Our Heroes' Valhalla', *Northampton Independent*, 810, 19 March 1921, p. 1; 'The Late Lieut. Eric Bostock, M.C.: Memorial at St. Sepulchre's', *Northampton Independent*, 823, 18 June 1921, p. 6; 'Memorials to the 5th & 7th: Windows Dedicated at St. Sepulchre's', *Northampton Independent*, 842, 15 October 1921, p. 4.
[149] 'Memorial Window to the 4th Northamptons', *Northampton Independent*, 805, 5 February 1921, p. 18.

Crusading imagery was supra-denominational. At the Roman Catholic Church of St Mary's Lowe House, St Helens, Lancashire, a memorial window representing the defeat of the Turks at Lepanto in 1571 and a window picturing St Louis gazing down on Jerusalem were erected as memorials to fallen parishioners. At the other end of the spectrum of denominations, nonconformists frequently utilised the language of crusade. A window in the Congregational church in Ashton-in-Makerfield, Lancashire, shows God presenting the crown of victory to returned crusaders.[150] A case study of the remembrance practices of middle-class Baptists in Norwich points out that waging war against 'Protestant' Germany was a cause of great distress to dissenters, whereas the thought of fighting and dying in the Holy Land was justifiable and even comforting. The notion of liberating Palestine gave the conflict a moral dimension lacking from the slaughter taking place in the trenches in the west. Thus nonconformists could overcome their aversion to militarism and attribute a positive meaning to physical sacrifice.[151]

The use of crusading motifs is very notable in the commemoration of individuals. An intriguing example can be found in Sledemere, East Yorkshire. The Eleanor cross, a nineteenth-century replica, bears a Gothic-style brass plaque depicting Sir Mark Sykes in the guise of a medieval knight.[152] During the war, Sykes had controlled British propaganda concerning the Palestine campaign and negotiated the secret Sykes–Picot Pact of 1916 which divided the Middle East into British and French spheres of influence. Appropriately enough, at Sledemere, Sykes is commemorated as a crusader. With his feet he is crushing a Muslim, the scroll above his head reads *Laetare Jerusalem*, and in the background is an outline of the city of Jerusalem. The diplomat had survived the war, but contracted influenza and died when attending the peace conference in Paris in 1919. By contrast, Lieutenant Kendall of the Norfolk Regiment had 'Died of wounds near Jerusalem' in November 1917 and was fittingly commemorated by his family with an image of Richard I.[153] Likewise, the Lionheart features in the

---

[150] IWM, WM 1031, box 1, Ashton-in-Makerfield, Lancs.
[151] Barry M. Doyle, 'Religion, Politics and Remembrance: A Free Church Community and its Great War Dead', in Martin Evans and Ken Lunn (eds.), *War and Memory in the Twentieth Century* (Oxford and New York, Berg, 1997), pp. 229, 233. See also Connelly, *Great War, Memory and Ritual*, p. 146. For a contrary opinion, see Bar-Yosef, 'Last Crusade?', pp. 89–90, 103–7.
[152] P. A. J. Banbury, 'The Sledemere Cross', *Yorkshire Archaelogical Journal*, 72 (2000), pp. 201, 207.
[153] IWM, WM 2945, box 15, Leasingham, Kesteven, Lincs.

stained-glass window dedicated to a namesake of his, Richard Knowles, killed in action near Salonika.[154]

Generally speaking, the operations in Palestine retained a stronger aura of crusading romance than the Dardanelles campaign. To be sure, pilgrimages of veterans and bereaved to Gallipoli – the largest organised tours became known as the 'Pilgrimage of Chivalry' – re-enacted the war as a crusade. Above all, Jerusalem acted as a magnet for 'battlefield tourists'. Between January and April 1930, the British-Imperial war graves cemetery on the Mount of Olives (inaugurated by Allenby in 1927) recorded over a thousand visitors. This was a landscape saturated with meaning, yet the cemetery design avoids any explicit reference to the Crusades, perhaps because this would have clashed with the notion of Mandate, that is internationally sanctioned trusteeship.[155] Still, in the middle stands the obligatory 'Cross of Sacrifice' bearing a 'Crusaders' Sword' and the entrance to the chapel is crowned with a figure of St George in full armour slaying the dragon designed by Gilbert Bayes (see figure 28).[156] Nevertheless, the location invited comparisons between the soldiers and the crusaders or Christ. *The Times* noted in a special War Graves Number that 'the British War Cemetery on the Mount of Olives [is] a site which not only recalls some of the most sacred incidents in the life of Our Lord but is inseparably associated with the Crusades of the middle ages'.[157]

In Jerusalem, nineteen German war casualties were interred in the cemetery beside their former enemies. Only the use of crosses in place of headstones distinguished their graves. The German dead were indirectly subsumed in the British crusading imagery.[158] Their country, however, had not only entered into an alliance with Turkey in 1914, but also attempted to incite a jihad against the Entente powers. This put post-war commemorators in an awkward position. Neither concept, the

[154] NIWM, 9930, Nantwich, Ches.

[155] Lloyd, *Battlefield Tourism*, pp. 17, 97–9, 219; Vance, *Death So Noble*, p. 60. See also Ilana R. Bet-El, 'A Soldier's Pilgrimage: Jerusalem 1918', *Mediterranean Historical Review*, 8 (1993), pp. 218–35; Ron Fuchs and Gilbert Herbert, 'Representing Mandatory Palestine: Auden St Barbe Harrison and the Representational Buildings of the British Mandate in Palestine, 1922–37', *Architectural History*, 43 (2000), pp. 283–4.

[156] CWGC, F 604, Minutes of the 78th Commission Meeting, n.d.; CWGC, Add 8/1/4, 'Jerusalem War Memorial: Worthy Monument to the Fallen', *The Times*, 44575, 7 May 1927, p. 11.

[157] 'In Three Continents: Distant Theatres of War', *The Times*, 45047, suppl., 10 November 1928, p. ix; *War Graves of the Empire: Reprinted from the Special Number of* The Times *November 10, 1928* (London, The Times, [1928]), p. 32. Compare also 'Design for Palestine Memorial', *Builder*, 121 (1921), p. 875.

[158] Compare Jon Davies, 'Reconstructing Enmities: War and War Memorials, the Boundary Markers of the West', *History of European Ideas*, 19 (1994), pp. 47–52.

Figure 28. St George by Gilbert Bayes for the Imperial War Graves Commission. Jerusalem, 1927.

Islamic jihad nor the Christian crusade, could plausibly serve as the grammar of war remembrance – at least not in the immediate post-war period. However, in 1935, when the *Totenburg* of Nazareth (see figure 29), by far the largest German war cemetery in Palestine with over 260 graves, was opened, the German war graves association recalled unabashedly the story of the Crusades (but this did not prevent it from honouring 'Turkish comrades' at the same time). The *Totenburg*'s interior design included a figure of St George killing the beast which was not dissimilar to the statue in the British-Imperial cemetery in Jerusalem:

Powerfully he plunges the lance into the monster's jaws, symbol of the battle which Germany waged against a world poisoned with lies and full of hate. Looking at him, we remember the crusaders from Nordic countries who, centuries ago, fought the holy battle of faith at this place. Our heroes of the world war also fought a fight of faith in the greatness and mission of their *Volk*. So far-off past and present join hands in this hall of honour.[159]

---

[159] [Franz] Hallbaum, 'Der Volksbund baut die Ehrenstätte Nazareth', *Kriegsgräberfürsorge*, 15, 3 (1935), p. 45: 'Machtvoll stößt er die Lanze in den Rachen des Ungeheuers, Symbol des Kampfes, den Deutschland gegen eine lügenvergiftete und haßerfüllte Welt geführt hat. Bei seinem Anblick gedenken wir der Kreuzritter aus nordischen Ländern, die vor Jahrhunderten an diesen Stätten den heiligen Kampf des Glaubens kämpften. Auch unsere Helden des Weltkrieges haben einen Kampf des Glaubens an

Figure 29. 'Fortress of the Dead' (*Totenburg*) from outside. Built by Volksbund Deutsche Kriegsgräberfürsorge. Nazareth, Palestine, 1935.

Such imaginings originated in a desire to give death on the battlefield a greater historical significance than a purely personal loss. To put this into perspective, the new diction was a belated phenomenon with a negligible effect on war remembrance as a whole. After all, Palestine represented, from the German point of view, a minor theatre of war with few casualties. Until 1935, the commemoration of the war dead in Palestine had principally developed along Biblical lines. Significantly, an article published in 1933 in *Kriegsgräberfürsorge*, the official journal of the German war graves association, made no mention of the Crusades: 'They rest in the Holy Land which was once blessed by Jesus's life on earth.'[160]

die Größe und Sendung ihres Volkes geführt. So reichen sich in dieser Ehrenhalle fernste Vergangenheit und Gegenwart die Hand.'

[160] Schlegel, 'Nazareth', *Kriegsgräberfürsorge*, 13,12 (1933), p. 178: 'Sie ruhen im heiligen Lande, das einst Jesu Erdenleben gesegnet hat.' Compare also [Otto] Kreß von Kreßenstein, 'Eine Schlacht im Heiligen Lande', in [Ernst] von Eisenhart Rothe (ed.), *Ehrendenkmal der deutschen Armee und Marine* (Berlin and Munich, Deutscher National-Verlag, 4th edn [1928]), pp. 522–33.

Tannenberg and eastern Europe

The path of the 146th [Regiment] was like Israel's journey through the desert. They passed through the east through the severest battles and deprivation, struggled right through to the south and stood battle-tried and victory-crowned in the Holy Land, at the places where the deepest yearning of our heart was relieved by Him who said about Himself: 'I am the Way, the Truth and the Life. I am the goal!' – So the heart opens to hope, so men learn to hope [. . .]. Death has led them to the goal. We continue to journey and struggle. But we want to learn hope from those pilgrims in steel helmets.[161]

Thus spoke the pastor at the dedication service of the memorial to the First Masurian Infantry Regiment No. 146 in 1923. He relocated the campaign 'in a foreign, historically memorable country' in the Biblical instead of the medieval tradition.[162] The omission of crusading imagery reflects the state of the commemorative discourse in the 1920s, and yet is remarkable if we consider the memorial's setting: the castle of Allenstein (Olsztyn), East Prussia, which was believed to have been built by the Teutonic Order.[163]

Founded in Acre during the Third Crusade, the Teutonic Order settled in north-eastern Europe in the thirteenth century. The crusader knights took possession of their new homeland by scattering castles over the region. The castles served as strong points to subjugate the native population, the ancient Baltic Prussians or *Pruzzen*, and as bases for raids over the border against the pagan Lithuanians. In 1410, an allied army of Lithuanian and Polish forces struck back and defeated the Teutonic Knights near the villages of Tannenberg (Stębark in Polish) and Grunwald (Grünfelde in German), a blow from which the order never recovered. By a stroke of fortune, Germany's greatest victory in the entire war happened to take place not far from the ancient battlefield – a coincidence which gave rise to the most powerful German myth of the war: the Tannenberg myth. The name of 'Tannenberg' for the battle of

---

[161] Vereinigung ehemaliger Offiziere des Regiments (ed.), *Das 1. Masurische Infanterie-Regiment Nr. 146 1897–1919* (Berlin, Wilhelm Kolk, 1929), p. 313: 'Der Weg der 146er glich der Wanderung Israels durch die Wüste. Unter schwersten Kämpfen und Entbehrungen durchzogen sie den Osten, schlugen sich durch bis zum Süden und standen kampferprobt und sieggekrönt im Heiligen Lande, an den Stätten, wo das tiefste Sehnen unseres Herzens gestillt worden ist durch den, der von sich sagte: "Ich bin der Weg, die Wahrheit und das Leben! Ich bin das Ziel!" – Da tut sich das Herz auf für die Hoffnung, da lernt der Mensch das Hoffen [. . .]. Sie hat der Tod ans Ziel gebracht. Wir wandern and kämpfen weiter. Aber wir wollen von diesen Pilgern im Stahlhelm das Hoffen lernen.' The passage from the Bible is misquoted from John 14:6.

[162] Ibid., p. 212.

[163] Ibid., p. 314.

August 1914 was a careful recollection of the clash of 1410. Initially, the press named the operation after the encounters at Gilgenburg (Dąbrówno) and Ortelsburg (Szczytno), but eventually Tannenberg gained acceptance. General Erich Ludendorff took credit for this, but his authorship is debatable. Perhaps the name sprang from the inventive genius of Theodor Wolff, editor of the left-liberal *Berliner Tageblatt*. Ironically, nationalist demagogues later condemned Wolff as a Jewish-pacifist traitor. In an article published on 31 August 1914, Wolff suggested that the fighting in East Prussia would enter history as the battle of Tannenberg.[164]

The triumph in the east caused great excitement in 1914 as it came at a time of bitter disappointments in the west. Yet without sustained efforts to recall the events of August 1914, Tannenberg would not have taken on mystic proportions as a celebration of a historic victory within the framework of defeat. Two focal points for rehearsals of the Tannenberg story evolved: first, the project of a Tannenberg monument, and secondly, the apotheosis of Hindenburg, commander of the victorious Eighth Army in East Prussia.

'There is a medieval flavour in the very name of Tannenberg, and it is hardly surprising that something resembling a medieval fortress, covering fifteen acres, should have been erected even now in the centre of an ancient battle zone of East Prussia', noted *The Times*.[165] A building of triumphal monumentality marked the site of the Tannenberg epic near Hohenstein, East Prussia (see figures 3–4 and 30). Eight massive clinker towers and high walls fence in an octagonal arena for rallies. The memorial's architecture was a hybrid of art history. The towers connoted prehistoric stone circles; the fortress-like structure reminded observers of the castles of the Teutonic Order or the Castel del Monte in Apulia, southern Italy, built by Frederick II of Hohenstaufen in 1240; and the simple but elegant design revealed the influences of expressionism,

---

[164] Detlef Lehnert, 'Die geschichtlichen Schattenbilder von "Tannenberg": Vom Hindenburg-Mythos im Ersten Weltkrieg zum ersatzmonarchischen Identifikationssymbol in der Weimarer Republik', in Kurt Imhof and Peter Schulz (eds.), *Medien und Krieg – Krieg in den Medien* (Zürich, Seismo, 1995), pp. 45–6. Compare Wolfgang Wippermann, 'Die Geschichte des "Reichsehrenmals Tannenberg": Ein historisches Lehrstück', *Niemandsland*, 1,2 (1987), pp. 59–60. Wippermann argues that Ludendorff's decision to name the battle 'Tannenberg' was crucial in the making of the myth. Russian popular culture during the war, by contrast, dwelt on the feat of Alexander Nevsky, the legendary victor over the Teutonic Order in 1242. See Hubertus F. Jahn, *Patriotic Culture in Russia during World War I* (Ithaca and London, Cornell University Press, 1995), pp. 6–7.

[165] 'Tannenberg and an Indiscretion', *The Times*, 44591, 20 September 1927, p. 15.

functionalism and Art Deco.[166] The diverse functions of the memorial added to its peculiarity. The Tannenberg memorial served as a monument, mausoleum, museum and meeting place. In the centre of the arena, a grave holding the mortal remains of twenty unknown soldiers from the eastern front had been erected. The towers accommodated youth hostels, exhibitions of military history, an archive, and commemorative rooms in honour of soldiers and generals; all functions were subject to frequent review.[167] In a sense, Tannenberg is better described as a memory workshop than a monument.

The project was launched as the Tannenberg National Memorial. Although a memorial of national attention and importance, it was not made an official Reich memorial during the Weimar Republic. The memorial never stood a chance of fulfilling the basic requirement of widespread acceptance; it was exclusive and polarising. Tannenberg was contested terrain, and the memorial enshrined the myth of the 'eastern front experience' for a nationalist audience. An examination of the participants in the unveiling ceremony on 18 September 1927 is revealing. The Generals Hindenburg, Ludendorff and Mackensen made grand entrances, cheered by the members of the assembled right-wing groups which belonged to an umbrella organisation called Vereinigte Vaterländische Verbände Deutschlands. The Social-Democratic Reichsbanner Schwarz-Rot-Gold deliberately stayed away from the spectacle, in which the colours of the Kaiserreich, black, white and red, were expected to dominate. The Social-Democratic state government of Prussia, though hosting the ceremony on its territory, pursued the same policy of conspicuous absence. The federal government, recently formed by centre-right parties including the German National People's Party, was represented by the Reich Chancellor, Wilhelm Marx of the Centre Party, and cabinet ministers.[168] The event of 1927 was an ostentatious display of nationalist sentiment and arguably a prelude to future Nazi ceremonies at Tannnenberg.[169]

---

[166] Tietz, *Tannenberg-Nationaldenkmal*, pp. 75–84; Heike Fischer, 'Tannenberg-Denkmal und Hindenburgkult: Hintergründe eines Mythos', in Hütt *et al.*, *Unglücklich das Land, das Helden nötig hat*, p. 31; Lurz, *Kriegerdenkmäler*, vol. IV, pp. 202–7.

[167] Tietz, *Tannenberg-Nationaldenkmal*, pp. 54, 127–44. On exhibitions and museums as memorials, see Susanne Brandt, 'Kriegssammlungen im Ersten Weltkrieg: Denkmäler oder Laboratoires d'histoire?', in Gerhard Hirschfeld, Gerd Krumeich and Irina Renz (eds.), '*Keiner fühlt sich hier mehr als Mensch. . .*': *Erlebnis und Wirkung des Ersten Weltkriegs* (Frankfurt am Main, Fischer, 1996), pp. 283–302.

[168] BArch, R 43 I/834, folio 15, Note by the Staatssektretär in der Reichskanzlei, 19 March 1927; ibid., fos. 82–93, Reichsminister des Innern to Preußischer Ministerpräsident, 3 August 1927. See also Lurz, *Kriegerdenkmäler*, vol. IV, p. 208.

[169] Hans-Ulrich Thamer, 'Nationalsozialismus und Denkmalskult', in *Historische Denkmäler: Vergangenheit im Dienste der Gegenwart?* (Bergisch-Gladbach, Thomas-

When Hitler finally declared the Tannenberg site a Reich memorial on 2 October 1935, the memorial makers could look back on more than fifteen years of planning and building. Veterans first expressed their wish to see a Tannenberg monument established during a review to mark the fifth anniversary of the battle of 1914. Five years later, in June 1924, a working committee comprising the heads of the associations of German officers and East Prussian veterans was brought into being. Hindenburg accepted the position of honorary chairman. Astonishingly, as early as 31 August 1924 the foundation stone was laid in a ceremony on the battle-field. The venture was a leap in the dark since the finances were on shaky ground. Moreover, not even an architectural plan existed at this stage. The architectural competition of 1925 was won by the brothers Walter and Johannes Krüger.

In September 1927, the committee, now known as the Tannenberg National Memorial Society, pressed ahead again with their undertaking. The shell of the unfinished monument was officially unveiled amid a blaze of publicity. Over the following years, building work continued. The building was nearing completion by the time Hitler, the 'artist-politician', ordered extensive alterations to the original plan. The re-building of the Tannenberg memorial reveals exemplarily the ability of the Nazis to recycle and reinvent *lieux de mémoire* for their own purposes. The grave of the unknown soldiers was removed from the centre of the arena, and one of the towers was rebuilt to create space for a crypt in which the bodies of the deceased Hindenburg and his wife were entombed in October 1935 (see figure 30).[170]

Hindenburg's ceremonial burial on the site of the historic battle crowned the memorial project. Cunningly, the Nazis coupled two interlinked yet not identical myths, the myths of Tannenberg and Hindenburg. Hindenburg had emerged as a legend from the war. Over-night, the victor of Tannenberg became a household name in Germany in 1914. The cult of the general gathered momentum during the war, and by 1918 he had grown into a 'living memorial' in his own right, a fact which helped him to win the German presidential election of 1925. Hindenburg seemed the embodiment of the war in general, and the Russian front in particular. Throughout the Reich, streets, places, schools et cetera were named after the general.[171]

Morus-Akademie, 1994), p. 18; Wippermann, 'Geschichte des "Reichsehrenmals Tannenberg"', p. 63. See, by contrast, Tietz, *Tannenberg-Nationaldenkmal*, pp. 51, 86.
[170] Fischer, 'Tannenberg-Denkmal', pp. 30, 38–9; Tietz, *Tannenberg-Nationaldenkmal*, pp. 85–154.
[171] See e.g. StdADO, 3–2031, 'Ehrungen für den Generalfeldmarschall von Hindenburg', 1917; Hubertus Adam, 'Hindenburgring und Grabmal Hohmeyer: Zwei Projekte

Figure 30. The Tannenberg memorial with the Hindenburg vault by
Walter and Johannes Krüger. Tannenberg, 1935.

In 1927, when the Reich President attained the age of eighty, the
Hindenburg Donation was introduced. This benevolent fund for the
welfare of ex-servicemen and the surviving dependents of soldiers killed
in the war paralleled, in a certain sense, the Haig Poppy Appeal in
Britain. Yet the German charity sold objects which encouraged the
personality cult surrounding Hindenburg, such as Hindenburg stamps,
Hindenburg postcards, a Hindenburg memorial volume and other
Hindenburg kitsch.[172] No other hero of the war either at home – including Ludendorff – or abroad – including Allenby and Lawrence – could
equal him in popular fame and adoration. At first, Hindenburg's
and Ludendorff's stars were in dual ascendance, like Allenby's and
Lawrence's. Soon, however, Hindenburg, the military figurehead,
surpassed Ludendorff, the strategic mastermind, in prominence. Ludendorff's attempts to emancipate himself from his superior and claim the
legacy of Tannenberg were in vain. His Tannenberg-Bund, a jingoistic

Berhard Hoetgers für Hannover aus den Jahren des 1. Weltkriegs', *Hannoversche
Geschichtsblätter*, new ser., 43 (1989), pp. 57–84.
[172] BArch, R 601/1100, 'Hindenburg-Spende: Allgemeines', 1927–36, esp. fos. 161, 249.
For a fine example of wartime Hindenburg kitsch, see Winter, *Sites of Memory*, p. 83.
On the Haig Poppy Appeal, see Gregory, *Silence of Memory*, ch. 3.

sect founded in 1925, shrilly ostracising Freemasons, Jesuits, Jews and Marxists, took Ludendorff to the fringes of the radical Right.[173]

Above all, war landmarks and memorials developed into foci of the public cult of Hindenburg. Berlin's colossal iron-nail figure of the general as a modern-day Roland (over twelve metres in height, fifty-six metric tonnes in weight), inaugurated on the first anniversary of the battle of Tannenberg, led the way (see figure 44).[174] Smaller communities followed suit.[175] The war landmark of Havelberg in Brandenburg, celebrated Hindenburg as a Teutonic Knight triumphing over the beast in the tradition of older representations of St George. In Graudenz (Grudziądz), West Prussia, too, Hindenburg appears as a Teutonic crusader 'as a symbol of northern German colonisation' (see figure 31).[176] At the unveiling ceremony, local girls sold miniature shields of Teutonic Knights carved out of wood by soldiers wounded at Tannenberg.[177]

After the war the popularity of this imagery abated. In an age of the 'democratisation' of remembrance, a general, however popular, could not represent the ordinary fallen soldier in the local communities. Of course, there are notable exceptions like the war memorial of Bad Reinerz (Duszniki Zdrój), Lower Silesia, which figured 'Reich President v[on] Hindenburg in the garb of the Order of [Teutonic] Knights with sword and shield'.[178] Hindenburg's long pedigree seemed to justify the drawing of analogies between the general and Teutonic Knights. Hindenburg was supposedly following in the footsteps of one of his forebears who had taken part in the 'bold, faith and culture disseminating Crusades' of the Teutonic Order, as we learn from a book entitled 'Hindenburg Memorial for the German People' of 1922.[179] This

[173] Lurz, *Kriegerdenkmäler*, vol. IV, pp. 380–1.
[174] Harald von Koenigswald, *Das verwandelte Antlitz* (Berlin, Kommodore, 1938), pp. 62–5; Diers, 'Nagelmänner', pp. 90–2, 95–6. See also Stefan Goebel, Kevin Repp and Jay Winter, 'Exhibitions', in Winter, Robert *et al.*, *Capital Cities at War*, vol. II.
[175] 'Die Enthüllung des Neuköllner Roland', *Neue Preußische Zeitung [Kreuz-Zeitung]*, 442, 31 August 1915; 'Die Nagelung des "Ritters von Neukölln"', *Neue Preußische Zeitung [Kreuz-Zeitung]*, 466, 13 September 1915.
[176] Weltzien, 'Kriegsnagelungen in Niederdeutschland', p. 39; Warburg-Haus, Bildindex 100/10, Postcard, Havelberg, n.d.
[177] 'Der Eiserne Hindenburg: Nagelungsfeiern in Berlin und Graudenz', *Berliner Illustrierte Zeitung*, 24 (1915), p. 503.
[178] BArch, R 32/351, folio 131, Stadtbauamt Bad Reinerz to Reichskunstwart, 14 December 1930: 'Reichspräsidenten v. Hindenburg in Ordensrittertracht mit Schwert und Schild'.
[179] Paul Lindenberg, 'Beim Armee-Oberkommando Hindenburgs während der Schlacht bei Tannenberg', in Paul Lindenberg (ed.), *Hindenburg-Denkmal für das deutsche Volk: Eine Ehrengabe zum 75. Geburtstage des Generalfeldmarschalls* (Berlin, C. U. Weller, 1922), p. 119: 'kühnen, Glauben und Kultur verbreitenden Kreuzzüge'.

Figure 31. Hindenburg as a Teutonic Knight. Wartime postcard depicting the iron-nail statue. Graudenz, *c.* 1915.

constitutes an interesting parallel to T. E. Lawrence, who had readily internalised crusading rhetoric, imagining himself to be a descendant of a crusader knight who had served in Richard Cœur de Lion's army at Acre.[180]

Wrapped in the habit of the Order of St John, Hindenburg's dead body lay in state at Tannenberg.[181] The costume signified that the German crusading fervour was directed towards north-eastern Europe. For Nazi ideologists, the endeavours of the Teutonic Knights perfectly exemplified the necessity of German territorial expansion into eastern Europe at the expense of Slavic *Untermenschen*. A book on the making of the new Reich memorial published in 1939 declared that

The name of Tannenberg is a symbol of the centuries-long battle of Germanness in the east for national self-assertion. Here, on old Germanic soil of settlement,

[180] Siberry, *New Crusaders*, p. 51.
[181] Ackermann, *Nationale Totenfeiern*, p. 116.

the Order of Teutonic Knights laid the foundation stone of its work of German state formation and German culture, which following generations time after time had to defend against alien force. [. . .] Only this work of settlement and culture, which will for ever be part of Prussian and German history, has created the imperative precondition for a universally recognised German Reich by giving the German people the indispensable basis for its living-space [*Lebensraum*].[182]

It is worth contrasting this statement with the unveiling volume of 1927:

For the conquest of Prussia, the Teutonic Order had gathered Saxon, Swabian, Thuringian and Franconian lords who were soon followed by a corresponding influx of burghers and peasants. The ancient Prussians [*Pruzzen*] were either exterminated or absorbed by the predominance of the settlers. Here tribal peculiarities ceased to exist. Here were simply German land and German people.[183]

On the one hand, both commentaries are pointedly aggressive and annexationist in tone; on the other, we can discern subtle differences between the two accounts. In 1927, the east was seen as a territory which could be manipulated and colonised (even allowing some mixture of races), whereas, in 1939, it appeared to be an eternal combat zone of racial struggle. Historical scholarship has highlighted the ahistorical tendencies behind the use of historical arguments in Nazi ideology. Historical phenomena were decontextualised and lumped together as racial clashes. The alleged *Drang nach Osten*, the 'drive to the east', of the Teutonic Order in particular (a notion of historical determinism advanced by historians during the nineteenth century) gave the Nazis ideological ammunition. But in contrast to the earlier writings of nationalist scholars, the Nazis regarded the Teutonic crusaders as racial

---

[182] [Hans] Pfundtner, 'Vorwort', in Kuratorium für das Reichsehrenmal Tannenberg (ed.), *Tannenberg: Deutsches Schicksal – Deutsche Aufgabe* (Oldenburg and Berlin, Gerhard Stalling, [1939]), p. 7: 'Der Name Tannenberg ist Symbol für den Jahrhunderte währenden Kampf des Deutschtums im Osten um seine national Selbstbehauptung. Hier auf altgermanischem Siedlungsboden legte der Deutsche Ritterorden den Grundstein zu einem Werk deutscher Staatenbildung und deutscher Kultur, das nachfolgende Geschlechter immer wieder gegen fremde Gewalt verteidigen mußte. [. . .] Erst dieses Siedlungs- und Kulturwerk, das für ewige Zeiten in die Annalen der preußisch-deutschen Geschichte eingetragen ist, hat die unerläßliche Voraussetzung für ein Deutsches Reich von Weltgeltung geschaffen, indem es dem deutschen Volke die unentbehrliche Grundlage für seinen Lebensraum gab.'

[183] *Festschrift zur Einweihung des Tannenberg-Denkmals am 18. September 1927* (Königsberg, Gräfe und Unzer, [1927]), pp. 25–6: 'Zur Eroberung Preußens hatte der Deutsche Orden sächsische und schwäbische, thüringer und fränkische Herren gesammelt, denen bald ein entsprechender Zuzug von Bürgern und Bauern gefolgt war. Die alten Pruzzen waren entweder vernichtet oder durch das Übergewicht der Einwanderung aufgesogen. Hier gab es keine Stammesbesonderheit mehr. Hier war einfach deutsches Land und deutsches Volk.'

warriors in pursuit of *Lebensraum*, 'living-space', rather than *Kulturträger*, upholders and apostles of a superior culture colonising the east.[184]

For the political Right, the Tannenberg memorial gave stony expression to Germany's ethnic or cultural aspirations in eastern Europe. The agitation would not have fallen on fertile ground if previous decades had not established categories for viewing the east and its history. Nineteenth-century historical research into the Teutonic Order certainly helped to shape the agenda. But above all, commemorative politics and signifying practices of the Wilhelmine era had a bearing on later developments. In 1902, Wilhelm II delivered an infamous speech at the restored castle of Marienburg (Malbork), West Prussia, the seat of the Grand Master of the Teutonic Order between 1309 and 1457, in which he defended German imperial interests and warned of the Polish danger in the east. The ceremonial framework of the speech is illuminating. The Kaiser received a delegation of the surviving branch of the Teutonic Order from Vienna. Some fifty years earlier, a similar invitation to Marienburg had scandalised the Austrian knights. For the historic reunion, Wilhelm and the Prussian aristocrats dressed in the habit of the Order of St John (Knights of St John had also accompanied the Kaiser to Jerusalem in 1898). To complete the pageant, the Prussian guards were in medieval dress as well.[185]

The Poles launched a commemorative counter-attack in the same year of 1902, by organising a celebration of the victory of Grunwald – the name under which the battle of 1410 is known in Poland – in Austrian-occupied Galicia. At the five hundredth anniversary of the battle in 1910, Great Polish agitators unveiled about sixty Grunwald memorials throughout Galicia, notably an impressive, twenty-four-metre high equestrian statue of Władysław II Jagiełło, King of Poland and champion of Grunwald, in Cracow.[186] German agitators had not lapsed into silence either. In 1901/02, one of the most prominent of the right-wing

---

[184] Wolfgang Wippermann, *Der Ordensstaat als Ideologie: Das Bild des Deutschen Ordens in der deutschen Geschichtsschreibung und Publizistik* (Berlin, Colloquium, 1979), pp. 218–19, 253. See also Gerd Althoff, 'Die Beurteilung der mittelalterlichen Ostpolitik als Paradigma für zeitgebundene Geschichtsbewertung', in Gerd Althoff (ed.), *Die Deutschen und ihr Mittelalter: Themen und Funktionen moderner Geschichtsbilder vom Mittelalter* (Darmstadt, Wissenschaftliche Buchgesellschaft, 1992), p. 161.

[185] Hartmut Boockmann, *Die Marienburg im 19. Jahrhundert* (Frankfurt am Main, Berlin and Vienna, Ullstein-Propyläen, 1982), pp. 38–9.

[186] Sven Ekdahl, 'Die Grunwald-Denkmäler in Polen: Politischer Kontext und nationale Funktion', *Nordost-Archiv*, new ser., 6 (1997), pp. 76–7, 80; Christoph Mick, '"Den Vorvätern zum Ruhm – den Brüdern zur Ermutigung": Variationen zum Thema Grunwald/Tannenberg', *zeitenblicke*, 3,1 (2004), URL: <http://zeitenblicke.historicum.net/2004/01/mick/index.html>, accessed 9 June 2004.

Vaterländische Verbände, the Deutscher Ostmarkenverein (founded in 1894 to campaign for further German settlement in the eastern provinces), pressed the provincial officials to set up a boulder in memory of the unfortunate Ulrich von Jungingen. 'Here Grand Master Ulrich von Jungingen died a hero's death on 15 July 1410 in the struggle for German character, German right', reads the inscription.[187] (Legend has it that Hindenburg fitted in a visit to Jungingen's memorial stone when commanding the Eighth Army in summer 1914.[188]) In anticipation of the Polish celebrations in 1910, German firebrands intended to reconstruct the Atonement Chapel, built by Heinrich von Plauen, the saviour of the Marienburg from the Polish-Lithuanian advance and Grand Master of the order between 1410 and 1414. The head of the provincial administration of East Prussia strongly advised the Berlin government against supporting the initiative. He reasoned that the reconstruction of the chapel would provide plenty of ammunition for Polish propaganda and hence increase already existing tensions between the Prussian state and its Polish subjects.[189]

The politics of intersecting and competing memories in the decade before the First World War had prepared the ground for the monumental assertion of an inevitable historic German surge to the east at Tannenberg. A second factor which helped to shape German perceptions of the east represented the memory of the 'eastern front experience' of the First World War. Having repelled the Russian invasion of East Prussia in summer and autumn 1914, the German army pushed deep into enemy territory in the following year. In the north-west of Russia, Ober Ost (Oberbefehlshaber Ost), a quasi-independent military state, was established under the Supreme Commander in the East, Hindenburg, assisted by his energetic chief of staff, Ludendorff. Ober Ost was more of a vision, a cultural and military utopia, than a bureaucratic experiment or programme; it opened up new spaces of thinking and created 'a German imperialist "mindscape" of the East'.[190]

[187] Kuratorium, *Tannenberg*, pp. 184–5: 'Im / Kampf für / deutsches Wesen / deutsches Recht / starb hier / der Hochmeister / Ulrich / von Jungingen / am 15. Juli 1914 / den Heldentod'. See Wippermann, 'Geschichte des "Reichsehrenmals Tannenberg"', p. 62. On the *Deutscher Ostmarkenverein* see Wippermann, *Ordensstaat als Ideologie*, pp. 185–97.
[188] Lindenberg, 'Beim Armee-Oberkommando Hindenburgs', p. 124.
[189] GStAPK, I. HA Rep. 77 Tit. 151 Nr. 15 Fasz. 48 (M), fos. 3–4, Oberpräsident der Provinz Ostpreußen to Minister des Innern und Minister für Landwirtschaft, Domänen und Forsten, 14 December 1908.
[190] Vejas Gabriel Liulevicius, *War Land on the Eastern Front: Culture, National Identity, and German Occupation in World War I* (Cambridge, Cambridge University Press, 2000), p. 151.

A key element of the mental conquest of eastern Europe was the juxtaposition of German *Kultur* and native *Unkultur,* 'unculture'. In their occupation zone, the German soldiers encountered an insistent but incomprehensible 'mess of history', a situation incompatible with western concepts of historical sense and order.[191] They faced a primitive society in which a bewildering array of traces of the past coexisted detached from all historical contexts. This unfamiliar chaos seemed to call for help from the German genius for organisation; this was the message Ober Ost's sophisticated propaganda machinery drummed into the heads of the soldiers and the indigenous people alike. In practice, German officials got down to cataloguing, exhibiting and preserving local art-historical treasures. The invaders would play the role of 'custodians of history for native populations, using German Work to interpret and define the area's past'.[192] In the end, the German ideas were frustrated by the resistance of the native people, who insisted on a national identity of their own. The military planners now discarded their positive approach to the east and gave way to radically racist notions of a dangerous 'dirty East of dirty populations' that had to be 'cleared and cleaned'.[193]

The radicalisation of the language of propaganda about the German cultural mission in the east is not necessarily reflected in subsequent representations of the war. In fact, spreading culture or securing 'living-space' was one but not the dominant theme of war remembrance. In effect, when the Nazis appropriated the Tannenberg memorial they singled out a sub-narrative of the 'eastern front experience' (that of Germanic 'living-space') for official use; a narrative which had evolved alongside others in the Weimar Republic. I now want to turn to two alternative narratives which emphasise either cultural mission *and* territorial defence, or solely national defence.

The Teutonic Order Infantry Regiment No. 152 was less traditional than its name implied. Founded only in 1897, the regiment and its members found in the war the opportunity to make a name for themselves as 'the new knights of the order'.[194] At the unveiling of the regimental memorial in Marienburg in 1925, the guard of honour was appropriately dressed as Teutonic Knights. The account of the the battle(s) of Tannenberg printed in the regiment's book of remembrance

---

[191] Ibid., p. 38.
[192] Ibid., p. 129. See also Koshar, *Germany's Transient Pasts*, pp. 92–4.
[193] Liulevicius, *War Land*, pp. 219–20, 272.
[194] Karl Strecker (ed.), *Das Deutsch Ordens-Infanterie-Regiment Nr. 152 im Weltkriege* (Berlin, Bernhard & Graefe, 1933), p. 11: 'die neuen Ordens-Ritter'.

(which also includes a list of the names of its fallen soldiers) is inconsistent. In places, the essays draw parallels between the cultural mission of the order and the achievements of the regiment: 'They [the soldiers] have matched them [the knights] and their brave leader, the great champion of Germanness, Ulrich von Jungingen, by suffering a heroic death while fighting gloriously under the sign of the black cross against a white background.'[195] Other passages, however, stress the defensive nature of the hostilities:

A young regiment – still without battle honours – the Teutonic Order Regiment 152 went out to defend their native soil. As once 500 years before the Teutonic Order had formed a living rampart against the Slavic invasions, so did their descendants, to whom the supreme commander had, with that proud name, entrusted the record of great history, defend the German *Heimat* against the superior Slavic force.[196]

The same ambiguity manifested itself in a second memorial of the Teutonic Order Infantry Regiment, unveiled in 1929, which was integrated into the Tannenberg site. The commemorative plaque showed a Teutonic Knight parrying an attack with his large shield and starting a counter-offensive with his sword raised to strike. The posture was understood to visualise both the ideal of iron defence and the 'ruthless spirit of the offensive'.[197]

Surprisingly, the Social Democratic Party (SPD) also saw Germany's war against Russia initially as a defensive *and* missionary measure, though for different reasons. The Social Democrats had for a long time despised the autocratic and reactionary regime of the Tsar. Already the founding fathers of the party had harboured thoughts of waging a revolutionary war against tsarist despotism.[198] In 1914, in a situation where the arch-enemy seemed to have gone on the offensive, the SPD

---

[195] Ibid., p. 30: 'sie haben es ihnen und ihrem tapferen Führer, dem großen Verfechter des Deutschtums, Ulrich von Jungingen, gleich getan, indem sie unter dem Zeichen des schwarzen Kreuzes auf weißem Felde ruhmvoll kämpfend den Heldentod erlitten haben'. For a photographic record of the unveiling ceremony, see ibid., fig. vi.

[196] Ibid., p. 9: 'Ein junges Regiment – noch ohne Kriegsruhm – zog das Deutsch Ordens-Regiment 152 hinaus zur Verteidigung der heimatlichen Scholle. Wie einst vor 500 Jahren der deutsche Ritterorden einen lebendigen Wall bildete gegen slawische Einfälle, so schützten die Nachfahren, denen vom obersten Kriegsherrn mit dem stolzen Namen die Ueberlieferung der großen Geschichte anvertraut war, deutsche Heimat gegen slawische Uebermacht.'

[197] Ibid., p. 76, and fig. vii: 'rücksichtslosen Angriffswillen'.

[198] Reinhard Rürup, 'Der "Geist von 1914" in Deutschland: Kriegsbegeisterung und Ideologisierung des Krieges im Ersten Weltkrieg', in Bernd Hüppauf (ed.), *Ansichten vom Krieg: Vergleichende Studien zum Ersten Weltkrieg in Literatur und Gesellschaft* (Königstein, Athenäum, 1984), pp. 9–10, 15. See also Lehnert, 'Die geschichtlichen Schattenbilder von "Tannenberg"', p. 47; Nicholas Stargardt, *The German Idea of*

readily joined the national camp and gave its consent for the war loans.[199] Until the split of the party in spring 1917, national defence against tsarist Russia was held up as a moral imperative. Although towards the end of the war the party dissociated itself from the German war effort and especially the declared annexationism of the Right, the Social Democrats could not close their minds to the notion of a war of defence in the east. After all, had not Russian troops devastated East Prussia in 1914–15? In November 1926, a Prussian government official suggested to the Prussian Minister of the Interior that the 'memory of the liberation of the German Eastern Marches [*Ostmark*] from the enemy can claim to be of especially extensive and outstanding significance'.[200] The argument carried conviction. The state government reconsidered its former negative attitude towards the projected Tannenberg memorial and granted its permission to organise fund-raising campaigns such as lotteries. Up to this time, the Social Democrats had obstructed the project on the grounds that the priority the welfare of the surviving war victims must take priority over the cult of the fallen soldier.[201]

The memory of the Russian invasion of East Prussia fired popular imagination in the inter-war period. Tannenberg was cited to refute the so-called 'war-guilt lie' enacted in article 231 of the Treaty of Versailles. All political parties were in agreement about fundamental opposition to the 'dictate of Versailles'. German politicians demanded in particular the revision of the new boundaries in the east and the repeal of the controversial war-guilt clause.[202] The Tannenberg memorial proved the ideal setting for agitation against the 'dictate'. In September 1927, Reich President von Hindenburg shocked the international public by declaring that Germany had entered the war as a 'means of self-assertion against a world full of enemies. *Pure* in heart we set off to the defence of the fatherland, and with *clean* hands the German army carried the sword. Germany is prepared to prove this before impartial judges at any

Militarism: Radical and Socialist Critics, 1866–1914 (Cambridge, Cambridge University Press, 1994), pp. 59–67.

[199] Wolfgang Kruse, *Krieg und nationale Integration: Eine Neuinterpretation des sozialdemokratischen Burgfriedensschlusses 1914/15* (Essen, Klartext, 1993), pp. 71–4. On the Social-Democratic press, see Verhey, *Spirit of 1914*, p. 20.

[200] GStAPK, I. HA Rep. 77, Tit. 1215 Nr. 3d Beiakten, Preußischer Staatskommissar für die Regelung der Wohlfahrtspflege to Preußischer Minister des Innern, 20 November 1926: 'Erinnerung an die Befreiung der deutschen Ostmark vom Feinde [kann] eine besondere umfassende und hervorragende Bedeutung für sich in Anspruch nehmen'.

[201] Ibid.; Lurz, *Kriegerdenkmäler*, vol. III, p. 180; Jeismann and Westheider, 'Wofür stirbt der Bürger?', p. 36.

[202] Ulrich Heinemann, *Die verdrängte Niederlage: Politische Öffentlichkeit und Kriegsschuldfrage in der Weimarer Republik* (Göttingen, Vandenhoeck & Ruprecht, 1983), esp. pp. 236, 254.

time!'[203] This very passage from his speech was recorded verbatim on a bronze plaque later erected at the Tannenberg site.[204]

It was a war without end. The Armistice silenced the guns, but the verbal gunfire never ceased in the east in the inter-war years. The conclusion of a second Locarno Treaty for eastern Europe was out of the question. The memory of the battles of 1410 and 1914 was used to remobilise the German people against the Slavic and especially the Polish 'threat'. Plebiscite memorials sprang up in addition to war memorials. In Allenstein, one such memorial takes the form of an abstract stone circle. In Marienburg, the memorial – with the castle in sight – features a Teutonic Knight. The inscription in Marienburg said: 'This land / remains German! / 11 July 1920'.[205] In July 1920, a plebiscite was held in parts of West and East Prussia on the region's territorial status. However, most of the provinces of Posen and West Prussia had been allocated to Poland in the Versailles Treaty. Embittered Germans turned towards the Tannenberg memorial for symbolic compensation. The memorial committee cleverly linked the two battles of Tannenberg to the border issue:

German! Do you think of Tannenberg? On the fields of Tannenberg, the knights of the Teutonic Order succumbed to the onslaught of a superior Slavic force in the Middle Ages. Five hundred years later, German heroic courage and genius of leadership stopped the further advance of the colossal Russian military masses, which, after overrunning East Prussia, sought to deal the deathblow to Germany. For this reason, Tannenberg is destiny in the east, perhaps German destiny in general. Today, people are fighting on there at the plough and the forge, not least for you, Germans in the Reich: alien subversives, memories of referenda mean that Tannenberg shall not fall into oblivion.[206]

[203] BArch, R 43 I/834, fos. 162–3, 'Ansprache des Herrn Reichspräsidenten bei der Einweihung des Tannenberg-Denkmals', 18 September 1927, italics in the original: 'Mittel der Selbstbehauptung einer Welt von Feinden gegenüber. *Reinen* Herzens sind wir zur Verteidigung des Vaterlandes ausgezogen, und mit *reinen* Händen hat das deutsche Heer das Schwert geführt. Deutschland ist jederzeit bereit, dies vor unparteiischen Richtern nachzuweisen!'
[204] See the illustration in Buchheit, *Reichsehrenmal Tannenberg*, p. 57.
[205] Vereinigung ehemaliger Offiziere, *1. Masurische Infanterie-Regiment Nr. 146*, fig. 36; Strecker, *Deutsch Ordens-Infanterie-Regiment Nr. 152*, fig. i: 'Dies Land / bleibt Deutsch! / 11. Juli 1920'.
[206] BArch, R 43 I/834, folio 33, Tannenberg-Nationaldenkmal-Verein e.V., 'Aufruf!', [*c.* 1927]: 'Deutscher! Denkst Du an Tannenberg? Auf den Gefilden von Tannenberg erlag im Mittelalter die Ritterschaft des Deutschen Ordens dem Ansturm slawischer Uebermacht. 500 Jahre später gebot hier deutscher Heldenmut und Führergenius dem weiteren Vordringen der gewaltigen russischen Heeresmassen Halt, die nach der Ueberflutung Ostpreußens Deutschland den Todesstoß versetzen sollten. Deshalb ist Tannenberg das Schicksal im Osten, vielleicht das deutsche Schicksal überhaupt. Heute wird dort noch an Pflug und Schraubstock weitergekämpft, auch für Euch, Ihr

The memorial of Tannenberg was intended to broadcast German determination to resist and fight Polish expansionism. To judge by international reactions, the memorial's founders succeeded in getting the
message across. As had happened twenty years before, nationalist Poles
embarked on anti-monuments. In 1931, a nephew of Marshal Piłsudski
unveiled a Grunwald monument at Uzdowo (Usdau), launched in symbolic retaliation for the building of the Tannenberg memorial on East
Prussian soil. Polish cultural memory was mobilised in an effort to
reassert the historical legitimacy of the post-Versailles Polish state. The
resurgence of Grunwald nationalism in Poland led to commemorative
frictions with now independent Lithuania which also claimed the legacy
of the battle of 1410 (named Žalgiris in Lithuanian). In 1932, Kaunas,
Lithuania's capital city, saw the dedication of a magnificent statue of
Vytautas the Great, a cousin of the Polish King Jagiełło. The iconography
was unambiguous. The memorial represented four symbolic figures,
easily identifiable as a Pole, a Russian, a Tartar and a Teutonic Knight,
surrendering to the Lithuanian Grand Prince. The final act of the
commemorative struggle over Tannenberg-Grunwald-Žalgiris in the
inter-war years was played out before the eyes of the world in 1939.
At the World's Fair in New York, an equestrian statue of Jagiełło
holding aloft two crossed swords adorned the Polish pavilion, while the
Lithuanian contribution featured a bronze sculpture of Vytautas. Later
in the same year, Hitler's Wehrmacht occupied Poland and demolished
the large figure of Jagiełło in Cracow, originally erected in 1910.[207]

The Tannenberg memorial did not escape the attention of former
enemies in the west either. 'According to one of the architects, the
fortress-like character of the building is meant to symbolize the position
of East Prussia as a German outpost surrounded by Slavs', reported The
Times about the unveiling.[208] To most viewers in 1927, it was clear that
the architecture of Tannenberg was supposed to recall the castles built
by the Teutonic Order in the region. Yet later, during the Third Reich,
the architects Walter and Johannes Krüger emphatically rejected allusions to Teutonic fortresses.[209] Instead, the Krügers insisted on the

Deutschen im Reich: Landfremde Wühler, Volksabstimmungserinnerungen lassen
Tannenberg nicht in Vergessenheit kommen.' For another appeal, see BArch, R 43 I/
834, folio 60, 'Helft das Tannenberg-Nationaldenkmal bauen!', [c. July 1927].

[207] Sven Ekdahl, 'Tannenberg – Grunwald – Žalgiris: Eine mittelalterliche Schlacht im
Spiegel deutscher, polnischer und litauischer Denkmäler', Zeitschrift für Geschichtswissenschaft, 50 (2002), pp. 108–10.

[208] 'Tannenberg Memorial: Fortresslike Monument', The Times, 44690, 19 September
1927, p. 11.

[209] Krüger and Krüger, 'Bauliche Gedanken', p. 230. See Tietz, Tannenberg-Nationaldenkmal, p. 75.

formative influence of Germanic stone circles. Their clients did not share the architects' point of view. The unveiling brochure explicitly linked the design of the façades to the example of the brick buildings of the Teutonic Order.[210] The Teutonic castles splendidly mirrored the renewed feeling of encirclement and the spirit of defensiveness. Their architecture set a precedent for memorial designs and offered an ideal framework for various remembrance activities. Guidebooks to the battlefield directed travellers towards the castles of the Teutonic Order.[211] Ex-servicemen used the castles as a location for commemorative services. The First Masurian Infantry Regiment No. 146, for instance, erected its memorial in Allenstein Castle:

No fairer site could have been chosen for the memorial: with a view of the magnificent castle of the order, a stronghold of Germanness against alien arrogance. [. . .] At the foot of the garrison church, which had been built to foster the spirit which inspired the soldiers to go to their deaths with the old German song of refuge and strength [Schutz- und Trutzlied] in their hearts: 'A mighty fortress is our God' [Ein feste Burg ist unser Gott].[212]

The commemoration of the war in the east was articulated around a complex historical geography. The Tannenberg story did not go unchallenged, to be sure. The efflorescence of variant encodings of the war at the eastern front testifies to the robustness of local and regional traditions. It shows that different people with different sets of values could draw different lessons from history. However, alternative narratives were rarely formulated as counter-narratives. Chance and convenience, rather than opposition to the Tannenberg myth, were crucial factors in the making of the memorial fountain in Lippstadt, Westphalia. It depicted Bernhard II of Lippe, founder of the city in 1168, hailed as the very epitome of Victorian values: 'a lauded hero, a devoted sovereign, a happy father, a man of strong faith in God'.[213] Initiated and

---

[210] Festschrift zur Einweihung des Tannenberg-Denkmals, pp. 38–9.

[211] Robert Traba, 'Kriegssyndrom in Ostpreußen: Ein Beitrag zum kollektiven Bewußtsein der Weimarer Zeit', Krieg und Literatur, 3–4 (1997–8), p. 408.

[212] Vereinigung ehemaliger Offiziere, 1. Masurische Infanterie-Regiment Nr. 146, p. 314: 'Kein schönerer Platz konnte für das Denkmal gewählt werden: angesichts des stattlichen Ordensschlosses, eines Horts des Deutschtums gegen fremde Übermut. [. . .] Zu Füßen der Garnisonskirche, die bestimmt war, den Geist zu pflegen, der die Soldaten in den Tod gehen hieß mit dem alten deutschen Schutz- und Trutzlied im Herzen: "Ein feste Burg ist unser Gott".' The hymn 'Ein feste Burg', which is based on Psalm 46, was written by Martin Luther around 1528. On the hymn and Protestant identity during the war, see Stefan Laube, Fest, Religion und Erinnerung: Konfessionelles Gedächtnis in Bayern von 1804 bis 1917 (Munich, C. H. Beck, 1999), pp. 382–3, 389.

[213] StAMS, OP 5626, folio 2, C. Laumanns, 'Der Gründer Lippstadts: Bernhard II. Edler Herr zur Lippe', 1914, p. 71: 'Ein gepriesener Held, ein treufolgender Landesherr, ein glücklicher Familienvater, ein glaubensstarker Gottesmann'.

completed in peacetime, the opening of the fountain was originally scheduled for August 1914, but then postponed until after the expected military victory. With the outbreak of hostilities, the life of Bernhard took on an unexpected topicality. As Bishop of Selonia, Livland, Bernhard had done missionary work in the Baltic region. His reputation as a 'warrior of God' invited comparisons with the German soldiers fighting at the Russian front.[214] Hence, after the war, it seemed logical and opportune to turn the fountain into a war memorial, the secular monument into a sacred one.

Bernhard II of Lippe had been a follower of one of the most enigmatic characters of German history, Henry the Lion, Duke of Saxony and Bavaria in the late twelfth century. Henry the Lion attracted scathing criticism but also effusive praise from nineteenth- and twentieth-century academics, poets and politicians.[215] His admirers regarded him as a pioneer of German expansion into eastern Europe, his critics as a traitor to the Reich and the Holy Roman Emperor. Henry the Lion had made the city of Brunswick the centre of his duchy; his putative tomb (re-designed by the architects Krüger for the Nazis in 1937) is situated in the cathedral church. A figure of the Saxon duke was therefore the natural choice for the iron-nail landmark of Brunswick, presented to the public in December 1915. The statue's grave facial expression, Roland-style deportment, and large shield conveyed stoicism and defensiveness rather than thirst for imperial adventure. This impression is confirmed by the picture of Henry's endeavours presented by the cathedral preacher at the dedication. He characterised the medieval ruler as a model protector of Germanness against Slavic aggression. (Interestingly, a local Social-Democratic newspaper criticised the nailing ritual and its bourgeois organisers, but did not object to the medievalist narrative.) In his dedication speech, the pastor suggested that

Following the path which the great duke showed us, a good deal of the energy of the German people has turned eastward. And when we think of the enemies all around in the north and west and south, who have been united with Slavdom in hatred against us, and when we remember that they were all unable to achieve anything against us through sixteen months of war, then our soul fills with humble gratitude to God, our Lord.[216]

[214] Vogt, *Den Lebenden zur Mahnung*, pp. 130–2. See also Bach, *Studien zur Geschichte*, pp. 290–1, 294.
[215] Johannes Fried, 'Der Löwe als Objekt: Was Literaten, Historiker und Politiker aus Heinrich dem Löwen machten', *Historische Zeitschrift*, 262 (1996), pp. 673–93; Stefanie Barbara Berg, *Heldenbilder und Gegensätze: Friedrich Barbarossa und Heinrich der Löwe im Urteil des 19. und 20. Jahrhunderts* (Münster and Hamburg, Lit, 1994).
[216] As cited in Wulf Otte, 'Heinrich der Löwe – in Eisen', *Braunschweigisches Landesmuseum: Informationen und Berichte*, 3 (1987), p. 37: 'Den Bahnen folgend, die der große

The paranoia about the Slavic threat took on new dimensions after the war. As I have noted, the territorial losses due to the Versailles Treaty fanned the flames of loathing for the eastern neighbours. First and foremost the populace of Silesia suffered the consequences of the peace treaty. In accordance with outcome of a referendum in March 1921, Upper Silesia remained mostly German, but the industrial heartland became Polish. Plans for a Reich memorial on Silesian ground had every prospect of succeeding. A Silesian initiative, backed by the local branch of the Centre Party, demanded that the national memorial be established on Mount Zobten, Lower Silesia, that 'outpost [. . .] of Germanness' surrounded by hostile Slavs.[217] The advertising campaign juxtaposed German cultural achievements with the aggressive instincts of the Mongolians, Slavs, Hussites and others. A turning-point in history, it argued, had occurred when Germans colonised Silesia in the thirteenth century: 'Silesia was German again as in prehistoric times and has remained so till the present, defying all the surging waves of the pugnacious latterday Slavdom.'[218] To be sure, such hatred was not universal and not every Silesian agent of remembrance presented history in black and white. In Namslau (Namysłów), Lower Silesia, the war memorial in the form of an 'old watch-tower' was placed at 'a historic spot [. . .], where the Slavic settlement had stood out of which the city developed'.[219]

Medievalist commemorations reconfigured the war in eastern Europe as a national mission (to spread culture or to secure 'living-space') or territorial defence. The former discourse represents a functional equivalent of the mystique attached to the Palestine campaign in Britain. Both narratives centre on a clash with 'inferior', non-western lands and peoples. Both commemorate victories which seemed to have 'corrected' history; Hindenburg reversed Jungingen's defeat while Allenby fulfilled Richard I's dream. The personalisation of the 'face of battle' was built

Herzog wies, hat jetzt ein gut Teil der Kraft des deutschen Volkes gen Osten sich gewandt. Und wenn wir an die Feinde ringsum denken in Nord und West und Süd, die sich mit dem Slaventum vereinten in Haß gegen uns, wenn wir daran denken, daß sie alle in sechzehn Kriegsmonaten nichts gegen uns vermochten, so erfüllt demütiger Dank gegen Gott, den Herren, unsere Seele.' See also Gerhard Schneider, 'Nageln in Niedersachsen im Ersten Weltkrieg', *Niedersächsisches Jahrbuch für Landesgeschichte*, 76 (2004), pp. 262–3.

[217] BArch, R 43 I/716, folio 79, Schlesisches Komitee für das Reichsehrenmal to Reichskanzler, 10 June 1930; ibid., folio 81, Theo Johannes Mann, 'Reichsehrenmal Zobtenberg', [c. 1930].

[218] Ibid.: 'Schlesien war wieder deutsch, wie in vorgeschichtlicher Zeit und ist es geblieben bis in die Gegenwart, allen anbrandenden Wellen des späteren kampfbereiten Slaventums trotzend.'

[219] BArch, R 32/350, folio 180, Magistrat Namslau to Reichskunstwart, 28 November 1930: 'an historischer Stelle [. . .], auf der die slawische Siedlung gestanden hat, aus der die Stadt sich entwickelte'.

into both scripts. In Germany, personalisation paved the way for a personality cult; Hindenburg became a demigod, whereas Allenby and Lawrence remained revered heroes. The respective 'crusades' which they embodied had contrary objectives: Allenby and Lawrence were imagined to have crusaded for universal values – justice and freedom; Hindenburg fought for German culture or 'living-space'. The Palestine narrative was socially integrating, the Tannenberg one proved politically polarising. Especially the political far Right subscribed to and disseminated the notion of a culturally or racially motivated 'drive to the east'. The Tannenberg memorial became the ceremonial focus for rehearsals of the tale of a German mission in the east; in Britain no particular site was designated to the memory of the war in Palestine.

The war in the west

The author of 'At Tannenberg in 1914 and 1410', a historical sketch of the two battles published in 1915, claimed that 'English envy' was the driving force behind the Russian attack on East Prussia in 1914.[220] In the early stages of the war, the familiar west rather than the 'unknown east' was the prime target for German propaganda. The prophets of the 'ideas of 1914' rendered the war as an unavoidable apocalyptic clash between artificial or superficial Anglo-French civilisation and genuine German *Kultur*. The social scientist Werner Sombart made a major contribution to the discourse on a positive German 'special path' in the war years. In 1915 his book 'Heroes and Merchants', which remained a best seller in the 1920s, Sombart traced the underlying cause of the war to a process of modernisation out of which Britain had emerged as a nation of shopkeepers. The commercialisation of British society, Sombart pointed out, had started in the early fifteenth century, that is long before the ideas of the Reformation – 'made in Germany' – had been imported to Britain.[221] British profiteering culminated in the declaration of war on Germany, that nation of heroes. For Sombart, the German war against British capitalism represented a crusade: 'All great

---

[220] Paul Fischer, *Bei Tannenberg 1914 und 1410: Die Schlacht bei Tannenberg-Grünfelde am 15. Juli 1410 und die Schlachten bei Gilgenburg-Hohenstein-Ortelsburg (Schlacht bei Tannenberg) 27., 28., 29. August 1914* (Lissa, Oskar Eulitz, 1915), p. 4.

[221] Werner Sombart, *Händler und Helden: Patriotische Besinnungen* (Munich and Leipzig, Duncker & Humblot, 1915), pp. 12–3, 30, 49. On Sombart's book, see Friedrich Lenger, *Werner Sombart 1863–1941: Eine Biographie* (Munich, C. H. Beck, 1994), pp. 246–52. Not all intellectuals subscribed to Sombart's xenophobia; see Steffen Bruendel, *Volksgemeinschaft oder Volksstaat: 'Die Ideen von 1914' und die Neuordnung Deutschlands im Ersten Weltkrieg* (Berlin, Akademie, 2003), pp. 88–91.

wars are wars of belief, have been in the past, are in the present and will be in future.'[222]

God was, of course, expected to side with the 'heroes', the Germans. 'God with Us' was the general tenor of popular wartime theology.[223] Bismarck's dictum, 'We Germans fear God, but nothing else in the world', was also frequently recalled in war posters and postcards.[224] In the 'world of enemies', it was England which incurred the wrath of God. *Gott strafe England*, 'May God punish England', sounded the battle cry of German propaganda. Indeed, in autumn 1914 'May God punish England' was recommended as a new greeting to replace the traditional *Guten Tag* (the appropriate reply was 'May He punish her'). In Wetter, Westphalia, a wounded soldier recited the propaganda slogan while hammering an iron-nail into the 'Iron Sword' war landmark.[225] 'England' stood for the United Kingdom as a whole. A German picture postcard visualised the slogan *Gott strafe England* by depicting a gigantic sword or cross falling from heaven on the British Isles and, actually, hitting Scotland.[226]

The aggressive rhetoric developed in parallel to claims of innocence. 'I have a clear conscience before God and history: I did not want the war!', a poster of 1915 quoted the Kaiser.[227] Shortly before the end of the war, his words 'I did not want it' were etched onto the fireplace in the great hall in the neo-medieval castle of Haut-Kœnigsbourg (Hohkönigsburg), Alsace, which had been (re)built under Wilhelm II at the turn of the century.[228] The stalemate at the Western Front dampened down

[222] Sombart, *Händler und Helden*, p. 3: 'Alle großen Kriege sind Glaubenskriege, waren es in der Vergangenheit, sind es in der Gegenwart und werden es in der Zukunft sein.'
[223] Heinrich Missalla, *'Gott mit Uns': Die deutsche katholische Kriegspredigt 1914–1918* (Munich, Kösel, 1968), pp. 67–75. On visual representations of the dictum, see Holsten, *Allegorische Darstellungen des Krieges*, p. 38.
[224] *Ein Krieg wird ausgestellt: Die Weltkriegssammlung des Historischen Museums (1914–1918)* (Frankfurt am Main, Dezernat für Kultur und Freizeit, 1976), pp. 170–1; Otto May, *Deutsch sein heißt treu sein: Ansichtskarten als Spiegel von Mentalität und Untertanenerziehung in der Wilhelminischen Ära (1888–1918)* (Hildesheim, Lax, 1998), fig. 138.
[225] Dietrich Thier, 'Das Kriegswahrzeichen von Wetter (Ruhr): die Nagelspende, das Eiserne Schwert', in Hans-Friedrich Kniehase and Dietrich Thier (eds.), *Projekte: Landeskundliche Studien im Bereich des mittleren Ruhrtals*, vol. I (Wetter a.d. Ruhr, Dierk Hobein, 1994), p. 219. See also Matthew Stibbe, *German Anglophobia and the Great War, 1914–1918* (Cambridge, Cambridge University Press, 2001), p. 18; Verhey, *Spirit of 1914*, p. 122.
[226] Private Collection, Hanover, Postcard 'Gott strafe England. Er strafe es', n.d.
[227] BfZ, Plakatsammlung Erster Weltkrieg, 2.0/27, 'An das Deutsche Volk', 1915: 'Vor Gott und der Geschichte ist Mein Gewissen rein: Ich habe den Krieg nicht gewollt!'
[228] Laurent Baridon and Nathalie Pinthus, *Le Château du Haut-Kœnigsbourg: A la recherche du Moyen Age* (Paris, CNRS Editions, 1998), pp. 110–13. On the restoration of the castle before the war, see Winfried Speitkamp, 'Die Hohkönigsburg und die Denkmalpflege im Kaiserreich', *Neue Museumskunde*, 34 (1991), pp. 121–30.

Germany's messianic zeal. Moreover, the increasing pressure on her defences in the second half of the war made the German side aware of their own passivity. Soldiers' private photographs of the battle of the Somme captured the spirit of military resistance to the Entente powers' offensive.[229] The soldiers' photographic testimonies were made available to a wider audience through publication in illustrated volumes in the 1920s – at a time when French imperialism seemed plainly visible with regard to the French presence in the Rhine, Ruhr and Saar regions, not to mention the annexation of Alsace-Lorraine. The conflict in the west which – in one discursive strand – had been mounted as a cultural mission against both French republicanism (the 'ideas of 1789') and British commercialism, became reconfigured as a defensive war against the ruthless expansionism of France. One commemorative trope, in particular, was used to revise the image of the war in the west: the mystification of the River Rhine.

In 1928, the Reichskunstwart counted over three hundred suggestions for a German national memorial.[230] By then, the idea had been under discussion for four years. Among the proposals put forward were a number of promising schemes for the Rhineland, notably Ehrenbreitstein Castle and the islands of Lorch and Hammerstein. The campaigners secured backing for the general plan for a memorial on the River Rhine from the provincial governor, local politicians and certain organisations of ex-servicemen. The issue split the veterans' camp in 1926. One association of war victims, the Zentralverband deutscher Kriegsbeschädigter und Kriegshinterbliebener, and some minor organisations gave their support to the Rhineland's campaign. The western branches of the leading veterans' organisations also endorsed the Rhine project. They rejected the historic consensus among the national leaders of the Reichsbanner (Social Democratic), Kyffhäuserbund (conservative), Stahlhelm (nationalist), Jungdeutscher Orden (Liberal, racist) and Reichsbund jüdischer Frontsoldaten (Jewish) for a Germanic heroes' grove at Bad Berka, near Weimar in Thuringia.[231] Apart from the Rhineland and Bad Berka, there were two other sites to be reckoned with: the heroes' grove

---

[229] Gerd Krumeich, 'Kriegsfotografie zwischen Erleben und Propaganda: Verdun und die Somme in deutschen und französischen Fotografien des Ersten Weltkriegs', in Ute Daniel and Wolfram Siemann (eds.), *Propaganda: Meinungskampf, Verführung und politische Sinnstiftung (1789–1989)* (Frankfurt am Main, Fischer, 1994), pp. 129–30.

[230] BArch, R 32/353a, folio 114, Reichskunstwart to Reichsminister des Innern, 10 October 1928.

[231] Heffen, *Reichskunstwart*, p. 256. See also Fritz Hilpert, *Das Reichsehrenmal und die Frontkämpfer: Nach authentischem Material der Frontkämpferverbände Reichskriegerbund Kyffhäuser, Reichsbanner, Stahlhelm und Reichsbund jüdischer Frontsoldaten* (Berlin, Deutsche Verlagsgesellschaft für Politik und Geschichte, 1927).

of Goslar, and the Neue Wache, the classical-style guard house on Unter den Linden in Berlin.[232]

The real issue at stake was neither regional loyalty nor a commemorative aesthetics but the contested meaning of the war. To place the Reich memorial on the Rhine would have put the stress on the war in the west against Germany's *Erbfeind*, 'hereditary enemy', France. Some critics wondered whether yet another monumental 'Watch on the Rhine' was indeed desirable.[233] The river landscape was already dotted with memorials to Franco-German conflicts of the previous century: Cologne Cathedral, completed during the nineteenth century, connoted the liberation from French occupation in 1813; the Niederwald National Memorial at Rüdesheim, unveiled in 1883, with the statue of a corpulent Germania, was dedicated to the Franco-Prussian war of 1870–1; finally, the future of the national monument to Bismarck, the victor of 1871, at Bingerbrück near Bingen was hanging in the balance.[234]

The Bismarck National Memorial had been due to be unveiled on 1 April 1915, to mark the hundredth anniversary of the former chancellor's birth. Following a public competition in 1909–10, the artistic jury had chosen the entry 'Siegfried Dolmen', a stone circle dominated by a huge figure of 'Young Siegfried', for the first prize. The members of the jury were by no means inclined to a reactionary *völkisch* position, but represented the German-speaking avant-garde and its supporters: among them were Max Klinger, Alfred Lichtwark, Hermann Muthesius, Fritz Schumacher and Franz von Stuck; Josef Hoffmann and the industrialist Walther Rathenau were elected deputies.[235] The prize winners, German Bestelmeyer and Hermann Hahn, explained that 'Bismarck as the liberator of the people from foreignness shall be embodied in Young Siegfried, that figure of light and strength in the German saga who was born by the River Rhine.'[236] A postponement of the ambitious

[232] Friedrich Deininger, 'Goslars Bemühungen um den Reichsehrenhain', *Niedersächsisches Jahrbuch für Landesgeschichte*, 55 (1983), pp. 311–69.

[233] See BArch, R 43 I/714, folio 62, Bürgermeister Ehrenbreitstein to Reichspräsident, 12 July 1926, for the use of the term 'The Watch on the Rhine'. Max Schneckenburger had written the song 'The Watch on the Rhine' ('Die Wacht am Rhein') in 1840. On the symbolism of the song, see Whalen, *Bitter Wounds*, pp. 23–4.

[234] Nipperdey, 'Kölner Dom', p. 597; Alings, *Monument und Nation*, pp. 167–76. On proposals to integrate the Reich memorial into the Niederwald monument, see StAMS, OP 5510, fos. 165–71, Carl Kuebart, 'Der Niederwald muß als Nationalhain der Platz für das Reichsehrenmal werden!', 1926.

[235] *Hundert Entwürfe aus dem Wettbewerb für das Bismarck-National-Denkmal auf der Elisenhöhe bei Bingerbrück-Bingen* (Düsseldorf, Düsseldorfer Verlags-Anstalt, 1911), p. 12.

[236] Ibid., p. 26: 'Bismarck als Befreier des Volkes von fremdem Wesen soll verkörpert sein in Jung-Siegfried, dieser Licht- und Kraftgestalt der deutschen Sage, die am Rhein geboren wurde.'

plan became inevitable because of the war. The project was taken up again around 1925.[237] Although the newly constituted committee stressed that they were not competing for the Reich memorial, they aimed to incorporate the remembrance of the Great War into the Bismarck National Memorial nevertheless:

> Today, a Bismarck National Memorial must [. . .], apart from the commemoration of the iron chancellor, also be consecrated to the memory of Germany's superhuman struggle against a world of enemies, in which the German people had to bear witness that they were worthy of Bismarck's legacy. The thousand-year struggle for the River Rhine [. . .] merely entered a new phase with the world war.[238]

Despite its declared neutrality, the committee had de facto entered the competition for the national memorial.[239] What is more, the Bingerbrück committee fell back on the notation established by the campaigners for a Reich memorial on the Rhine. The notion of a 'thousand-year struggle' for the river pervaded their campaign.[240] The history of the Middle Ages provided them with compelling evidence of German defensiveness: the defeat of the West Franks under Ludwig (Louis) III in 876, the liberation of Lorraine by Henry I in 925, the consolidation of German rule over the region in the age of Otto the Great in 939 and so on.[241] Some proposals read like a *Who's Who* of the early Holy Roman Empire. The history of German *Reichsherrlichkeit* (literally 'Reich sovereignty' or 'Reich nobility') 'has always been the "struggle for the Rhine"'. The fate of the Rhineland has always been Germany's fate. In the River Rhine lies the treasure of the Nibelungen,

---

[237] BArch, R 32/17, folio 7, Oberbürgermeister Duisburg to Reichskunstwart, 4 June 1926.

[238] BArch, R 43 I/834, folio 230, Chairman of Verein zur Errichtung eines Bismarck-National-Denkmals e.V. to Reichspräsident, 13 October 1932: 'Ein Bismarck-National-Denkmal muss heute [. . .] neben dem Gedenken an den eiseren Kanzler auch der Erinnerung an das übermenschliche Ringen Deutschlands gegen eine Welt von Feinden geweiht sein, in dem das deutsche Volk Zeugnis dafür ablegen musste, dass es Bismarcks Erbe würdig war. Der tausendjährige Kampf um den Rhein, [. . .] trat ja mit dem Weltkrieg nur in einen neuen Abschnitt.'

[239] BArch, R 43 I/713, folio 155, 'Nachtrag zur Zusammenstellung der Vorschläge für die Errichtung eines Nationaldenkmals für die Gefallenen im Weltkriege', 15 February 1926.

[240] BArch, R 43 I/714, folio 146, 'Das Schwergewicht der offiziellen Rheinprojekte zum Reichsehrenmal', *Rheinisch-Nassauische Tageszeitung*, 176, 30 July 1926; BArch, R 43 I/716, folio 45, Albert Maennchen, 'Wohin das Reichsehrenmal?', April 1930. See also chapter 5.

[241] Ibid.; GStAPK, I. HA Rep. 77, Tit. 1215 Nr. 3c Bd. 1, fos. 148–9, C. Burger, 'Das Reichsehrenmal auf der Insel Hammerstein im Rhein', n.d. On history and the Rhine in German and French propaganda generally, see Franziska Wein, *Deutschlands Strom – Frankreichs Grenze: Geschichte und Propaganda am Rhein 1919–1930* (Essen, Klartext, 1992), pp. 123–51.

our promise.'[242] In addition to 'real' history, the *Song of the Nibelungen* – the story of which is predominantly set in the Rhineland – was commonly cited to legitimise German claims and, conversely, to alert people to the ongoing French threat.

While the memory of the Rhineland's occupation by French troops loomed large in people's mind, the messianic aspirations of 1914 (and the actual advance into French territory) sank into oblivion. Medieval and Germanic imagery was instrumental in redefining the war in the west as a defensive struggle for national survival. Once again, the Middle Ages were deployed after 1918 to assert Germany's distinctive national identity and destiny in the wake of French occupation. In contrast, in Britain there was no coherent medievalist narrative of the conflict with Germany. To many there was not a shadow of doubt that 'the boys' at Ypres or on the Somme were a model of chivalry, but the imagined nature of the war they fought remained vague. The messiness of the Western Front may have hindered the process of medievalisation.[243] The task was complicated by the absence of historical models for remembering the clash with Germany. Some local memorial projects overcame both obstacles by re-locating the front from the Continent to the British North-Sea coast where Viking and Norman invaders had landed in the past.

The city of Bedford commissioned Charles Sargeant Jagger, the famous creator of the Royal artillery memorial in Hyde Park, London, to design a monumental tribute to the fallen soldiers of the local community. Jagger sculptured an eclectic representation of 'Justice', an open-eyed – not blindfolded – figure, carrying a sword and scales, and clad in 'Crusader's armour' (see figure 32).[244] Beneath her feet is a chained dragon. Originally, it was planned to unveil the memorial on 'the thousandth anniversary of the defeat of the Danes by the English',

---

[242] GStAPK, I. HA Rep. 77, Tit. 1215 Nr. 3c Bd. 1, folio 70, Richard Klapheck, *Das Reichsehrenmal für unsere Gefallenen: Die Toteninsel im Rhein* (Düsseldorf, Staatliche Kunstakademie, 1926), p. 2: 'Immer, bis auf die Gegenwart, war die Geschichte deutscher Reichsherrlichkeit der "Kampf um den Rhein". Rheinlands Schicksal war stets Deutschlands Schicksal! Im Rheine liegt der Schatz der Nibelungen, unsere Verheißung.'

[243] On the puzzling character of the Western Front, see Jay Winter, 'Representations of War on the Western Front, 1914–18: Some Reflections on Cultural Ambivalence', in Joseph Canning, Hartmut Lehmann and Jay Winter (eds.), *Power, Violence and Mass Death in Pre-Modern and Modern Times* (Aldershot and Burlington, VT, Ashgate, 2004), pp. 205–16. On representations of 'German atrocities', see chapter 4.

[244] 'Bedford War Memorial: Arrangements for the Unveiling', *Bedfordshire Times and Independent*, 3992, 14 July 1922, p. 7; 'A Description by Mr. Rowland Hill', *Bedfordshire Times and Independent*, 21 July 1922, p. 7. See also John Glaves-Smith, 'Realism and Propaganda in the Work of Charles Sergeant Jagger and their Relationship to Artistic Tradition', in Ann Compton (ed.), *Charles Sargeant Jagger: War and Peace Sculpture* (London, Imperial War Museum, 1985), p. 68.

Figure 32. Justice by Charles Sargeant Jagger. Bedford, 1922.

for the battle had taken place not far from the chosen site of the war memorial.[245] But a delay in the memorial's execution thwarted the plan.

The villagers of Greenock, Renfrewshire, would not have subscribed to the intended symbolism at Bedford. Their monument, an obelisk, features the prow of a Viking ship as an acknowledgment of the role 'the fighting peoples of Scandinavia' had played in the maritime and early history of the town. On the deck of the warship of the dragon class – 'These are the Tenth Century equivalents of our modern ships' – is a winged Figure of Victory holding aloft a laurel wreath.[246] The brutality

---

[245] Bedford Central Library, Local Studies Collection, Report by the Chairman of the Memorial Committee, 1920. The archival material kept at the Bedfordshire and Luton Archives and Records Service, Bedford, is exclusively concerned with practicalities like time and cost. Interestingly, the memorial of Bedford School also refers to the defeat of the Danes. See 'The War Memorials', *Ousel*, 556, 10 June 1921, pp. 48–9.

[246] *A Memorial Record of Men of Greenock Who Fell in the Great War, 1914–1918* (Greenock, Greenock Telegraph, 1924), p. 49. On the cult of the Vikings in the Victorian era, see Andrew Wawn, *The Vikings and the Victorians: Inventing the Old North in Nineteenth-Century Britain* (Cambridge, D. S. Brewer, 2000).

of the Viking raiders belonged to the arsenal of (southern) English rather than British historical imagination.

English determination to resist a 'Germanic' invasion had no better embodiment than St Edmund, king of the East Angles in the ninth century. A memorial window at Bracknell, Berkshire, depicts the martyrdom of the king who had refused to forswear Christianity; tied to a tree he is shot to death by the arrows of the heathen Danes.[247] The scene of St Edmund's execution is also captured in a window in a Roman Catholic church in St Helens, Lancashire. For centuries, his memory had been held in great esteem, especially in East Anglia. His burial place at Bury St Edmunds had evolved into a shrine of especial veneration. Naturally, Suffolk war memorials drew heavily on this tradition.[248] At Yoxford, St Edmund was claimed as 'the Suffolk martyr'.[249] A Cambridgeshire peculiarity is evocations of Byrhtnoth (see figure 33).[250] In a window in Ely Cathedral, the ealdorman of Essex is shown exhorting his men before the battle of Maldon in 991, when he was defeated and killed by a Danish force.[251]

Hereward the Wake ('the watchful one') appears in the same window in Ely Cathedral.[252] Victorian upholders of Anglo-Saxonism had extolled Hereward, the leading figure in the fenland revolt against William the Conqueror in 1071, as the symbol of English resistance to Norman oppression. However, mid-nineteenth-century theories about the 'Norman yoke', the suppression of Anglo-Saxon liberty by the Norman conquerors, did not flare up again after the war – a war in which Britain had, after all, stood side by side with France.[253] After 1918, agents of remembrance spoke of the Norman takeover in neutral terms as 'the last conquest of England'.[254] Already Edwardian discourse had shown a tendency to water down or smooth over the historical caesura of 1066,

---

[247] IWM, WM 2988, box 3, Bracknell, Berks.

[248] NIWM, 4714, Burgate, E. Suff.; 4732, Creeting St Mary, E. Suff.; 4426, Erwarton, E. Suff.; 4788–9, Mendlesham, E. Suff.; 5608, Yoxford, E. Suff.

[249] 'In Remembrance: Window Unveiled in Yoxford', *Suffolk Chronicle and Mercury*, 4561, 30 April 1920, p. 6.

[250] IWM, WM 2554, box 8, St Mary's, Ely, Cambs.

[251] 'In Memory of the Fallen: Cambs. and Isle of Ely Memorial Chapel in Ely Cathedral', *Cambridge Independent Press*, 5521, 12 May 1922, p. 3.

[252] NIWM, 12936, Ely, Cambs.

[253] On the nineteenth century, see Asa Briggs, 'Saxons, Normans and Victorians', in *The Collected Essays of Asa Briggs*, vol. II, *Images, Problems, Standpoints, Forecasts* (Brighton, Harvester, 1985), pp. 215–9; Clare A. Simmons, *Reversing the Conquest: History and Myth in Nineteenth-Century British Literature* (New Brunswick and London, Rutgers University Press, 1990), pp. 198–9; Wawn, *Vikings and the Victorians*, pp. 315–21; Barczewski, *Myth and National Identity*, p. 235; Readman, 'Place of the Past', pp. 193–4.

[254] Edgar A. Hunt (ed.), *The Colchester Memorial Souvenir* (Colchester, Essex Telegraph, 1923), p. 20. Colchester's war memorial is situated at the entrance to the Norman castle.

Figure 33. Byrhtnoth of Essex. Stained-glass window. Church of St Mary the Virgin, Ely, 1920s.

and this trend continued after 1918. The mayor of Todmorden, West Yorkshire, was reported to have said the following at the opening of the town's garden of remembrance in 1921: 'The people of Todmorden ought to be proud [. . .] of the lads who went out, when the war began, to do their duty and to help to keep the foreigner from coming to our shores. Only once [. . .] had our shores been invaded – when William the Conqueror came – and they hoped they would never be invaded again.'[255]

Father King, a padre based in Gallipoli in 1915, preached to his men that the war was, paradoxically, 'Hell' and, at the same time, 'a holy war'. This he regarded as 'instrumental in drawing from men deeds of unparalleled heroism and self-sacrifice'.[256] The nature of the war mattered; it determined the righteousness and importance of the cause for which the soldiers fought and died. Wartime sermons, posters and other forms of propaganda had pre-formulated themes which were later adapted for commemorative purposes. The intellectual architects of propaganda themselves often drew on a rich repertoire of symbols developed well before the war. War commemorations revived images and figures from the nation's cultural memory (such as Richard I and the crusaders or Teutonic Knights and Roland) in an effort to give death on the battlefield a greater historical significance than a purely personal tragedy.

Agents of memory configured the Great War as a crusade, a mission of bringing culture, order or liberal values, but also as a defence of the realm, the home, or civic liberty and national freedom. Broadly speaking, in the British discourse of remembrance the concept of a new crusade prevailed, whereas German commemorations put emphasis on aspects of national defence. The universality of the aspirations of the victor contrasts with the self-centredness of the loser. However, it is necessary to differentiate between dominant narratives about 'the war' in general and sub-narratives about particular theatres of operation. Notably, two variants of the Tannenberg story departed significantly from the established pattern of war commemoration in Germany. The rhetoric of spreading *Kultur* and conquering *Lebensraum* reflected the mindset of the right-wing and *völkisch* milieux. In this socio-political context, war remembrance blended into political re-mobilisation. The occupation of German territory in the east – which was, in contrast to the Rhineland, supposed to be a permanent settlement – seemed like a prolongation of the war.

---

[255] 'A Garden of Remembrance: Todmorden's Unique War Memorial', *Todmorden and District News*, 14 October 1921, p. 2.
[256] As cited in Wilkinson, *Church of England*, p. 149.

Ultimately, most discussions of the nature of the conflict in Germany and Britain centred on the human toll of the war. The legitimisation of death and suffering was critical in the search for meaning, both existential and political. Defensive and missionary narratives attributed positive meanings to physical sacrifice. Both narratives asserted that fallen soldiers had not died in vain: they had either given their lives to avert a national disaster and shield German territorial integrity (the peace treaty was, after all, not within their influence) or they had, in the imagined footsteps of the historic crusaders, struggled to achieve a military-cum-ethical victory and uphold British liberal principles.

3   Destruction and endurance: the war experience

The German dream of crushing military victory over the Entente in the early stages of the war failed to materialise. As the army's westward advance ground to halt, commentators had to adjust their language to the reality of a stalemate. By 1915, expressions of holding out or resilience instead of advance proliferated: 'In the east and west, in the north and south, we clench our enemies in an iron fist.'[1] To be sure, the Russian retreat from Poland in summer 1915 aroused new excitement. Germans at home imagined that the imperial 'mailed fist hovered menacingly in the air for the ultimate, crushing blow'.[2]

The 'iron fist' – an implicit reference to the story of Reich Knight 'Götz von Berlichingen with the Iron Hand' (the title of Johann Wolfgang von Goethe's drama) – was firmly established in the corpus of propaganda. It symbolised the army's unbreakable determination to resist the enemy attack and to achieve a lasting 'peace'. 'This / is the way to peace – / the enemy wills it so!', reads a 1918 poster by Lucian Bernhard depicting a clenched mailed fist.[3] Propaganda of this kind backfired on the Kaiserreich. Abroad, the image of the iron fist – dating back to Wilhelm II's infamous 'mailed fist speech' on the German occupation of Tsingtao in 1897 – was identified with German ruthlessness. 'Have you read the Kaiser's speeches? [. . .] They are full of the glitter and bluster of German militarism – "mailed fist", and "shining

---

[1] 'Der Eiserne Roland in Bremen: Die Einweihungsfeier', *Bremer Nachrichten*, 195, 16 July 1915: 'Im Osten und Westen, in Nord und Süd halten wir die Gegner mit eiserner Faust umklammert.'

[2] 'Einweihung des "Schmiedes von Essen"', *Rheinisch-Westfälischer Anzeiger*, 205, 26 July 1915, p. 5: 'daß die gepanzerte Faust zum letzten, vernichtenden Schlage drohend in der Luft schwebte'.

[3] BfZ, Plakatsammlung Erster Weltkrieg, 2.5/32, 'Das ist der Weg zum Frieden', 1918. See also ibid., 2.6/1, 'Deutsche Kriegsausstellung', 1916. On posters, see Peter Paret, Beth Irwin Lewis and Paul Paret, *Persuasive Images: Posters of War and Revolution from the Hoover Institution Archives* (Princeton, Princeton University Press, 1992).

armour"', said Lloyd George in the winter of 1914.[4] Even years after the
war, the frightful diction of Imperial Germany had not been forgotten in
Britain. Remembrance ceremonies and war memoirs recalled the horror
of the Kaiser's 'gory mailed fist'.[5]

The iron fist was an ambiguous symbol, a symbol of steadfast endurance as well as of ruthless destruction. Destruction and endurance were
two sides of the same coin, the novel experience of industrialised mass
warfare. For the brutality with which the generals waged the war, the
First World War, especially the Western Front, was experienced as a
turning-point in the history of armed conflict.[6] The contemporaries were
aware that the Great War marked, in the words of Lloyd George, an
unprecedented 'engineers' war'.[7] Yet this did not prevent them from
couching the violent modernity of the war in medieval imagery. This
chapter is concerned with medievalist representations of the experience
of the First World War (rather than reconstructions of an 'authentic'
experience of combat). I concentrate on three commemorative motifs
that projected something of the 'experience' of the Great War and its
connection to history and modernity: the mystique surrounding iron and
steel; evocations of rocks and castles; and, finally, medieval ruins, the
restoration of historic ruins, and the ruin of art-historic treasures at the
front.

Iron and steel

The *Materialschlacht*, the battle of *matériel*, in the world war put an
immense and often intolerable strain on the combatants. Politicians
and generals pushed their soldiers beyond the boundaries of endurance.
Invocations of 'cold steel' offered a symbolic compensation to Germans.
Propagandists pictured countering the nerve-racking drumfire with iron
will-power. Iron determination would overcome the enemy within: anxiety. Anxiety was attributed to an almost pathological lack of will-power

---

[4] David Lloyd George, '"Through Terror to Triumph!" Why Our National Honour is
Involved', in F[rances] L. Stevenson (ed.), *Through Terror to Triumph: Speeches and
Pronouncements of the Right Hon. David Lloyd George, M.P., since the Beginning of the
War* (London, New York and Toronto, Hodder and Stoughton, 1915), p. 10. On the
speech of 1897, see Lothar Reinermann, *Der Kaiser in England: Wilhelm II. und sein Bild
in der britischen Öffentlichkeit* (Paderborn, Ferdinand Schöningh, 2001), pp. 180–1.

[5] Stewartry Museum, Acc. 7216, vol. 2, n.p., David Clark, 'Rejoice!', unspecified newspaper cutting, n.d.; Chesterton, *Autobiography*, p. 246.

[6] Bernd Hüppauf, 'Introduction: Modernity and Violence: Observations Concerning a
Contradictory Relationship', in Bernd Hüppauf (ed.), *War, Violence and the Modern
Condition* (Berlin and New York, Walter de Gruyter, 1997), esp. pp. 23–4.

[7] Lloyd George, 'A Holy War', in *Through Terror to Triumph*, p. 81.

and self-control – not to the overpowering force of total war. Werner Sombart illustrated the ideal of calmness in wartime by analogy with an armour-clad warrior resting stoically on his gigantic sword in the midst of battle.[8]

Commemorations, both during and after the war, echoed Sombart's vision; the knight in armour represented the archetypal man of steel who was both mentally and physically invulnerable.[9] This image informed a language which contemporaries devised to acknowledge the soldiers' achievement, a language which posited the soldiers' ability to abide unimaginable harshness. Victory and defeat in the conventional sense did not matter in this discursive context; the soldier's iron endurance of the *Materialschlacht* meant a victory over human nature. It is little wonder that, after the war, veterans encouraged the use of this language. Their special status in post-war Germany, the strength of their associations and societies and their involvement in public rituals of commemoration enabled them to do so. At the same time, iron masculinity was the cure prescribed for crippled veterans to help them triumph over their disabilities. Time and again, orthopaedic surgeons and medical technicians praised Götz von Berlichingen as a role model. A number of new designs for prosthetic arms even bore Götz's name. The famous knight with his iron fist became the archetypal German warrior disabled by injury but armed with a steel prosthesis and sustained by his unbreakable spirit.[10]

Imposed on war cripples by medical experts, the notion of iron endurance provided able-bodied but disgruntled veterans with a welcome collective myth which underscored their special station in post-war German society. British political culture, in contrast, was unprepared to assign a special role to ex-servicemen, a group whose national association, the British Legion, was, in comparative terms, notable for its numeric weakness. Veterans were not usually party to the initiating committees since war memorials were meant to be tributes from citizens to soldiers. The soldier's experience could rarely be fully articulated

[8] Sombart, *Händler und Helden*, pp. 131–2.
[9] Aribert Reimann, *Der große Krieg der Sprachen: Untersuchungen zur historischen Semantik in Deutschland und England zur Zeit des Ersten Weltkriegs* (Essen, Klartext, 2000), pp. 39–68, 280.
[10] Sabine Kienitz, 'Der Krieg der Invaliden: Helden-Bilder und Männlichkeitskonstruktionen nach dem Ersten Weltkrieg', *Militärgeschichtliche Zeitschrift*, 60 (2001), pp. 384–7. See also Tim Armstrong, *Modernism, Technology, and the Body: A Cultural Study* (Cambridge, Cambridge University Press, 1998), ch. 3. On the place of disabled veterans in post-war society, see Deborah Cohen, *The War Come Home: Disabled Veterans in Great Britain and Germany, 1914–1939* (Berkeley, Los Angeles and London, University of California Press, 2001).

within the framework of communal commemorations, which were mostly managed by those who had remained at home.[11] As a consequence, the British story lacks a precise analogue to the cult of the *Kriegserlebnis*, the 'war experience', and its 'eyewitnesses' in German commemorative culture.[12] Instead, the British First World War experience was encoded in a language of suffering and sacrifice which validated soldiers' vulnerability.[13]

While the military authorities maintained that nervous breakdown was an evasion of duty, large parts of the British public saw mental devastation (especially if suffered by officers) as a legitimate wartime injury. In the English-speaking world, the term 'shell-shock', coined by the British physician C. S. Myers in 1915, was transformed from a medical diagnosis to a metaphor of the experience of the First World War.[14] What is more, the imagery of cold steel, discredited by the shadow of the Kaiser's 'mailed fist' rhetoric, was unavailable for the expression of the soldier's ordeal.[15] Since a distinct medievalist discourse of unshakable endurance of adversity was virtually non-existent in the British context, this chapter will chiefly deal with the German case.

Knights in armour

Iron-nail war landmarks swept German towns in 1915 and 1916.[16] Countless war landmarks represented *Eiserne Wehrmänner* or 'Iron Defenders'. Consider the 'Iron Defender' of Halberstadt, Prussian Province of Saxony, which was unveiled in January 1916. The local press described the body language of the figure as follows: 'Not in an offensive posture, armed for battle, but with shield lowered and sword sheathed; and yet clad in full armour to repel attacks directed against him. And in this state of calmness he is a model of steady

---

[11] Gaffney, *Aftermath*, pp. 26–33; Gregory, *Silence of Memory*, ch. 2; Barr, 'British Legion'; Connelly, *Great War, Memory and Ritual*, p. 190. For a contrary opinion, see King, *Memorials of the Great War*, pp. 29, 90; Grieves, 'Common Meeting Places'.

[12] Bernd Ulrich, *Die Augenzeugen: Deutsche Feldpostbriefe in Kriegs- und Nachkriegszeit 1914–1933* (Essen, Klartext, 1997).

[13] Laurinda S. Stryker, 'Languages of Sacrifice and Suffering in England in the First World War', Ph.D. dissertation, University of Cambridge, 1992. See also Peter Leese, '"Why Are They Not Cured?" British Shellshock Treatment during the Great War', in Mark S. Micale and Paul Lerner (eds.), *Traumatic Pasts: History, Psychiatry, and Trauma in the Modern Age, 1870–1930* (Cambridge, Cambridge University Press, 2001), pp. 206–8, 212.

[14] Winter, 'Shell-Shock', pp. 7–11. See also Winter and Baggett, *1914–18*, pp. 212–29.

[15] For positive images of 'cold steel' contrast Joanna Bourke, *An Intimate History of Killing: Face-to-Face Killing in Twentieth-Century Warfare* (London, Granta, 1999), pp. 55, 58.

[16] On iron-nail war landmarks, see chapter 1.

strength.'[17] Composure, not brutality, distinguished this iron warrior. Calmness was the keyword here. Halberstadt's 'calm' knight was a typical product of the 'age of nervousness'.[18] Observers of western societies had been increasingly preoccupied with nervous disorders since the late nineteenth century. Some doctors had diagnosed a correlation between the acceleration in socio-economic modernisation and an increase in nervous complaints. Underlying their research was a pessimistic critique of the modern condition. In search of an antidote to the perceived degeneration of modern society, psychiatric specialists had extolled the 'natural' wartime environment. Yet the outbreak of war in 1914 presented the medical profession with a new situation. Nervous symptoms spread rapidly among formerly healthy men, and effective treatment for mental diseases under the conditions of industrialised warfare became a pressing military need.

German psychiatrists, eager to prove their field's utility in wartime, classified nervous symptoms as hysterical rather than traumatic reactions and thus as a particular form of mental disposition (that required medical attention) rather than genuine shell-shock.[19] The medical discourse of the war years has attracted considerable attention from scholars. A feature which is worth noting here is the representation of the soldier's psyche in public ceremonies. War landmarks were commonly identified as 'a symbol of iron will'.[20] Note the slippage and oscillation between the material and the mental, from iron nails to iron will; metallic qualities became charged with psychic values. The war landmark provided a focus for rituals to exorcise nervousness and promote calmness as a wartime virtue. The practice of hammering iron nails into wooden objects signified the collective steeling of nerves. Driving iron nails into oak meant, as Karl-Ernst Osthaus put it, 'to greet and to peel away the hard with the

---

[17] 'Die Einweihung des Eisernen Wehrmannes', *Halberstädter Zeitung und Intelligenzblatt*, 23, suppl., 28 Jan. 1916, p. 5: 'Nicht in Angriffsstellung, zum Kampfe gerüstet, sondern den Schild gesenkt und das Schwert in der Scheide; aber in voller Rüstung gewappnet, um Angriffen, die gegen ihn erhoben werden sollen, die Spitze zu bieten. Und in dieser Ruhe ist er ein Bild der sicheren Kraft.'

[18] Joachim Radkau, *Das Zeitalter der Nervosität: Deutschland zwischen Bismarck und Hitler* (Munich and Vienna, Carl Hanser, 1998).

[19] Paul Lerner, *Hysterical Men: War, Psychiatry, and the Politics of Trauma in Germany, 1890–1930* (Ithaca and London, Cornell University Press, 2003) and 'Psychiatry and Casualties of War in Germany, 1914–18', *Journal of Contemporary History*, 35 (2000), pp. 13–28. See also Joachim Radkau, 'Das Stahlbad der Nervenkur? Nervöse Ursprünge des Ersten Weltkrieges', *Newsletter des Arbeitskreises Militärgeschichte*, 10 (1999), pp. 6–8. For comparison, see Peter Leese, *Shell Shock: Traumatic Neurosis and the British Soldiers of the First World War* (Basingstoke and New York, Palgrave, 2002).

[20] Hans Sachs, 'Vom Hurrakitsch, von Nagelungsstandbildern, Nagelungsplakaten und anderen – Schönheiten', *Das Plakat*, 8,1 (1917), p. 10.

even harder [material]'.[21] Wooden objects were thus turned into steeled figures, the organic metaphor into metal. Communal action created a protective suit of iron: 'Iron is the word of our time! Germany's power wears an iron garment': thus Bremen sung the praises of its 'Iron Roland' (see figure 22).[22] The 'iron garment' was a standard formula in ceremonies held at war landmarks.[23] The symbolism was most persuasive where iron nails were used to describe the figure or image of a medieval knight clad in a suit of armour such as the 'Gallant Swabian in Iron' of Stuttgart.

Stuttgart's 'Wackerer Schwabe in Eisen' exemplifies the strength of regional traditions and identities in narratives of destruction and endurance. Judging from its design, the war landmark of Stuttgart was nothing out of the ordinary: a conventional representation of a knight armed with a sword and shield. Moreover, the figure was unveiled on 2 September 1915 – Sedan Day. Sedan Day dramatised annually the founding myth of Imperial Germany, the formation of a national phalanx against France in the war of 1870–1. Although a celebration of national union, the flavour of the event differed between states and regions.[24] The unveiling ceremony of 1915 accentuated Swabian (rather than German) steadfastness in the ongoing conflict. The main speaker, the president of the Red Cross of Württemberg, highlighted the *Ausharren*, 'endurance', of the soldiers at the front which he related to the legendary *Schwabenstreiche*, reported the local Social-Democratic newspaper.[25]

The term *Schwabenstreich*, 'Swabian trick' or 'Swabian blow', originally a mocking expression for a piece of folly, had been refashioned by Ludwig Uhland. In 1814, Uhland, a leading protagonist of German Romanticism and a medievalist at the University of Tübingen, had

[21] Karl Ernst Osthaus, 'Die Kunst und der Eiserne Schmied in Hagen', *Westfälisches Tageblatt*, 214, 13 September 1915: 'das Harte mit dem Härteren zu grüßen und zu häuten'. See also Reimann, *Krieg der Sprachen*, pp. 48–68; Diers, 'Nagelmänner', p. 86.
[22] StAB 7,60/2–9.b.1, 'Der Eiserne Roland in Bremen: Die Einweihungsfeier', *Bremer Nachrichten*, 195, 16 July 1915: 'Eisen ist das Wort der Zeit! Deutschlands Kraft trägt eisernes Kleid.' See also Zentral-Hilfsausschuß, 'Der Eiserne Roland zu Bremen', *Bremer Nachrichten*, 170, 21 June 1915; StAB, 10-B-Al-875, Postcard 'Der Eiserne Roland zu Bremen', [c. 1915].
[23] *Der Eiserne Schmied von Hagen*, p. 3; 'Im Zeichen des Sedantages: Der "Wackere Schwabe" in Eisen', *Stuttgarter Neues Tagblatt*, 443, 2 September 1915, p. 5.
[24] On celebrations of Sedan Day in Württemberg, see Alon Confino, *The Nation as a Local Metaphor: Württemberg, Imperial Germany, and National Memory, 1871–1918* (Chapel Hill and London, University of North Carolina Press, 1997).
[25] 'Die Einweihung des "Wackeren Schwaben"', *Schwäbische Tagwacht: Organ der Sozialdemokraten Württembergs*, 205, 3 September 1915, p. 5. See also 'Einweihung des "Wackeren Schwaben"', *Stuttgarter Neues Tagblatt*, 444, 2 September 1915, p. 2; BArch, R 8034 II/7690, folio 30, 'Der "wackere Schwabe in Eisen": Denkmalsnagelung in Stuttgart', *Berliner Tageblatt*, 448, 2 September 1915.

written the humorous poem 'Swabian Intelligence' ('Schwäbische Kunde'). It tells the story of the 'Gallant Swabian', a paladin of the crusader Frederick I Barbarossa who always remains cool, calm and collected in battle. He endures the assaults launched on him by the Turks with disdain and plays a passive role up to a point when he unexpectedly, but vigorously, strikes back with his sword: the *Schwabenstreich*. In short, the poem could be read as a tale of both iron resilience and resilient humour. A local newspaper remarked on the iron-nail figure: 'With an expression of humorous contempt, winking, twisting his mouth into a slight smile, he looks back over the massive shield which has blocked a few arrows; but with his right hand he grasps the good sword, and woe betide anyone who comes too close to him! He will taste what the *Schwabenstreiche* mean'.[26]

After the war, the 'Gallant Swabian in Iron' fell, like many other war landmarks, into oblivion. Yet in the final years of the Weimar Republic, the figure, meanwhile transferred to a storeroom in Stuttgart's old castle, captured Swabian imagination once again. The castle was badly damaged by fire, but by a strange twist of fate the 'Gallant Swabian' survived intact. In the aftermath of the fire disaster the discourse of endurance flared up temporarily, and the 'Gallant Swabian' was once again pronounced a role model. 'Thus the "Gallant Swabian" [. . .] has, before all eyes, truly risen again from the ashes of the Württembergian mother castle as a wonderful symbol of Swabian toughness and victorious steadfastness', reported the bourgeois press.[27] The story of the miraculous survival of the 'Gallant Swabian' was also spread by means of picture postcards showing the knight surrounded by the rubble of the castle (see figure 34). The caption stated that 'he "gallantly" stood firm during the fire disaster of the Old Castle in Stuttgart [. . .]. Practically undamaged he rises from the rubble.'[28]

[26] 'Im Zeichen des Sedantages: Der "Wackere Schwabe" in Eisen', *Stuttgarter Neues Tagblatt*, 443, 2 September 1915, p. 5: 'Mit einem Ausdruck humoristischer Verachtung, das eine Auge zuzwinkernd, den Mund zu einem leichten Schmunzeln verzogen, lugt er rückwärts über den mächtigen Schild weg, der schon ein paar Pfeile aufgefangen hat; aber mit der Rechten greift er nach dem guten Schwert, und wehe dem, der ihm zu nahe kommt! Er wird verschmecken, was Schwabenstreiche sind.'

[27] Wilhelm Schussen, 'Der Wackere Schwabe', *Stuttgarter Neues Tagblatt*, 277, 17 June 1932, p. 2: 'So ist der [. . .] "Wackere Schwabe" als ein herrliches Sinnbild schwäbischer Zähigkeit und sieghafter Beharrlichkeit aus den Brandtrümmern der württembergischen Mutterburg in Wahrheit vor aller Augen wiedererstanden.'

[28] Stadtarchiv Stuttgart, Postkartensammlung, 'Wackerer Schwabe', [*c*. 1931]: 'hielt auch der verheerenden Brandkatastrophe des Alten Schlosses in Stuttgart [. . .] "wacker" stand. Fast unbeschädigt steigt er aus den Trümmern wieder empor.'

Figure 34. 'Gallant Swabian'. Postcard depicting the iron-nail statue of
1915 by Josef Zeitler after the fire disaster of 1931.

The steel-helmeted man

The use of iron in the creation of war landmarks synthesised medievalist and modernist sentiments. Iron evoked images of both medieval warriors and industrialised warfare. It is noteworthy that iron-nail monuments swept the country in 1915–16. The notion of iron resilience was born of the experience of a prolonged war of position and entrenchment at the Western Front in 1914–15. The symbolism of iron predated both Verdun and the Somme, the two battles which revolutionised the meaning of the word 'endurance'. In the aftermath of the battles of *matériel* at Verdun and on the Somme in 1916, a new icon of hardness proliferated alongside the established metaphors of medieval armour. The *Stahlhelm*, the distinctive flat-topped steel helmet, was introduced in early 1916 to replace the decorative, but inefficient, spiked *Pickelhaube*, a relic of the mid-nineteenth-century army.

Although it was the progeny of modern engineering, the shape of the *Stahlhelm* conjured up archaic helmets. Erich Maria Remarque observed that cavalrymen 'in their steel helmets resemble knights of a forgotten time'.[29] The editor of the magazine of the Kyffhäuserbund noted in an essay on the 'Struggle on the Somme – The Emotional Experience of a Front Fighter': 'But those soldiers! Those German soldiers with their German Siegfried helmets, with their fists on their hot rifles, with iron features of valour, love and horror [. . .] – those men on the Somme are our defence in the most monstrous hurricane of this war.'[30] Official war propaganda had probably set the tone. In poster art, the steel helmet blended with medieval armour.[31] In the course of time, the steel helmet evolved into the quintessential German symbol of the Great War. Countless war memorials featured 'the German steel helmet in its wonderful, almost ancient form' (see figure 24).[32] However, for some agents of memory notions of hardness associated with the steel helmet had more radical, ideologically far-reaching implications. I now want to turn to this sub-discourse which emphasised the transformative power of the ordeal at the front.

---

[29] Remarque, *All Quiet*, p. 67.
[30] Otto Riebicke, 'Ringen an der Somme – Das seelische Erleben eines Frontkämpfers', in Bernd Ulrich and Benjamin Ziemann (eds.), *Krieg im Frieden: Die umkämpfte Erinnerung an den Ersten Weltkrieg: Quellen und Dokumente* (Frankfurt am Main, Fischer, 1997), doc. 21b, pp. 155–6.
[31] IWM, PST 3213, 'VIIte Kriegsanleihe', 1917. See also IWM, PST 5985, 'Brigarde Reinhard', [c. 1919].
[32] Ludwig Kittel, 'Heldenehrung in Ostfriesland', *Ostfreesland: Ein Kalender für Jedermann*, 15 (1928), p. 101: 'der deutsche Stahlhelm mit seiner wundervollen, fast antiken Form'.

The steel helmet connoted the imagined *Kriegserlebnis* of the front-line combatant. Not for nothing was the Stahlhelm, Bund der Frontsoldaten, the anti-republican 'League of Front Soldiers', founded in November 1918, named after the new helmet (later, however, non-combatants and youngsters could enlist in sub-organisations of the Stahlhelm league).[33] Many veterans joined the league in order to dissociate themselves from the boozy atmosphere of the traditional *Kriegervereine*, warriors' societies, established in the nineteenth century. No better emblem could have been found to outline a symbolic demarcation between the Great War and previous conflicts than the helmet of Verdun and the Somme. A new type of soldier, the 'Verdun fighter', was hammered into being in 1916, as Bernd Hüppauf has argued.[34] Hardened by the battle of *matériel*, the front-fighter typified a dehumanised race, a war machine with an iron soul – a notion not dissimilar to the steely-bodied machines characteristic of Wyndham Lewis's idiosyncratic paintings of the later 1930s.[35] Externally, the 'new man' was distinguished by the steel helmet crowning his head (some German soldiers wore, in addition, full chest armour).

To Ernst Jünger, the poet of the machine war, the steel-helmeted man appeared to be 'the inhabitant of a new, mysterious and harder world'.[36] Jünger's detached, clinical descriptions of the Western Front capture the imbalance between man and material. The soldier who endured hell on earth, the artillery's *Stahlgewitter*, 'storm of steel', emerged as a new (super-)human species. There is a degree of resemblance between the writings of Jünger and those of German psychiatrists. Psychiatric doctors concerned with war neuroses did not blame the shocks of the battlefield

---

[33] On the Stahlhelm association generally, see Volker R. Berghahn, *Der Stahlhelm: Bund der Frontsoldaten 1918–1935* (Düsseldorf, Droste, 1966).

[34] Bernd Hüppauf, 'Schlachtenmythen und die Konstruktion des "Neuen Menschen"', in Gerhard Hirschfeld, Gerd Krumeich and Irina Renz (eds.), *'Keiner fühlt sich hier mehr als Mensch. . .': Erlebnis und Wirkung des Ersten Weltkriegs* (Frankfurt am Main, Fischer, 1996), esp. pp. 81–4. See also Mosse, *Fallen Soldiers*, pp. 132, 184–5.

[35] Andrew Causey, 'Wyndham Lewis and History Painting in the Later 1930s', in David Peters Corbett (ed.), *Wyndham Lewis and the Art of Modern War* (Cambridge, Cambridge University Press, 1998), pp. 164, 169.

[36] Ernst Jünger, *In Stahlgewittern: Ein Kriegstagebuch* (Berlin, E. S. Mittler, 20th edn 1940), p. 97. The twentieth edition is a reprint of the sixteenth edition (fourth revised version) of 1935. Jünger revised his novel four times in the years 1921 to 1935. *Inter alia* he altered the wording of the passage cited above, putting additional emphasis on the *Stahlhelm*. On Jünger's vision of a 'steeled' human, see Klaus Theweleit, *Male Fantasies*, vol. II, *Male Bodies: Psychoanalyzing the White Terror* (Cambridge, Polity, 1989), pp. 159–62, 197–210; Eric J. Leed, *No Man's Land: Combat & Identity in World War I* (Cambridge, Cambridge University Press, 1979), pp. 95, 145–62; Midgley, *Writing Weimar*, pp. 242–3, 247; Matthew Biro, 'The New Man as Cyborg: Figures of Technology in Weimar Visual Culture', *New German Critique*, 62 (1994), pp. 97–108.

for the onset of nervous symptoms. On the contrary, they pointed out the spiritually invigorating effect of battle on man's psyche, and envisaged war as a kind of therapy or cure, a *Stahlbad*, a 'bath of steel'.[37]

How widespread was the idea of a 'new man' surfacing in the aftermath of the 'storm of steel' or 'bath of steel'? A recent study of German war memorials suggests that monuments erected after *c.* 1928, when mourning was supposedly on the decline, were vectors for the dissemination of notions of the 'new man'.[38] The figure of the steel-helmeted man with a stern face was indeed a popular choice – maybe even the most popular choice – for figurative war memorials, especially regimental memorials, even before 1928. For example, the sculptor Hermann Hosaeus modelled, according to one contemporary expert, the soldier who 'marched through the "Storm of Steel"' to perfection.[39] The expert regarded Hosaeus' Roland-style figure for the town of Norden, Hanover (see figure 24), unveiled in 1927, as exemplary memorial art:

One glance at this face and one understands why the enemy must hate him and seeks to bring him to his knees with diabolic cunning. Because one cannot cope with him in any other way. He is genuine, that is why one needs craftiness against him; he is deep and spiritualised [*verinnerlicht*], that is why one has to defame him; he is upright, that is why one has to humiliate him; he is steadfast against inner distress and outer threat, hard as iron and steel, solid as a rocksteady stone, that is why one has to murder him. He can win, lead, fight and die. His power is as strong and quick as a hammer whistling down. His weapon is as sure as death. His faith is as true as his eye. His death is an ancient epic of heroism and ruin. He is greater than the material of battle, because he embodies defiance, spirit and will.[40]

Literary and visual representations of the steel-helmeted warrior complemented each other. They enshrined one particular facet of the First

---

[37] As cited in Radkau, *Zeitalter der Nervosität*, p. 404. See Lerner, 'Psychiatry and Casualties of War', p. 27.
[38] Sabine Behrenbeck, 'Zwischen Trauer und Heroisierung: Vom Umgang mit Kriegstod und Niederlage nach 1918', in Jörg Duppler and Gerhard P. Groß (eds.), *Kriegsende 1918: Ereignis, Wirkung, Nachwirkung* (Munich, R. Oldenbourg, 1999), pp. 336–7.
[39] Seeger, *Denkmal des Weltkriegs*, p. 35.
[40] Ibid.: 'Ein Blick in dieses Gesicht, und man versteht, warum der Feind ihn hassen muß und ihn mit diabolischer Raffiniertheit auf die Knie zwingen will. Denn anders kann man mit ihm nicht fertig werden. Er ist wahr, darum braucht man Tücke gegen ihn, er ist tief und verinnerlicht, darum muß man ihn verleumden, er ist aufrecht, darum muß man ihn demütigen, er ist tapfer gegen innere Not und äußere Bedrängnis, hart wie Eisen und Stahl, wuchtig wie ein felsenschwerer Stein, darum muß man ihn morden. Er kann siegen, führen, kämpfen und sterben. Seine Kraft ist stark und rasch wie ein niedersausend geschwungener Hammer. Seine Waffe ist sicher wie der Tod. Sein Glaube wahr wie sein Auge. Sein Sterben ein uraltes Epos von Heldentum und Untergang. Er ist größer als die Materie der Schlacht, denn er ist Trotz, Geist und Wille.'

World War experience, namely operations in the front line of the western battlefields. Ernst Jünger himself had joined one of the elite storm-troop units formed in answer to the British bombardment on the Somme. These units were given full freedom of action. The new tactics relied on the storm trooper's savage energy and imagination and thus re-invented individualism in the midst of a mechanical war. Consequently, Jünger's experience of the conflict was anything but representative of the legendary 'front generation'.[41] Nonetheless Jünger, one of the most prolific writers of his generation, was enormously influential in shaping the veterans' ideal of the front-line fighter, an ideal which excluded a significant proportion of ex-servicemen. The Weimar Republic saw a bitter wrangle over the question of who did and who did not belong to this exclusive group. Did army railwaymen, for instance, share the front experience? Their association was anxious to stress the unity of 'sword and track', which was the theme of their war memorial in the Berlin suburb of Schöneberg. 'Does it not take a whole heart [. . .] to drive the trains onto the battlefield amidst the storm of steel of the enemy artillery?', their leader asked. 'The army railway-service, with all its privations, called for hearts and nerves of steel and iron fists.'[42]

After the war, the imagery of memorialisation frequently borrowed and transformed that of wartime visual culture and discourses depicting the 'metallisation' of the German soldier. That imagery may have been bourgeois in its origin, since metaphors of iron determination and endurance reflected long-established fears about psychical degeneration, fears which predominated among the middle classes. They were the instigators of iron-nail landmarks in 1915–16. But after the war, such metaphors became most seductive among the minority of soldiers who joined in the Jüngerian chorus. The 'steeled' superman was the brain-child of a counter-revolutionary elite, eagerly embraced by equally reactionary spokesmen of conservative veterans' associations and regimental societies.[43] In contrast, the silent majority of demobilised soldiers, keen

---

[41] For a social history of the 'front generation', see Richard Bessel, 'The "Front Generation" and the Politics of Weimar Germany', in Mark Roseman (ed.), *Generations in Conflict: Youth Revolt and Generation Formation in Germany 1770–1968* (Cambridge, Cambridge University Press, 1995), esp. pp. 123, 126.

[42] Max Heubes (ed.), *Ehrenbuch der Feldeisenbahner* (Berlin, Wilhelm Kolk, 1931), n.p. [preface]: 'Oder gehört nicht ein ganzes Herz dazu, im Stahlgewitter feindlicher Artillerie [. . .] die Züge auf das Kampffeld zu fahren?'; 'Stählerne Herzen und Nerven, eiserne Fäuste gehörten zum entsagungsvollen Dienst der Feldeisenbahner'. See also Landesarchiv Berlin, Gesch 921, 'Weihe des Ehrenmals für die gefallenen Kameraden der Deutschen Eisenbahntruppen in Berlin Schöneberg', 1929, p. 6.

[43] See the critique of Bernd Hüppauf's thesis by Benjamin Ziemann, '"Macht der Maschine": Mythen des industriellen Krieges', in Rolf Spilker and Bernd Ulrich

to return to their civilian lives, held themselves aloof from veterans' politics,[44] and although workers participated in the nailing rituals, the working-class press proved by and large immune to the mystique of metal.[45]

Rocks and castles

'The powers of our people grow in the storm of steel, in the iron cure of the war',[46] preached a pastor in summer 1914 during a service held at the gigantic Völkerschlacht memorial – a colossus built of reinforced concrete, a hitherto unknown building material for commemorative architecture (see figure 35).[47] The centenary monument for the victory over Napoleon's army in the Battle of the Nations had been inaugurated in Leipzig, Kingdom of Saxony, in October 1913. Owing to the Kaiser's indignant refusal to partake fully in the festivities of 1913, the Leipzig monument was regarded as a bastion of German *Bürgerlichkeit*, 'middle classness'. Wilhelm II had harboured profound suspicions about the memorial, which expressed bourgeois nationalist pride, was planned by liberal-minded Freemasons, and was designed in a novel style.[48] Aesthetically, the memorial consisted of a pot-pourri of architectural and sculptural forms and materials of Germanic-*völkisch*, medieval-sacral, and industrial-modern origin. The ambiguity of its architectural language notwithstanding, after 1914 the Völkerschlacht monument was widely acclaimed as a model German war memorial.[49] In the eyes of

---

(eds.), *Der Tod als Maschinist: Der industrialisierte Krieg 1914–1918* (Bramsche, Rasch, 1998), p. 184.

[44] Ziemann, *Front und Heimat*, pp. 419–20, 437.

[45] Reimann, *Krieg der Sprachen*, pp. 67–8.

[46] Rendtorff, *Bittgottesdienst am Völkerschlachtdenkmal*, p. 8: 'Im Stahlbad, in der Eisenkur des Kriegs wachsen unserem Volk die Kräfte.' The Leipzig monument evolved into a focal point of remembrance activities; see BArch, R 8034 II/7690, fos. 107–8, 'Das Völkerschlachtdenkmal als Helden-Urnenhalle?', *Deutsche Tageszeitung*, 359, 15 July 1916; BArch, R 8034 II/7691, folio 53, 'Der Heldenfriedhof am Völkerschlacht-Denkmal', *Berliner Lokal-Anzeiger*, 595, 21 November 1915; ibid., folio 79, 'Eine Gedenkfeier für die im Weltkriege gefallenen Land- und Gastwirte', *Deutsche Tageszeitung*, 312, 7 July 1921.

[47] Hans-Ernst Mittig, 'Dauerhaftigkeit, einst Denkmalargument', in Michael Diers (ed.), *Mo(nu)mente: Formen und Funktionen ephemerer Denkmäler* (Berlin, Akademie, 1993), pp. 16–17. On the Völkerschlacht monument, see Hutter, *'Die feinste Barbarei'*. On the symbolism of concrete, see Fuhrmeister, *Beton, Klinker, Granit*, pp. 81–120.

[48] Stefan-Ludwig Hoffmann, 'Sakraler Monumentalismus um 1900: Das Leipziger Völkerschlachtdenkmal', in Reinhart Koselleck and Michael Jeismann (eds.), *Der politische Totenkult: Kriegerdenkmäler in der Moderne* (Munich, Wilhelm Fink, 1994), p. 258.

[49] BArch, R 43 I/713, folio 55, Staatssekretär in der Reichskanzlei to Reichskunstwart, 17 June 1925; BArch, R 32/359, folio 1, 'Ehrenmal auf dem Brocken?', *Braunschweiger Neueste Nachrichten*, 238, 11 October 1930; Lurz, *Kriegerdenkmäler*, vol. III, p. 27.

Figure 35. The Völkerschlacht memorial in Leipzig. Wartime postcard depicting the building designed by Bruno Schmitz and opened in 1913. Leipzig, 1915.

British art critics, the Leipzig memorial stood as an anti-model. The *Architectural Review* condemned the Völkerschlacht monument in 1916 as 'a mammoth embodiment of "frightfulness"'.[50] In Germany, Willy Lange, the inventor of the heroes' grove, was among the memorial's admirers. He compared it to the 'elemental quality of grown rock' characteristic of ancient Germanic monuments.[51]

'Grown rock', evocative of primeval firmness, constitutes the second leitmotif of narratives of endurance, an 'organic' motif lacking the sinister undercurrent of some interpretations of 'steel'. Generally, 'grown rock' was linked to medieval fortifications rather than Germanic remains. The guidelines for the erection of war memorials issued by the Württembergian Conservation Committee in 1916 recommended that 'The grown rock can be integrated into the foundation of the memorial structure (as was often the case with medieval castles).'[52] A host of architects and memorial committees took heed of the advice, perhaps inadvertently. The war memorial at Kloppenheim, a village near Wiesbaden, Hesse-Nassau, was designed in the manner of a feudal keep which blended into a hilltop.[53] Elsewhere, surviving castles were directly adapted for commemorative use. Rhinelanders campaigned for the establishment of the German national memorial at Feste Ehrenbreitstein, a fortress towering over the River Rhine opposite Koblenz. Built in the tenth century, Ehrenbreitstein Castle had been razed to the ground by French invaders in 1801, reconstructed under Prussian rule, and partly dismantled in 1920 according to the Versailles Treaty: 'the rock massif of Feste Ehrenbreitstein rises defiant. Its cubic blocks grow solidly out of the rock', a publicity leaflet of 1928 stated.[54] The mayor of Ehrenbreitstein suggested that the 'fortress massif' signified 'the invincible and undefeated

---

[50] 'Memorials of War: – VIII. German', *Architectural Review*, 40 (1916), p. 107. See King, *Memorials of the Great War*, pp. 156–8.
[51] GStAPK, I. HA Rep. 77 Tit. 1215 Nr. 3d Bd. 1 (M), folio 40, Willy Lange, 'Heldeneichen und Friedenslinden: Ein Ruf und Widerhall', n.d., p. 3: 'das Urwüchsige gewachsenen Felsens'.
[52] HStAS, M 746, Bü 1, Württemb. Landesausschuß für Natur- und Heimatschutz, 'Richtlinien für die Erstellung von Kriegserinnerungszeichen', 1916, p. 7: 'Der gewachsene Fels kann in den Unterbau des Denkmalbaues einbezogen sein (wie auch an mittelalterlichen Burgen oft der Fall).'
[53] *Deutscher Ehrenhain*, p. 236.
[54] StAMS, OP 5510, folio 202, Ausschuß für das Reichsehrenmal auf dem Ehrenbreitstein (ed.), *Der Ehrenbreitstein als Reichsehrenmal* (Koblenz, Breuer, 1928), p. 6: 'erhebt sich trotzig das Felsmassiv der Feste Ehrenbreitstein. Wuchtig wachsen ihre kubischen Baublöcke aus dem Felsen heraus.' See also BArch, R 43 I/715, folio 89, H. Jacobi, 'Vorschlag zu einem Reichsehrendenkmal am Rhein auf dem Ehrenbreitstein bei Koblenz', 1927.

Figure 36. The Scottish National War Memorial by Robert (later Sir Robert) Lorimer. Edinburgh Castle, 1927.

iron wall of the German army'.[55] The imagery of rock-solidness stood in the tradition of an older memorial project for Bingerbrück, a few miles up river. Franz Brantzky's design for the Bismarck national memorial, which had been awarded a second prize in 1910, 'grows organically out of the rock as the old castles did'.[56]

Allusions to the hardness of rocks and castles were not completely absent from British commemorations. As I noted in chapter 2, fortresses conveying a defensive Celtic tradition played a role in Scottish remembrance culture. Notably, the imposing national memorial of Scotland was integrated into Edinburgh Castle (see figure 36). A *Times* journalist stressed the rock-hard character of the ensemble, yet it is significant that

---

[55] BArch, R 43 I/714, folio 62, Bürgermeister Ehrenbreitstein to Reichspräsident, 12 July 1926: 'das Massiv der Festung [. . .] als Abbild der unbesiegbaren und nicht besiegten ehernen Mauer des deutschen Heeres'.

[56] *Hundert Entwürfe*, p. 38: 'aus dem Felsen organisch erwachsen, wie es die alten Burgen ja waren'. On the symbolism of rocks and castles, see Mittig, 'Dauerhaftigkeit', pp. 13–14.

he made no attempt to link this observation to the First World War experience. He merely noted

the firmness with which the buttressed shrine is rooted to its rocky foundation, the 'batter', or inward slope of the buttresses, giving a great effect of stability. The effect is increased at close quarters owing to the fact that the shrine starts not from levelled ground, but from the broken surface of the Rock itself, the hollows in which are to be filled with soil for such hardy plants as will grow at that elevation.[57]

Some historians like to point out that such imaginings had nothing to do with or indeed blurred the 'reality' of modern, trench warfare.[58] Be that as it may, contemporaries, at least in Germany, sensed the ambiguity of the modernity of the world war; they often felt as if they had been taken back to a bygone age.[59] Positional warfare, particularly on the Western Front, bore a puzzling resemblance to a castle in a state of siege. This impression informed a memorial design drawn up by a Viennese building contractor around 1915 (see figure 37). He proposed a star-shaped tower with battlements girdled by a trench (Schützengraben) and embankments. The tower would provide sufficient space for plaques; war trophies such as cannons could be placed on the tower's roof, as the designer explained.[60] Around the same time, the architect Oskar Strnad, a professor at the Kunstgewerbeschule in Vienna, sketched out a similar memorial concept. Strnad, a collaborator of Josef Hoffmann in a project on modernist solutions to memorial art, revived the architecture of moated castles. A ditch filled with water protected a simple but massive cylindrical building topped with stylised iron battlements in allusion to the historic example.[61] An almost exact copy of Strnad's design, but without the characteristic battlements, was realised at Frankfurt am Main, Hesse-Nassau (see figure 38).[62]

Moated memorial towers reflected popular feelings of encirclement. From 1914 onwards, Germany was given over to siege mentality. A commentary on a local Württembergian memorial stated in 1926:

just as the people of old, in times of ungoverned strife, retreated finally, when hard beset, into the 'churchyard', and felt secure within its four sturdy walls, in

---

[57] 'Scottish Art: Academy and War Memorial', The Times, 44557, 16 April 1927, p. 11.
[58] See, for example, the critique by Laube, Fest, Religion und Erinnerung, p. 393.
[59] 'Schützengraben-Ritter des Weltkriegs', Zeiten und Völker, 12 (1916), p. 152.
[60] GStAPK, I. HA Rep. 77 Tit. 1215 Nr. 3d Bd. 1 (M), folio 6, Johann Hermuth, Drawing, [c. 1915].
[61] K. K. Gewerbeförderungs-Amt (ed.), Soldatengräber und Kriegsdenkmale (Vienna, Anton Schroll, 1915), pp. 176–9.
[62] Deutscher Ehrenhain, p. 234.

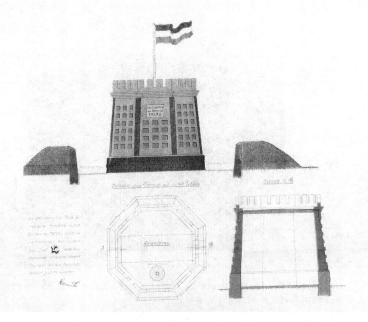

Figure 37. Moated tower by Johann Hermuth. Drawing, *c.* 1915.

their 'moated castle', so we, beset on all sides in the great world war, for years enjoyed the hopeful feeling of security behind the protective wall of our gallant warriors at the front.[63]

Ruins and restorations

By enduring battle, Germany's iron soldiers of the world war had en-sured, as remembrance activities reasserted, that the *Heimat* remained a 'mighty fortress'. In the past, however, the homeland had not always

[63] HStAS, M 746, Bü 64, Section Fellbach, *Dem Gedächtnis unserer Toten im Weltkrieg 1914–1918: Fellbach, am Reichstrauertag, den 28. Februar 1926* (Fellbach, G. Conradi, 1926), p. 6: 'wie jene Alten in wilden Kampfeszeiten, hart bedrängt, letztlich sich in den "Kirchhof" zurückgezogen haben, und wie sie da innerhalb des ringsum festgemauerten Vierecks und hinter dem Graben ihrer "Wasserburg" sich sicher fühlten, so genossen auch wir, die allseits Bedrängten des großen Weltkriegs, hinter dem Schutzwall unserer wackeren Kämpferfronten jahrelang das hoffnungsvolle Empfinden des Geborgenseins'. See also Müller-Loebnitz, *Ehrenbuch der Westfalen*, p. 2.

Figure 38. Moated tower by H. Senf and Paul Seiler. Main cemetery, Frankfurt am Main, 1928.

been fortunate enough to be spared from havoc and humiliation. Ruins of medieval buildings, castles in particular, survived as unavoidable and sometimes disturbing testimonies to the ravages of war on German soil. The remnants of the *Kaiserpfalz* of Gelnhausen, Hesse-Nassau, an imperial palace put up in the reign of Frederick I Barbarossa, 'call to mind that our heroes, by laying down their lives, saved our fatherland from the devastation caused here by the war-storms of bygone days'.[64] At the same time, the idyllic, ivy-covered ruin summoned up memories of the 'former greatness and splendour of the old German empire'.[65] Broken-down edifices like the Gelnhausen palace provided a paradoxical scenery for war commemorations reminiscent of both the beauty of romantic landscapes and the surrealistic anti-landscape of no man's land. Ruins in war remembrance were imaginative productions halfway between the paintings of Caspar David Friedrich and the rubble of the Second World War.

[64] BArch, R 43 I/713, folio 161v, 'Nationaldenkmal für die Gefallenen im Weltkriege', [c. 1926]: 'ins Gedächtnis rufen, daß unsere Helden Verwüstungen, wie sie hier Kriegssturm vergangener Zeiten anrichteten durch Hingabe ihres Lebens unserem Vaterlande ersparten'.
[65] Ibid.: 'einstiger Größe und Herrlichkeit des alten deutschen Reiches'.

Historic ruins at home

The Rhineland has a wealth of picturesque vestiges of medieval keeps and castles. Situated on the hills and river banks, they could, however, be perceived as sublime reminders of historic tragedies and French invasions, of the 'eternal "struggle for the Rhine"'.[66] Bodo Ebhardt, the restorer of the neo-medieval castle of Haut-Kœnigsbourg in Alsace, wrote in 1915 that the ruins along the River Rhine 'teach us what our fate would be if the hordes of our enemy descended on us again'. For Ebhardt, the visible legacy of military destruction did not merely raise frightening vistas, but represented a call to 'hatred, revenge, and battle to the bitter end'.[67] The orgy of destruction in the Great War motivated Ebhardt, who had already been notorious for his aggressive nationalism before 1914, to embrace rather than reject violence. Yet other agents of remembrance, bewildered by the seemingly uncontrolled, destructive energy unleashed by the war, considered the war experience as unrepresentable in traditional literary and artistic notation. A Protestant clergyman concluded, at the unveiling of a regimental war memorial in Bremen in 1924, that there was 'no way that language could describe how terrible it was where the atrocious machine of war hit town or village. We have been protected from this horror.'[68] Accordingly, the memorial makers did not even attempt to reproduce the hideousness and scale of the war. In a sense, the memorial chapel situated in the restored Tresekammer, Bremen's treasure-house, which prior to 1924 had merely been a shell of an early Gothic chapel, smoothed over the physical traces and scars of the war.[69]

After the war, Winston Churchill (himself a veteran of the Western Front) proposed that the British government should acquire from the

[66] BArch, R 43 I/713, folio 203v, Richard Klapheck, *Das Reichsehrenmal für unsere Gefallenen: Die Toteninsel im Rhein* (Düsseldorf, Staatliche Kunstakademie, 1926), p. 8: 'Burgruinen rahmen auf Bergeshöhen die Toteninseln ein. Sie alle können erzählen vom ewigen "Kampf um den Rhein".'
[67] As cited in Koshar, *Germany's Transient Pasts*, p. 87. Generally, see Koshar, *From Monuments to Traces*, ch. 2.
[68] StAB, 3-B.13. Nr. 92, folio 9, '75er Regiments-Appell', *Bremer Nachrichten*, 263, suppl., 21 September 1924: 'kein Mittel der Sprache, um zu schildern, wie furchtbar es war, wohin die grauenvolle Maschine des Krieges in Stadt und Dorf schlug. Vor diesem Entsetzlichen sind wir bewahrt geblieben.' On the notion of unprecedented and uncontrolled destruction, see Bernd Hüppauf, 'Räume der Destruktion und Konstruktion von Raum: Landschaft, Sehen, Raum und der Erste Weltkrieg', *Krieg und Literatur*, 3 (1991), p. 114.
[69] StAB, 3-B.13. Nr. 92, folio 8, Pastor Groscurth, 'Das Heldenmal in der Liebfrauenkirche', *Bremer Nachrichten*, 261, 19 September 1924.

Belgians the ruins of Ypres, including the thirteenth-century Cloth Hall and cathedral, and maintain them as war memorials. His effort was for nought. Unsurprisingly, the citizens of Ypres, who were returning to their war-wrecked city, could not warm to the idea.[70] More importantly, Churchill's proposal was out of touch with the commemorative mainstream in Britain too. Historic restorations rather than ruins dominated the British commemorative scene.

The restoration of the Five Sisters Window in York Minster was the most spectacular undertaking in this field. During the war, York had been the target of air raids by German Zeppelins. After a bomb had exploded in the proximity of the minster, the precious window of grisaille stained glass was removed for safe keeping. On closer inspection, it was established that both the glass and lead were in urgent need of repair.[71] Over the next decade, the Five Sisters Window underwent a careful restoration, using lead from the ruined Cistercian abbey of Rievaulx, North Yorkshire. In June 1925, the window was reinaugurated, now as a memorial to the women of the Empire who had died in the war. 'It is a true restoration: for what we now see is what our fathers saw 600 years ago', reported *The Times*.[72] According to the souvenir programme, it was a work of 'handing down to the future the greatest treasures of the art of mediaeval craftsman in coloured glass'.[73] Still, the *Manchester Guardian* expressed pessimism about the preservation of the national heritage. It was the prospect of future destruction that loomed large in its account:

For 600 years it has been a wonder of stained glass; now it has a second significance, a significance of profound historical importance, a significance definitely sinister and uneasy. It marks a new stepping-stone in social custom. It stands to attest, till perhaps itself by some casual bomb shall be sent to join the dust of the women it commemorates.[74]

Limited though it was, the bombing of York manifested the trend towards 'total war', revealing the enormous technical potential for destruction and blurring the boundaries between battle front and home

---

[70] Heffernan, 'For Ever England', p. 308; Longworth, *Unending Vigil*, pp. 86–7. See Beckles Willson, *Ypres: The Holy Ground of British Arms* (Bruges, C. Beyaert, 1920), pp. xii–xiii, 7–9.

[71] 'The Five Sisters: Women's Memorial to Women', *The Times*, 43986, 12 June 1925, pp. 19–20.

[72] 'Five Sisters Window: Unveiling by the Duchess of York', *The Times*, 43997, 25 June 1925, p. 17.

[73] York Minster Library and Archives, YM/LB 5.94 YOR, 'Souvenir and Form of Service for the Unveiling of The Five Sisters Window and the War Memorial', 1925, p. 23.

[74] 'Women and War: Empire Memorial at York', *Manchester Guardian*, 24599, 25 June 1925, p. 8.

Figure 39. Recumbent soldier in a ruined castle. Contemporary post-card depicting the effigy by Friedrich Bagdons. Hohensyburg castle, Dortmund, 1925.

front.[75] Nevertheless, in 1914–18 both the British and German heart-lands had been largely unaffected by the devastation of war. Ruins could, therefore, still be seen through rose-coloured spectacles. Negligible in Britain, ruins were of paramount importance to German commemor-ations (see figure 39). In the German popular mind, ruined castles maintained their association with heroism and beauty. At Kaiserswerth near Düsseldorf, Rhine Province, a war memorial was erected in 1922 adjacent to the fragments of the ancient *Kaiserpfalz*, originally built in the age of the Hohenstaufen dynasty.[76] The monument, a 'symbol of the faithfulness of the fallen', featured a steel helmet on a wedge-shaped plinth, designed by Bernhard Lohf.[77] (In 1936, a Hitler Youth memorial

---

[75] On the concept of 'total war', see Stig Förster, 'Das Zeitalter des totalen Kriegs, 1861–1945: Konzeptionelle Überlegungen für einen historischen Strukturvergleich', *Mittelweg 36*, 8,6 (1999), pp. 12–29; Roger Chickering, 'Total War: The Use and Abuse of a Concept', in Manfred F. Boemeke, Roger Chickering and Stig Förster (eds.), *Anticipating Total War: The German and American Experiences, 1871–1914* (Cambridge, Cambridge University Press, 1999), pp. 13–28.

[76] StdAD, XVI 1670, 'Das Rheinland und Westfalen: Kriegergedenkfeier', *Düsseldorfer Nachrichten*, 260, 23 May 1921.

[77] As cited in Hubert Delvos, *Geschichte der Düsseldorfer Denkmäler, Gedenktafeln und Brunnen* (Düsseldorf, L. Schwann, 1938), p. 181.

fountain, also a work by Lohf, was opened near the 'massive walls of the Barbarossa palace, witnesses to a time of German greatness'.[78]) Similarly, in 1926, the committee of Volmarstein, Westphalia, integrated the figure of a naked steel-helmeted warrior into the 'weathered walls, of Volmarstein's great past'. The 'keep of iron strength' dominated the commemorative ensemble, entitled *Schildwacht*, literally 'shield sentry'.[79]

The memorial makers of Kaiserswerth and Volmarstein fused the Romanticism of time-honoured vestiges with images of steely endurance. Frequently, however, the mining of eighteenth- or nineteenth-century motifs accommodated notions of natural beauty or historical edification. In the competition for the Reich memorial, much care was taken to emphasise the pictorial quality of landscapes with ruins. Two crumbling castles formed a dramatic backdrop to the proposed Reich memorial on a hill at Bensheim, Hesse.[80] One of its competitors, Aschersleben in the Prussian Province of Saxony, on the other hand, dwelt on the lure of history. Its mayor proposed to establish the national memorial at Mount Wolf, crowned by an eroded tower 'which in folk tradition is regarded as part of the castle of the great Ascanian'.[81] Albrecht I the Bear, forefather of the Ascanian dynasty, he elucidated, had colonised the Mark of Brandenburg and made Aschersleben its capital around 1150. Hence, Aschersleben could legitimately claim to be the 'starting point of the German empire'.[82]

The ruin of cultural treasures at the front

Historic ruins at home carried ambiguous messages; they could be understood as objects of delight as well as harbingers of doom. The latter image derived from representations of the uncanny landscapes of destruction at the front.[83] Total war and modern explosives exposed

---

[78] StdAD, XXIV 1178, folio 61, 'Ein HJ.-Brunnen in Kaiserswerth: Pimpf mit der Landsknechtstrummel als Brunnenfigur', *Rheinische Landeszeitung*, 26 November 1936: 'den wuchtigen Mauern der Barbarossa-Pfalz, Zeugen einer Zeit deutscher Größe'. See also Fuhrmeister, *Beton, Klinker, Granit*, pp. 226–8.
[79] As cited in Vogt, *Den Lebenden zur Mahnung*, p. 148.
[80] BArch, R 43 I/713, fos. 51–2, Vorsitzender des Verkehrsausschusses der Bergstraße to Reichskanzler, 10 June 1925.
[81] BArch, R 32/359, folio 63v, Oberbürgermeister Aschersleben to Reichskunstwart, 4 May 1926: 'der im Volksmunde als ein Teil der Burg des grossen Askaniers gesehen wird'.
[82] Ibid.: '1150 erwarb er die Mark Brandenburg und machte Aschersleben zum Ausgangspunkt für das Deutsche Reich.'
[83] On British war artists, see Sue Malvern, *Modern Art, Britain, and the Great War: Witnessing, Testimony and Remembrance* (New Haven and London, Yale University Press, 2004).

irreplaceable cultural treasures to new dangers. Buildings that had defied history and seemed indestructible went up in smoke. The ruins of Belgium, France and East Prussia mapped out a mental landscape of cultural destruction. Against this mental landscape, war memorials credited the German soldiers, the protectors of the *Heimat*, with containing the impending disaster.[84] However, in the British context, ruined landscapes bore witness to cultural atrocities rather than notions of destruction; in other words, they are concerned with soldiers' conduct in war (see chapter 4) rather than their experience of mass-industrialised warfare. Typically, stained-glass windows depicted St George in armour against a background of burning cathedrals, thus contrasting British righteousness with German ruthlessness.[85]

The Germans have committed an atrocious act which will turn the hands of every civilized nation in the world against them. They have utterly destroyed the peaceful and historic old city of Louvain, the Oxford of Belgium. The beautiful Hôtel de Ville – a wonderful example of pointed Gothic – the stately church of St. Pierre, the famous University, all are gone. Even the library of 70,000 volumes and priceless manuscripts was committed to the flames by the ruthless barbarians who have set forth to spread 'German culture' throughout the globe. Louvain, the most celebrated seat of learning in the Low Countries, is to-day 'nothing more than a heap of ashes'.[86]

News about the German outrages at Louvain, the 'Oxford of Belgium', as *The Times* put it, scandalised the international public. Panicked by misunderstood troop movements and friendly fire as well as rumours about irregular snipers or *francs-tireurs*, the occupiers had apparently aimed to give a demonstration of their military might by setting fire to the historic city in late August 1914. The torching of the university library, in particular, provoked an outcry from educated men all over the world, as the measure seemed to be an unforgivable assault on cultural memory *per se*.[87] In the aftermath of the war, under the

---

[84] Ziemann, *Front und Heimat*, p. 455. See also ibid., pp. 44, 378.

[85] See, for instance, IWM, Eph. Mem., K 74907–1, 'Westminster Abbey: Dedication of a Window in Memory of the Officers, Non-Commissioned Officers and Private Riflemen of the Queen's Westminster Rifles', 1923; Patricia Utechin, *The Trumpets Sounded: Commemoration of the War Dead in the Parish Churches of Oxfordshire* (Oxford, Robert Dugdale, 1996), p. 17.

[86] 'The March of the Huns', *The Times*, 40691, 29 August 1914, p. 9. In reality, almost 300,000 books, manuscripts and incunabula were destroyed.

[87] Wolfgang Schivelbusch, *Die Bibliothek von Löwen: Eine Episode aus der Zeit der Weltkriege* (Munich and Vienna, Carl Hanser, 1988), esp. pp. 19, 27, 26. See also Mark Derez, 'The Flames of Louvain: The War Experience of an Academic Community', in Hugh Cecil and Peter H. Liddle (eds.), *Facing Armageddon: The First World War Experienced* (London, Leo Cooper, 1996), pp. 617–29.

Versailles Treaty, German libraries were forced to hand over books, incunabula and manuscripts out of their own stock to the re-established library of Louvain. In addition, the Belgians received financial support from the international Louvain relief organisation. Its New York committee intimated their wish to see the ruins of the old library preserved as a monumental accusation of German barbarity (here, amidst the rubble, an honorary doctorate was conferred on President Woodrow Wilson in June 1919), a wish which the Belgians declined.[88]

German intellectuals were also somewhat taken aback by the events of Louvain. Many were, after all, in the vanguard of the German *Kultur* mission. In summer 1914, Theodor Wolff of the *Berliner Tageblatt* expressed regret at the 'tragedy of Louvain': 'We do not take those things lightly and do not wear the supercilious smile with which once the French Count Mélac departed from the rubble of Heidelberg Castle.'[89] German apologists repeatedly quoted the precedent of Heidelberg's medieval castle, razed by the troops of Louis XIV, the Sun King, at the end of the seventeenth century, in order to qualify the worldwide condemnation of the damage inflicted on Belgium and France. Even after 1918, the German side countered French plans for the conversion of the defaced cathedral of Rheims into an architectural necropolis and 'souvenir de la barbarie allemande' with images of the havoc wreaked on Heidelberg.[90] A comparison of wartime and post-war references to the fate of Heidelberg Castle attests to a degree of continuity in journalistic coverage of the Western Front between the Kaiserreich and the Weimar Republic.[91]

The treatment of Rheims Cathedral in the German media confirms this continuity. In September 1914, the cathedral was severely damaged by German artillery fire. The shelling breached the postulate of a shared, international cultural heritage, codified in the Hague Convention of 1907. Article 27 laid down that historic monuments not used by the

[88] Schivelbusch, *Bibliothek von Löwen*, pp. 57, 130–1.
[89] T[heodor] W[olff], 'Der Brand von Löwen', *Berliner Tageblatt*, 444, 2 September 1914, p. 1: 'Nein, wir nehmen diese Dinge nicht leicht und haben nicht das überlegene Lächeln, mit dem einst der französische Graf von Mélac von den Trümmern des Heidelberger Schlosses schied.' See also Koshar, *From Monuments to Traces*, p. 86.
[90] Klaus H. Kiefer, 'Die Beschießung der Kathedrale von Reims: Bilddokument und Legendenbildung – Eine Semiotik der Zerstörung', *Krieg und Literatur*, 3–4 (1997–8), p. 142.
[91] Generally, see Susanne Brandt, 'Bilder von der Zerstörung an der Westfront und die doppelte Verdrängung der Niederlage', in Gerhard Hirschfeld *et al.* (eds.), *Kriegserfahrungen: Studien zur Sozial- und Mentalitätsgeschichte des Ersten Weltkriegs* (Essen, Klartext, 1997), pp. 439–50. On the discourse surrounding the restoration of Heidelberg Castle around 1900, see Speitkamp, *Verwaltung der Geschichte*, pp. 97–102.

military were to be marked with appropriate symbols and spared by the attackers.[92] On 19 September 1914, however, the Germans determined that French artillery spotters were positioned on the roof of the cathedral and opened fire. The bombardment of Rheims Cathedral was to become another propaganda goldmine for the Entente powers, much to the annoyance of the German command. French propaganda re-invented Rheims as a 'moral cathedral' signifying the immorality of cultural damage and the moral superiority assumed by France.[93] Patriotic Germans were still smarting from the long-term effects of Allied propaganda in the 1920s. A journalist of the conservative *Berliner Lokal-Anzeiger* reported of his trip to the former battlefields:

We are still ten kilometres away from Rheims, and already there rises from the plain, soaring hugely over the landscape, the cathedral with her twin towers, clearly visible with the naked eye. We know what a convenient propaganda tool this very cathedral was during the war; and now, as I see the huge towers rising from such a distance, I am convinced that observers sat on the top, because there can never have been a better view over many miles around.[94]

Furthermore, the author accused the French of continuing to exploit the cathedral as a propaganda weapon and delaying the restoration work (which was not completed until 1938), because the wreckage turned out to be a profitable attraction for wealthy American and British battlefield tourists. In fact, after the Armistice, the ruined cathedals of north-eastern France soon became objects of pilgrimage for those curious to inspect the damage at first hand. At Rheims, tourists could even purchase souvenirs of war damage, such as jewellery made from pieces of shattered stained glass, and thus support the work of the Société des Amis de la Cathédrale de Reims.[95]

Relics of the ruin of Rheims Cathedral were brought to America and Britain during the war to document the destruction of a prime French

---

[92] Kiefer, 'Beschießung der Kathedrale von Reims', p. 121.

[93] Nicola Lambourne, '"Moral Cathedrals": War Damage and Franco-German Cultural Propaganda on the Western Front 1870–1938', Ph.D. dissertation, University of London, 1997.

[94] BArch, R 8034 II/7692, folio 63, Hans Heil, 'Fahrt zu den Gräbern: Drama und Satire von den französischen Schlachtfeldern', *Berliner Lokal-Anzeiger*, 196, 27 April 1926: 'Wir sind noch zehn Kilometer von Reims, und schon hebt sich aus der Ebene, gewaltig das Land überragend, die Kathedrale mit ihren beiden Türmen, mit bloßem Auge deutlich erkennbar. Wir wissen, was für ein willkommenes Propagandamittel gerade diese Kathedrale im Kriege gewesen ist, und jetzt, da ich die riesigen Türme aus solcher Entfernung ragen sehe, bin ich überzeugt, daß damals Beobachter oben gesessen haben, denn einen besseren Ueberblick auf viele Meilen in der Runde hat es nie gegeben.' See also Brandt, *Vom Kriegsschauplatz zum Gedächtnisraum*, pp. 29, 165.

[95] Lambourne, 'Moral Cathedrals', pp. 266–7.

lieu de mémoire. A shell-shattered pilaster from the cathedral was incorporated like a holy relic into the pedestal of a statue of Joan of Arc unveiled in New York in December 1915. The Maid of Orleans had taken the dauphin to Rheims to be crowned and 'anointed in that august cathedral at Rheims, which was never defaced by sacrilegious hands until the present day', the French ambassador told the American audience.[96] He made it plain that in France the injury to Rheims, the old city of coronations, was, in Jacques Le Goff's phrase, 'felt as a wound to memory itself'.[97] A fire-damaged bronze crucifix found in the cathedral ruin was taken to Almondbury, West Yorkshire, where it was made part of the parochial war memorial (together with the vicar's correspondence with the Archbishop of Rheims).[98] Significantly, the scars of war were removed from the crucifix in the process of its restoration at Almondbury; war-caused fragmentation gave way to commemorative wholeness. Similarly, a war memorial window by the Arts and Crafts designer Louis Davis in Harrow church, Middlesex, incorporated a restored fragment of glass from the shattered windows of Ypres Cathedral, sent to Britain by an officer who was later killed in action.[99]

Official German propaganda was at pains to refute the image of the diabolical German as the modern-day 'Hun' wiping out Europe's cultural patrimony. What is more, the German side endeavoured to create the impression that major damage to historic buildings had instead been done by Allied guns. The destruction of the cathedral of St Quentin at the Somme allegedly proved that the French themselves had no scruples about setting their own country ablaze. In 1917, the results of an official enquiry into the razing of St Quentin Cathedral were published. Unsurprisingly, the British and French were accused of shattering a masterpiece of the European Gothic comparable to the cathedrals of Cologne and Rheims: 'Deeply shaken we stand in front of the ruin of one of the most beautiful buildings in France. St Quentin has redeemed Rheims.'[100] The booklet was heavily illustrated with pictures showing

---

[96] 'Joan of Arc Statue Unveiled in Drive: Cannon Boom a Salute', *New York Times*, 21136, 7 December 1915, p. 13. On the commemoration of Joan of Arc, see Gerd Krumeich, *Jeanne d'Arc in der Geschichte: Historiographie – Politik – Kultur* (Sigmaringen, Jan Thorbecke, 1989).

[97] Jacques Le Goff, 'Reims, City of Coronation', in Pierre Nora (ed.), *Realms of Memory: The Construction of the French Past*, vol. III, *Symbols* (New York, Columbia University Press, 1998), p. 195.

[98] Boorman, *At the Going Down of the Sun*, p. 23.

[99] NIWM, 11135, Harrow, Mddx.

[100] *Die Zerstörung der Kathedrale von St. Quentin: Im amtlichen Auftrage zusammengestellt* (Berlin, Karl Curtius, 1917), p. 3; and ibid., p. 22: 'Tief erschüttert stehen wir vor der Ruine eines der schönsten Bauwerke Frankreichs. Reims ist durch St. Quentin abgelöst.' See Lambourne, 'Moral Cathedrals', pp. 140–3.

the scope and scale of the destruction. Photography proved a seemingly credible tool in sustaining German claims of innocence during the inter-war years. An illustrated volume of 1930, edited by a revisionist historian at the Reich archive, included four photographs of St Quentin. One caption reads: 'Eventually, through the year-long bombardment, the French also systematically destroyed their own works of art. The pillar of smoke, on the right in the picture, came from a French incendiary shell.'[101]

While the German side condemned the Entente for defiling the Euro-pean cultural heritage, it prided itself on doing everything in its power to restrict the damage. The report of 1917 pointed out that German soldiers had rescued movable works of art from the burning cathedral of St Quentin at the risk of their own lives.[102] The most spectacular measure was the removal from Colmar, Alsace, to Munich of Matthias Grünewald's Isenheim altar in 1917 under the pretext of restoration and safekeeping. The altarpiece, which had miraculously escaped destruction during the Reformation, was on show in the Munich Alte Pinakothek until September 1919 and proved an enormous success with the public. 'German loot', cried the British and French press in unison, whereas the German authorities presented themselves as the saviours of a masterpiece threatened by bombardment and decay.[103]

Cultured Germans did not merely safeguard historic monuments but also expedited the scientific task of classifying, cataloguing and inter-preting art-historical treasures. The government, pressurised by the preservationists' lobby, appointed a Reich commissioner in 1914–15 to co-ordinate monument conservation in the occupied territories of the west and east. Some twenty-five German experts and their support staffs assisted the new Reich commissioner, Paul Clemen, in assessing the damage, supervising the preservation work and conferring with military strategists.[104] Spurred on by genuine scholarly interest as well as a feeling of cultural superiority, particularly over the east, German

---

[101] *Der Weltkrieg im Bild: Originalaufnahmen des Kriegs-Bild- und Filmamtes aus der modernen Materialschlacht*, [ed.] George Soldan (Berlin and Oldenburg, National Archiv, 1930), p. 70: 'Durch den jahrelangen Beschuß vernichteten schließlich die Franzosen auch systematisch ihre Kunstwerke. Die Rauchentwicklung rechts im Bild stammt von einer französischen Brandgranate.' On photographs of destruction, see Krumeich, 'Kriegs-fotografie zwischen Erleben und Propaganda', pp. 125, 129, 131. See also Brandt, *Vom Kriegsschauplatz zum Gedächtnisraum*, pp. 36, 106, 120.

[102] *Die Zerstörung der Kathedrale von St. Quentin*, p. 7.

[103] Ann Stieglitz, 'The Reproduction of Agony: Toward a Reception-History of Grüne-wald's Isenheim Altar after the First World War', *Oxford Art Journal*, 12, 2 (1989), pp. 92–4; Winter, *Sites of Memory*, pp. 92, 163.

[104] Koshar, *Germany's Transient Pasts*, p. 81.

preservationists fancied themselves custodians of art history in the midst of a frenzy of destruction. Admittedly, they often produced valuable inventories. In occupied north-west Russia, for example, Ober Ost surveyed and classified castles, churches, cloisters and statues, as well as art collections, libraries and museums.[105]

However, Ober Ost's reports greatly exaggerated its achievements in monument preservation vis-à-vis the previous neglect, and played down the damage caused by German fire vis-à-vis Russian vandalism.[106] The German military (but also 'private' propagandists) obviously went through a learning curve; in the east, they aimed to win the propaganda battle by emulating the methods and language of the western Allies. 'Swarms of Asiatic and half-Asiatic barbarians' – namely Huns, Mongolians, Poles and Lithuanians – 'have for a thousand years repeatedly descended on "the West" and devastated the home of European culture', claimed the author of a book on the battle of Tannenberg published in 1915.[107] In the prevailing circumstances, the imagery made perfect sense. Russian advances in the early stages of the war had reduced great tracts of East Prussia to a shambles. With regard to the havoc created in East Prussia, the Bund Deutscher Heimatschutz promulgated the idea of future war memorials in the 'Eastern Marches' in the form of 'defensive fortifications [*Sperrfesten*] [. . .] that will for ever protect our *Heimat* from a renewal of the frightful destruction wreaked by our enemies'.[108]

In the past, the strongholds of the Teutonic Order had functioned as barriers against the threatening east. The Great War, however, had left its mark on the Teutonic bulwarks. In 1916, an initiative was formed with the support of the provincial governor to restore or indeed to 'heal' the damage inflicted on the late-fourteenth-century Neidenburg Castle, and to launch it as a national site of Tannenberg worship:

Five hundred years ago, she [Neidenburg Castle] saw the wild hordes of the Polish King Władysław Jagiełło and the Lithuanian Prince Witowd before her walls; at the time of the Great Elector [Frederick William], she repelled a Tartar

---

[105] Ibid., pp. 92–4; Liulevicius, *War Land*, pp. 129–31.

[106] Liulevicius, *War Land*, p. 129.

[107] Fischer, *Bei Tannenberg 1914 und 1410*, p. 4: 'asiatische und halbasiatische Barbarenschwärme haben seit einem Jahrtausend wiederholt den "Westen" heimgesucht und europäisches Kulturland verwüstet'. On the notion of eastern 'barbarism', see Aviel Roshwald and Richard Stites, 'Conclusion', in Aviel Roshwald and Richard Stites (eds.), *European Culture in the Great War: The Arts, Entertainment, and Propaganda, 1914–1918* (Cambridge, Cambridge University Press, 1999), pp. 351–2.

[108] Deutscher Bund Heimatschutz, *Kriegergräber und Denkmäler*, pp. 24–5: 'wehrhafte Sperrfesten [. . .], die unsere Heimat auf alle Zeit vor der Wiederholung feindlicher Verwüstungsgreuel schützten'. On the Bund Deutscher Heimatschutz, see Lurz, *Kriegerdenkmäler*, vol. III, pp. 167–70.

invasion; two years ago, she looked down again on a struggle between nations, and defied the Russian shells with her iron-solid walls. Let us turn it into a national Tannenberg memorial for the entire German *Volk*![109]

The plan, which came to nought, was absolutely in line with nineteenth-century remembrance culture. The crumbling castle of Marienburg, the former residence of the Grand Master of the Teutonic Order, had been reconstructed between 1817 and 1830. A second phase of rebuilding had begun under the Kaiser's patronage in 1882. In the Wilhelmine era, Marienburg Castle was widely regarded as an architectural assertion of fortified Germanness in the east, a notion which a romantic ruined castle could not have conveyed.[110] The war years interrupted the restoration work and gave the project a new significance. The idea emerged of mending the decaying towers of the Plauenbollwerk, 'Plauen bulwark' (an extension to Marienburg Castle erected under Heinrich von Plauen in the aftermath of the first battle of Tannenberg), in honour of famous generals of the world war. The reconstruction of the central tower as a Hindenburg shrine was at the core of the project.[111] In September 1927, shortly before the Reich President's eightieth birthday, the Reich Minister of the Interior granted the requested subsidy of 50,000 marks for the undertaking, which was nothing but a monumental celebration of German defiance in an age of destruction.[112] Hence, memorial makers in the east championed the imagery of 'restoration' instead of the preservation and celebration of ruins as they were.

Castles, rocks and armour connoted the spirit of endurance, while ruins implied that destruction was imminent. These medievalist motifs – including modernised medievalist motifs such as the steel helmet – proved instrumental in framing the mythical *Kriegserlebnis* or 'war experience' of the first mass-industrialised conflict in Europe. Neither 'traditionalist' nor 'modernist' in the conventional sense, medievalist

---

[109] BArch, R 8034 II/7690, folio 110, 'Tannenberg-Gedächtnishalle auf der Neidenburg', *Deutsche Tagezeitung*, 412, 13 August 1916: 'Vor fünf hundert Jahren sah sie die wilden Scharen des Polenkönigs Wladislav Jagiello und des Litauerfürsten Witowd vor ihren Mauern, zur Zeit des Großen Kurfürsten wehrte sie den Einfall der Tataren ab, vor zwei Jahren blickte sie wieder herab auf ein Völkerringen und bot mit ihren eisenfesten Mauern den russischen Granaten Trotz. Machen wir aus ihr ein Nationaldenkmal des ganzen deutschen Volkes für Tannenberg!' See also ibid., folio 106, 'Tannenberger Gedächtnis', *Deutsche Tageszeitung*, 326, 28 June 1916.

[110] Boockmann, *Marienburg*, p. 36.

[111] BArch, R 43 I/834, folio 62, Regierungspräsident Marienwerder to Reichskanzler, 7 July 1927.

[112] BArch, R 43 I/834, folio 164, Reichsminister des Innern to Staatssekretär in der Reichskanzlei, 30 September 1927.

imagery reveals striking ambiguities in negotiations of modernity under the impact of total war. Such representations helped to accommodate the violent modernity of the war in collective remembrance. They refute the common assumption that the consciousness of the modern hinged on a dominant sense of historical rupture expressed in iconoclastic language.[113]

Above all, the Western Front was paradigmatic for the formulation of the First World War experience. The *Materialschlacht* or battles of *matériel* in France and Flanders radically changed the meaning of the words 'destruction' and 'endurance'. A sense of devastation was all-pervasive during the period. Yet the imaginative productions of middle-class 're-actionary modernists' such as Ernst Jünger, who reduced modern war to an aesthetic phenomenon, a 'storm of steel' forging a superior man destined to rule, were not identical with the German mindset *per se*.[114] Nevertheless, German society was prepared to see battle through the soldier's eyes, to recognise the harsh conditions the combatants had endured in the nerve-racking gunfire. In Germany, the soldier's perspective won a public recognition unknown across the Channel. In Britain, with no 'militaristic' tradition, the soldiers' ordeal of battle, though acknowledged, could not and did not gain cult status. Conduct in war, rather than the experience of war, was at the heart of war remembrance in Britain. Broadly speaking, British agents of memory – who were predominantly civilians – cultivated the ideal of the gentlemanly, not the iron, knight, as I shall argue in the following chapter.

---

[113] See Bernhard Rieger and Martin Daunton, 'Introduction', in Martin Daunton and Bernhard Rieger (eds.), *Meanings of Modernity: Britain from the Late-Victorian Era to World War II* (Oxford and New York, Berg, 2001), pp. 1–21.

[114] On the aestheticisation of violence as the hallmark of German culture in the age of the First World War, see Eksteins, *Rites of Spring*. The term 'reactionary modernists' is borrowed from Herf, *Reactionary Modernism*.

4   Chivalry and cruelty: the soldiers' character and conduct

The Storm of Steel by Ernst Jünger, first published in German in 1921, is now one of the most celebrated accounts of the experience of the trench war. Prior to 1929, both the novel and its author were little known outside the Reichswehr, the veterans' camp and radical nationalist circles.[1] Jünger achieved overnight fame in the literary world when the distinguished publishing house of Chatto & Windus brought out the English-language edition of *Storm of Steel* in 1929. Within a year of publication, the translation of the so-called 'diary' not only went through five editions, but was also given more – and mostly favourable – reviews than the German original throughout the era of the Weimar Republic. British reviewers, however, demonstrated a conspicuous naivety about Jünger's reactionary agenda.[2] In 1930, one critic commented on one of Jünger's later works, *Copse 125*, that in the publisher's announcement 'we are told, the book "is an epic of action, endurance, and courage". I fail to see this. A greater part is concerned with reflections on the nobility of being noble and how noble it is to slaughter or be slaughtered for my country, right or wrong.'[3]

Is it possible that Jünger fooled his British readership? The literary historian Hans-Harald Müller holds that the foreword to the English edition of *Storm of Steel* was one factor in moulding British readings of Jünger's work.[4] In the foreword, Jünger shifts the emphasis from the German 'war experience' to British conduct in war:

Time only strengthens my conviction that it was a good and strenuous life, and that the war, for all its destructiveness, was an incomparable schooling of the

[1] Hans-Harald Müller, '"Herr Jünger Thinks War a Lovely Business" (On the Reception of Ernst Jünger's *In Stahlgewittern* in Germany and Britain before 1933)', in Franz Karl Stanzel and Martin Löschnigg (eds.), *Intimate Enemies: English and German Literary Reactions to the Great War 1914–1918* (Heidelberg, C. Winter, 1993), p. 328.
[2] Ibid.
[3] 'Copse 125', *Life and Letters*, 5 (1930), p. 142. See Müller, 'Herr Jünger', p. 334.
[4] Ibid., p. 331.

heart. The front-line soldier whose foot came down on the earth so grimly and harshly may claim this at least, that it came down cleanly. Warlike achievements are enhanced by the inherent worth of the enemy. Of all the troops who were opposed to the Germans on the great battlefields the English were not only the most formidable but the manliest and most chivalrous.[5]

Jünger reiterated a British popular sentiment. Chivalry dominated British imaginings of the Great War. It was a commemorative trope which tended to obscure the harshness of war captured in Jünger's writings. Britons showed little understanding of the kind of warfare the First World War epitomised, warfare which, according to the *Daily Chronicle*, 'requires deathless endurance, but no chivalry'.[6] The ghastliness of the war, however, did not diminish the glory of the warrior. 'War is not glorious [. . .] but oftentimes in war men are', public commemorations reasserted.[7] Moreover, those men were 'not only glorious, but a glorious part of a long and a great line. Chivalry, knighthood, heroism, self-sacrifice from age to age are knit together here', remarked a visitor to British war cemeteries.[8] Soldiers were deemed glorious when they adhered to the principles of chivalry. The centrality of chivalry in war remembrance points to the profound force of civil society (that field of cultural and social life that spans the space between the individual and the state) in Britain. Memory work was by and large in the hands of middle-aged civilians who, in contrast to their German counterparts, lacked first-hand army experience (since conscription had not been introduced until January 1916) as well as a militaristic socialisation in peacetime.[9] Consequently, agents of remembrance failed to translate the experience of combat into a public discourse, for they had little specific to say about the 'war experience' analysed in the previous

---

[5] Ernst Jünger, *The Storm of Steel: From the Diary of a German Storm-Troop Officer on the Western Front*, intro. R. H. Mottram (London, Chatto & Windus, 1929), pp. xii–xiii. The English edition is based on the fifth edition (second revised version) of *In Stahlgewittern* (1924).

[6] Hall Caine, 'The Coming of Peace', *Daily Chronicle*, 17304, 3 August 1917, p. 2. See Reimann, *Krieg der Sprachen*, p. 46.

[7] Stewartry Museum, Acc. 7216, vol. 3, pp. 11–12, 'Kirkcudbright Parish Church: War Memorial Unveiled', unspecified newspaper cutting, 16 January 1921.

[8] William Pulteney and Beatrix Brice, *The Immortal Salient: An Historical Record and Complete Guide for Pilgrims to Ypres* (London, John Murray, 4th edn 1926), p. 54; Beatrix Brice, 'If You Seek a Monument', *The Times*, 42505, 2 September 1920, p. 13.

[9] On militarism (or the absence thereof) in Britain before 1914, see Jay Winter, 'Representations of War', pp. 206–7; DeGroot, *Blighty*, pp. 14–16; Ferguson, *Pity of War*, ch. 1. For a contrary opinion, see Anne Summers, 'Militarism in Britain before the Great War', *History Workshop*, 2 (1976), pp. 104–24; Olive Anderson, 'The Growth of Christian Militarism in Mid-Victorian Britain', *English Historical Review*, 86 (1971), pp. 46–72; Paris, *Warrior Nation*, esp. chs. 4–5.

chapter. Instead, they exalted the soldiers' chivalry, a code of conduct not specific to the First World War, but firmly anchored in British public life prior to 1914.

The first section of this chapter traces primarily the origins and the ramifications of the concept of chivalry in Britain. By comparison, the German discourse of chivalry was unsophisticated and underdeveloped. Nonetheless, conduct in war proved a sensitive issue for Germans also. After all, the man of war was a death-giver on behalf of society as a whole. Stories about German atrocities in 1914 hit a raw nerve at home. Commemorations not only refuted Allied allegations but also launched the counter-image of the *Unritterlichkeit*, 'un-chivalry', of the enemy – an image which indirectly reaffirmed the nobility of the German soldier. The latter part of the first section centres the discussion on representations of *Unritterlichkeit* or atrocities. Two further sections explore aspects of the discourse of chivalry which deserve treatment in greater detail: first, the identification of soldiers with knightly sportsmen, and secondly, the elevation of flyers to knights of the sky.

Knights and butchers

The reinvention of chivalry was by no means a product of the First World War. Modernised chivalry had entered the arena of British high culture by the beginning of the nineteenth century.[10] The concept operated on two interrelated levels. On the one hand, chivalry manifested itself as an aesthetic phenomenon among the governing classes. The Eglinton Tournament, fancy-dress balls with Queen Victoria and Prince Albert, Sir Walter Scott's novels and Pre-Raphaelite paintings seemed to offer aesthetic redemption to the perceived ugliness of the modern world. On the other hand, romantic images of chivalry were transformed into a normative force. Medieval knighthood constituted a resource for people who wanted to ennoble and improve the existing world. The concept of the gentleman came into being in part as an adoption of the medieval idea of chivalry designed for modern everyday life.[11] The gentlemanly paradigm was in essence a code of behaviour which prescribed a set of virtues such as fairness, kindness and loyalty. The ability to conform to these standards was seen as a function of

[10] Mark Girouard, *The Return to Camelot: Chivalry and the English Gentleman* (New Haven and London, Yale University Press, 1981). On the inter-war period, see Marcus Collins, 'The Fall of the English Gentleman: The National Character in Decline, c. 1918–1970', *Historical Research*, 75 (2002), pp. 90–9.
[11] Girouard, *Return to Camelot*, esp. pp. 260–74.

character.[12] Character, in turn, demanded conquering one's weaker self. Modern knights were engaged in a permanent struggle; 'life was a battlefield on which a gentleman had to fight impure thoughts in himself, injustice or ignorance in others', writes Mark Girouard.[13] The language of fighting permeated the gentlemanly community; it brought about the moral rearmament of civil society. Cultural historians have therefore suggested that the knights of Edwardian Britain were mentally equipped for combat when war broke out in 1914.[14]

The case of the monument to the Black Prince in Leeds highlights the continuities between representations of chivalry before and after 1914–18. In 1903, the statue of the Black Prince, imposing and magnificent, sitting on horseback, in full armour, was unveiled in City Square. Edward, Prince of Wales, known as the Black Prince, had been chosen due to the absence of a heroic figure with local associations. At any rate, the local worthies intended to teach 'a population devoted very much to sordid occupations' a lesson, not in history, but in practical philosophy. In the Black Prince they recognised a man 'who was universally considered as the best type of the Age of Chivalry, and whose character was adorned by so manly and unselfish virtues which in all times go to make the true gentleman'.[15] They got the message across. In the 1920s, there was discussion of whether the monument of the Black Prince should be incorporated into the city's war memorial. 'We shall see', one citizen wrote, 'the Chivalry of "Tommy Atkins" in the 20th century associated with that of the Middle Ages [. . .] showing that English patriotism and self-sacrifice have not lapsed with the centuries.'[16] In the event, the Black Prince was removed from City Square in order to make room for the new war memorial: an equally chivalric figure of St George slaying the dragon, sculptured by H. C. Fehr (see figure 40).

Victorian medievalism had furnished a repertoire of cultural forms and idioms that could be drawn on in the inter-war years. Apart from soldier saints such as St George, Arthurian knights were the common currency among artists before and after the war. In war memorials,

[12] On 'character', see Stefan Collini, *Public Moralists: Political Thought and Intellectual Life in Britain 1850–1930* (Oxford, Clarendon, 1991), ch. 3.

[13] Girouard, *Return to Camelot*, p. 281.

[14] Ibid.; Michael C. C. Adams, *The Great Adventure: Male Desire and the Coming of World War I* (Bloomington and Indianapolis, Indiana University Press, 1990), ch. 5. See also Allen J. Frantzen, *Bloody Good: Chivalry, Sacrifice, and the Great War* (Chicago and London, University of Chicago Press, 2004).

[15] 'Leeds City Square: The Decorative Scheme Complete', *Yorkshire Post*, 17533, 3 September 1903, p. 8.

[16] LCL, LQ 940.465 L 517, 'Leeds Memorials', *Yorkshire Post*, 2 December 1920.

Figure 40. St George by H. C. Fehr. Leeds, 1922.

Christian and Arthurian iconography tended to converge, frequently to such an extent that they became indistinguishable. Alfred Turner, for one, designed two identical figures clad in armour holding out a sword combined with a crucifix; at Kingsthorpe, Northamptonshire, the knight was identified as St George, whereas his courterpart at Victoria College, Jersey, was meant to represent Sir Galahad (see figure 41).[17]

These were not Turner's first medievalist sculptures. In 1912, he had received a commission to design an effigy of Owen Glendower as part of a series of statues of great Welshmen (among them King Arthur) for Cardiff's town hall. Due to the outbreak of war, the ceremonial unveiling did not take place until October 1916. Lloyd George – probably the greatest British orator of the age – dwelt in his opening address on the Welsh code of honour originally inculcated by King Arthur: 'a new code of honour, that restrained, ennobled, exalted, engentled the brute forces of Europe for centuries. That is the civilisation of Wales.'[18] Lloyd George's speech reflects the reawakened interest in the legend of King Arthur and his knights in Wales. During the nineteenth century, Anglo-Saxon nationalists had appropriated the Arthurian mythology, thus turning a British into an English national epic. In the decade before the Great War, Welsh authors began to lay claim to the legacy of Camelot by emphasising its Celtic origins.[19] However, their endeavours had practically no impact on the commemorative practices. If anything, Arthurian heroes were underrepresented in Welsh war memorials. (Interestingly, the same applies to commemorations in the West Country, and Cornwall in particular, the quintessential Arthurian *lieux de mémoire* in the nineteenth century.)[20] A study of war remembrance in Wales has refuted the idea that commemorations were used to promote an exclusively Celtic identity. On the contrary, commemorative projects reveal the existence of multiple loyalties, loyalties to the locality, Wales, Britain and the Empire.[21] Even representations of the English patron

---

[17] 'Kingsthorpe War Memorial: Graceful Cenotaph Unveiled by the Mayor', *Northampton Independent*, 818, 14 May 1921, p. 12; 'Dedication of the War Memorial', *Victorian*, 11 (1924), pp. 273–7.

[18] David Lloyd George, 'The Great Men of Wales', in *The Great Crusade*, p. 29. On Turner's sculptures, see *Alfred and Winifred Turner*, pp. 18–19.

[19] Barczewski, *Myth and National Identity*, pp. 160, 236. On early twentieth-century debates about the historicity of Arthur, see N. J. Higham, *King Arthur: Myth-Making and History* (London and New York, Routledge, 2002), ch. 1.

[20] NIWM, 33593, Paul, Cornwall, which features Sir Galahad, is an exception. See Barczewski, *Myth and National Identity*, p. 202, on the evolution of the Arthurian legend in the nineteenth century.

[21] Gaffney, *Aftermath*, pp. 161–9. On the pre-war period, see Jones, *Last Great Quest*, pp. 206–9, 226.

Figure 41. Sir Galahad by Alfred Turner. Victoria College, St Helier, Jersey, 1924.

saint, St George, triumphing over the dragon were unproblematic, although the Welsh dragon, which had evolved into a quasi-official symbol during the war, was depicted in war memorials too.[22]

It is important to recognise that alongside rehearsals of Victorian sentiments, one finds disturbing or subversive imaginings. Exchanging the metaphorical battlefield for the real one meant a shattering blow to some gentlemen's belief in the pre-war order in general and chivalry in particular. 'The chivalrous temper had had a set-back', wrote the liberal journalist C. E. Montague; 'it was no longer the mode; the latest wear was a fine robust shabbiness'.[23] 'Big words' like chivalry seemed not merely inadequate but obscene after the futile slaughter on the Western Front. Notably, the war poets posed, in form of irony and anger, a challenge – however incomplete – to traditional representations of war.[24] Seemingly unimpressed by this, the managers of public war remembrance fell back on just the sort of high diction that appalled the war poets. Ambivalence and multivocality characterise, as Jay Winter has observed, the cultural imprint of the Great War.[25] Today, the overblown chivalric rhetoric of the 1920s seems unwittingly ironic. Take the memorial to a veteran called 'Warrior' in Southampton, Hampshire. The inscription praises 'HIS FAMOUS WAR RECORD' (he had served on the Western Front throughout the war and was wounded by shrapnel once), devotion to 'DUTY' and 'NOBLE CHARACTER'. Having survived the war, 'Warrior', a white gelding, passed away in 1935 at the age of twenty-six years.[26]

Chivalric diction

An emphasis on character is the salient mark of the language of chivalry. It is the knightly or gentlemanly character that sets the modern knight apart from ordinary mankind. The system of high diction in war remembrance which defined the chivalric character can be divided broadly into five categories: courage, duty, honour, fairness and faith. All five

[22] NIWM, 7173, Johnstown, Clwyd; NIWM, 6962, Saundersfoot, Pembs.; and NIWM, 6730, Aberdare, Glam., represent St George. For images of the Welsh dragon, see NIWM, 6812, Haverfordwest, Pembs.; and NIWM, 6850, Rhayader, Powys. See also Prys Morgan, 'From a Death to a View: The Hunt for the Welsh Past in the Romantic Period', in Eric Hobsbawm and Terence Ranger (eds.), The Invention of Tradition (Cambridge, Cambridge University Press, 1983), p. 90; Gaffney, Aftermath, pp. 161–4.
[23] C[harles] E. Montague, Disenchantment (London, Chatto & Windus, 1922), p. 148.
[24] Fussell, Great War; Hynes, War Imagined. On the ambiguities of war poetry, see Winter, Sites of Memory, ch. 8.
[25] Winter, 'Representations of the War', p. 212.
[26] NIWM, 21626, Southampton, Hants.

elements do not necessarily occur together in any given memorial project. For example, at Redgrave, East Suffolk, stress was laid on 'chivalry, courage, faith'.[27] In aggregate, however, the five constituents stand out.

Convention dictated that knights were courageous, brave, gallant or valiant – the four most popular adjectives in inscription lines and unveiling speeches. Fallen soldiers were remembered collectively as those 'WHOSE DAUNTLESS COURAGE / WAS THE LIVING BREATH / OF FREEDOM AND OF CHIVALRY / AND TRUTH',[28] or individually as 'A man of courage, unshakable / and chivalrous as strong'.[29] Codes of courageous behaviour made explicit a specific pattern of relations between the sexes. The ideal of the brave knight was premised on a strong sense of the female 'other'. The polarisation of gender was much in evidence in commemorative speeches and occasionally manifested itself in the iconography of war monuments. The Leeds war memorial, dedicated in October 1922, features ideal bronze figures of peace and war (see figure 40). 'That of Peace is a beautiful draped female figure, holding aloft a palm branch while on the opposite side, a figure of St. George slaying the Dragon typifies War, and the everlasting struggle of good against evil.'[30] Later, the designer, H. C. Fehr, replaced the palm branch by a dove, thus underlining the identity of the figure. An almost identical memorial, sculptured by the same artist, was unveiled at Colchester in the same year. Again, the design amounted to a massive reaffirmation of gender stereotypes. St George as 'symbolical of the chivalry and the manhood of England' contrasted with the figure of peace (with a dove perched on one of her fingers) representing 'the Womanhood of England'.[31] Interestingly, Fehr configured the contrast between manhood and womanhood as one between medievalism and classicism. The female embodiment of peace was classicised in her costume, while St George as the male embodiment of war and chivalry was clad in medieval armour.[32]

---

[27] SROI, FB 132, E 3/3, Faculty for memorial to Captain the Hon. Lyon Playfair, Redgrave, 21 February 1916.

[28] NIWM, 6777, Mountain Ash, Glam. See also Utechin, *Trumpets Sounded*, p. 40.

[29] NIWM, 18007, Harrow, Mddx.

[30] WYASL, LC/TC/R 17, T. W. Harding, Press statement, 26 January 1921; ibid., LC/TC/R 26, 'City of Leeds: Unveiling of the War Memorial', 1922, p. 2.

[31] EROC, Acc. C 3, vol. 17, p. 358, 'The Colchester War Memorial', *Essex County Telegraph*, 26 May 1923; Hunt, *Colchester Memorial Souvenir*, p. 25.

[32] On gendered commemorative forms, see Susan R. Grayzel, *Women's Identities at War: Gender, Motherhood, and Politics in Britain and France during the First World War* (Chapel Hill and London, University of Northern Carolina Press, 1999), ch. 7; Ana Carden-Coyne, 'Gendering Death and Renewal: Classical Monuments of the First World War', *Humanities Research*, 10,2 (2003), pp. 40–50.

Memorial makers indulged in masculine heroics. Nevertheless, Paul Fussell's argument that chivalry connoted total bravery, an idea which could not admit of human weakness, does not withstand scrutiny.[33] In contrast to representations of iron warriors in Germany discussed in chapter 3, visual representations of British knights were in many cases not stridently heroic. The figure of St George at Leeds, although victorious, has a pensive look on his face. His opposite number at Colchester, also sculptured by H. C. Fehr, bows his head as a sign of mourning.[34] Similar to depictions of the British Tommy, knights represented a nation 'drawn into war by necessity, not design'.[35] Even official propagandists did not necessarily uphold total bravery. In a speech to an American audience on St George's Day 1918, John Masefield embraced a model of chivalry which allowed for the human factor. He suggested that England's patron saint 'went out, I think, as the battalions of our men went out, a little trembling and a little sick and not knowing much about it, except that it had to be done, and then stood up to the dragon in the mud of that far land, and waited for him to come on'.[36] Representations of the British as a martial race or 'warrior nation' flourished at the margins of inter-war culture, especially in boys' magazines, but were not part of the imagery of public commemoration. The British knight of the Great War was remembered as a man and civilian in uniform who had showed great courage by simply doing his bit.

The concept of courage was intrinsically tied up with the notion of dutiful service to the community. A private from Chatteris, Cambridgeshire, was posthumously awarded the Victoria Cross 'for most conspicuous bravery and devotion to duty'.[37] He had been killed in action in France in 1917 after rescuing wounded comrades. Accordingly, his memorial window in Chatteris parish church features a knight in gleaming armour. Knights were supposed to have a rigid sense of duty and to be ready to serve. 'The word knight [. . .] means "servant"', emphasised a wartime agitator.[38] Selfless service entailed willingness to

[33] Fussell, 'Fate of Chivalry', p. 222.
[34] EROC, Acc. C 4, Minutes of Colchester Borough War Memorial Committees and Sub-Committees, 1919–25.
[35] J[ay] M. Winter, 'British National Identity and the First World War', in S[imon] J. D. Green and R. C. Whiting (eds.), *The Boundaries of the State in Modern Britain* (Cambridge, Cambridge University Press, 1996), pp. 269–70. See also Borg, *War Memorials*, p. 50.
[36] John Masefield, *St. George and the Dragon* (London, William Heinemann, 1919), pp. 42–3.
[37] CUL, EDR, D 3/4c, pp. 21–2, and D 3/5, Faculty for window for G. W. Clare, Chatteris, 4 May 1918. See also NIWM, 18908, Lanhydrock, Cornwall.
[38] Edward S. Woods, *Knights in Armour* (London, Robert Scott, 1916), p. 16.

die, that is to make the 'supreme sacrifice': 'Tranquil you lie, your
knightly virtue proved', reads the famous line in 'O Valiant Hearts'
('The Supreme Sacrifice').[39] John Arkwright's wartime hymn set the
tone of commemorations throughout the British Isles. It was obligatory
to sing the hymn at remembrance services. In addition, the text was
inscribed on many war memorials.[40] The dutiful aspect of service had
been accentuated by wartime propaganda prior to the passing of the
Military Service Act in January 1916, for in Britain a mass army had to
be raised by consent. As Britain's war effort relied initially on voluntary
recruitment, early propaganda appealed to men's chivalrous feelings.
Service to the nation became the crucial test of chivalry and manhood.
A well-known poster issued by the Parliamentary Recruiting Committee
in 1915 proclaiming 'BRITAIN NEEDS / YOU AT ONCE' depicted St George in
full armour fighting the beast.[41]

Britain's deepening manpower crisis in the second year of the war
coincided with the execution of Edith Cavell, a British nurse in German-
occupied Belgium shot in October 1915 for helping Allied soldiers cross
enemy lines. Cavell's death became not only one of the most powerful
symbols of the German violation of womanhood, but also a symbol of
British bravery. To contemporary observers, Cavell's courage seemed to
contrast sharply with those male 'slackers' unwilling to sign up voluntar-
ily for military service. Female self-sacrifice posed a challenge to notions
of male chivalry. One Anglican vicar pronounced that 'If ever a challenge
rang out to the chivalry of our young men [. . .] it is surely to be heard
in the dastardly execution of an Englishwoman at the hands of an
enemy [. . .]. What will be the answer of those "nearly two million
unmarried men who could enlist without disaster to the munitions
supply [. . .]"? If chivalry and manhood are not extinct in them they will
make their answer as one man.'[42]

The language of volunteering of 1914–15 lived on in the rhetoric of
war remembrance in spite of conscription. Failure to answer the call of
duty courageously resulted in dishonour. A Welsh-language epitaph

---

[39] John S. Arkwright, 'The Supreme Sacrifice', in John S. Arkwright, *The Supreme Sacrifice and Other Poems in Time of War* (London, Skeffington, 2nd edn 1919), pp. 17–18.

[40] IWM, Eph. Mem., K 3820, 'Borough of Talbot: War Memorial in Remembrance of Those of This Borough Who Fell in the Great War', 27 June 1925, may serve as an example.

[41] IWM, PST 4902, PRC 108, 'Britain Needs You', [*c.* 1915].

[42] Jooelyn Henry Speck, 'The Execution of Miss Cavell' [letter to the editor], *The Times*, 40989, 19 October 1915, p. 9. See Nicoletta F. Gullace, *'The Blood of Our Sons': Men, Women, and the Renegotiation of British Citizenship during the Great War* (New York and Basingstoke, Palgrave, 2002), pp. 99–101.

dedicated to a 'true and very gallant Welsh gentleman' stated that it was
'A thousand times better to die as a brave boy than to live as a cowardly
boy'.[43] The highest form of honour at which a soldier knight could
aim was a 'death of honour'.[44] Honour was the knight's reward for
sacrificial death in Britain's great crusade. At the same time, commitment to honour imposed a moral obligation on the soldier. He was not
to hate his enemy, but was bound, by the brotherhood of arms, to
respect him even while he did his best to kill him. It was the absence of
personal hatred that transformed the killing enterprise into a chivalrous
blood-letting:

During one of the very few months of open warfare a cavalry private of ours
brought in a captive, a gorgeous specimen of the terrific Prussian Uhlan of
tradition. 'But why didn't you put your sword through him?', an officer asked,
who belonged to the school of Froissart less obviously than the private. 'Well,
sir', the captor replied, 'the gentleman wasn't looking'.[45]

It is noteworthy that this quotation is taken from *Disenchantment* by
C. E. Montague, first published in 1922. The author is, as maintained
by Samuel Hynes, a prime authority for the turn of mind produced by
the war.[46] Yet the title of the book is misleading and Montague's attitude
to the war more nuanced than literary critics have admitted.[47] Some
passages evince his bitterness and disillusionment, others convey his
belief in the survival of personal morality. The common man is portrayed
as a hero, the commander as a villain. Characteristically, the paragraph
cited above was reprinted in a volume containing uplifting prose and
poetry for private remembrance on Armistice Day, thus converting an
'anti-monument' (if it was one at all) into an affirmation of Victorian
notions of chivalry and decency. Public commemorations, too, assured
the bereaved that the war dead were not bloodthirsty killers. 'Not only

---

[43] NIWM, 6977, Aberystwyth, Cardigan.
[44] NIWM, 3465, Wisbech, Cambs.
[45] C[harles] E. Montague, 'Christmas 1914', in Thomas Moult (ed.), *Cenotaph: A Book of Remembrance in Poetry and Prose for November the Eleventh* (London, Jonathan Cape, 1923), p. 102; Montague, *Disenchantment*, p. 140. On chivalry and military killing, see Bourke, *Intimate History*, pp. 67, 169–70.
[46] Hynes, *War Imagined*, pp. 307–10. For a similar argument, see Peter Buitenhuis, *The Great War of Words: Literature as Propaganda 1914–18 and After* (London, B. T. Batsford, 1989), pp. 149–51. On the construction of disillusionment in post-war writings, see Janet S. K. Watson, *Fighting Different Wars: Experience, Memory, and the First World War in Britain* (Cambridge, Cambridge University Press, 2004).
[47] See Keith Grieves, 'C. E. Montague and the Making of *Disenchantment*, 1914–1921', *War in History*, 4 (1997), esp. pp. 44–5, for a revisionist account of Montague's work.

were they gallant in action, they were chivalrous to their enemies.'[48]
Gentility rather than aggression marked the knight. Fairness towards
the opponent was axiomatic in the chivalric code, a code which essentially described a person in his relation to others. Scrupulously fair
conduct involved recognised formalities like straightforward attack,
and courtesies like kindness towards prisoners of war.

The chivalrous bearing of medieval warriors in battle testified to the
fact 'that you need not cease to be a Christian or a gentleman because
you have to fight', as pointed out by Arthur Winnington-Ingram in
1917.[49] Chivalry and Christianity went hand in hand; violence and piety
converged. The Black Prince, the Bishop of London pointed out, had
treated the captured King of France with the utmost courtesy. The
unwritten laws of chivalry allegedly resonated with Christian dogma;
chivalrous conduct meant the translation of sound religion into action.
Church propagandists even pictured heaven itself as a breeding-ground
for chivalry. Fanatical preachers did not shy away from calling Jesus 'the
one perfect chivalrous Gentleman that the world has ever seen', or
'the most perfect and knightly character in the whole history of chivalry'.[50] Canon Scott Holland, the Oxford theologian, conceived
the Sermon on the Mount as 'the book of Christian Knighthood' – the
Gospel revisited.[51]

Some outspokenly belligerent churchmen gave their blessing to the
perpetuation of these images on the local level. A memorial plaque
mounted by members of a soldiers' home in Avonmouth, Gloucester-
shire, honoured those who by their sacrifice had 'upheld the cause of
justice and true Christian chivalry'.[52] In memorial windows and figurative monuments the iconography could establish a link between chivalry
and faith.[53] The connection is especially striking where knights are
depicted holding their swords aloft but with the point downwards. In
an upturned position, the sword, the prime symbol of chivalry, becomes

---

[48] 'Pembrokeshire's War Memorial: Unveiling by Milford V. C.', *Pembrokeshire Telegraph*,
3575, 7 September 1921, p. 5.
[49] Arthur F. Winnington-Ingram, *The Potter and the Clay* (London, Wells Gardner and
Darton, 1917), p. 62.
[50] Woods, *Knights in Armour*, p. 25; Marrin, *Last Crusade*, p. 153. See also Shannon Ty
Bontrager, 'The Imagined Crusade: The Church of England and the Mythology of
Nationalism and Christianity during the Great War', *Church History*, 71 (2002), pp.
780–93.
[51] As cited in Wilkinson, *Church of England*, p. 231.
[52] NIWM, 7363, Avonmouth, Glos.
[53] See, for instance, J. Gurr Reed, *Sir Galahad's Quest: Addresses on the War Memorial
Window, Richmond Hill Congregational Church, Bournemouth* (London, Congregational
Union of England & Wales, [1925]).

a cross, as in the case of the Pearl Assurance war memorial by Sir George Frampton (see figure 42). At the unveiling ceremony in London in July 1921, the chairman of the company commented on the memorial design that it

is crowned by a figure of a chivalrous Knight, holding a shield on which is engraved the Cross of Christianity – the emblem of sacrifice. In the Right hand aloft is the sword of glorious victory: at the feet lies a dead monster – the embodiment of all that is brutal, treacherous and unholy – slain and obliterated from our life, we fervently hope, for all time by those other 435 valiant and chivalrous knights whose names are cut in everlasting granite, which will be a perpetual reminder to posterity and ourselves of our great indebtedness to them.[54]

Chivalry provided a language for commending soldiers across socio-economic boundaries. This was an essentially classless rhetoric about national virtues. Evocations of chivalry elevated the common soldier and thus diminished the gulf of understanding between classes. In the wake of the First World War, every one of the fallen could be regarded a courageous, dutiful, honourable, fair and holy knight. The class dichotomy, typical of the medieval revival in the previous period, dissolved after 1914–18. To label this development 'chivalric egalitarianism' or 'feudalisation of war remembrance' is to miss the main point. Crucial to an understanding of chivalric diction in war remembrance is the fact that the war dead were not only victims but also executioners.[55] Languages of chivalry reconfigured the act of killing as a bloody yet noble deed, a deed which followed a code of conduct which was deeply entrenched in the conventions of civil society. What is more, the foregrounding of chivalry as a characteristic of the Tommy in commemorative discourse was paralleled by political debates that pictured the use of violence as uniquely 'un-British' (or 'un-English'). In the wake of the Great War – and escalating violence in Ireland – the 'national character' was being construed by politicians and political commentators as peculiarly peaceable. Acts of violence in Ireland and the Empire seemed a negation of an imagined British way. Plagued by specific post-war fears about the consequences of wartime 'brutalisation', contemporaries embraced a reassuring view of themselves, namely that they were a non-violent and chivalrous nation.[56]

---

[54] 'Pearl War Memorial', *Insurance Gem*, 139, August 1921, p. 7.
[55] Winter, 'Representations of War', p. 212.
[56] Jon Lawrence, 'Forging a Peaceable Kingdom: War, Violence, and Fear of Brutalization in Post-First World War Britain', *Journal of Modern History*, 75 (2003), pp. 557–89; Gregory, 'Peculiarities of the British?', esp. p. 57.

Figure 42. St George by Sir George Frampton. Pearl Assurance, Peter-borough (formerly London), 1921.

Gentlemanliness and chivalry had long been the identifying code of many in public service and political life. After 1914, chivalric diction translated the slaughter of the Great War into a narrative which was intelligible to Britons, a predominantly unmilitary nation which was not prepared to elevate military virtues to social norms of national life. By contrast, scholars have noted that Germans had been socialised into a 'nation-at-arms' in the late nineteenth century through victory parades, veterans' societies and compulsory military service.[57] The fact that combat entailed killing did not come as a shocking revelation to the German public in 1914–18. Rather the enormity and novelty of the event had to be located in a symbolic order to make it tolerable. As I argued in the previous chapter, the mythical *Kriegserlebnis*, the 'experience' of industrialised mass warfare, became encoded in a language of steely endurance; the iron knight preceded the gentlemanly knight. Notably, war landmarks conveyed German tenacity. In Dortmund, Westphalia, the iron-nail monument, unveiled in September 1915, represented the city's patron saint, St Reinoldus, in a suit of armour shouldering a large sword. In 1920, a local clergymen compared the 'Iron St Reinoldus' to a fourteenth-century effigy of the warrior saint: 'The Reinoldus created by the sculptor Bagdons [. . .], is of shattering force and steadfast warriorness [*Reckenhaftigkeit*], whereas the saint of the church will remain an exemplar of Christian faith and chivalrous piety.'[58]

Chivalric diction was also conspicuously absent from a commemoration in the Westphalian capital, Münster. Erected in the Gothic town hall in 1931 and dedicated to the fallen soldiers of the 47th Reserve 'Iron' Division, the stained-glass memorial window featured a stylised St George as a symbol of the German spirit overcoming war.[59] Overall, there was a marked contrast between the prevalence of visual representations of knights – ranging from St George to Roland – and the

[57] Jakob Vogel, *Nationen im Gleichschritt: Der Kult der 'Nation in Waffen' in Deutschland und Frankreich, 1871–1914* (Göttingen, Vandenhoeck & Ruprecht, 1997). On the middle classes, see Frank Becker, *Bilder von Krieg und Nation: Die Einigungskriege in der bürgerlichen Öffentlichkeit Deutschlands 1864–1913* (Munich, R. Oldenbourg, 2001).
[58] Hans Strobel (ed.), *Dortmund: Ein Blick in eine deutsche Industriestadt* (Dortmund, C. L. Krüger, 1922), pp. 50–2: 'Der vom Bildhauer Bagdons geformte Reinoldus [. . .] ist dagegen von erschütternder Wucht und standfester Reckenhaftigkeit, während der Kirchenheilige ein Vorbild christlichen Glaubens und ritterlicher Frömmigkeit bleiben soll.' In addition, see Uwe Fleckner and Jürgen Zänker (eds.), *Friedrich Bagdons (1878–1937): Eine Bildhauerkarriere vom Kaiserreich zum Nationalsozialismus* (Stuttgart, Gerd Hatje, 1993), pp. 48–9.
[59] 'Das Ehrenmal der "Eisernen Division" im Rathaus zu Münster i.Westf.: Die Kampfgeschichte der 47. Res.-Division', *Münstersche Zeitung*, 37, 20 September 1931.

insignificance of (affirmative) chivalric notation in German war remembrance.[60] Explicit references to the fallen soldiers' *Ritterlichkeit*,
chivalry, were relatively rare and vague, with the exception of one
commemorative strand: the Langemarck legend.

Lost elites

The Langemarck legend enshrined the 'war enthusiasm' of the nationalist *Bildungsbürger*, the educated middle classes.[61] A great many grammar
school boys and university students rushed to the colours in the summer
and autumn of 1914. The battle of Langemarck near Ypres became their
mythical baptism of fire. An army communiqué of 11 November 1914,
reprinted on the front pages of most newspapers, turned into the stuff of
myth for decades after 1918: 'West of Langemarck youthful regiments
stormed the first lines of the enemy trenches and took them, singing
Deutschland, Deutschland über alles.'[62] Later, after the Second World War,
military historians set out to unmask the legend, revealing the futility of
the German offensive and the lack of substance to the story (only a small
percentage of the casualties had been students). In the era of the Great
War, however, these circumstances – if they were known at all – were
subsumed in a tale of willing self-sacrifice by Germany's academic
volunteers. Langemarck stood for the triumph of youthful idealism in
the wake of military defeat. Subsequently, a narrative crystallised which
was filled with images reminiscent of the spirit of the Wars of Liberation
and notions of tragic knighthood.[63] Werner Beumelburg's account of the
first battle of Ypres, which appeared as part of a multi-volume series of
popular battle narratives edited by the Reich archive, illustrates these
features:

For the last time, combat takes place in those bloody forms of the Middle Ages
and antiquity. For the last time, the youth of Germany storms like the grenadiers
of Frederick the Great or old Blücher's musketeers, scorning all protection,
throwing up a wall of bodies in a bloody shambles before the borders of
the fatherland. As a century of military history was buried in the battle of the

---

[60] Compare Frantzen, *Bloody Good*, p. 165, who relies entirely on iconographic evidence.
[61] Mosse, *Fallen Soldiers*, pp. 70–4; Uwe-K. Ketelsen, '"Die Jugend von Langemarck": Ein
poetisch-politisches Motiv der Zwischenkriegszeit', in Thomas Koebner, Rolf-Peter
Janz and Frank Trommler (eds.), *'Mit uns zieht die neue Zeit': Der Mythos der Jugend*
(Frankfurt am Main, Suhrkamp, 1985), pp. 68–96; Karl Unruh, *Langemarck: Legende
und Wirklichkeit* (Koblenz, Bernard & Graefe, 1986). Contrast Brandt, *Vom Kriegsschauplatz zum Gedächtnisraum*, pp. 193–5, 204.
[62] As cited in Mosse, *Fallen Soldiers*, p. 70, my italics.
[63] Hüppauf, 'Schlachtenmythen', pp. 54, 60.

iron-clad knights against the confederate lansquenets at Sempach and Morgaten; as the ossified tactics of Frederick's army broke before the living impact of the Corsican troops at Jena and Auerstedt: so the battle of Ypres represents the last, monstrous, blood-red signal for the mass onslaught against the hundredfold power of the machine. The new experience cost us the best of our youth.[64]

Bernd Hüppauf has characterised the opposition between the myths of Langemarck and Verdun as one of idealism versus nihilism, enthusiasm versus hardness, devotion versus experience, youth versus maturity, nostalgia versus futurism, heroism versus technology.[65] While the Langemarck legend reflected the *bildungsbürgerlich* frame of mind, the Verdun myth constituted the intellectual property of 'reactionary modernists' on the fringes of the Weimar society. However, the Langemarck legend, too, carried revolutionary overtones; the idealism of the student martyrs contrasted sharply with the perceived decadence of the Wilhelmine bourgeoisie.[66] The mystification of Langemarck clearly stood in the rebellious tradition of pre-1914 German youth movements. The neo-Romantic quest for 'authenticity' among the middle-class youth of Imperial Germany climaxed in the Langemarck panegyric. In fact, the bourgeois youth movement and students' organisations considered themselves the legitimate heirs to the legacy of Langemarck and played a dominant role in its commemorations. It is no coincidence that the students' branch of the Stahlhelm league bore the name 'Langemarck'.[67]

Weimar's nationalist youth spread the gospel through a variety of media, primarily rallies on Langemarck Day (coincidentally, 11 November), the anniversary of the battle (which overshadowed memories of the Armistice), but also through memorials. In 1924, two thousand members

---

[64] Werner Beumelburg, *Ypern 1914* (Oldenburg and Berlin, Gerhard Stalling, 2nd edn 1926), pp. 9–10: 'Zum letztenmal vollzieht sich der Kampf in jenen blutrünstigen Formen des Mittelalters und des Altertums. Zum letztenmal stürmt die Jugend Deutschlands wie die Grenadiere Friedrichs des Großen und die Musketiere des alten Blücher, jeden Schutz verachtend, den Damm der Leiber hinwerfend in blutiger Verschwendung vor die Grenzen des Vaterlandes. Wie bei Sempach und Morgaten im Kampf der eisengepanzerten Ritter gegen die eidgenössischen Landsknechte ein Jahrhundert der Kriegesgeschichte begraben wurde, wie bei Jena und Auerstedt die erstarrten Kampfformen der friderizianischen Armee auseinanderbrachen vor dem lebendigen Aufprall der Korsentruppen: so steht die Ypernschlacht da als letztes, ungeheuerliches, blutrotes Fanal des Massensturms gegen die verhundertfachte Macht der Maschine. Die neue Erfahrung kostete uns die besten Teile unserer Jugend.' See Ziemann, 'Macht der Maschine', p. 181.

[65] Hüppauf, 'Schlachtenmythen'. Compare Brandt, *Vom Kriegsschauplatz zum Gedächtnisraum*, pp. 191–5.

[66] Ziemann, 'Macht der Maschine', p. 179.

[67] Mosse, *Fallen Soldiers*, pp. 73–4; Berghahn, *Stahlhelm*, p. 107.

of the Bündische Jugend gathered in the Rhön mountains to inaugurate a monument to the dead of Langemarck.[68] At the same time, pedagogues discovered the legend as an educational tool. Take the Langemarck memorial of a *Gymnasium*, or grammar school, in Rheine, Westphalia (see figure 43). It immortalised the names of thirty-five fallen pupils and two trainee teachers who had volunteered between 1914 and 1918, though only one pupil had actually been killed in Flanders in 1914; the names of 113 dead conscripts were effaced from memory. The memorial commemorated only those pupils who had suffered of their own free will. The dedication was intended to teach future generations a lesson in selfless service: 'LANGEMARCK / THE FATHERLAND CALLED YOU [*PATRIA VOCAVIT VOS*] / WE DIED FOR YOU, DO NOT LAMENT, FIGHT!' Characteristically, the memorial depicts two naked adolescents, a drummer signalling for the attack to begin and a warrior falling under the fatal blow. Regarding the imagery, the school authorities had vacillated between classicism and medievalism. They asked the sculptor to revise his model six times. The first and third proposals showed a medieval knight in armour; the fourth, a nude warrior armed with an antique sword and a medieval shield; the fifth and sixth, nude classic figures. The seventh design was accepted and the memorial was unveiled in October 1934.[69]

Under the name of Langemarck, the educated middle classes grieved for their progeny. The bourgeois elite had been deprived of their successors; the normal succession from one generation to the next had been reversed. The Langemarck legend in Germany coincided with the myth of 'the lost generation' in Britain. Like the heroes of Langemarck, Britain's lost soldiers had been men of promise. They embodied 'the more chivalrous, the more virile, the more courageous, the more patriotic, and the high death-rate among combatants compared with non-combatants meant [. . .] an impoverishment of the race – a reversed selection'.[70] The term 'the lost generation' made a life-long impact on the surviving and later-born members of the British establishment. An abiding sense of admiration, as well as guilt, became part of the *esprit de*

---

[68] Hüppauf, 'Schlachtenmythen', p. 60. For further examples, see Schneider, '. . . nicht umsonst gefallen'?, pp. 214–15.

[69] Holger Dickmänken *et al.*, 'Das Langemarck-Denkmal des Gymnasiums Dionysianum in Rheine', in Verein Alter Dionysianer (ed.), *Langemarck und ein Denkmal: Nachdenken über unsere Geschichte* (Berlin, News & Media, 1994), pp. 68–77. The inscription in Latin and German reads: 'LANGEMARCK / PATRIA VOCAVIT VOS / WIR STARBEN FÜR EUCH, KLAGT NICHT, KÄMPFT!'

[70] John Keay, 'War and the Burden of Insanity', *Journal of Mental Science*, 64 (1918), p. 326. See Winter, 'Legende der "verlorenen Generation"', p. 118.

Figure 43. Langemarck memorial by Albert Mazzotti. *Abitur* (A-level) certificate depicting a school war memorial. Gymnasium Dionysianum, Rheine, 1934.

corps of public-school-educated Britons. School and university war memorials, largely financed by parents and old boys, evolved into elite foci of reflections on 'the lost generation'. Clifton College, which had produced Field Marshal Earl Haig, for instance, saluted its fallen members' chivalry and self-sacrifice: 'From the great Marshal to the last recruit, These, Clifton, were thy Self, thy Spirit in Deed, Thy flower of Chivalry, thy fallen fruit, And thine immortal Seed'.[71]

It is not hard to discern a degree of converging *habitus* between establishment memory agents in Britain and Germany. They exalted their respective lost elites as a generation apart, as shining models of duty and purity, for the dead had willingly 'laid down' their lives as innocent volunteers (which also meant, by implication, that the state and its agents could not be blamed for their premature deaths). Duty and purity functioned as elegant synonyms for chivalry, although this association is stronger in the British case. Nevertheless, there is a notable difference in tone. The blood sacrifice of Britain's youth was tragic; Germany's redemptive. The myth of 'the lost generation' was an elegy not only for 'the lost generation' but also for the lost sense of historical progress; the Langemarck legend was a gospel of catharsis leading to a brighter future.[72]

Atrocities

The German preoccupation with the *Kriegserlebnis* did not imply indifference towards human life; the iron knight was no agent of the brutalisation of German society.[73] Chivalry often loomed as an unspoken assumption in commemorative discourses. Significantly, accounts of enemy *Unritterlichkeit* or 'un-chivalry' presumed that German conduct was beyond reproach. French authorities and soldiers (particularly coloured soldiers), supposedly thrown into ecstasy over their victory in 1918, stood accused of abusing their position and eroding chivalrous standards. Reports about the defilement or obliteration of German war graves and cemeteries in northern France – measures in breach of the Versailles Treaty – and the defacement or demolition of monuments

---

[71] Kernot, *Public Schools War Memorials*, p. 49. See, in general, Jamet-Bellier de la Duboisière, 'Commemorating "the Lost Generation"'.

[72] Baird, *To Die for Germany*, p. 4; Winter, 'Representations of War', p. 213.

[73] On the brutalising effects of the Great War, see Mosse, *Fallen Soldiers*, ch. 9; Eksteins, *Rites of Spring*. See also the critique of the brutalisation thesis by Bessel, *Germany after the First World War*, pp. vi, 258; Ziemann, *Front und Heimat*, pp. 9–18, 412–13; Dirk Schumann, 'Europa, der Erste Weltkrieg und die Nachkriegszeit: eine Kontinuität der Gewalt?', *Journal of Modern European History*, 1 (2003), pp. 24–43.

from the Franco-Prussian war in Alsace-Lorraine provoked public outcries from the revisionist camp. In 1923, Hindenburg cited in front of veterans the removal of the memorials to the First and Third Guards Regiments from the *Walstatt* (the word used for 'battlefield' in Nordic mythology) of St Privat as manifestations of French 'un-chivalry'.[74] French iconoclasm was, to a degree, a natural reaction considering that the memorials of St Privat figured a roaring lion of 1900 and the German patron saint, St Michael the archangel, in full armour based on a design by Wilhelm II of 1899. On the whole, however, respect towards the dead enemy predominated over vengeful outbursts.[75]

While the French were branded as brutes, the British were – after 1918 – often recognised as gentlemen.[76] Placing the two national stereotypes in juxtaposition highlighted the wickedness of Germany's 'archenemy'. British gentlemen were purportedly horrified by French violations of the memory of German war dead by their late wartime Allies. 'I asked them whether this was their conception of French chivalry and, as a result, was cut dead by all of them for the remainder of the journey': thus the national-liberal *Deutsche Allgemeine Zeitung*, quoting a British battlefield tourist who had allegedly witnessed French incivilities at German war graves.[77] Britons, in contrast, were reported to pay tribute to friend and foe equally. When British officers attended the opening of the military cemetery of Nazareth in 1935, the Volksbund Deutsche Kriegsgräberfürsorge complimented the delegates on their 'chivalrous ethos'.[78]

[74] BArch, R 8034 II/7691, folio 130, 'Denkmalsweihen der Garde: Der Löwe von Döberitz', *Der Tag*, 108, 8 May 1923. For further examples, see BArch, R 8034 II/7690, fos. 153–5, 'Französische Ritterlichkeit: Schmähungen gegen die deutschen Toten und ihre Ruhestätten', *Berliner Neue Woche*, 300, 15 June 1917; BArch, R 8034 II/7692, folio 45, 'Frankreichs Kampf gegen unsere Toten: Von 3000 Soldatenfriedhöfen 2750 aufgelöst', *Deutsche Zeitung*, 88, 22 Feb. 1926; BArch, R 8034 II/7691, folio 48, 'Die Nation der Leichenschänder', *Deutsche Tageszeitung*, 328, 10 July 1920. See also Brandt, *Vom Kriegsschauplatz zum Gedächtnisraum*, pp. 114, 122, 142–3.
[75] Annette Maas, 'Politische Ikonographie im deutsch-französischen Spannungsfeld: Die Kriegerdenkmäler von 1870/71 auf dem Schlachtfeld um Metz', in Reinhart Koselleck and Michael Jeismann (eds.), *Der politische Totenkult: Kriegerdenkmäler in der Moderne* (Munich, Wilhelm Fink, 1994), pp. 203–9. On the demolition of memorials, see Speitkamp, *Denkmalsturz*.
[76] See chapter 2 on the reconfiguration of the conflict in the west as a primarily defensive war against France. On the decline of Anglophobia in inter-war Germany, see Stibbe, *German Anglophobia*, p. 194.
[77] BArch, R 8034 II/7691, folio 135, 'Französische Achtung vor Kriegergräbern', *Deutsche Allgemeine Zeitung*, 289, 25 June 1923: 'Ich fragte sie, ob das ihre Auffassung von französischer Ritterlichkeit wäre und wurde daraufhin für den Rest der Fahrt von allen geschnitten.'
[78] [Franz] Hallbaum, 'Die Einweihung der deutschen Kriegsgräberstätte Nazareth in Palästina', *Kriegsgräberfürsorge*, 15,8 (1935), p. 116.

Naturally, diplomatic etiquette shaped and constrained the language of government officials and quasi-officials. In his memorandum on the festivities to mark the 'liberation' of the Rhineland from French occupation in 1930, Reich Art Custodian Edwin Redslob emphasised 'the chivalrous custom of paying mutual respects to the graves', a custom to which both French and Germans adhered.[79] Moreover, he suggested that the French cult of the Tricolour 'exemplarily revealed the chivalrous features of the French character'.[80] But Redslob added that, for the German viewer, the French custom came close to ritualism. Redslob's commemorative *Realpolitik* failed to impress vociferous revisionists. Regimental societies and groups on the political Right were hotbeds of revisionism and accusations of French 'un-chivalry', sentiments of which Weimar's nationalist press became a mouthpiece. Organs of German nationalism disseminated the image of French *Unritterlichkeit* in an effort to restore a sense of moral superiority to the German people. The wartime atrocity propaganda of the Allies continued to be a thorn in the German flesh throughout the 1920s. 'But we have been decried as "Huns". And how did we honour the graves of the French dead in the war of 1870?', wrote the national-liberal *Zeit* in 1924, incensed at French contempt for the German fallen.[81]

During the war, news about alleged outrages perpetrated by the German army, navy, and air force stirred emotions on the British home front. Initially, horror stories about the rape and murder of Belgian civilians made good newspaper copy, and journalists hurled the epithet 'Hun' at the Kaiser and his troops. The German or, in propagandaspeak 'Germ-hun', invasion of Belgium in August 1914 appeared as 'The March of the Huns' reincarnate.[82] The imagery was compelling. After all, no less a person than the Kaiser himself had released into public imagination the identification of the German soldier with the Hun. In July 1900, Wilhelm II had enjoined on his troops in Bremerhaven, ready for dispatch to China, not to show mercy to the insurgent Boxers. They should, he trumpeted, forever gain a reputation in China like that of the Huns under King Etzel (the name for legendary Attila the Hun in the

[79] BArch, R 32/281, folio 118, 'Die Rheinische Befreiungsfeier als Ausdruck deutscher Festkultur', [*c.* June 1930]: 'der ritterliche Brauch der wechselnden Verehrung der Gräber'.

[80] Ibid., folio 136: 'die ritterlichen Züge des französischen Wesens vorbildlich offenbarten'.

[81] BArch, R 8034 II/7691, folio 145, 'Ein Trauertag des Deutschen Volkes', *Zeit*, 60, 11 March 1924: 'Uns aber hat man als "Hunnen" verrufen. Und wie haben wir die Gräber französischer Toten im Krieg von 1870 geehrt?'

[82] 'The March of the Huns', *The Times*, 40691, 29 August 1914, p. 9.

Song of the Nibelungen) in Germany. At the time, Wihelm's imperialistic sabre-rattling did not create a diplomatic scandal. The official version, carefully edited by Foreign Secretary Bernhard von Bülow, omitted the Kaiser's allusion to the Huns and emphasised soldierly 'discipline' and 'self-control' instead.[83] What is more, Whitehall itself, Britain being a partner in the six-nation expeditionary force in China, pursued colonial affairs with an iron fist, most obviously in South Africa. But fourteen years later, British propagandists dusted off the Kaiser's phrase. Henceforth, the label 'Hun' encapsulated German transgressions of basic human values. Propaganda stigmatised the German as a brutal savage living, like his Hunnish 'ancestors', outside the bounds of decency and humanity.

Visions of a nation besieged had served as building blocks of national identity in nineteenth-century Continental Europe. Imperial Germany entered the war in 1914 as a 'fatherland of enemies'.[84] In Britain, by contrast, the pressures and consequences of the First World War brought to light aspects of Britishness that had been blurred or ill-defined in Victorian and Edwardian times.[85] In the aftermath of the war, British identity was reformulated in two ways; first, with negative reference to the enemy, the perpetrator of gruesome war crimes, and, secondly, by holding up the war dead as the embodiment of British chivalry. These were, to some extent, complementary imaginings. Even though, after the war, many Britons came to see German atrocities as essentially propaganda fabrications, chivalry remained a cornerstone of the imagery of Britishness. The war had a clarifying effect which the author-cum-propagandist John Masefield stylised as follows:

I know what England was, before the war. She was a nation which had outgrown her machine, a nation which had forgotten her soul [. . .]. And then, at a day's notice, at the blowing of a horn, at the cry from a little people in distress, all that was changed, and she re-made her soul, which was the soul of St. George who fought the dragon.[86]

---

[83] Bernd Sösemann, 'Die sog. Hunnenrede Wilhelms II.: Textkritische und interpretatorische Bemerkungen zur Ansprache des Kaisers vom 27. Juli 1900 in Bremerhaven', *Historische Zeitschrift*, 222 (1976), pp. 342–58. See also Reinermann, *Der Kaiser in England*, pp. 206–11.

[84] Jeismann, *Vaterland der Feinde*.

[85] Winter, 'British National Identity', pp. 262–8. See also Aribert Reimann, 'Popular Culture and the Reconstruction of British Identity', in Hartmut Berghoff and Robert von Friedeburg (eds.), *Change and Inertia: Britain under the Impact of the Great War* (Bodenheim, Philo, 1998), pp. 99–120.

[86] Masefield, *St. George and the Dragon*, p. 43.

General Erich Ludendorff, who made a name for himself as the bold conqueror of Liège in August 1914, tells a different story. In his memoirs, published in both German and English as early as 1919, Ludendorff contends that the alleged German atrocities were a myth. Indeed, it was poor little Belgium which had broken the rules of civilised warfare: 'For my part, I had taken the field with chivalrous and humane conceptions of war. The *franc-tireur* warfare was bound to disgust any soldier. My soldierly spirit suffered bitter disillusion.'[87] The German military had been haunted by images of insidious *francs-tireurs* or 'free-shooters', irregular snipers firing from behind, since the war against France in 1870–1. Veterans' tales and literature had kept the concept of the *franc-tireur* as a distorted mirror image of the chivalrous German soldier very much alive in Imperial Germany. In the course of the advance through Belgium, memory transmuted into paranoia. German soldiers, surprised and frustrated by the stiff resistance put up by the underequipped army of a supposedly inferior nation, pinned the blame for their military difficulties on phantom *francs-tireurs*. Innocent Belgians were seen as underhand enemies. Army units wreaked vengeance on civilians, first spontaneously, later with official approval. It seems that many a culprit genuinely believed in the fantasy of the *franc-tireur* war. Wounds on German corpses were perceived as mutilations, and members of the Belgian civil guard, who wore only rudimentary uniforms, were identified as irregulars.[88]

Belgium was not the only theatre of operations where Germans encountered alien 'un-chivalry'. German women and children, the *Deutsche Allgemeine Zeitung* recollected in 1921, had suffered from the 'hunger blockade' enforced by the British 'iron squadrons'.[89] Animated by the revived spirit of the Hanseatic League, the newspaper suggested, Germany's lost submariners had undermined the naval blockade and thus rendered their country great service. Notably, Otto Weddigen, commander of the submarines *U-9* and *U-29*, emerged as a naval idol

[87] [Erich] Ludendorff, *My War Memories 1914–1918*, vol. I (London, Hutchinson, [1919]), p. 32.
[88] John Horne and Alan Kramer, *German Atrocities, 1914: A History of Denial* (New Haven and London, Yale University Press, 2001); Alan Kramer, '"Greultaten": Zum Problem der deutschen Kriegsverbrechen in Belgien und Frankreich 1914', in Gerhard Hirschfeld, Gerd Krumeich and Irina Renz (eds.), '*Keiner fühlt sich hier mehr als Mensch . . .': Erlebnis und Wirkung des Ersten Weltkriegs* (Frankfurt am Main, Fischer, 1996), pp. 104–39. See also Christophe Prochasson, 'Sur les atrocités allemandes: la guerre comme représentation', *Annales*, 58 (2003), pp. 879–94.
[89] BArch, R 8034 II/7691, folio 104, Walter Wauer, 'Den toten U-Bootshelden!', *Deutsche Allgemeine Zeitung*, 595, 25 December 1921.

from the otherwise unspectacular war at sea. Having sent 'Britain's floating fortresses' to the bottom of the North Sea, Weddigen's U-boat sank near the Orkney Islands in March 1915 after a collision with a dreadnought.[90] In a 'chivalrous battle', as the mayor of Dortmund put it on Navy Sacrifice Day 1916, Weddigen had also 'cleared up' among the enemy trading vessels. Yet his was a tragic story. Weddigen typified, in the eyes of the mayor, the reborn 'Siegfried who succumbed to malicious assault' by his foe (note the absence of a sense of *Dolchstoß*, 'stab in the back', here).[91] The Dortmund home front honoured the hero with a memorial stone and lime tree in October 1916 – four months before the start of unrestricted submarine warfare in February 1917. In addition, a figurative monument, a statue of 'Young Siegfried', had been under discussion between 1915 and 1917, but did not materialise in the end.[92]

The inauguration of the Weddigen site in Dortmund coincided with the completion of a related war memorial in Osnabrück, Hanover: a redone façade of a sixteenth-century half-timbered house, owned by a local arms dealer, richly adorned with allegories of war. It featured, among other things, St Michael in the guise of a medieval knight, the sinking of three British cruisers by *U-9* in October 1914, and a Zeppelin bombing raid.[93] The same imagery occurred in a stained-glass window of 1919 in Swaffham Prior parish church, Cambridgeshire. Here, however, U-boats and Zeppelins symbolised, according to the inscription, 'THE AGGRESSION AND BARBARITIES OF GERMAN MILITARISM'.[94] From the

[90] StdADO, 3–3085, folio 76, 'Marine-Opfertag', *Dortmunder Zeitung*, 500, 2 October 1916. See also ibid., folio 56, 'Marine-Opfertag', *Dortmunder Zeitung*, 21 September 1916. See also René Schilling, *'Kriegshelden': Deutungsmuster heroischer Männlichkeit in Deutschland 1813–1945* (Paderborn, Ferdinand Schöningh, 2002), ch. 4.

[91] StdADO, 3–3085, folio 74, Mayor Ernst Eichoff, Manuscript of the unveiling speech, [c. October 1916]: 'Siegfried, der tückischem Überfall erlag'. On the symbolism of Siegfried generally, see Herfried Münkler and Wolfgang Storch, *Siegfrieden: Politik mit einem deutschen Mythos* (Berlin, Rotbuch, 1988).

[92] StdADO, 3–3085, folio 12, Magistrat Dortmund, Minutes with notes by Hans Strobel, 5 July 1915; StdADO, Ep 39, Hans Strobel (ed.), *Führer durch die Kriegsausstellung Dortmund 1917 im Fredenbaum, August–Oktober* (Dortmund, Verlag der Ausstellungsleitung, 1917), pp. 88–91. See also Fleckner and Zänker, *Friedrich Bagdons*, pp. 50–1. On the rhetoric of the U-boat campaign, see Holger H. Herwig, 'Total Rhetoric, Limited War: Germany's U-Boat Campaign, 1917–1918', in Roger Chickering and Stig Förster (eds.), *Great War, Total War: Combat and Mobilization on the Western Front, 1914–1918* (Cambridge, Cambridge University Press, 2000), pp. 189–206.

[93] Gisela Schirmer, 'Osnabrück im Jahr 1916: Die Hausfassade Kranstraße 53', in Jutta Held (ed.), *Symbole des Friedens und des Krieges im öffentlichen Raum: Osnabrück, die 'Stadt des Westfälischen Friedens'* (Weimar, VDG, 1998), pp. 128, 133.

[94] NIWM, 3573, Swaffham Prior, Cambs. See CROC, P 150/06/19, C. P. Allix, Description of the war memorial windows, 1920; CROC, P 150/3/13, Restoration Book, 1805–1932.

German perspective, submarines and Zeppelins took reprisals for enemy acts of 'un-chivalry'. In Britain, new kinds of weapons, the weapons of 'total war', generated a propaganda campaign of hatred, hatred not of the German command but of the entire German nation and its *Kultur*. The term 'German atrocities' did not merely describe atrocities committed by Germans: 'their "Germanness" was what made them atrocious'.[95]

The 'belief in ruthless war which distinguishes modern Germany', the *Architectural Review* claimed in 1916, was not confined to soldiers but shared by the home front also.[96] Civilian cruelty seemed to find expression in the wartime practice of driving nails into wooden figures designed as war landmarks. Notoriously, the three-storey colossus of the 'Iron Hindenburg' in central Berlin (see figure 44) caught the attention of British observers.[97] In the inter-war years, however, public awareness of this monstrosity faded away, and yet the figure was not entirely forgotten. John Wheeler-Bennett's 1936 biography of Hindenburg, written under the impact of Nazism, was characteristically subtitled *The Wooden Titan*. It is worth citing the author's interpretation of iron-nail monuments at full length:

These statues [of Hindenburg] were symbolic. They were huge, crude, and rugged, and recalled the primitive sculptures of an earlier civilization. They were indeed a 'throw-back' to the images of Thor and Odin, the Nordic war-gods so dear to an earlier German tradition, and to them were made sacrifices in a truly Nordic spirit, sacrifices not of garlands or of doves but of iron nails hammered into the figure till they stood out 'like quills upon the fretful porcupine'. The proceeds of the sale of the nails to the faithful who desired the privilege of knocking them in went to the German Red Cross. Here the underlying streak of paganism in the German character was combined with Christian humanity, the worship of the war-god with alleviation of the ghastly results of such worship. The contrast is sharp; the incongruity almost frightening. The strange problem of German psychology is here displayed, a fierce and pagan sadism mingling in the German character with the Christian spirit of human kindliness. And if the figures and their cult were significant of the German people as a whole, they were even more symbolic of Hindenburg. A Wooden Titan he had become, and remained so to the end.[98]

There were Germans who also raised objections to iron-nail landmarks. Socialist critics denounced the 'Iron Hindenburg' in 1922 as a

---

[95] Winter and Baggett, *1914–18*, p. 134.

[96] 'Memorials of War: – VIII. German', *Architectural Review*, 40 (1916), p. 107.

[97] Goebel, Repp and Winter, 'Exhibitions'.

[98] John W. Wheeler-Bennett, *Hindenburg: The Wooden Titan* (London, Macmillan, 1936), pp. 79–80. Margaret Goldsmith and Frederick Voigt, *Hindenburg: The Man and the Legend* (London, Faber & Faber, [1930]), p. 139, argue in a similar vein.

Figure 44. 'Iron Hindenburg'. Wartime postcard depicting the iron-nail statue by Georg Marschall. Berlin, 1915.

prime symbol of German savagery, and a Berlin Dada artist caricatured the iron field marshal as an obscene and violent monstrosity.[99] Middle-class commentators rejected the figure as an example of 'bad taste', primarily on aesthetic grounds.[100] Participants were troubled by the idea of knocking nails into the effigy of a human – a kind of crucifixion. Hence the organisers of nailing ceremonies throughout Germany were anxious to stress that only armour or garments would be made of iron; the face and hands would not. In Hagen, Westphalia, Karl Ernst Osthaus tried to capitalise on popular reservations against this practice. In his campaign for Ernst Ludwig Kirchner's stylised 'Iron Blacksmith', and against Friedrich Bagdons's naturalistic figure, Osthaus pointed out that 'it was not an embarrassment to drive iron nails into this block, which is not a human but an oak tree' (see figures 9–10).[101]

The Iron Cross (which derived from the emblem of the Teutonic Order),[102] embellished by the date and Imperial initial, was one of the most common and ethically unproblematic motifs for war landmarks. When inaugurating the 'Iron Cross' landmark of Rinteln, Hanover, in October 1915, the deputy mayor invoked the persecution of the elderly, women and children of East Prussia by the 'Asiatic hordes of Russia'.[103] As early as 3 August 1914, the *Kölnische Volkszeitung*, a newspaper which maintained close contact with the Centre Party, had dubbed the Russian people the modern-day 'Huns'.[104] In the aftermath of the Russian invasion in 1914, German propagandists grossly exaggerated the suffering of the civilian population of East Prussia during the brief period of occupation. The torrent of stories of Russian atrocities in the German media mirrored allegations of the German ravaging of Belgium made by the Entente; German journalists were obviously taking their cue from the

---

[99] BArch, R 8034 II/7691, folio 27, 'Hindenburg auf Abbruch', *Freiheit*, 473, 31 August 1919; Biro, 'The New Man as Cyborg', p. 77. See also Schneider, 'Hannoversche Nagelfiguren', p. 223 n. 48.

[100] P[eter] Loth (ed.), *Das Kriegswahrzeichen der Stadt Zweibrücken: Unserem tapferen Heere gewidmet* (Zweibrücken, Friedrich Lehmann, 1916), p. 4; O[tto] Weltzien, 'Kriegsna-gelungen in Niederdeutschland', *Niedersachsen*, 22,3 (1916), p. 39.

[101] Karl Ernst Osthaus, 'Die Kunst und der Eiserne Schmied in Hagen', *Westfälisches Tageblatt*, 214, 13 September 1915: 'Es hat nichts Peinliches, in diesen Klotz, der nicht Mensch, sondern Eichbaum ist, eiserne Nägel zu treiben.' See Diers, 'Ernst Ludwig Kirchner', pp. 26–7. The figure's face and hands were excluded; see *Der Eiserne Schmied von Hagen*, pp. 24–6.

[102] Benno Fitzke and Paul Matzdorf, *Eiserne Kreuz-Nagelungen zum Besten der Kriegshilfe und zur Schaffung von Kriegswahrzeichen: Gebrauchsfertiges Material für vaterländische Volksunterhaltung durch Feiern in Schulen, Jugendvereinigungen und Vereinen* (Leipzig, Arwed Strauch, 1916), p. 15. See Boockmann, *Marienburg*, p. 18.

[103] As cited in Schneider, 'Mobilisierung der "Heimatfront"', p. 45.

[104] Reimann, *Krieg der Sprachen*, pp. 172–3.

western Allies.[105] While the western Allies labelled such acts 'Hunnish' viciousness, German propagandists preferred to speak of the 'onslaught of the twentieth-century Mongols'.[106] German women raped by the Russian invaders, having their breasts cut off and their genitalia maimed, were favoured images. Sex murder featured equally prominently in British accounts of the Western Front. One historian suspects 'that the stories allowed the discussion of topics ordinarily considered taboo' in British society.[107]

Some historians have posed the question whether the combatants of 1914–18 were driven by a subconscious 'death instinct' to kill the enemy, and whether the act of killing another person could even incite feelings of pleasure.[108] If that was the case, it had no bearing on signifying practices. Neither British nor German architects of war remembrance indulged in blood-lust. On the contrary, both sides claimed moral integrity and charged one another with 'un-knightly' or atrocious behaviour. Although they painted a similar picture of the decline of chivalry in the First World War, the commentators reached different conclusions: British agents reaffirmed their own commitment to the tenets of chivalrous warfare, whereas their German counterparts embraced a concept of total war. Ludendorff in Belgium, Weddigen at sea, Hindenburg in East Prussia, were imagined as waging total war against a 'world full of enemies', enemies who had unilaterally annulled the laws of chivalry.

Sportsmen and flyers

In his introduction to the English edition of Jünger's *Storm of Steel*, R. H. Mottram hinted that the brutal character of total war did not necessarily pave the way for a culture of brutalisation. He remarked of Jünger that 'He had no conception of himself as the man of violence [. . .]. He must have been astonished to find himself described as a "Hun". There was nothing petty or mean about his deliberate destruction of property in the German retreat in 1917. It was part of the game.'[109] British players in

---

[105] Hynes, *War Imagined*, pp. 52–6. On the Social-Democratic press, see Kruse, *Krieg und nationale Integration*, p. 72. On the Russian perspective, see Jahn, *Patriotic Culture*, pp. 18–19, 165–6.

[106] Fischer, *Bei Tannenberg*, p. 34, and pp. 4, 40, 45, 110.

[107] DeGroot, *Blighty*, p. 188. See also Nicoletta F. Gullace, 'Sexual Violence and Family Honor: British Propaganda and International Law during the First World War', *American Historical Review*, 102 (1997), pp. 714–47.

[108] Ferguson, *Pity of War*, pp. 357–66; Bourke, *Intimate History*, esp. 369–75.

[109] R[alph] H. Mottram, 'Introduction', in Jünger, *Storm of Steel*, pp. v–vi.

'the game', though, followed a different set of rules. In Britain, sport provided the experience around which ideas of proper warfare coalesced.

Iron and gentlemanly sportsmen

The prevalence of sport and sporting images in commemorative practices is striking. In both Britain and Germany, organised games and races were considered appropriate entertainments on days of remembrance. The British Legion as well as the Stahlhelm league held sporting events for their members.[110] Furthermore, memorial schemes could incorporate playing-fields or stadiums. At Reigate and Redhill, Surrey, memorial sports grounds were laid out.[111] Similarly, in 1916–17, Hanover planned a grand memorial complex including an arena. After the war, the provincial capital built a *Kampfbahn*, literally 'fighting ground', dedicated to Hindenburg, where 'Langemarck competitions' took place.[112] The draft plan for the Tannenberg memorial included a sports field and a memorial room to fallen athletes.[113] The nexus between sport and commemoration goes back to the nineteenth century. Sporting events had rounded off Sedan Day, and large stadiums for the national monuments at Mount Kyffhäuser and Bingerbrück had been under discussion.[114] In the event, Hans Poelzig's 1910 design of a 'stadium for the German youth' at Bingerbrück was rediscovered after the war but never built.[115]

The respective sporting ethoses of Britain and Germany, however, were worlds apart. Hand-grenade throwing, for example, was a discipline uncommon in the British Isles. Germany witnessed the militarisation of its sporting scene in the aftermath of the Great War. Sport fitted in perfectly with the aim of regaining moral and physical strength after military humiliation. In a sense, the bourgeois sport boom during the Weimar Republic constituted an act of defiance vis-à-vis the terms of

---

[110] Barr, 'British Legion', p. 218; Berghahn, *Stahlhelm*, p. 59. On the construction of a dichotomy between decent and indecent celebrations on Armistice Day, see Gregory, *Silence of Memory*, pp. 66–86. On sport in the British army during the war, see J[ohn] G. Fuller, *Troop Morale and Popular Culture in the British and Dominion Armies 1914–1918* (Oxford, Clarendon, 1990), pp. 85–94.

[111] Boorman, *At the Going Down of the Sun*, p. 93.

[112] Schneider, '... *nicht umsonst gefallen'?*, pp. 122, 161.

[113] Tietz, *Tannenberg-Nationaldenkmal*, pp. 71–2, 141–2; Fischer, 'Tannenberg-Denkmal', pp. 33–4.

[114] Kerssen, *Interesse am Mittelalter*, p. 104; Schneider, '... *nicht umsonst gefallen'?*, p. 225, and pp. 156, 161 on sporting events after the war; Tietz, *Tannenberg-Nationaldenkmal*, p. 71.

[115] BArch, R 32/353, folio 43, 'Vorschläge für das Reichsehrenmal', n.d. Compare *Hundert Entwürfe*, pp. 21, 42.

the Versailles Treaty.[116] Some construed sport as a peacetime surrogate for the hardening effects of the 'war experience'. The campaigners for the proposed Reich memorial at Ehrenbreitstein Castle, Rhine Province, meant to fortify German lads through exercise. The draft plan integrated '*Kampfbahnen* for peaceful contest and the physical steeling of German youth' into the memorial fortress.[117] Similarly, Remscheid, Rhine Province, planted a heroes' grove alongside a *Kampfbahn* in memory of those who had held the 'iron rampart' at the front. The *Kampfbahn*, the local sport official elucidated, would foster the physical fitness so essential for the cause of national 'rebirth'.[118] At this point we enter a new discursive field. Invocations of sport and steel linked the discourse of endurance (chapter 3) to that of regeneration (chapter 5).

Not every sport, Werner Sombart believed, furthered the condition of young men to the same extent. Principally, athletics, gymnastics and mountaineering – as opposed to English 'merchants' sports' like cricket or football – would help 'to steel the body'.[119] In England, Sombart argued, 'sportism' had taken the place of sport; the forces of commercialisation and professionalisation had perverted its true character. Sombart was not alone in attacking this development in British sport. Old public-school boys expressed dismay at the consequences of the social diffusion of former elite pastimes, particularly association football. From the vantage point of the Pall Mall club, the growth of professionalism and spectating threatened to destroy the authentic ethos of sportsmanship. True gentlemen were, after all, amateurs; and amateurism afforded them a certain disinterestedness. Calls to abandon the professional football league in 1914–15 have to be seen against a background of mounting anger and frustration of establishment sportsmen. Even though recruiting for the army went on at half-time during matches, wartime games seemed to some gentlemen to endanger the national war

---

[116] Christiane Eisenberg, '*English sports*' *und deutsche Bürger: Eine Gesellschäftsgeschichte 1800–1939* (Paderborn, Ferdinand Schöningh, 1999), pp. 322–3, 329; Mosse, *Fallen Soldiers*, pp. 151, 156. To be sure, the Weimar era also saw the emergence of an alternative, modern or 'Americanised' sports culture. See Frank Becker, *Amerikanismus in Weimar: Sportsymbole und politische Kultur 1918–1933* (Wiesbaden, Deutscher Universitäts Verlag, 1993).

[117] StAMS, OP 5510, folio 202, Ausschuß für das Reichsehrenmal auf dem Ehrenbreitstein (ed.), *Der Ehrenbreitstein als Reichsehrenmal* (Koblenz, n.p., 1928), p. 6: 'Kampfbahnen zum friedlichen Wettstreit und zur körperlichen Stählung der deutschen Jugend'.

[118] BArch, R 36/2099, n.folio, Stadtturnrat Karl Grüber, 'Ehrenhain: Urkunde zur Grundsteinlegung', 2 December 1923. See also Lurz, *Kriegerdenkmäler*, vol. III, p. 123, and vol. IV, pp. 253–4.

[119] Sombart, *Händler und Helden*, p. 121; Stibbe, *German Anglophobia*, pp. 76–7.

effort. Eventually, in April 1915, the Football Association gave in and cancelled all fixtures for the duration of the war.[120]

'NO DOUBT / YOU CAN MAKE MONEY IN THIS FIELD, MY FRIEND, / BUT THERE'S ONLY ONE FIELD TO-DAY WHERE YOU / CAN GET HONOUR', said Mr Punch to a professional association player in October 1914. The cartoon was later adopted for a propaganda poster.[121] Playing 'the greater game', ideally in a sportsman's battalion, was the order of the day. Colonel Edgar Mobbs, a professional with the Northampton rugby team, was among those who led the way. At the outbreak of war, he raised a local sportsmen's battalion, officially the Seventh Battalion of the Northampton-shire Regiment. Mobbs was killed at Passchendaele in 1917. His memorial in Northampton, designed by Alfred Turner, tries to recapture these two facets of Mobbs's life (see figure 45). The side panels depict scenes from the rugby pitch and the battlefield. 'He played the game [in both civilian and military life]' was the tenor of the ceremonial unveiling in July 1921.[122] A few month earlier, Mobbs's former club had initiated an immaterial memorial to its hero. The Mobbs memorial match, first held in February 1921, has remained an annual event to the present.[123] In addition, Mobbs's name is engraved on the war monument outside the clubhouse. 'THEY PLAYED / THE GAME', reads the dedication.[124]

'May their example inspire those who read these words to play the game': thus the memorial of the Aylesbury football club in Buckingham-shire appealed to survivors.[125] Commitment to 'the game' was not exclusive to the commemoration of athletes, however. Local war memorials throughout the country configured the war as a higher form of sporting contest. At Kirkcudbright (where a programme of sports for children and ex-servicemen had rounded off the 1919 peace celebrations), the lord lieutenant said at the unveiling of the war memorial in 1921: 'Mindful of our individual responsibility to the community, let the heart and not only the head direct our action, and as true sportsmen play the game, not for our own hand or even for our own side but let us *play the game*.'[126]

[120] Colin Veitch, '"Play up! Play up! and Win the War!" Football, the Nation and the First World War 1914–15', *Journal of Contemporary History*, 20 (1985), pp. 363–78.
[121] IWM, PST 830, 'The Greater Game', [c. 1914]; 'The Greater Game', *Punch*, 147 (1914), p. 331.
[122] 'Honouring our Great Hero: Mobbs' Memorial Unveiled', *Northampton Independent*, 830, 23 July 1921, p. 16.
[123] 'Mobbs Memorial Match', *Northampton Independent*, 805, 5 February 1921, p. 20.
[124] NIWM, 14946, Northampton.
[125] NIWM, 8047, Aylesbury, Bucks.
[126] Stewartry Museum, Acc. 7216, vol. 3, p. 14, 'Kirkcudbright War Memorial: Unveiled by Lord-Lieutenant', unspecified newspaper cutting, 14 April 1921, italics in the

Figure 45. Edgar Mobbs by Alfred Turner. Northampton, 1921.

The ubiquitous phrase 'to play the game' had been coined by Henry (later Sir Henry) Newbolt in his poem 'Vitai Lampada' published in 1897. It implied two moral imperatives: devotion to the team spirit and conformity to the standards of fair play. Newbolt, a best-selling author of boy's fiction, stated in his 1907 *Book of the Happy Warrior* (the title is cribbed from William Wordsworth's poem 'Character of the Happy Warrior', 1807) that 'the love of games, the "sporting" or "amateur" view of them [derived] from the tournament and chivalric rules of war'.[127] E. B. Osborne, the editor of trench poetry, wrote in a similar vein that 'sportsmanship is our new homely name, derived from a radical predilection

original. See also ibid., vol. 2, p. 194, 'Kirkcudbright War Memorial: The Successful Design', unspecified newspaper cutting, 18 July 1919.

[127] Henry Newbolt, *The Book of the Happy Warrior* (London, Longmans and Green, 1917), p. vii. For a compelling study of the chivalry of sport see Girouard, *Return to Camelot*, pp. 232–48, 285–6. See also Paris, *Warrior Nation*, pp. 133–4.

for comparing great things with small, for the *chevalerie* of the Middle Ages'.[128] A section of his anthology was characteristically headed 'Chivalry of Sport'. Small wonder 'O Valiant Hearts' ('your knightly virtue proved') set the tone for the inauguration of the Mobbs memorial.[129] Sport was regarded as the modern equivalent to the chivalrous duel or tournament. Games like football, rugby and cricket signified a collective – British (or British-Imperial) – code of sportsmanlike behaviour.[130]

By conjuring up notions of sportsmanship, Britons were able to evoke feelings of respect for their opponents. The trouble was that one could not expect the enemy to play the game properly. In April and May 1915, the German army disgusted the chivalric community by employing chlorine-filled shells in the second battle of Ypres. 'It was a new device in warfare and thoroughly illustrative of the Prussian idea of playing the game', remarked a Canadian sergeant of poison gas.[131] Sportsmanship and personal integrity seemed alien to German militarism. A memorial window in Winchester Cathedral contrasted the chivalry of Saints Michael, George and Hubert – the latter being 'the Patron of Sport, and thus, incidentally, of Clean life, Discipline and Fair-play' – with German acts of destruction.[132] The stained-glass widow, which commemorates an individual victim of the Great War, was mounted by the soldier's friends in 1916. A brochure published on the occasion of the unveiling recalls the subject's life:

It is, however, such men as he who make a country worth fighting for and belonging to – men who consistently 'play the game' at the wickets, on the football and hockey ground, and in the field with the gun no less than in their profession or calling, who by proving themselves reliable, thoroughly straightforward, and in every way true sportsmen, exercise what is after all, the only real lasting influence, that of personal example, on those with whom they come in contact.[133]

---

[128] E[dward] B. Osborn (ed.), *The Muse in Arms: A Collection of War Poems for the Most Part Written in the Field of Action, by Seamen, Soldiers, and Flying Men Who Are Serving, or Have Served, in the Great War* (London, John Murray, 1917), p. ix, italics in the original.

[129] 'Mobbs' Memorial: Arrangements for the Unveiling', *Northampton Independent*, 827, 2 July 1921, p. 2.

[130] Reimann, 'Popular Culture', pp. 110–13; Eksteins, *Rites of Spring*, pp. 120–6.

[131] Reginald Grant, *S.O.S. Stand To!* (New York and London, D. Appleton, 1918), p. 32. On sport metaphors in Canadian remembrance culture, see Vance, *Death So Noble*, pp. 97, 237.

[132] IWM, Eph. Mem., K 9702, 'An Account of the Memorial in Winchester Cathedral to Edward Henry Swinburn Bligh Together with the Order of the Dedication Service', 1916.

[133] Ibid. On the significance of brochures commemorating individuals, see Oliver Janz, 'Zwischen privater Trauer und öffentlichem Gedenken: Der bürgerliche

Cricket, hockey and rugby were, of course, a privilege of the leisured classes. Their sons had been inculcated with the games ethos in the late-Victorian and Edwardian public schools. Team sports were deemed vital to the formation of character. Pedagogues, often imbued with anti-intellectualism, bred up British youths as sportsmen and gentlemen. 'Schools of this kind are a particular British institution. [. . .] Boys learn to play the game, to obey, to command, and loyalty to their Old School – a very beautiful thing': thus the speaker at the inauguration of the memorial organ at Worcester Grammar School.[134] The rhetoric of sportsmanship and team spirit was everywhere. In the public-school context, however, 'playing the game' also resonated with religious overtones. The ideal of muscular Christianity, epitomised by the Victorian public schools, combined physical fitness with purity and piety. Bedford School chose to depict 'Muscular Christians' on its memorial reredos (St Alban, King Alfred, Sir Galahad, St George, St Martin of Tours and St Michael), so as to typify the old boys' spirit.[135] In *Knights in Armour*, a book for cadets, the chaplain of Sandhurst set out to define the Christian team spirit. He noted that 'as a Christian, you are not spectator, linesman or referee: you are one of the team; and it's "up to" you to strip and get going and play the game for all you are worth'.[136]

Despite the persistence of muscular Christianity in the public schools (and its imitation by the lesser schools), chivalric elitism became a casualty of the First World War. After 1914, national cohesion through the widening of the chivalric fellowship was imperative. Commemorations represented chivalry as the common aspiration of men in all walks of life. Even though, for many middle-class commentators the British worker was at best a sort of 'gentleman-in-training',[137] many applauded the sportsmanship and chivalry of the former private without a trace of condescension. Consider the 1918 memorial volume of fallen soldier poets. Alongside poems by Etonian knights errant-cum-sportsmen,

---

Gefallenenkult in Italien während des Ersten Weltkriegs', *Geschichte und Gesellschaft*, 28 (2002), pp. 561–2.

[134] Kernot, *Public Schools War Memorials*, p. 28. Generally, see J[ames] A. Mangan, *Athleticism in the Victorian and Edwardian Public School: The Emergence and Consolidation of an Educational Ideology* (Cambridge, Cambridge University Press, 1981); Frantzen, *Bloody Good*, pp. 138–44.

[135] 'The War Memorials', *Ousel*, 556, 10 June 1921, pp. 47–8. On the imitation of muscular Christianity by the lesser schools, see Connelly, *Great War, Memory and Ritual*, pp. 76–7.

[136] Woods, *Knights in Armour*, pp. 8–9.

[137] Collins, 'Fall of the English Gentleman', p. 99.

one finds the verse of John William Streets, a coal miner from north Derbyshire who had attended a Weslyan Sunday school:

Some of us used to say, perhaps too complacently, that Waterloo was won on the playing-fields of Eton. Be that as it may, it is clear to all eyes that the greater, more terrible battles of this war were won on the playing-fields and in the class-rooms of the Council Schools, as well as the Colleges, and in the homes of the whole nation – in cottages and workmen's dwellings no less than in town and country mansions. The Public School spirit is a splendid and a potent tradition, but it does not account for such men as Streets and, in our days, there are not a few of them. I honour their memories too profoundly to think for a moment that it was just their Public School training which made such dear and heroic souls as [The Hon. Julian] Grenfell, [The Hon. Colwyn E. A.] Philipps, [The Hon. Herbert] Palmer, or [The Hon. E.] Wyndham Tennant the fearless and perfect gentle knights that they were; for without that training at least as many have risen, like [Francis] Ledwidge from his scavengering, like [Clifford] Flower from his clerking, like Streets from toiling in the mine, fired by the same shining ideals, the same hatred of cruelty and scorn of wrong, the same selfless love of country, and have died for these things with a chivalry and courage that are no school but of all schools, that are of no class, no limited section of the community, but are in the very blood and bones of our people, in the large tradition of the race.[138]

Knights of the sky

Sport connoted fair play in Britain, but physical steeling in Germany. However, the two concepts were not mutually exclusive. German pilots pursuing the ultimate sport – *Flugsport* or 'flight sport' – identified themselves (or were identified) as sportsmen.[139] Manfred Baron von Richthofen, Germany's air ace with the 'iron fist',[140] spoke highly of *sportlich* or 'sporting' gestures (although he principally saw his acts as analogous to hunting).[141] A German fellow pilot of Richthofen's was reported to have said that 'Every fight is a tournament for us, a chival-rous or [. . .] sporting duel. I do not have anything against the individual

---

[138] A. St John Adcock, *For Remembrance: Soldier Poets Who Have Fallen in the War* (London, New York and Toronto, Hodder and Stoughton, 1918), pp. 170–1, and see also pp. 64–5, 73–4.

[139] Peter Fritzsche, *A Nation of Fliers: German Aviation and the Popular Imagination* (Cambridge, MA and London, Harvard University Press, 1992), pp. 75, 87.

[140] BArch, R 8034 II/7691, folio 44, Rudolf Bieler, 'Dein Werk ist unsterblich! Richthofen an seinem Todestage zum Gedächtnis!', *Deutsche Zeitung*, 165, 18 April 1920.

[141] Manfred von Richthofen, *Der rote Kampfflieger* (Berlin and Vienna, Ullstein, 1917), p. 109, and see pp. 50, 111. On Richthofen's memoirs, see Mosse, *Fallen Soldiers*, p. 122; Robert Wohl, *A Passion for Wings: Aviation and the Western Imagination 1908–1918* (New Haven and London, Yale University Press, 1994), pp. 227–9.

man with whom I fence – I merely want to put him and his aeroplane out of action.'[142] Apparently, he gladly shook hands with opponents who had to make a forced landing. An American rival flyer conceded that 'It is natural that the chivalric spirit should be strong. Even the Boche, treacherous and brutal in all other fighting, has felt its influence and battles in the air with sportsmanship and fairness.'[143] Significantly, his reminiscences are entitled *Knights of the Air*.

Celebrations of knights of the air show that chivalry was not vulnerable to industrial technologies *per se*. The war in the air fought by the new, one-seater planes was portrayed as the last arena for true chivalric endeavour in the machine war; aerial encounters seemed to resemble knightly tournaments.[144] On occasions, even *Vorwärts*, the Social-Democratic daily, enthused over the rebirth of what had been believed to be a vanishing breed: the individual hero descended from the knights of bygone days.[145] But, above all, airmen – the initiated – themselves helped to popularise the myth of knights of the sky. A large number of memoirs by Great War pilots recall the Arthurian legends. The structural similarities between the two genres are remarkable: 'the catalogues of warriors, the repeated trials by combat, the attention to gestures and the set pieces of dialogue, the relishing of all mechanical description, and the avowal of moral purpose throughout', writes one literary historian.[146] The overall impression conveyed in (auto)biographical or fictional accounts of the air war is of a clean, small-scale, face-to-face fight, that is a re-creation of the duel entailing obedience to an unwritten code of behaviour. A British pilot, Cecil Lewis, writes that 'It was like the lists of the Middle Ages, the only sphere in modern warfare where a man saw his adversary and faced him in moral combat, the only sphere

---

[142] Johannes Werner (ed.), *Briefe eines deutschen Kampffliegers an ein junges Mädchen* (Leipzig and Berlin, Hase & Koehler, 1930), p. 67: 'Jeder Kampf bei uns ist ein Turnier, ein ritterlicher oder [. . .] sportmäßiger Zweikampf. Gegen den einzelnen Mann, gegen den ich fechte, habe ich gar nichts – ich will nur ihn und sein Flugzeug außer Kraft setzen.'

[143] Molter, *Knights of the Air*, pp. 21–2.

[144] See John H. Morrow, 'Knights of the Sky: The Rise of Military Aviation', in Frans Coetzee and Marily Shevin-Coetzee (eds.), *Authority, Identity and the Social History of the Great War* (Oxford and Providence, Berghahn, 1995), pp. 315–21; George Mosse, 'The Knights of the Sky and the Myth of the War Experience', in Robert A. Hinde and Helen E. Watson (eds.), *War: A Cruel Necessity? The Bases of Institutional Violence* (London and New York, I. B. Tauris, 1995), pp. 133–5; Paris, *Warrior Nation*, pp. 135–6; Reimann, *Krieg der Sprachen*, pp. 68–73; Schilling, *Kriegshelden*, chs. 4–5; Eksteins, *Rites of Spring*, pp. 264–5.

[145] 'Flieger Richthofen gefallen', *Vorwärts*, 112, 24 April 1918, p. 2. See Schilling, *Kriegshelden*, pp. 253, 281.

[146] Laurence Goldstein, *The Flying Machine and Modern Literature* (Basingstoke and London, Macmillan, 1986), p. 89.

where there was still chivalry and honour.'[147] In short, the fighter pilot managed to reconcile his moral integrity with his duty of having to kill.

Almost identical descriptions can be found in the popular literature of most combatant nations. Chivalry of the air evolved into an international myth, a myth of a fraternity of knights transcending national barriers. Jean Renoir, the director who served in the French air service during the war, created a powerful monument to the cliché of the communion of airborne knights in form of a feature film. *The Grand Illusion*, released in 1937, tells the story of two aristocratic flyers, one German and the other French, captor and captive, bound together by a gentlemanly code of honour. The Frenchman is torn between chivalry and nationality. At first, his ethos prevents him from plotting against the German brother-in-arms to help his French comrades escape from the fortress prison (the scene was shot in the neo-medieval castle of Haut-Kœnigsbourg, Alsace). In the end, the national bond and the bonds of camaraderie prevail.[148]

The opening scene features a German orderly preparing a wreath to be parachuted on to a French aerodrome as a salute to an opponent killed in action. Noble gestures of exchange in particular made up the romance of knights of the sky. While propaganda from all sides bombarded the soldiers in the trenches with atrocity stories, airmen cultivated the image of an honest fight with worthy contenders. In June 1916, when air ace Max Immelmann was killed on a combat mission due to a technical hitch, the Royal Flying Corps (RFC, which became the Royal Air Force in April 1918) dropped a wreath with a note behind German lines announcing the death of the 'sportsman'.[149] Four month later, following the news of the death of Oswald Boelcke, then the German celebrity of the sky, the RFC wrote another letter of condolence: 'To the memory of Captain Boelke [*sic*], our brave and chivalrous opponent.' (After the war, the document was reproduced in facsimile in Johannes Werner's memoir of Boelcke.)[150] Boelcke was eventually superseded in fame by his pupil, Manfred von Richthofen. The 'Red Baron' himself claimed in his memoirs to have erected a tombstone in memory of the first enemy pilot he had shot down.[151] The cult of the honourable opponent culminated

[147] Cecil Lewis, *Sagittarius Rising* (London, Peter Davies, 1936), p. 45.

[148] Michael Paris, *From the Wright Brothers to Top Gun: Aviation, Nationalism and Popular Cinema* (Manchester and New York, Manchester University Press, 1995), pp. 49–50; J[ay] M. Winter, *The Experience of World War I* (London and Basingstoke, Macmillan, 1988), p. 246.

[149] Wohl, *Passion for Wings*, fig. 292.

[150] Johannes Werner, *Boelcke der Mensch, der Flieger, der Führer der deutschen Jagdfliegerei* (Leipzig, von Hase & Koehler, [1932]), pp. 192–3, 214.

[151] Richthofen, *Rote Kampfflieger*, p. 93.

in the funeral honours for the dead Richthofen provided by the Allies in April 1918. Such was the power of the myth of a brotherhood of knights that when Richthofen's body was repatriated to Berlin in November 1925, two Allied officers attended the impressively orchestrated event and placed a floral aeroplane propeller on the hero's coffin.[152]

National narratives of chivalrous airmen intersected; German air aces captured British imagination. The British public was perhaps even more fascinated by the chivalry of Immelmann, Boelcke and Richthofen than the Germans themselves. Biographies and autobiographies of German flyers appeared quickly in English translation; C. W. Sykes alone translated a dozen works. A comparison between the German and English editions of Werner's memoir of Boelcke is illuminating. The German original, published in 1932 under the uninspiring title 'Boelcke the Man, the Flyer, the Leader of German Military Aviation', contains few instances of chivalric diction. The English edition of 1933, prepared by Sykes and marketed imaginatively as *Knight of Germany: Oswald Boelcke: German Ace*, implies that book is about the chivalrous exploits of the German air ace.[153] Sykes himself wrote a biography of Richthofen, characteristically entitled *Richthofen: The Red Knight of the Air*.[154]

Chivalry sold well in Britain, but there was a gap in the market. The RFC failed to satisfy the popular demand for knightly champions. While the German command lionised the names of top pilots in despatches and awarded them the most prestigious decorations, especially the *Pour le mérite* cross (which derived from the cross of the Knights of Malta), the RFC frowned on the celebration of individual heroes. This egalitarian policy is reflected in a parliamentary speech delivered by Lloyd George in October 1917: 'They [the airmen] are the knighthood of this war [. . .]. They recall the old legends of chivalry, not merely by the daring of their exploits, but by the nobility of their spirit, and, amongst the multitudes of heroes, let us think of the chivalry of the air.'[155] The RFC refrained from singling out fine fighter pilots such as Lanoe Hawker, whom the Germans considered 'the English Boelcke', as was done in Germany.[156] Local communities, though, cheered their heroes. A number of parish churches house stained-glass windows dedicated to

---

[152] Whalen, *Bitter Wounds*, p. 34; Fritzsche, *Nation of Fliers*, pp. 89–90.
[153] Werner, *Boelcke der Mensch*; Johannes Werner, *Knight of Germany: Oswald Boelcke: German Ace* (London, John Hamilton, 1933).
[154] 'Vigilant' [Claud W. Sykes], *Richthofen: The Red Knight of the Air* (London, John Hamilton, [1934]). See also Floyd Gibbons, *The Red Knight of Germany: Baron von Richthofen* (London, Cassell, 1930).
[155] Lloyd George, 'A Nation's Thanks', in *The Great Crusade*, p. 149.
[156] Wohl, *Passion for Wings*, p. 216. Compare 'Vigilant', *Richthofen*, pp. 103–13.

home-grown knights of the sky.[157] The most notable memorial to a dead British airman is located in the grounds of Nottingham Castle, a place resonant with chivalric images. Albert Ball V. C. was the local war hero of Nottingham. His official biographer described him as 'a young knight of gentle manners'.[158] At the unveiling of the Ball memorial in September 1921, the speakers acknowledged the pilot's aggressiveness in combat but, at the same time, underlined his 'admiration for those he conquered'. 'His whole desire', the mayor said, 'seemed to be not to destroy life, but to destroy the machines that made it possible for our enemies to destroy life.'[159] In other words, Ball was not a brutal killer but an honest fighter.

In sum, the tale of chivalrous air warfare fulfilled a compensatory function. It pictured the kind of battle the war as a whole should have been but was not: a fair and straightforward man-to-man fight.[160] 'Air-fighting came to be pretty well the old duel, or else the medieval mêlée between little picked teams. The clean element, too, may have counted – it always looked a clean job from below', noted C. E. Montague. He contrasted the noble conduct of the knights of the sky with demands to employ the air force to 'bomb German women and children'.[161] The bomber pilot, cruel and cowardly, belonged to the lowest warrior caste. Boelcke distanced himself from strategic bombing. His biographer suggested that impersonal aerial bombardments from the security of the skies offended the 'chivalrous nature' of the German fighter pilot.[162]

Commentators, especially in Britain, constructed a dichotomy between (chivalrous) air duels and (atrocious) air raids. The enemy bomber pilot embodied the anti-knight. A British placard figured Hindenburg in conversation with Ludendorff: '"KNIGHTS OF THE AIR" / LOOK HINDENBURG! MY GERMAN HEROES!'.[163] In the background, German aeroplanes bombard a field hospital unmistakably marked with a Red Cross sign. In a similar fashion, Escott Lynn's novel for boys (*Knights of the Air*, 1918) recollected the sufferings of 'men, women, and children – on

---

[157] NIWM, 4732, Creeting St Mary, E. Suff., features St George and St Edmund; NIWM, 15216, Prescot, Lancs., shows *inter alia* St George and St Michael.

[158] Walter A. Briscoe and H. Russell Stannard, *Captain Ball V. C.: The Career of Flight-Commander Ball, V. C., D. S.O.* (London, Herbert Jenkins, 1918), p. 23.

[159] 'Homage to V. C. Airman: The Ball Memorial Unveiled', *Nottingham Guardian*, 20430, 9 September 1921, p. 6.

[160] Leed, *No Man's Land*, p. 134; Eksteins, *Rites of Spring*, pp. 264–5.

[161] Montague, 'Christmas 1914', in Moult, *Cenotaph*, p. 100; Montague, *Disenchantment*, p. 138.

[162] Werner, *Knight of Germany*, p. 92; Werner, *Boelcke der Mensch*, p. 86: 'ritterlichen Sinn'. See Morrow, 'Knights of the Sky', pp. 318–19; Paris, *Wright Brothers to Top Gun*, p. 27.

[163] IWM, PST 472, 'Knights of the Air' [*c.* 1915].

whom the bestial Hun was indiscriminately raining down bombs'. Furthermore, the reader is informed that 'unlike German aviators, the British were anxious to obtain their military results with as little danger to the civilian population as possible'.[164] Conversely, the *Deutsche Tageszeitung*, the organ of the agrarian conservatives, sought to reveal the hypocrisy of British chivalric rhetoric. The newspaper recalled the RFC's aerial depredations on 'defenceless women and children'.[165]

The Zeppelin was the ultimate symbol of German frightfulness. Total war arrived on the British doorstep when Zeppelins dropped bombs on London and other cities in 1915–16, ostensibly in direct retribution for Allied air attacks on German towns. The purpose of these air raids was psychological rather than strategic. The German command hoped to break enemy morale on the home front, but to no effect. Instead, Zeppelin raids played into the hands of British propaganda. Wilfred Owen's letters may serve as a measure of British defiance. Owen wrote to his mother in August 1916 that he did not want to destroy 'Fritz, whom I did not hate. To battle with the Super-Zeppelin, when he comes, this would be chivalry more than Arthur dreamed of. Zeppelin, the giant-dragon, the child-slayer, I would happily die in any adventure against him.'[166] Germans, however, had great expectations of what their wonder weapon could achieve. It is revealing that two Zeppelins, products of a technology widely proclaimed a 'modern wonder' in Imperial Germany, circled the Victory Column (inaugurated in 1873, two years after the victory of Sedan) opposite the Reichstag building at the unveiling of the 'Iron Hindenburg' monument in September 1915.[167] The Zeppelin gave the public confidence in Germany's invincibility. Wartime commentators described the airship as a 'steel-blue fortress' or 'iron-clad armament'.[168]

Images of iron proliferated in the German discourse of air warfare. Richthofen's squadron was remembered as an 'Iron Band', and the

---

[164] Escott Lynn, *Knights of the Air* (London, W. & R. Chambers, 1918), pp. 15, 204.

[165] BArch, R 8034 II/7690, folio 177, 'Dem Frhrn. v. Richthofen zum Gedächtnis', *Deutsche Tageszeitung*, 207, 27 April 1918.

[166] Wilfred Owen, *Collected Letters*, ed. Harold Owen and John Bell (London and Oxford, Oxford University Press, 1967), p. 408. See Felix Philipp Ingold, *Literatur und Aviatik: Europäische Flugdichtung 1907–1929* (Basle and Stuttgart, Birkhäuser, 1978), p. 225 n. 17.

[167] 'Die Enthüllung des Eisernen Hindenburg', *Berliner Lokal-Anzeiger*, 452, 4 September 1915. On the notion of the 'modern wonder', see Bernhard Rieger, *Technology and the Culture of Modernity in Britain and Germany, 1890–1945* (Cambridge, Cambridge University Press, 2005), pp. 20–50.

[168] As cited in Fritzsche, *Nation of Fliers*, pp. 28–9.

leader himself as superman 'hard as steel' with 'steely blue eyes'.[169]
Peter Fritzsche has made the point that Germany cultivated, side by
side with that of the knight of the sky, the image of the 'steeled machine-
man'. In open defiance of chivalric standards, this public image of
military masculinity not only legitimised but also celebrated violence
among aviators. Like the steel-helmeted man in the trenches (discussed
in chapter 3), the airborne 'new man' was an exponent of the steel
character of the technological age. More specifically, innovations in air
warfare forged the 'steeled machine-man'. There was no room for
jousting man to man, Fritzsche argues, after the creation of *Jagdstaffeln*,
echelons of five to ten planes, in late summer 1916 and *Geschwader*,
squadrons of up to fifty planes in 1918. The new pilot, operating in a
group, was actuated by a will to destroy, sustained by iron nerves.[170]

   In conclusion, the re-invention of the individual in aerial combat
clashed with the anonymity of operations in the trenches. The overemphasis on individualism in the lionisation of air aces may explain
why narratives of air warfare, although ingrained in popular culture,
had a negligible influence on public war remembrance.[171] The purpose
of war memorial sculpture was to portray the typical, common victim
rather than the exceptional hero. The managers of communal memorial
projects were charged with finding a commemorative language which
both idolised and equalised all fallen soldiers. As a result, the concept of
heroic ordinariness was brought into being; the soldier's normal military
duty could become a source of heroism as long as it was conscientiously
executed.[172] At any rate, it was character rather than outstanding
achievement which distinguished the modern knight.

French historian Antoine Prost has noted that 'behind every hero,
there is also a brute, without whom the hero would not exist'.[173] The
Great War brought into being a new kind of armed confrontation that
generated unprecedented levels of violence among combatants and
cruelty against civilians. The soldier was a death-giver, an agent of

[169] BArch, R 8034 II/7691, folio 44, 'Ein ganzer Mann', *Fränkischer Kurier*, 163, 16 April
    1920; Mosse, 'Knights of the Sky,' p. 137.
[170] Fritzsche, *Nation of Flyers*, pp. 71, 91–8. Compare Rieger, *Technology and the Culture of
    Modernity*, pp. 254–73.
[171] See Schilling, *Kriegshelden*, p. 291. The combined war memorial and Boelcke monu-
    ment in Dessau is an exception. See Paul Rieß, 'Das Denkmal auf dem Ehrenfriedhof
    zu Dessau', *Anhalter Anzeiger: Dessauer Neueste Nachrichten*, 255, 30 October 1921.
[172] King, *Memorials of the Great War*, p. 184.
[173] Antoine Prost, 'Representations of War in the Cultural History of France, 1914–1939',
    in Antoine Prost, *Republican Identities in War and Peace: Representations of France in the
    Nineteenth and Twentieth Centuries* (Oxford and New York, Berg, 2002), p. 101.

slaughter, but the reconfiguration of wartime brutality in post-war commemorations created a purified memory of the dead soldiers and their conduct in war. This was an essential component of the process of mourning. For the survivors it was 'easier, however painful, to accept the idea that one's grandfather or father was killed in combat than that he might have killed others. In the context of personal or family memory', Stéphane Audoin-Rouzeau and Annette Becker suggest, 'it is better to be a victim than an agent of suffering and death.'[174]

Public discourses of remembrance offered reassurance by eliding the war with a set of chivalric notations, notations which suggested a triumph over violence itself. Through symbolic language, the survivors asserted that their soldiers had remained untouched by the brutality of war, that they had not been transmuted into cold-blooded mass murderers. In Britain, chivalric diction ennobled combatants and obscured the act of killing; in Germany, by contrast, notions of alien *Unritterlichkeit* sanctified the conduct of total war. Both encodings rehabilitated the soldier. His goodness was important to memorial makers since, as Sir Henry Newbolt noted, 'it is impossible to honour men who have been guilty of barbarous cruelty'. Only 'clean fighters' could be venerated for their bloody deeds.[175] Chivalric notation provided one solution to the moral dilemmas of the post-war years. The soldiers of 1914–18 were both defenders and killers, mobilised by civilian society in their defence. Evocations of chivalry on your side and 'un-chivalry' on the enemy's side resolved doubts as to the moral character of the actions of the soldiers, both those who survived and those who died in the war.

[174] Stéphane Audoin-Rouzeau and Annette Becker, *1914–1918: Understanding the Great War* (London, Profile, 2002).
[175] Newbolt, *Book of the Happy Warrior*, pp. 278–9.

5   Regeneration and salvation: the prospects for the living and the dead

The slaughter of 1914–18 meant a significant lowering of the threshold of physical and verbal violence. Images of chivalry and *Unritterlichkeit*, discussed in chapter 4, sanctified the status of soldiers as killers and thus solved the moral predicament of the survivors. However, the ultimate challenge facing the architects of war remembrance was to make sense of mass death and respond to the accumulated presence of death in society. A British sample *Order of Memorial Service for those Fallen in the War*, issued in 1917, proffered the belief that a knight's death did not end life but rather enriched it. The service booklet evoked George Frederick Watt's painting *The Happy Warrior* of 1884, a product of the Arthurian revival in Victorian art, depicting an angel cradling the head of a dying youth:

Do not think of your sons, then, as sinking into the grave, but as ascending radiantly into life, winning in that high moment the crown of their earthly sacrifices. It is this thought that has made Watt's 'Happy Warrior' so rich in comfort to those whose brave sons have fallen in the fight. At the very moment of death, when to the world all seems lost, this Happy Warrior sees that all is gained. With the clear eyes of death he beholds the vision of his dreams; that which before could only be apprehended by faith is now revealed to sight, the happiness of victory vanquishes even the pain of death; so for him the heavens open, and he enters gloriously into Life! No broken pillar or funeral urn for such as he. For it is not when we die but how we live that counts; and as we think of those young knights of ours, splendid in their courage, splendid in their sacrifice, risking all, and yielding all, how can we think of their deaths with bitterness? Death becomes suddenly a radiant and a holy thing, purged for ever in our minds from what is shallow and unworthy.[1]

Knights of unimpeachable character, it seemed, were on the road to rebirth. Central to all war commemoration was the question of how salvation would actually come about. War remembrance placed itself

---

[1] J[ames] Burns, *Order of Memorial Service for those Fallen in the War* (London, James Clarke, [1917]), pp. 10–11.

right between death and life, recalling the soldier's nobility and consoling the bereaved. This chapter analyses how the spiritual dimension of medievalism established a 'domain of the sacred, the no man's land between the living and the dead'.[2] More precisely, I review three variants of spiritual medievalism: first, commemorative forms and practices of medieval-Christian inspiration; secondly, the concept of death as a deep, enchanted sleep derived from national mythologies and folk tale; and thirdly, prophecies based on Germanic saga and its nineteenth-century revival forms.

Christian redemption

The Great War left a paradoxical legacy of religious awakening and ecclesiastical decline. On the one hand, the strain of war and the confrontation with mass death strengthened religious imagination and created novel expressions of religiosity among the soldiers and their relatives. On the other hand, the quest for the sacred did not drive people into the arms of the churches. Contrary to the high expectations of some clergymen in 1914, the war accelerated the late nineteenth-century trend towards religious diversity or privatisation and decline of organised religion.[3] Even so, churches remained central sites of commemorative activity, and Christian notation – redemptive sacrifice and benevolent intercession in particular – flourished in the aftermath of the First World War because it offered an accessible and consolatory language. It empowered the bereaved or their agents to convert death into a gift, a noble sacrifice promising entry into everlasting life rather than a pointless passing. Such appropriations of Christian doctrine tended to be eclectic and unorthodox. Far from communicating anything specific about Christianity, religious diction helped to create a spiritual aura around the dead, the war and commemoration itself.

Patri-passionism

The notion of the reversibility of suffering, the conversion of gravest pain into everlasting joy, was critical to the spiritual fervour of the Great War. The archetypal suffering and resurrection of Christ provided the

---

[2] Winter, *Sites of Memory*, p. 221.
[3] K[en] S. Inglis, 'Foreword', in Annette Becker, *War and Faith: The Religious Imagination in France, 1914–1930* (Oxford and New York, Berg, 1998), pp. ix–x; Audoin-Rouzeau and Becker, *1914–1918*, ch. 5; Reimann, *Krieg der Sprachen*, pp. 91–113, 280. See also Harris, *Private Lives*, ch. 6.

principal point of religious reference in war remembrance. The Passion of Christ, endlessly recalled in war memorials, conceptualised and channelled the religious imagination: the fallen soldiers were presented as Christ-like characters, just as Jesus – as we have seen in the previous chapter – was imagined as a chivalrous soldier. Theologically, the equation of the combatants' self-sacrifice with Christ's was questionable; it obscured the uniqueness of the latter and thus came close to heresy. But in spite of theological objections, 'patri-passionism' evolved into the creed of the commemorative communion.[4] Popular sentiment overrode implicit doubts from some pulpits.

As for the design of war memorials, patri-passionism led to an enormous proliferation of crosses.[5] Uncontroversial in Germany, the cross, particularly the crucifix, could stir up heated disputes and sometimes even violent reactions in Britain. When the street shrine of the Roman Catholic parish of Croydon, Surrey – a Calvary – was smashed in May 1918, the press blamed anti-Catholic and anti-Irish sentiments for the outrage.[6] The Croydon incident must have dismayed the reader of the Roman Catholic *Tablet* who, earlier in the same year, had proposed war shrines as 'a favourable opportunity of making the Protestant public familiar with Catholic emblems'.[7] As a type of monument, the cross had largely disappeared from British ecclesiastical art in the sixteenth century and was, therefore, commonly associated with the 'Catholic' Middle Ages and with papalism. While patri-passionism enjoyed popularity in all denominations, its most potent symbol, the cross, seemed to many Protestants to reek of medieval superstition.[8] The Imperial War Graves Commission, charged with the representation of all war dead, realised that a delicate balancing act was needed in order to satisfy all shades of Catholicism and Protestantism at the same time. In the end, they established the 'Cross of Sacrifice' bearing the 'Crusaders' Sword'. The cross, Herbert (later Sir Herbert) Baker concluded, 'has been the accepted sign of self-sacrifice throughout Christendom [. . .], and even if the Presbyterians have a general objection to the principle of symbolism

---

[4] Gregory, *Silence of Memory*, pp. 34–5, 186. On nonconformists, see Doyle, 'Religion, Politics and Remembrance', p. 231. By contrast, Wilkinson, *Church of England*, pp. 295–6, highlights the evangelical critique of patri-passionism.

[5] Catherine Moriarty, 'Christian Iconography and First World War Memorials', *Imperial War Museum Review*, 6 (1991), pp. 69–74; King, *Memorials of the Great War*, pp. 129–30; Kathrin Hoffmann-Curtius, 'Das Kreuz als Nationaldenkmal: Deutschland 1814 und 1931', *Zeitschrift für Kunstgeschichte*, 48 (1985), pp. 85–100. See also Stieglitz, 'Reproduction of Agony', pp. 89–92.

[6] 'Croydon: War Shrine Smashed', *Tablet*, 131 (1918), pp. 627–8.

[7] 'War Shrines', *Tablet*, 131 (1918), p. 158.

[8] Inglis, 'The Homecoming', pp. 585–96. See also Gaffney, *Aftermath*, pp. 120–1.

they cannot reject the symbol of self-sacrifice which the wooden crosses on the graves of their fallen have sanctified'.[9]

In contrast to the French term *monument aux morts*, its English equivalent, *war memorial*, determines neither the form nor the subject of remembrance.[10] A war memorial may or may not be monumental, and may or may not represent suffering and sacrifice. Protestants, motivated by iconophobia and a preference for amenities to serve the living, tended to favour utilitarian schemes such as hospitals and village halls over monuments to the dead. Generally speaking, however, the adherents of utilitarian tributes were outvoted by the advocates of sacred memorials. According to one estimate, utilitarian offerings made up less than ten per cent of all Great War memorials in the British Isles.[11] The voluntarist tradition of British Protestantism struggled to accommodate the wistful yearning to visualise the sacred. Catholicism, on the other hand, proved more amenable to the sanctification of death in war, and often gained the upper hand in war commemoration. The conflict between upholders of Protestant utilitarianism and Catholic mysticism informs G. K. Chesterton's humorous vignette of small-town life in Beaconsfield, Buckinghamshire. In Beaconsfield, the proposed memorial cross met with considerable scepticism:

Other objections to the [. . .] symbol were adduced, probably to cover the real objection; such as the monument as an obstacle to traffic. The local doctor, an admirable physician but a sceptic of rather a schoolboy sort, observed warmly, 'If you do stick up a thing like this, I hope you'll stick a light on it, or all our cars will smash into it in the dark.' Whereupon my wife, who was then an ardent Anglo-Catholic, observed with an appearance of dreamy rapture, 'Oh, yes! How beautiful! A lamp continually burning before the Cross!' Which was not exactly what the man of science had proposed [. . .]. A renewed shock went through the anti-clerical party on finding that the Cross was a Crucifix. This represented, to many amiable and professedly moderate Nonconformists and other Protestants, exactly that extra touch that they could not tolerate.[12]

---

[9] CWGC, WG 18, Herbert Baker to Fabian Ware, 9 November. 1917. See also CWGC, SDC 30, 'Proposal for a Cruciform Headstone', 1919. Compare Frederic Kenyon, *War Graves: How the Cemeteries Abroad will be Designed* (London, HMSO, 1918), pp. 10–1. For dissenting voices, see Mansfield, 'Class Conflict', p. 80. On the 'Cross of Sacrifice', see chapter 2.

[10] Inglis, *Sacred Places*, p. 138.

[11] Moriarty, 'Narrative and the Absent Body', p. 77.

[12] Chesterton, *Autobiography*, pp. 241–2. See Inglis, 'The Homecoming', pp. 585, 595–6. Generally, see Ian Boyd, 'Chesterton's Medievalism', *Studies in Medievalism*, 3 (1991), pp. 243–55. For a similar design, see 'Lingfield War Memorial', *Builder*, 121 (1921), p. 193.

The *lanterne aux morts* at Beaconsfield, on the traditional medieval pattern, with a perpetual flame for the souls of the dead, was a clear manifestation of Anglo-Catholic pride. In search for a Catholicity distinct from contemporary Roman Catholicism, ritualistic-minded Anglicans had discovered medievalism in the previous century. Notably, the Ecclesiologists of the Cambridge Camden Society helped to establish the neo-Gothic style as the trade mark of Anglo-Catholicism (as opposed to the neo-Baroque preferred by the Roman church).[13] The Ecclesiologists idealised the Middle Ages as a model for their own time, and medieval spirituality as a vital counterbalance to the secular ethos of Victorian Britain. In architecture, they found an effective locus for the dissemination of their sacro-medievalism – so effective that even nonconformist chapels appropriated the Gothic externally. In this respect, the Ecclesiologists departed from the original Tractarians of the 1830s and 1840s. John Keble and his associates in the Oxford Movement had taken little if any interest in architectural and ceremonial matters. Keble's disapproval of ostentation notwithstanding, the chapel of Keble College, Oxford, consecrated in 1876, ten years after the death of the church reformer, was executed in ornate neo-Gothic. Predictably enough, the college war memorial, a shrine on the side of the approach to the chapel, embellished with figurative representations of St George and St Martin, is one of the most lavishly decorated memorials in Oxford. Initially, the college had also envisaged a memorial cross. In 1919, Ninian (later Sir Ninian) Comper, the last of the Gothic revivalists and devout Anglo-Catholic, sketched a huge Gothic-style cross for the college, crowned by a crucifix, and with figures of soldier saints in niches midway up the shaft (see figure 46).[14]

In 1917, in the footsteps of the Ecclesiologists, a new pressure group, the Wayside Cross Society, was formed to further the use of roadside crosses and calvaries for public commemorative purposes and as places of private prayer. Since the numberless calvaries at crossroads in Belgium and France were reported to have made a great impression on British soldiers of all denominations, the society expected that such visual reminders 'of the great fact of our Redemption' would accomplish

[13] James F. White, *The Cambridge Movement: The Ecclesiologists and the Gothic Revival* (Cambridge, Cambridge University Press, 1962); Raymond Chapman, 'Last Enchantments: Medievalism and the Early Anglo-Catholic Movement', *Studies in Medievalism*, 4 (1992), pp. 174–6.
[14] Keble College Archives, Oxford, Building Plans/OFF/S/01, Drawings of a war memorial cross by John Ninian Comper, 1919; 'Oxford War Memorials', *Oxford Magazine*, 41 (1923), p. 456.

Figure 46. Cross with statues of knights by Ninian (later Sir Ninian) Comper. Drawing of a proposed memorial cross for Keble College, Oxford, 1919.

similar ends in Britain.[15] In order to appeal to a wider public than
could be reached by memorials in the precincts of churches, the society
campaigned for the erection of new (and the restoration of ancient)
crosses along the highways of Britain. In 1919, however, the society
announced its dissolution due to lack of support from the public.[16]

Perhaps the society admitted defeat prematurely. In March 1920, the
townsfolk of Edwardstone, West Suffolk, raised a memorial cross at the
junction of two roads. The setting was carefully chosen in allusion to the
roadside calvaries at the entrance to French villages. Could there be a
more appropriate symbol than the crucifix, the parish priest asked in his
sermon. 'It spoke of suffering and it spoke of triumph through suffering.
Those brave comrades of theirs lost their lives, and fought bravely, and it
was their suffering which led to triumph.'[17] In the following month, the
East Suffolk village of Westhorpe dedicated a Calvary to its fallen sons.
Contrary to the agenda of the Wayside Cross Society, the memorial was
placed in the churchyard 'near the beautiful 15th century porch', as the
local newspaper stressed.[18] Nonetheless, the order of the service was that
of the Wayside Cross Society.

The use of the crucifix distinguished High Church parishes. It is
hardly a coincidence that the parish of St Mary the Less in Cambridge,
a well-known bastion of Anglo-Catholicism, settled on a 'war shrine'
featuring a crucifix accompanied by two candlesticks and a kneeler (see
figure 47).[19] But contrary to what one might expect, the Scottish National War Memorial in Edinburgh also incorporated a crucifix. 'Take
particular note of the figure itself', a contemporary guidebook points
out, 'it is not nailed to the Cross; it is free. No longer does its posture
represent Suffering and Death, but Resurrection and Ascension.'[20]
However, some Protestants discovered alternative ways of visualising
salvation and harking back to a remote past without renouncing the
Reformation. Celtic crosses, particularly widespread in Scotland, did
not have Catholic connotations.[21] Likewise, old market crosses, or

[15] Wayside Cross Society, *Wayside Crosses* (London, Chiswick, 2nd edn 1917), p. 5. On the
impact of wayside calvaries on British imagination, see Fussell, *Great War*, pp. 117–20.
[16] King, *Memorials of the Great War*, pp. 73–4.
[17] 'Memorials to the Fallen: Dedication of Cross and Window at Edwardstone', *East
Anglian Daily Times*, 16092, 16 March 1920, p. 4.
[18] 'Westhorpe Calvary Unveiled', *Suffolk Chronicle and Mercury*, 4560, 23 April 1920, p. 5.
[19] CUL, EDR, D 3/4c, pp. 35–6, and D 3/5, Faculty for War Shrine, St Mary the Less,
Cambridge, 12 August 1918.
[20] Hay, *Their Name Liveth*, p. 138.
[21] Bell, 'Monuments to the Fallen', pp. 225, 420, 431, 436–7; King, *Memorials of the Great
War*, p. 129.

Figure 47. Crucifix. Church of St Mary the Less, Cambridge, 1920s.

mercat crosses in Scotland, were acceptable non-sectarian symbols. Architectural historians highlighted the secular importance of these crosses which had served as focal points of town life prior to the advent of modernity. Moreover, there was a utilitarian dimension to the public cross where a roof supported by pillars had been added to its structure, as in the case of the late-Gothic market cross in Chichester, West Sussex. Such a 'gracefully-designed shelter' might even delight, it was hoped, the out-and-out utilitarian.[22]

Crucifixes, Celtic crosses and market crosses conjured up redemptive suffering and sacrifice. Eleanor crosses, by contrast, primarily represented statements by the survivors of grief and loss of loved ones. They were modelled on the monuments erected by Edward I between 1291 and 1294 to mark the progress of the funeral cortège of his queen Eleanor of Castile from Lincolnshire to Westminster. These stone crosses, put up by a man 'stricken with grief at the loss of his Queen', as the Herefordshire memorial committee put it, inspired a number of First World War memorials in England.[23] Fine examples can be found in Hereford, Wigan in Lancashire (by Sir Giles Gilbert Scott; see figure 48), and – unusual for Wales – in Prestatyn, Flintshire.[24] At St Albans, Hertfordshire, one of twelve places where Eleanor's body had rested for a night, local notables presented the abbey with a painting showing the honour paid to the dead queen in 1290.[25] Eleanor crosses had already undergone a revival before the Great War. At Sledemere, East Yorkshire, Sir Tatton Sykes, an enthusiastic supporter of the Gothic revival with an affinity for Catholicism, had commissioned an Eleanor cross. Completed in 1899, it is almost an exact replica of the Hardingstone monument near Northampton, one of three surviving medieval originals. After 1918, the Sledemere cross was turned into a war memorial. Brass effigies in Gothic style, depicting Sykes's son Mark and other distinguished members of the Fifth Battalion of the Yorkshire Regiment in the guise of crusader knights, were mounted on the cross.[26]

The symbolism of the cross had important ramifications for commemoration in Britain. By comparison, the semiotics of remembrance did not open up such deep divisions in German society. First of all, few Germans thought of a hospital, a library or a scholarship as a suitable memorial.

[22] Walter H. Godfrey, 'War Memorials: Suggestions from the Past. III. – Market Crosses and Halls', *Architectural Review*, 46 (1919), p. 67. See also Bell, 'Monuments to the Fallen', pp. 230, 525.

[23] Herefordshire Record Office, Hereford, BH 45/20, 'Order of Proceedings: Unveiling of the Hereford County & City War Memorial', 1922, p. 1.

[24] NIWM, 3236, Wigan, Lancs.; NIWM, 7157, Prestatyn, Flints. See also Moriarty, 'Narrative and the Absent Body', pp. 302, 320; Borg, *War Memorials*, pp. 9, 95.

[25] NIWM, 14682, St Albans, Herts.

[26] Banbury, 'Sledemere Cross', pp. 193–7.

Figure 48. Eleanor cross by Sir Giles Gilbert Scott. Wigan, 1925.

The provision of amenities and welfare was, by and large, considered to be the responsibility of the state, not its citizens. To be sure, the Baden advice centre for war commemoration reasoned, in 1916, that the economic and medical well-being of war-disabled veterans had to take

precedence over the desire for costly monuments.[27] Members of the
Social Democratic Party in particular defended the priority of war charity over war memorials.[28] What distinguished German proponents of
utilitarianism from their British counterparts, apart from their marginality, was the fact that they did not conceive of amenities as proper
commemorations, but as alternatives to war memorials at a time of tight
budgets. The real issue at stake in the discussion of utilitarian schemes
was the distribution of monies (possibly a combination of public funds
and private donations) rather than the ideal form of war remembrance.[29]

Second, the cross seldom aroused controversy in Germany, but was
almost universally accepted as the symbol of sacrificial death in war. The
exception only proves the rule. The sculpture 'Kruzifixus' by Ludwig
Gies, exhibited in the Lutheran cathedral of Lübeck in December 1921,
provoked an uproar, and was soon defaced by vandals.[30] Yet it was not so
much the depiction of the crucifixion as such than Gies's expressionist,
unheroic treatment of suffering that was contentious. The crucifix,
though, was something of a rarity in the predominantly Protestant
regions of northern and eastern Germany, and was largely confined to
Roman Catholic congregations. For instance, a 'carved medieval crucifix' commemorated the fallen of Holy Trinity, a Franciscan church in the
free city of Danzig (Gdańsk).[31] While Lutherans took a fairly relaxed
attitude towards religious emblems, a streak of iconophobia runs
through Calvinist commemorations. Crosses were conspicuously absent
from the war-memorial scene of East Friesland, Hanover, where Dutch-
influenced Calvinism had gained a firm foothold in the early modern
period. Only the war memorials of the city of Leer (see figure 12),
situated in the Lutheran cemetery, and the isle of Norderney represented

[27] *Kriegerdenkmal und Soldatengräber: Ratschläge der Badischen Beratungsstelle für Kriegerehrungen* (Karlsruhe, Braun, 1916), p. 1.
[28] Lurz, *Kriegerdenkmäler*, vol. III, p. 180. See also Alexander-Seitz-Geschichtswerkstatt
(ed.), *'Furchtlos und Treu': Die Geschichte des Marbacher Kriegerdenkmals* (Marbach,
Alexander-Seitz-Geschichtswerkstatt, 3rd edn 1994), p. 30; GStAPK, I. HA Rep. 191
Nr. 4368 (M), 'Ehrenmal für die im Weltkriege Gefallenen', 1924–6.
[29] To be sure, iconophobia was not the only motivation behind amenity memorials in
Britain. See Grieves, 'Common Meeting Places', esp. pp. 184–6; Mansfield, 'Class
Conflict', pp. 77–8.
[30] Bushart, *Geist der Gotik*, pp. 164–5, 187; Ursel Berger, '"Immer war die Plastik die
Kunst nach dem Kriege": Zur Rolle der Bildhauerei bei der Kriegerdenkmalproduktion
in der Zeit der Weimarer Republik', in Rainer Rother (ed.), *Die letzten Tage der Menschheit: Bilder des Ersten Weltkrieges* (Berlin, Deutsches Historisches Museum, 1994), pp.
426–7, 432. For a contemporary point of view, see Victor Klemperer, *Leben sammeln,
nicht fragen wozu und warum*, vol. I, *Tagebücher 1918–1924*, ed. Walter Nowojski (Berlin,
Aufbau, 1996), p. 891.
[31] BArch, R 32/348, folio 53, Friedrich Fischer, 'Kriegerehrungen in Danzig', 1927.

the cross.[32] The design of the latter, by Hermann Hosaeus, is faintly reminiscent of the Iron Cross. Hosaeus himself deemed the cross a sacred symbol independent of the dogmas of the church, a sentiment which struck a chord with many believers in patri-passionism.

Intercessions

Compared to the relative acceptance of the cross, the representation of saints in commemorative art was a sensitive issue that threatened to polarise the denominations, or residual denominational persuasions of the secularised population in Germany. While the notion of saintly intercession on behalf of the dead had the power to give comfort to Catholic-inclined audiences, it could antagonise Protestants. The problems involved in the invocation of saints did not escape the attention of official arbiters of taste in Germany. Concerned about both aesthetic standards and social harmony, a Westphalian advisory body recommended St George, St Martin and St Michael as appropriate figures for use in Roman Catholic commemoration only.[33] In practice, the soldier saints were preponderant in the rural Catholic districts of the province, whereas the more mixed urban population tended to settle for non-sectarian imagery.[34]

The war memorial in Albachten, a village near Münster, Westphalia, called on St Michael to safeguard the absent dead. Initiated by the local veterans' association, of which virtually all male adults were members, the monument was sited in the precincts of the Roman Catholic parish church – despite the priest's initial reluctance to cede the plot to the veterans. But as it happened, two out of the ten members of the memorial committee also sat on the parish council. The committee entrusted the design to Wilhelm Haverkamp, a Berlin-based sculptor with roots in the Münsterland, whom they appreciated for his earlier war memorials featuring the archangel in nearby Lüdinghausen 1907, and in Senden 1909. In a niche of the foundation stone, the villagers deposited a *Sekt*

---

[32] TUB, Ho 848, Photographs Norderney, n.d. See Weinland, *Kriegerdenkmäler in Berlin*, p. 121. For a contemporary survey of war memorials in East Friesland see Ludwig Kittel, 'Heldenehrung in Ostfriesland', *Ostfreesland*, 15 (1928), pp. 97–101.

[33] StAMS, OP 5603, folio 15, Westfälische Bauberatungsstelle *et al.*, 'Ehret die Krieger! Merkblatt für Kriegerehrungen', 1915, p. 4. On Roman Catholicism and cultural memory before the war, see Uta Rasche, 'Geschichtsbilder im katholischen Milieu des Kaiserreichs: Konkurrenz und Parallelen zum nationalen Gedächtnis', in Clemens Wischermann (ed.), *Vom kollektiven Gedächtnis zur Individualisierung der Erinnerung* (Stuttgart, Franz Steiner, 2002), pp. 25–52.

[34] Bach, *Studien zur Geschichte*, p. 23.

bottle containing an historical sketch of their monumental tribute to the dead. The iconography was explained as follows:

It represents a sarcophagus on which the names of the fallen and of those who died in the war have been chiselled. It also bears the names of the missing and the names of the fallen in the wars of 1864, 1866 and 1870–71. Above the sarcophagus lies a block of stone with an inscription mounted on the front, and on both sides kneel praying angels in armour. The figure of the Archangel Saint Michael adorns the upper part of the memorial. He is clad in a suit of armour; he holds the flaming sword vertically pointing to the ground; he shields, as it were, the heroes' grave and the fallen which rest therein. This is the meaning of the memorial.[35]

A flaming sword distinguished the archangel at Albachten. Elsewhere, St Michael, holding a pair of scales, appeared less martial. At Weingarten, Württemberg, St Michael, clothed in a curious ancient-Roman-medieval outfit, carries a banner (to lead the heavenly hosts) plus a pair of scales (to weigh the souls of the deceased). 'Standard-bearer, Saint Michael', the inscription beseeches him, 'take the heroes to their eternal goal.'[36] St George stands side by side with St Michael; they represent the Sixth Württembergian Infantry Regiment No. 124 and the municipal and parochial parishes respectively (see figures 49–50).

An inventory of the war memorials of Württemberg, compiled by a retired general in the inter-war years, confirms that soldier saints possessed a potent appeal to memorial makers in districts with a Catholic majority. Yet the inventory also reveals that saints were occasionally drafted into Protestant service. For visual representations of St George, the ratio is 20 (in Catholic-dominated districts) to 6 (in Protestant-dominated districts) to 4 (in mixed districts), and, for St Michael, 9 to

[35] As cited in Johannes Ahrendts, 'Wenn ein Denkmal rissig wird: Geschichte und Bedeutungswandel des Albachtener Kriegerdenkmals', in Heinrich Avenwedde and Heinz-Ulrich Eggert (eds.), Denkmäler in Münster: Auf Entdeckungsreise in die Vergangenheit (Münster, Schriftproben, 1996), p. 190: 'Er stellt einen Sarkophag dar, in welchem die Namen der Gefallenen und im Kriege Gestorbenen eingemeißelt sind. Auch trägt er die Namen der Vermißten und die Namen der Gefallenen der Kriege 1864, 1866 und 1870–71. Oberhalb des Sarkophags liegt ein Steinblock, in dem auf der Vorderseite eine Inschrift angebracht ist, an beiden Seiten knien gepanzerte betende Engel. Den oberen Teil des Denkmals schmückt die Figur des heiligen Erzengels Michael. Derselbe ist mit einer Rüstung angetan, das Flammenschwert hält er senkrecht zur Erde, er beschützt gleichsam das Heldengrab und die darin ruhenden Gefallenen. Das ist der Sinn des Denkmals.' See also Bach, Studien zur Geschichte, pp. 202–4, 210–11.
[36] HStAS, M 746, Bü 47, Section Ravensburg, Questionnaire, c. 1925: 'Bannerträger, heiliger Michael, fahre die Helden zum ewigen Ziel'; HStAS, M 746a, Offiziersverein und Landesverband ehem. 124er, 'Ehrentafel des Infanterie-Regiments König Wilhelm I. (6. Württ.) Nr. 124: Namentliches Verzeichnis der im Weltkrieg 1914–1918 gefallenen 3562 Offiziere, Unteroffiziere und Mannschaften', 1932.

Figure 49. St George by F. H. Eberhard. Minster church, Weingarten, 1923.

Figure 50. St Michael by F. H. Eberhard. Minster church, Weingarten, 1923.

2 to 1 (out of a total of 996 entries).[37] Notably, the memorial of the garrison of Ulm, prominently positioned in the minster, represents the archangel. According to Paul Schmitthenner, a professor of architecture at Stuttgart, the Ulm memorial successfully reintroduced art and beauty into the Protestant church: 'The figure of the angel in "armour and arms [Wehr und Waffen]" ideally encapsulates a Protestant idea in artistic form. Here is an exceptionally fortunate opportunity to let art speak in the Protestant church in an exemplary manner, that art which, unfortunately – not to the advantage of churches – has too often been banished from it.'[38]

The distinctly Protestant character of the monument remains vague, although in popular Protestantism heavenly mediators would typically take the form of angels rather than saints. The iconography of the minster memorial seemed to signify hope of deliverance in the aftermath of an apocalyptic experience. With his sword St Michael watches over the graves of the dead, but his opened wings speak of resurrection, as the local newspaper explained (see figure 19).[39] Catholics would have welcomed the symbolism. After all, St Michael was believed to be the guardian angel of all Germans regardless of their religious affiliation. Since St Michael represented a unifying national symbol, it was quite appropriate to invoke his spirit in a sermon touching on the legendary 'August experience' of 1914 that had allegedly united the German people. On the twentieth anniversary of the outbreak of the First World War, the dean of Ulm preached in 1934: 'But you, herald of God, tutelary genius of the German people, warrior Michael, be a sign to us [. . .] and fight against the evil and ungodly spirit in our people, so that the power of God may forever come upon us anew, as it came upon Germany at the outbreak of the great war 20 years ago'.[40]

[37] HStAS, M 746, 'Denkmäler und Ehrentafeln für die Gefallenen des Ersten Weltkrieges', 1923–31.

[38] StdAU, E 603/11, 'Das Gefallenendenkmal im Münster', Ulmer Tageblatt, 113, 15 May 1928: 'In der Gestalt des Engels in "Wehr und Waffen" findet ein protestantischer Gedanke eine vorbildlich künstlerische Gestaltung. Es bietet sich hier eine selten glückliche Gelegenheit, die Kunst in der protestantischen Kirche in vorbildlicher Weise sprechen zu lassen, die – nicht zum Besten der Kirchen – leider zu oft aus ihr verbannt wird.'

[39] Ibid., 'Das Gefallenendenkmal im Münster', Ulmer Tageblatt, 38, 15 February 1928.

[40] StdAU, E 603/17, 'Totengedenken und alter Frontgeist in Ulm: Denkmalsweihe im Münster', Ulmer Tageblatt, 180, 6 August 1934: 'Du aber, du Bote Gottes, Schutzgeist des deutschen Volkes, du Streiter Michael, sei uns Zeichen [. . .] und wehre dem bösen und widergöttlichen Geist in unserem Volk, daß Gottes Kraft immer neu über uns komme, wie sie über Deutschland kam vor 20 Jahren beim Ausbruch des großen Krieges.'

Supernatural Allies, first and foremost the English patron saint, St George, were mobilised in aid of 'Tommy Atkins' also. Paradigmatic in this respect was the reception of the legend of the Angels of Mons in wartime Britain. Unlike most myths of war, the Angels of Mons has a known originator: Arthur Machen, a journalist with the London *Evening News*, who had made a name for himself as a writer of wonder stories before the war. On 29 September 1914, his short story 'The Bowmen' appeared in the *Evening News*. It tells the story of a miracle that saved the British Expeditionary Force in a desperate situation during the retreat from Mons in August 1914. Nearly overwhelmed by the vastly superior German force, the British troops are delivered by St George and his army of resurrected Agincourt bowmen. Inexplicably, the bowmen's arrows kill the enemy without leaving visible wounds. Interestingly, only a week before publication of 'The Bowmen', the *Evening News* had printed Machen's 'The Ceaseless Bugle Call' which was a variation on the same theme: an appeal to St George and King Arthur to save the British.[41]

Even though the author vigorously claimed that the tale of 'The Bowmen' was entirely fictional, mixing a piece by Rudyard Kipling with what he called 'the medievalism that is always there', this did not prevent the story from spreading as gospel truth all over the country, preached in sermons and reinforced by rumours from the front.[42] To Machen's astonishment, independent witnesses stepped forward corroborating the apparition, but exchanging St George for angels. Harold Begbie was among those who acted as the seers' self-appointed mouthpiece. In his book *On the Side of the Angels: A Reply to Arthur Machen*, Begbie recounted the eyewitnesses' evidence in order to expose Machen as a liar and plagiarist. Whether or not one chose to believe these testimonies, Begbie stated, was a matter outside his argument. But it was not 'to be wondered at, in an hour of such universal bereavement, that curiosity and interest in a story of this kind should intensify into hunger and thirst of the soul – a hunger and thirst that life on this earth is bound up with universal existence'.[43] Begbie's intervention was part of a stream of newspaper reports, pamphlets and books in 1915 which immortalised the Angels of Mons. Two years after the phenomenal success of the angel

---

[41] Arthur Machen, *The Angel of Mons: The Bowmen and Other Legends of the War* (London, Simpkin, Marshall, Hamilton Kent, 2nd edn 1915). See David Clarke, 'Rumours of Angels: A Legend of the First World War', *Folklore*, 113 (2002), pp. 154, 167.

[42] Machen, *Angel of Mons*, p. 11. See Buitenhuis, *Great War of Words*, pp. 102–5; Becker, *War and Faith*, p. 97.

[43] Harold Begbie, *On the Side of the Angels: A Reply to Arthur Machen* (London, New York and Toronto, Hodder and Stoughton, 3rd edn 1915), p. 9.

legend, the market for the paranormal had still not been saturated. In 1916, Charles L. Warr, a wounded soldier who later became a minister in the Church of Scotland, published an anthology of war fiction entitled *The Unseen Host*, a book that remained popular throughout the 1920s. The title story was a variation on Machen's 'Bowmen'. This time, an unseen host of angels led by St Gabriel and St Michael intervenes in the battle and puts the German aggressors to flight.[44]

The legend of the Angels of Mons is significant for two reasons. First, it testifies to the robustness of supernaturalism in Britain. The origins of wartime superstition can be traced to the spiritualist movement of the Victorian period which tried to reconcile the modern condition with the need for spiritual antidotes.[45] The industrial war with its attendant shocks and uncertainties deepened the visionary and emotional attraction of both secular and religious spiritualism. Some people embraced occult mediums or escaped into seances and the like; others had visions of the divine, angels or saints – not only in Britain, but throughout war-torn Europe. In 1917, a shepherd girl from the small Portuguese village of Fatima was vouchsafed a vision of the Virgin Mary. A new ritual was born, closely following the nineteenth-century pattern of Lourdes in 1858, Marpingen in 1876 and Knock in 1879.[46]

Like the apparitions of the Blessed Virgin, the 'vision' of Mons was triggered by a larger crisis which had unleashed millenarian hopes and fears. Furthermore, both were movements which prospered outside the confines of organised religion. In fact, the churches harboured deep suspicion of the unpredictable turns of popular piety. With respect to the Church of England in 1914–18, it has been noted that the three prevailing lines of thought within Anglicanism were 'nervous of folk religion: its evangelicalism was too puritan, biblicist and pietistic, its liberalism too detached and academic, its catholicism too self-conscious, dogmatic and nostalgic.'[47]

The legend of the Angels of Mons is significant for a second reason: its reception illustrates the demarcation between Catholic and Protestant

---

[44] C[harles] L. Warr, *The Unseen Host: Stories of the Great War* (Edinburgh, Robert Grant, repr. 1928). See Stewart J. Brown, '"A Solemn Purification by Fire": Responses to the Great War in Scottish Presbyterian Churches, 1914–19', *Journal of Ecclesiastical History*, 45 (1994), pp. 88–9.

[45] Winter, *Sites of Memory*, pp. 67–8. See also Jenny Hazelgrove, *Spiritualism and British Society between the Wars* (Manchester and New York, Manchester University Press, 2000); Malcolm Gaskill, *Hellish Nell: Last of Britain's Witches* (London, Fourth Estate, 2001).

[46] David Blackbourn, *Marpingen: Apparitions of the Virgin Mary in Bismarckian Germany* (Oxford, Clarendon Press, 1993), pp. 360–1.

[47] Wilkinson, *Church of England*, p. 196.

discursive fields. It is noteworthy that saintly intervention was subsequently transformed into angelic help. Machen himself observed that

We have long ceased in England to take much interest in saints, and in the recent revival of the cultus of St. George, the saint is little more than a patriotic figurehead. And the appeal to the saints to succour us is certainly not a common English practice; it is held Popish by most of our countrymen. But angels, with certain reservations, have retained their popularity, and so, when it was settled that the English army in its dire peril was delivered by angelic aid, the way was clear for general belief, and for the enthusiasms of the religion of the man in the street.[48]

While Anglican evangelicals and Free Churchmen warned against hagiolatry, Anglo-Catholics were inclined to reinstate the worship of the saints in an effort to counter the challenge of secular spiritualism. Just as the Reformation had extirpated medieval idolatry, High Churchmen argued that it was necessary to go to opposite extremes in the prevailing circumstances.[49] This appeal fell on deaf ears among committed Protestants. Wherever St George appeared in nonconformist chapels in England, it was exclusively for his association with chivalry and the English nation rather than divine intervention. The Leys, a Wesleyan public school in Cambridge, commemorated its fallen former schoolboys with an elaborate sculpture of the English patron saint mounted on the outer wall of the school chapel (see figure 51). The monument was meant to be 'an inspiration of those ideals of chivalry, self-sacrifice and patriotism which were essential to the highest conduct of character'.[50] In Scotland, patriotism and Presbyterianism forbade the invocation of St George.[51] The interior designers of the Scottish National War Memorial were reminded 'that they were building something for *Scotland* – a land of certain definite and jealously guarded ecclesiastical traditions. This meant that they were committed to a design which precluded anything in the shape of ritualistic suggestion or exotic adornment'.[52] Even so, a figure of St Michael, a work by Alice Meredith Williams, occupies a central place in the Edinburgh shrine, for the archangel is the 'judge' and 'Conductor and Guardian of the spirits of the dead' (see figure 18).[53]

---

[48] Machen, *Angel of Mons*, pp. 19–20.
[49] Mews, 'Religion and English Society', p. 107.
[50] 'Speech Day', *Leys Fortnightly*, 46 (1922), p. 309.
[51] Brookfield, Renfrew., and Kelso, Roxburgh. – both in the Border – are notable exceptions in the Scottish war-memorial scene. See IWM, WM 2490, Brookfield, Renfrew.; Bell, 'Monuments to the Fallen', p. 479.
[52] Hay, *Their Name Liveth*, pp. 26–7, italics in the original.
[53] Weaver, *Scottish National War Memorial*, p. 13.

Figure 51. St George by G. P. Hutchinson. Leys School, Cambridge, 1922.

The fact that the bloodshed came to an end on 11 November 1918, St Martin's day, and soon after the feasts of All Saints and All Souls, seemed a mere coincidence to the secular mind, but a divine providence to some believers. In any case, the proximity of the events allowed Armisticetide and religious observances to mingle, especially in Catholic-oriented circles. For them, All Souls' Day (2 November) in particular offered a conceptual framework for commemorative practices. In Germany, the Bavarian Catholics insisted on concentrating their activities in the period of All Souls, thus hindering the introduction of a national holiday, the *Volkstrauertag*, on the fifth or sixth Sunday before Easter.[54]

In the German context, there was nothing particularly medieval about All Souls, in contrast to Britain, where the legacy of the Reformation appeared to be at stake. Uncommon among mainstream Anglicans before 1914, prayers of intercession were reincorporated in the burial and communion services of the Church of England during the First World War. Even some ministers of the Church of Scotland and the United Free Church ventured to encourage prayers for the dead and belief in an 'intermediate state' between life and death. Grief and bereavement, as one historian of religion has pointed out, were 'sweeping away the latent Protestantism of the English people in this matter'.[55] On 2 November 1914, Randall Thomas Davidson, the Archbishop of Canterbury, delivered an illuminating sermon on the subject of All Souls. The Primate of All England conceded the existence of excesses in the later Middle Ages but suggested that

the abuses of the chantry system and the extravagances of Tetzel need not now, nearly four centuries afterwards, thwart or hinder the reverent, the absolutely trustful prayer of a wounded spirit who feels it natural and helpful to pray for him whom we shall not greet on earth again, but who, in his Father's loving keeping, still lives, and, as we may surely believe, still grows from strength to strength in truer purity and in deepened reverence and love.[56]

Ritualistic Anglicans eagerly translated such revisionist ideas into monumental statements. At St Mary the Less in Cambridge, the dedication

---

[54] Fritz Schellack, *Nationalfeiertage in Deutschland von 1871 bis 1945* (Frankfurt am Main, Peter Lang, 1990), pp. 232–42; Ziemann, *Front und Heimat*, p. 459.

[55] Wilkinson, *Church of England*, p. 178. On Scottish Protestants, see James Lachlan MacLeod, '"Greater Love Hath No Man than This": Scotland's Conflicting Religious Responses to Death in the Great War', *Scottish Historical Review*, 81 (2002), pp. 85–8. See also Gregory, *Silence of Memory*, pp. 190–1; Connelly, *Great War, Memory and Ritual*, pp. 141–2.

[56] 'The Pulpit: Sermon by the Primate', *Guardian*, 69 (1914), p. 1232. See Wilkinson, *Church of England*, p. 176.

inscribed on the memorial crucifix reads: 'Pray for the souls of the men of this Parish and Congregation, / who gave their lives in the Great War, 1914–1918. / Rest eternal grant unto them, O Lord, and / let light perpetual shine upon them.' Memorials such as this one remain emotive testaments to a Catholic spirituality prompted by the war and encouraged by the Anglo-Catholic wing of the church. The Catholic spectrum of the Established Church witnessed the reinvigoration of the notion of purgatory, that bond of sympathy and empathy between the living and the dead, a concept deriving from medieval theology.[57] Public prayer for the dead represented a powerful rite of passage which effectively bidged the gap between Anglo-Catholicism and Roman Catholicism. This convergence did not, however, foster ecumenical approaches. On the contrary, the Roman clergy was anxious not to bestow legitimacy on what it considered a heretical church.[58]

The memorial chapel of St Mary's Lowe House in St Helens, Lancashire, was one of the grandest commemorations launched by the Roman Catholic church in inter-war Britain. The interior design of the chapel, opened in 1923, is dominated by representations of soldier saints such as St George and St Louis of France. One stained-glass window is particularly noteworthy, for it depicts the faces of those in purgatory, faces which convey resignation coupled with joy at their forthcoming release into paradise. The iconography is in keeping with the dedication of this Chapel of the Holy Souls. A pamphlet of 1918 elucidates the central idea behind the memorial scheme:

The proposed scheme is entirely in accord with Catholic tradition, for in the old days of Faith in this country, chantries as they were called, were erected after great battles, not merely as monuments, but as chapels where daily the Holy Sacrifice of the Mass might be offered for the souls of those who had fallen. Thus, in the reign of Henry V., the Chapel of All Souls, Oxford was built and endowed for the relief of the souls of those who had fallen in the French Wars. But, we need not go so far afield for examples of this practice. After the battle of Agincourt, A.D. 1415, Sir Thomas Gerard of Bryn built the little chapel of which the Tower still remains, known as Windleshaw Abbey, where Mass should be offered daily for the souls of his ancestors.[59]

Just as All Souls' observances integrated the war dead into an established ritual (visits to the cemetery on 2 November used to mark the

[57] Jon Davies, 'The Martial Uses of the Mass: War Remembrance as an Elementary Form of Religious Life', in Jon Davies (ed.), Ritual and Remembrance: Responses to Death in Human Societies (Sheffield, Sheffield Academic Press, 1994), pp. 159–60.
[58] Gregory, Silence of Memory, p. 197.
[59] St Helens Local History and Archives Library, C/LH/1.6, St Mary's Lowe House, 'Proposed Memorial Chapel', 1918.

annual peak of family mourning), the war-memorial chapel of St Mary's Lowe House was intended to provide a setting for 'ordinary' funeral rites in peacetime. The parish priest, a Jesuit and the driving force behind the memorial project, proposed to use the chapel for the bodies of the departed to rest in overnight. In addition, he expected that it would become the rule to have a requiem mass said in the memorial chapel.[60] The priest envisaged an extraordinary compounding of images of death on the battlefield and in bed. Whether or not he succeeded with his project is, due to the patchy records, unfortunately beyond our knowledge. While prayers and requiems for the dead had the virtue of enabling the survivors to maintain spiritual links with their loved ones in the next world, the use of the memorial chapel for civil occasions risked blurring the special character of patri-passionism.

The tradition of the College of All Souls at Oxford, invoked at St Helens, also provided inspiration outside the Catholic spectrum. Notably, the historian R. H. Tawney, once described as the 'saint of socialism', recalled or appropriated this commemorative precedent. In 1917, he published anonymously ('By an officer wounded on the Somme', thus underlining the author's moral authority) in *The Times Educational Supplement* an (unsuccessful) appeal for a National College of All Saints to be established after the Great War. Typically for a social reformer, Tawney took an approach to the subject of memorialisation which was both idealistic and pragmatic, enriched with the distinct flavour of socialist medievalism that was peculiar to Britain. The underlying idea was the institutionalisation of what he understood as the liberal wartime spirit – 'the absolute claim of personality' over materialism – through education. In spite of its name, the proposed new All Souls' College would have catered for future brains rather than the souls of the deceased:

A little less than 500 years ago, a great man desired to commemorate the end of one of the most miserable of wars in which the English nation was ever engaged. He endowed a college 'to pray for the souls of all those who fell in the grievous wars between France and England.' We stand for a moment where Chichele stood, because we stand upon a world of graves. With a nobler cause we ought not to be content with a memorial less noble. We ought to perpetuate in peace the idealism of war, because that alone can deliver us from the selfish appetites that lie in wait for us in both. And if we desire to perpetuate it, how can we begin better than by founding upon it the educational system to whose influence generation after generation is submitted? It is no time for minimum standards, but for an effort corresponding to the sacrifice which it commemorates.

---

[60] Ibid.

A reconstruction of education in a generous and liberal spirit would be the noblest memorial to those who have fallen, because, though, many of them were but little 'educated,' it would be the most formal and public recognition of the world of the spirit for which they fell.[61]

To summarise this section, Christianity – or rather medieval(ist) forms of Christian notation – yielded a repository of consolatory images that could be drawn on in the aftermath of the carnage. Religious vocabulary located death in a symbolic order to make it tolerable. The bereaved found solace in two ways: first, by emulating medieval (or more recent 'medievalist') encodings of Christ's suffering and resurrection, and secondly, by appealing to benevolent mediating agencies represented in medieval guise or by reviving pre-Reformation practices of spiritual mediation. Mostly uncontroversial in Germany, Christian medievalism proved an explosive subject in Britain, where it often clashed with the iconophobic attitudes of evangelicals and dissenters. The iconography of commemoration caused a split within British communities of remembrance, which, in effect, brought Anglo-Catholics and German Roman Catholics much closer than either might have realised. Medievalist diction resulted in a rift between the denominations in a secularising age which overshadowed the real problem: the appropriation of Christian dogma. Those theologians who voiced their concern were in the minority in both Britain and Germany. They were overridden by their colleagues, who only too willingly gave in to popular sentiment, thus lending credence to patri-passionism and the nationalisation of heavenly intercessors.

Enchanted sleep

In creating everlasting life out of untimely death Christian-medievalist notation gave structure to the memory of the war dead. This section explores a commemorative trope inspired by national mythologies and folk tale which borrowed the idea of resurrection from Christianity but subsumed it into the concept of death as a deep and joyous sleep. Enchanted sleep marked an intermediate stage between the departure and the return of the dead. The widespread popular appeal of this concept, especially in Germany and to a much lesser extent also in

---

[61] [Richard H. Tawney], 'A National College of All Souls', *The Times Educational Supplement*, 97, 22 February 1917, p. 66. Unfortunately, no documents relating to war remembrance at All Souls College, Oxford, have been preserved in the college archives. For a description of the college war memorials, see Utechin, *Sons of This Place*, pp. 24–6.

Britain, is a remarkable indication of the public denial of death and, sometimes, of the refusal to perceive the Great War as totally over.

The sleeping dead

During the war, museums and designers' associations endeavoured to put the sepulchral sculpture of the Middle Ages back on the artistic agenda. The resource of medieval funerary statuary was mobilised with recumbent figures in order to visualise the 'sleeping dead'.[62] In 1916, the art gallery of Mannheim, Baden, organised a well-received exhibition about war graves and war memorials that afterwards toured Germany. It encompassed *inter alia* examples of knightly graves.[63] In the following year, a group of progressive artistic institutions, amongst others the Deutscher Werkbund, published an illustrated book of historic memorials including a number of recumbent effigies of 'ballad-like power' (see figure 52).[64] They set a trend. Figures of recumbent soldiers gained currency after 1918. Sculptors adapted the medieval model, often imaginatively, in casting the dead as modern combatants rather than medieval knights. It was the combination of motif and setting that alluded to the source of inspiration. Customarily, the reclining figures were placed in either a crypt or a chapel like the relics of a saint, or in specially designed sanctuaries.

The recumbent figure was a highly ambiguous symbol that could convey diametrically opposite views depending on the memorial designers and clients. Käthe Kollwitz – artist, socialist and bereaved mother – re-worked the motif for commemorative sculpture, as did the Weltkriegsbücherei (now the Bibliothek für Zeitgeschichte) in Stuttgart, the gymnastics and sports club Fortuna Düsseldorf, and the *Gau* Mecklenburg of the Nazi party.[65] For analytical purposes it is sensible to distinguish between the funerary type and heroic variants. However, it

---

[62] Florian Matzner, 'Der "schlafende" Krieger: Ikonographische Aspekte zum ideologischen Stellenwert von Leben und Tod', in Michael Hütt *et al.* (eds.), *Unglücklich das Land, das Helden nötig hat: Leiden und Sterben in den Kriegsdenkmälern des Ersten und Zweiten Weltkrieges* (Marburg, Jonas, 1990), pp. 57–74.

[63] *Kriegergrabmal und Kriegerdenkmal: Führer durch die 20. Ausstellung des Freien Bundes: Städt. Kunsthalle Mannheim 2. Januar–6. Februar 1916* (Mannheim, Haas, 1916), p. 13. On the exhibition, see Lurz, *Kriegerdenkmäler*, vol. III, pp. 84–6.

[64] Jessen, *Kriegergräber im Felde*, pp. 30, 35, 38, and p. 62: 'balladenhaften Schlagkraft'.

[65] Ulrich Linse, '"Saatfrüchte sollen nicht vermahlen werden!" Zur Resymbolisierung des Soldatentodes', in Klaus Vondung (ed.), *Kriegserlebnis: Der Erste Weltkrieg in der literarischen Gestaltung und symbolischen Deutung der Nationen* (Göttingen, Vandenhoeck & Ruprecht, 1980), p. 271; Brandt, 'Kriegssammlungen im Ersten Weltkrieg', pp. 296–7; Lurz, *Kriegerdenkmäler*, vol. IV, pp. 176–86.

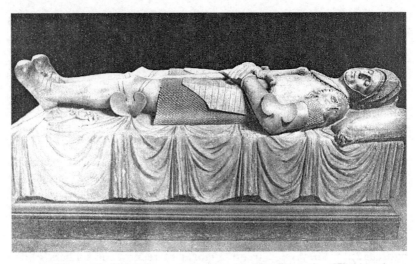

Figure 52. Knight's tomb suggested by the Deutscher Werkbund as a model for war memorials. Ravenna, fifteenth century.

is important to recognise that this distinction is purely conceptual, and that occasionally contemporaries remained unsure about the exact meaning of recumbent effigies, as in the case of the tragicomic making and demolition of Ewald Mataré's 'Dead Warrior' (or 'Lying in State of a Hero') at Kleve, Rhine Province.[66]

The establishment of a war memorial was a matter of prestige for the new rulers of Kleve after their 'seizure of power'. In autumn 1933, local Nazis held a design competition from which Mataré emerged as one of the winners. Shortly after the jury had awarded the prizes, the mayor got wind of Mataré's recent dismissal from the Düsseldorf art college as a consequence of the *Gleichschaltung* policy, the streamlining of German society. But due to the intervention of an open-minded Nazi functionary, Mataré's modernist solution was finally accepted and inaugurated with great pomp and circumstance in October 1934. The stylised figure represents a laid-out soldier wrapped in a flag. There is a bullet hole in his breast in which are placed a roll of honour, an Iron Cross and a copy of the seventh stanza of Friedrich Hölderlin's patriotic poem 'Germania'

[66] Inge Zacher, *Ewald Mataré: Der 'Tote Krieger' in Kleve* (Kleve, Boss, 1985), esp. pp. 9–18, 31–67.

of 1801.[67] The memorial was neither stridently heroic nor funerary in character – a reflection of the artist's ambivalence about the Great War, his admiration of the soldiers' courage and his awareness of the meaninglessness of their struggle. Nevertheless, for the Nazis, the 'Dead Warrior' embodied the final triumph of strength over death: 'The body shall not be a body, but only greatness and strength, wrapped up in a cloth, a protecting, holy cloth, the flag.'[68] The inclusion of works by Mataré in the Munich exhibition of 'Degenerate Art' in 1937 left this interpretation untenable. The 'Dead Warrior' of Kleve was removed and destroyed in May 1938.

The memorial of Rheingönheim in the Bavarian Palatinate offers a striking example of a purely funerary monument. Under a *Trauerweide*, a weeping willow, and next to a fire bowl with a perpetual flame, rests the figure of a fallen soldier on a large, tomb-like plinth. Architecture, sculpture and vegetation together formed an ensemble which was understood to be an (unspecified) 'allegory of history'.[69] All military insignia and even the obligatory steel helmet are missing. 'In the centre lies only the human being whom we mourn.'[70] Funerary memorials like this one spoke of death but also of regeneration. Statuary re-membered and repatriated the dis-membered and displaced male body: a resurrection. In battle, soldiers' bodies were mutilated and disfigured, frequently to such a degree that identification of the dead became impossible. Consequently, the bereaved had not only to come to terms with the mere absence of the corpses, but were, in addition, afflicted with the image of their loved ones being torn apart beyond recognition (and even swallowed in mud). Signifying practices reversed the process of physical fragmentation and disintegration. War memorials representing

---

[67] Ibid., p. 43; Friedrich Hölderlin, 'Germania', in *Poems and Fragments*, trans. Michael Hamburger (London, Anvil, 3rd edn 1996), p. 428: 'Once only, daughter of holy Earth, / Pronounce your Mother's name. The waters roar on the rock / And thunderstorms in the wood, and at their name / Divine things past ring out from time immemorial. / How all is changed! And to the right there gleam / And speak things yet to come, joy-giving, from the distance. / Yet at the centre of Time / In peace with hallowed, / With virginal Earth lives Aether / And gladly, for remembrance, they / The never-needy dwell / Hospitably amid the never-needy, / Amid your holidays, / Germania, where you are priestess and / Defenceless proffer all round / Advice to the kings and the peoples.' (seventh stanza).

[68] Karl Ahlers, 'Kleve dankt den Toten des großen Krieges: Weiheschrift zum 22. Oktober 1934', in Zacher, *Ewald Mataré*, p. 126: 'Der Leib soll nicht Leib sein, ist nur Größe und Kraft, die ein Tuch umhüllt, ein schützendes, heiliges Tuch, die Fahne.'

[69] G. Schmidt, *Kriegerdenkmale in der Pfalz: In Treue zur Heimat: 1914–1918* (Ludwigshafen, Waldkirch, 1934), p. 141.

[70] Ibid.: 'Im Mittelpunkt liegt nur der Mensch, um den wir trauern.'

anatomically whole humans provided a literal and metaphorical replacement for the absent and incomplete bodies of the war dead.[71]

Heroic variants of recumbent effigies went beyond merely re-membering and embodying the 'fallen' soldier. Physical wholeness was a necessary precondition for the impending awakening – as opposed to the ascension – of the fallen. But how could the living speed up resuscitation? When would they finally be reunited with the dead? The instigators of heroic monuments answered these questions by recourse to a combination of Biblical, classical, Germanic and medieval traditions. 'YOUR DEAD SHALL LIVE' (Isaiah 26:19) promises the inscription in a joint parochial-regimental memorial chapel in Bremen. The medieval chapel is an austere, dark and chilly building in which nothing distracts attention from the effigy of a soldier lying in its centre: a masculine, unscathed figure, protected by his steel helmet, clasping a sword (see figure 53). The ceremonial dedications in September 1924 (separate occasions for the parishioners and the soldiers) insisted that Isaiah's phrase was not a shallow expression of transcendence. 'He has fallen, but he is not dead', the pastors told their respective congregations, 'This is not death. He sleeps – on the authority of the majestic words of Jesus, the victor over death and the grave. [. . .] He sleeps until a better awakening. He lives. Those eyes will open again.'[72] Yet the living had to come to his assistance and hence to overcome their own lethargy. It was up to the survivors to suit their actions to the words:

Deep peace surrounds the site where the book [of remembrance] is to be placed. It radiates from the figure of the steel-helmeted warrior who rests there from battle and fight. Do not let us rob him and them of this peace; they have done what they could and all now is well with them. Their self-sacrifice, self-abandonment and devotion have unfortunately not secured the reward which the fallen and we had hoped for. Our fatherland has lost a goodly store of honour, freedom and power, because we retired before we had sacrificed our greatest and our last, because we did not prove worthy of the blood which they shed for us. Therefore, let us make good what we have ruined; let us erase the letters which since their deaths have been written in the book of history, let us take a new page

---

[71] Catherine Moriarty, 'The Absent Dead and Figurative First World War Memorials', *Transactions of the Ancient Monuments Society*, 39 (1995), pp. 20, 37; Carden-Coyne, 'Gendering Death and Renewal', p. 40. On representations of the dismembered body, see Bourke, *Dismembering the Male*, p. 210; Kienitz, 'Der Krieg der Invaliden'.

[72] StAB, Ag–9993–11, 'Weihe der Ehrentafeln für die aus der Gemeinde von Unser Lieben Frauen Gefallenen in der Gedächtniskapelle', 1924, p. 5: 'Er ist gefallen, aber er ist nicht tot. Das ist kein Tod. Er schläft – nach den Majestätsworten Jesu, des Siegers über Tod und Grab. [. . .] Er schläft zu besserem Erwachen. Er lebt. Diese Augen werden sich wieder öffnen.' See also Seeger, *Denkmal des Weltkriegs*, p. 33. The inscription reads in German: 'DEINE TOTEN WERDEN LEBEN'. On the chapel, see chapter 1.

Figure 53. Recumbent soldier by Friedrich Lommel in the *Tresekammer* memorial chapel. Unser Lieben Frauen church, Bremen, 1924.

and write the word of the holy fatherland onto it. Thus we waken the slumbering from their sleep, thus they will descend to help us live, suffer and fight and win, so that we also fulfil the word 'Greater love hath no man than this, that a man lay down his life for his friend.'[73]

The attempt to revive the dead was directed towards helping the living. Yet which chapters of history had to be rewritten? The pastors

[73] StAB, 3–B. 13. Nr. 92, folio 9, '75er Regiments-Appell', *Bremer Nachrichten*, 263, suppl., 21 September 1924: 'Tiefer Friede umweht die Stätte, an der das [Gedenk-] Buch seinen Platz finden soll. Er geht aus von der Gestalt des Kriegers mit Stahlhelm, der dort von Kampf und Streit ausruht. Laßt uns ihm und ihnen diesen Frieden nicht rauben; sie haben getan, was sie konnten und haben es jetzt gut. Ihre Aufopferung, ihre Hingebung und Treue, sie haben leider den Lohn nicht gefunden, den die Gefallenen und wir davon erhofft haben. Unser Vaterland hat an Ehre, Freiheit und Macht ein gutes Stück verloren, weil wir uns zur Ruhe begeben haben, ehe wir unser Letztes und Größtes hingegeben hatten, weil wir uns des Blutes, das sie für uns vergossen haben, nicht würdig gezeigt haben. Darum laßt uns gut machen, was wir verdarben; laßt uns die Schrift, die seit ihrem Tode ins Buch der Geschichte eingeschrieben worden ist, auslöschen, ein neues Blatt nehmen und darauf das Wort schreiben vom heiligen Vaterland. So wecken wir die Schlummernden aus ihrem Schlaf, so steigen sie herab zu uns und helfen und leben, leiden und kämpfen und siegen, auf das auch wir das Wort erfüllen "Niemand hat größere Liebe als daß er sein Leben lässet für sein [*sic*] Brüder".' The quotation is from John 15:13 and the translation follows the King James Version.

presumed a tacit agreement as to what the plot should be. Certainly, they envisaged erasing the contentious 'dictate of Versailles' and possibly the republican constitutions of the Reich and the city state of Bremen. But should this take the form of political change or military revenge? The message of the Bremen memorial remained nebulous; after all, it was raised in the first place as a symbolic focus of bereavement. Notions of revision or revenge – often fuzzy and generalised – were an integral part of this memory script, a script of hope for a brighter future. Exclusively political readings of war memorials, treating them as monumental manifestos, have overlooked this aspect of their significance. A large grey area divided the political and the personal, and it was precisely this grey space into which the memorial makers were venturing. Conventionally, historians have treated mourning and revenge as antithetical concepts or as sequential phases: the supposed decline of affliction allegedly gave rise to outpourings of revengeful feelings in the late 1920s.[74] By contrast, transcendence and revenge were two sides of the same coin. Both were integral to the search for meaning and consolation (both emotional and political) of a traumatised society.

Scholars have tended to exaggerate the significance of monumental accusations against the peace settlement and the revolution of 1918–19; they were spectacular but not prevalent.[75] Admittedly, overt displays of 'revanchism' created a great deal of noise. Consider two examples. The recumbent figure dedicated to the members of the Queen Augusta Guards Grenadier Regiment No. 4 killed in the war acquired notoriety for neo-Wilhelmine warmongering in 1925 (see figure 54). The unveiling at the garrison cemetery in the Berlin suburb of Neukölln on 11 October 1925 coincided with the summit conference at Locarno. Contrary to the Locarno spirit of reconciliation (at least with the west), the Latin inscription, a quotation from Virgil's *Aeneid* IV, 625, openly incited the educated visitor to overturn the peace settlement: 'May an avenger one day rise from my bones.' A German-language dedication was added to reach men of humble origin too: 'WE DIED / SO THAT GERMANY MIGHT LIVE / SO LET US LIVE IN YOU!'

The memorial was at the centre of a public scandal in autumn 1925. Monarchists set the tone at the inauguration attended by Hindenburg, the newly elected head of state. That, however, was to become a familiar

---

[74] Lurz, *Kriegerdenkmäler*, vol. IV, p. 438; Jeismann and Westheider, 'Wofür stirbt der Bürger?', pp. 43–4; Schneider, '. . .*nicht umsonst gefallen*'?, pp. 207–8. See also Bartov, 'Trauma and Absence', p. 353.

[75] Nabrings, '. . .*eine immerfort währende Mahnung*. . .', pp. 133–4; Koselleck, *Zur politischen Ikonologie*, p. 37; Ziemann, *Front und Heimat*, p. 454.

Figure 54. Recumbent soldier by Franz Dorrenbach. Memorial of Königin Augusta Garde-Grenadier-Regiment No. 4. Garrison cemetery, Berlin, 1925

scene. It was another representative of the republic, General Sixt von Arnim, who outraged the democrats. He laid a wreath at the memorial in the name of the exiled Kaiser. The conservative press applauded; the liberal and socialist newspapers cried high treason.[76] Strangely, the striking memorial design received virtually no coverage at all. It features a fallen soldier completely covered by a cloth; a sword and steel helmet are placed on top of his chest. Only his clenched right fist protrudes from

---

[76] 'Hindenburg bei den Augustanern: Die Denkmalsweihe auf dem Garnisons-Friedhof', *Der Montag: Sonderausgabe des Berliner Lokal-Anzeiger*, 39, 12 October 1925; 'Eine monarchische Denkmalsfeier: In Anwesendheit der Reichswehr', *Berliner Tageblatt*, 483, 12 October 1925. A full documentation of the press coverage is in BArch, R 8034 II/7692, fos. 20–34. See also Koselleck, *Zur politischen Ikonologie*, pp. 33–6; Saehrendt, *Stellungskrieg der Denkmäler*, pp. 97–104. The inscriptions read in the original: 'Exoriare aliquis nostris ex ossibus ultor' and 'WIR STARBEN, AUF DASS DEUTSCHLAND LEBE, / SO LASSET UNS LEBEN IN EUCH!'

the cover, signalling defiance, like a mirror image of the dead Siegfried's hand rising to prevent Hagen from taking the ring in the third act of Richard Wagner's *Götterdämmerung*.

The funeral march from *Götterdämmerung* provided the perfect accompaniment to the unveiling of the 'sleeping warrior' in Munich in December 1924 (see figure 55). In harmony with the inscription, 'THEY SHALL RISE AGAIN', the speaker of the local branch of the Bavarian veterans' association, Bayerischer Kriegerbund, pictured the imminence of national regeneration: 'Beneath the image of the resting warrior his sleep of death slumbers the heroic spirit and self-sacrifice of our Bavarian troops, waiting for the holy seeds in our own soil to ripen some day soon into a blessed day of resurrection. God grant it!'[77] In numerous commentaries, the recumbent figure by Bernhard Bleeker, although in modern uniform, was held to be analogous to the sepulchral sculpture of the Middle Ages.[78] The architectural frame heightened the medieval aura surrounding the sculpture. Critics compared the intimate atmosphere of the interior to the vaults of medieval churches, but related the rough-hewn style of the exterior to megalithic remains.[79] Thus commentators put together a composite picture of the art-historical roots of the Munich monument. A patchwork in terms of style, the memorial was, however, built on a consistent ideology: the myth of the eternal Reich.

The Reich reawakened

The Munich memorial evoked the mystical intent to reinstate the first Reich personified by Frederick I Barbarossa, who, according to the saga, reinvented in the nineteenth century, was sleeping in Mount Kyffhäuser

---

[77] BArch, R 8034 II/7691, fos. 189–90, 'Enthüllung des Münchner Kriegerdenkmals', *München-Augsburger Abendzeitung*, 348, 15 August 1924: 'Unter dem Bilde des im Todesschlaf ruhenden Kriegers schlummert der Heldengeist und der Opfermut unserer bayerischen Truppen harrend, daß diese heilige Saat in heimischer Erde einst und bald einem segensreichen Tage der Auferstehung entgegenreife. Das walte Gott!' See also StdAM, ZA Denkmäler/Kriegerdenkmäler, G. v. Pechmann, 'Der schlafende Krieger des neuen Münchner Denkmals', *Münchner Neueste Nachrichten*, 26, 27 January 1925, p. 1; August Alckens, *Die Denkmäler und Denksteine der Stadt München*, ed. Kulturamt der Stadt München (Munich, Georg D. W. Callwey, 1936), pp. 182–5; Lurz, *Kriegerdenkmäler*, vol. IV, pp. 183–6, 267, 365; Tietz, *Tannenberg-Nationaldenkmal*, pp. 108–14; Jürgen Tietz, '"Es soll ein Ort der Begegnung sein" – Zur Geschichte des Münchner Kriegerdenkmals', *Jahrbuch der Bayerischen Denkmalspflege*, 47–8 (1993–4), pp. 238–53. The German inscription reads: 'SIE WERDEN AUFERSTEHEN'.
[78] StdAM, ZA Denkmäler/Kriegerdenkmäler, 'Das Münchener Kriegerdenkmal', *Münchener Zeitung*, 337–8, 6–7 December 1924.
[79] Ibid., Alois Wurm, 'Das Münchener Kriegerdenkmal', *Augsburger Postzeitung*, 296, 21 December 1924.

Figure 55. Recumbent soldier by Bernhard Bleeker. Munich, 1925.

in Thuringia until the restoration of the Holy Roman Empire. The story of 'Barbarossa in the Kyffhäuser suggests itself with regard to the "sleeping" German youth', one journalist observed.[80] What is more, an equestrian statue of Otto I of Wittelsbach, Duke of Bavaria, originally unveiled in 1911, towered above the Great War memorial. Duke Otto, the founder of the Wittelsbach dynasty, was remembered as a loyal follower of Barbarossa.[81] In 1180, following the deposition of Henry the Lion, the Kaiser had granted Otto the dukedom of Bavaria, a territory which the Wittelsbachers had thereafter continuously ruled until the revolution of November 1918. The choreography of the unveiling ceremony in 1924 strengthened this association. Special seats were reserved for Duke

---

[80] Ibid.: 'die [Sage] Barbarossas im Kyffhäuser legt sich ja angesichts des "schlafenden" deutschen Jüngling im Innern so nahe'. On the Barbarossa revival, see Arno Borst, 'Barbarossas Erwachen – Zur Geschichte der deutschen Identität', in Odo Marquard and Karlheinz Stierle (eds.), *Identität* (Munich, Wilhelm Fink, 1979), pp. 29–60.

[81] Alckens, *Denkmäler und Denksteine*, pp. 84–5, 102–3. See also StdAM, BuR 551, Staatsministerium für Unterricht und Kultus to Bayerischer Kriegerbund Obmannsbezirk München-Stadt, 9 June 1925; Britta-R. Schwahn, 'Otto I. von Wittelsbach – ein politisches Denkmal im Münchner Hofgarten', in Ekkehard Mai and Stephan Waetzoldt (eds.), *Kunstverwaltung, Bau- und Denkmal-Politik im Kaiserreich* (Berlin, Mann, 1981), esp. pp. 203, 206.

Otto's twentieth-century descendants, whereas the Social-Democratic veterans of the Reichsbanner Schwarz-Rot-Gold had not even been invited to attend the function. (Berthold von Deimling, a general turned pacifist, writing in the *Berliner Tageblatt*, denounced this decision as 'medieval outlawing'.)[82] Despite its name, the Reichsbanner championed the republic, the very institution which the Reich myth called into question.

As a right-wing credo that helped to undermine the foundations of the Weimar Republic, particularly in the early 1930s, the Reich myth has attracted considerable attention from historians in this field.[83] Unlike a state, the Reich, as the legatee of the Roman empire, connoted a dynamic polity with a special socio-political mission in Europe. So far as foreign policy was concerned, the myth of the Reich legitimised German aspirations for supremacy in the west and, as regards domestic affairs, the overthrow of Weimar's constitutional settlement. There were, of course, delicate differences between the visions of reactionary Catholics, old-fashioned conservatives and *völkisch* nationalists dreaming of a 'Third Reich'. Rather than reiterating the ideological nuances revealed by scholars of intellectual history, I want to concentrate on the neglected links between the remembrance of the war dead and the quest for a political utopia. The saga of Barbarossa provided the symbolism around which the ideas of the rebirth of a thousand-year Reich and the resurrection of the dead coalesced, thus bridging the gap between the nation and the individual, between the political and the personal realms.

Though it was a myth in the service of the attainment of national unity, an intense rivalry grew up between the upholders of the Staufen tradition in the inter-war years. Walter Schott, a favourite of Wilhelm II, campaigned for a Barbarossa-cum-war memorial on Mount Brocken in the Harz.[84] Mount Hohenstaufen in Württemberg, which gave its name

---

[82] Staatsarchiv Munich, Pol.-Dir. 6889, Section General Deimling, folio 9, Berthold von Deimling, 'Die Verfemung des Reichsbanners: Ein Wort zur Verständigung', *Berliner Tageblatt*, 18, 11 January 1925: 'mittelalterlichen Verfemungen'. See also Martin H. Geyer, *Verkehrte Welt: Revolution, Inflation und Moderne, München 1914–1924* (Göttingen, Vandenhoeck & Ruprecht, 1998), pp. 124–6.

[83] Kurt Sontheimer, *Antidemokratisches Denken in der Weimarer Republik: Die politischen Ideen des deutschen Nationalismus zwischen 1918 und 1933* (Munich, dtv, 1978), pp. 222–43; Berg, *Heldenbilder und Gegensätze*, pp. 161–77; Winkler, *Long Shadow of the Reich*; Lothar Kettenacker, 'Der Mythos vom Reich', in Karl Heinz Bohrer (ed.), *Mythos und Moderne: Begriff und Bild einer Rekonstruktion* (Frankfurt am Main, Suhrkamp, 1983), pp. 261–89.

[84] BArch, R 32/359, folio 2, 'Reichsehrenmal auf dem Brocken! Ein Vorschlag von Professor Walter Schott, Berlin', *Magdeburger Tageszeitung*, 264, 9 November 1930; ibid., folio 1, 'Ehrenmal auf dem Brocken?', *Braunschweiger Neueste Nachrichten*, 238, 11 October 1930.

to the Staufen dynasty, was briefly under discussion too.[85] Designers came up with still more proposals, such as a Reich war memorial on Mount Untersberg near Salzburg. The Untersberg was pronounced a 'holy' mountain of which the 'people know that "old Kaiser Frederick" slumbers in this mountain awaiting the new glory of the German Reich'.[86] There seems to have been some confusion over who actually rested beneath the Untersberg. Folk myth has it that Charlemagne resided there (although other versions tracked him down to Mount Oden-berg in Hesse), and local industry had a vested interest in seeing him in the Untersberg. A monument supplier advertised his products during the war as follows:

Untersberg marble is a German stone unlike any other. Its reputation is age-old and world-famous. Through the great Kaiser Charles, who as popular belief has it slumbers in the legendary Untersberg, this marble is solemnly linked to the restoration of the powerful German empire for whose continued existence and growth millions of German men are fighting today.[87]

The Kaiser saga was a hotly contested terrain, but in the event the Kyffhäuser retained its position as the foremost incarnation of medieval glory. In contrast to the other magic mountains, the Kyffhäuser was ingrained in a pre-existing commemorative milieu. Between 1892 and 1896, the German veterans' associations (which amalgamated between 1892 and 1900 to form the Kyffhäuserbund) had taken possession of the monumental landscape of Thuringia. Amidst the ruins of Kyffhausen Castle, a team of artists headed by Bruno Schmitz built a gigantic temple to Frederick I Barbarossa ('Redbeard') and his latter-day successor, Wilhelm I 'Barbablanca' ('Whitebeard').[88] The figure of Barbarossa

---

[85] BArch, R 43 I/713, folio 119v, 'Zusammenstellung der dem Reichsministerium des Innern bekannt gewordenen Vorschläge zur Errichtung eines Nationaldenkmals für die Gefallenen im Weltkriege', November 1925, p. 14; BArch, R 32/473, folio 14, Julius Baum, 'Mahnmale', *Schwäbischer Merkur*, 14 February 1925.

[86] BArch, R 32/473, folio 91, Oscar Doering, 'Vom Reichsehrenmal', *Dortmunder Zeitung*, 565, 2 December 1928: 'Das Volk weiß, daß in jenem Berge der "alte Kaiser Friedrich [*sic*]" einer neuen Herrlichkeit des deutschen Reiches entgegenschlummert.'

[87] HStAS, M 400/2, Fasz. 189, folio 46, Marmor-Industrie Kiefer A.-G. Kiefersfelden, 'Soldatengrabsteine, Erinnerungszeichen, Gedenksteine', n.d.: 'Der Untersberger Marmor ist ein deutscher Stein wie kaum ein anderer. Uralt und weltbekannt ist sein Ruf. Durch den großen Kaiser Karl, den der Volksglaube im sagenumworbenen Untersberg schlummern läßt, ist dieser Marmor mit der Wiederaufrichtung des machtvollen deutschen Weltreiches weihevoll verknüpft, für dessen Bestand und Wachstum heute die Millionen deutschen Männer kämpfen.'

[88] Monika Arndt, 'Das Kyffhäuser-Denkmal – Ein Beitrag zur politischen Ikonographie des Zweiten Kaiserreiches', *Wallraf-Richartz-Jahrbuch*, 40 (1978), pp. 75–127; Kerssen, *Interesse am Mittelalter*, pp. 97–105; Jakob Vogel, 'Zwischen protestantischem Herrscherideal und Mittelaltermystik: Wilhelm I. und die "Mythomotorik" des

captures the moment of his awakening, while the Whitebeard is shown mounted and in military uniform, interpreting medieval history as the prelude to the foundation of the Kaiserreich in 1871. As a focal point of the quasi-religious rituals and rhetoric of the conservative veterans' movement, the Kyffhäuser monument maintained its significance in the wake of the revolution. After 1918, the Hohenzollern monarchy seemed to be a mere interlude between the medieval empire and the Reich to come.

In anticipation of the new millennium, the veterans set out to recast the Mecca of Wilhelmine nationalism in order to incorporate the memory of the 1914–18 dead. Individual death on the battlefield was reconfigured as the vehicle of collective redemption and renewal. In the mid-1920s, the Kyffhäuserbund considered plans for an underground 'Hall of Honour' dedicated to the fallen soldiers, crowned with a majestic 'Hall of Fame' above ground.[89] The right-wing Nationalverband deutscher Offiziere (founded in 1918) seconded in principle the idea of a central monument at Mount Kyffhäuser. 'In my opinion', the officers' leader, Admiral von Schröder, stated, 'only one site in our fatherland is possible, and that would have to be sought in the proximity of the Kyffhäuser memorial. Since it came into existence it has been as a place of pilgrimage for German warriors as well as all German-feeling hearts'.[90] These efforts did not bear fruit until 1934, when the Nazi successor organisation to the Kyffhäuserbund redesigned the existing monument to accommodate urns holding soil from the lost territories, and busts of Scharnhorst, Bismarck, Hitler and others.[91] The deliverance of the war dead was linked to the coming of a national messiah, a new Barbarossa, who would invoke the feats of a heroic past. In a sense, the Nazis simply accentuated the leadership cult that had been built into

Deutschen Kaiserreichs', in Gerd Krumeich and Hartmut Lehmann (eds.), 'Gott mit uns': Nation, Religion und Gewalt im 19. und frühen 20. Jahrhundert (Göttingen, Vandenhoeck & Ruprecht, 2000), pp. 222–8; Assmann, Arbeit am nationalen Gedächtnis, pp. 53–6.

[89] BArch, R 8034 II/7692, folio 18, 'Für ein Reichsehrenmal auf dem Kyffhäuser: Die Vertreterversammlung des Kyffhäuserbundes', Deutsche Tageszeitung, 432, 14 September 1925. See also Lurz, Kriegerdenkmäler, vol. III, p. 16; Bucher, 'Errichtung des Reichsehrenmals', p. 362.

[90] GStAPK, I. HA Rep. 77, Tit. 1215 Nr. 3c Beiheft 'Pressestimmen', 'Deutschlands Ehrenmal: Schinckels Hauptwache oder ein Heldenhain in Thüringen?', Berliner Lokal-Anzeiger, 100, 28 February 1926: 'M. E. käme nur ein Platz in unserem Vaterlande in Frage, und dieser wäre in der Nähe des Kyffhäuser-Denkmals zu suchen. Seit seinem Bestehen bildet es den Wallfahrtsort der deutschen Krieger sowie aller deutschfühlenden und empfindenden Herzen.' On languages of pilgrimage, see Lloyd, Battlefield Tourism.

[91] Arndt, 'Kyffhäuser-Denkmal', p. 89 n. 75.

the monument of 1896, promising individual and national rebirth through subordination to a great *Führer* – a notion which had been completely absent from the Barbarossa revival of the early nineteenth century.

The folklorists Jacob and Wilhelm Grimm were among those who had rediscovered the Barbarossa saga. The Grimms' collection of ancient German fairy tales, a *lieu de mémoire* first published in the early nineteenth century, figured Barbarossa waiting in the Kyffhäuser for the day of judgment. In the Grimms' version, however, the emperor is awake rather than asleep.[92] The sleep motif which they introduced into the tale of *Dornröschen*, 'Sleeping Beauty', dating from the fourteenth century, became another favoured image of war remembrance. 'The thousand-year-old stronghold above the River Inn has been wakened from its *Dornröschenschlaf* [sleep of the Sleeping Beauty]', a journalist noted on the opening of the Austro-German memorial at Geroldseck Castle, Kufstein in the Tyrol.[93] The resurgence of historic settings that had sunk into a long sleep evoked echoes of the legendary revitalisation of the court of the sleeping princess. The analogy allowed the war (or its memory) to be configured as a liberating kiss rather than as a curse. Arneburg, a small town in the Prussian Province of Saxony 'far removed from the great hurly-burly of the world', had fallen into a thousand-year *Dornröschenschlummer*, i.e. slumbered like the Sleeping Beauty, until local dignitaries decided to apply for the Reich memorial.[94] 'Arneburg [. . .] wakened by the remembrance of a thousand-year meaningful past! A sleep! But now, the few bumpy streets, which lead to the erstwhile Kaiser stronghold and Zollern castle, show the way! This Arneburg, symbol of our future [. . .]: both bulwark and gateway to the east!'[95]

---

[92] Borst, 'Barbarossas Erwachen', pp. 30–1.

[93] StAMS, OP 5510, folio 285, 'Tönendes Denkmal: Zur Einweihung der Kufsteiner Heldenorgel am 3. Mai', unspecified newspaper cutting, 1931: 'Die tausendjährig Trutzburg über dem Inn ist aus ihrem Dornröschenschlaf erwacht'.

[94] BArch, R 32/360c, fos. 29–31, Hans Wegener, 'Das Reichsehrenmal in der Altmark', 1925: the 'Städtchen, das dem großen Getriebe der Welt entrückt ist, das jetzt still in der altmärkischen Heimat schlummert, [. . .] ruht in der jetzigen Zeit in einer Art Dornröschenschlummer'. See also ibid., fos. 35–41, Karl Hohmann-Eichwalde, 'Arneburg in vorgeschichtlicher Zeit', 1925; BArch, R 32/360b, folio 7, Kreis-Ausschuß Altmark to Reichskunstwart, 26 February 1926; ibid., fos. 32–9, 'Vortrag gehalten im Schwarzen Adler zu Stendal', 17 October 1925.

[95] BArch, R 32/360c, folio 44, Waldemar Müller Eberhart, *Tausend Jahre wie ein Tag: Die Chronik von Arneburg: Ein deutsches Spiel* (Berlin, August Scherl, 1925): 'Arneburg [. . .] durch das Erinnern an eine tausendjährige bedeutsame Vergangenheit aufgeweckt! Ein Schlaf! Jetzt aber, die wenige holprigen Straßen, die hinanführen zur ehemaligen Kaisertrutzburg und Zollernfeste, weisen den Weg! Dies Arneburg, Symbol für unsere Zukunft [. . .]: Bollwerk und Pforte nach Osten zugleich!'

The return from Avalon

The tales of Barbarossa and the Sleeping Beauty provided the mental equipment for Germans to summon up visions of the rebirth of both the Reich and the dead. By comparison, Britons seldom seized on the legend of King Arthur, a potent script from their own arsenal of historical imagination, to recover their losses. The legend had it that Arthur, betrayed and wounded by his only son, had not died but rested on the Isle of Avalon where gentle queens had taken him to heal his battle wounds. On some distant day, Arthur would rise again to rally the British nation in a time of dire need. The lost kingdom would be regained and Arthur's dream of an ideal world fulfilled. The prospect of the return of the redeemer represents a striking parallel between the legends of King Arthur and Kaiser Barbarossa. However, while German commemorations fused notions of individual and national regeneration, British discourses tended to emphasise the aspect of personal rebirth and bypass the political utopia.

The Arthurian mythology was mobilised for commemorative purposes at the King's School, Chester. An image of King Arthur fills the centre of the memorial window in the school chapel, with the legend 'Such a / sleep they sleep / the men / I love [sic]'.[96] This line, slightly misquoted from Alfred Lord Tennyson's 'The Passing of Arthur' (in *Idylls of the King*, 1859), had been given the Victoria and Albert Museum's seal of approval. In 1919, the museum had issued a booklet of edifying memorial inscriptions borrowed from the corpus of English literature.[97] In practice, Tennyson's Arthurian verses did not prove a popular choice for grass-roots commemorations. Far more widespread was John S. Arkwright's hymn 'O Valiant Hearts', especially the verse 'Tranquil you lie, your knightly virtue proved', which conjured up notions of chivalry and enchanted sleep but lacked the Arthurian subtext of political awakening. The hymn was sung at the burial service for the Unknown Warrior (see figure 2) – the 'Unknown Arthur' as one newspaper strangely dubbed him – in Westminster Abbey in 1920, and evolved subsequently into a leitmotif of war remembrance in inter-war Britain.[98] Some imagined the Unknown Warrior resting until the day of his triumphant return. 'Here Sleeps, until the Great Reveille, An

[96] Kernot, *Public Schools War Memorials*, p. 149. The last line reads 'the men I lov*ed*' in the original.
[97] Cecil Harcourt Smith [ed.], *Inscriptions Suggested For War Memorials* (London, HMSO, 1919), p. 32.
[98] WAML, 58667, 'The Funeral Service of a British Warrior on the Second Anniversary of the Signing of the Armistice', 11 November 1920, pp. 3–4. The complete text of the

Unknown Warrior' reads the epitaph suggested by one Mr T. H. Lewis for the abbey tomb.[99] A journalist on the *Daily Chronicle*, reporting the funeral of the Unknown Warrior, tried to capture the atmosphere in Westminster Abbey by quoting a passage from Sir Walter Scott's *Marmion* of 1808 aimed at two 'sleeping dead', Pitt the Younger and Charles James Fox:

> Sacred be his [*sic*] last long rest
> Here, where the end of earthly things
> Lays heroes, patriots, bards, and kings;
> Here, where the fretted aisles prolong
> The distant notes of holy song,
> As if some angel spoke again,
> 'All peace on earth, goodwill to men.'[100]

The interment of a humble soldier in a church of national importance would have been unthinkable before 1914. Yet the democracy of suffering in the years 1914–18 called for an egalitarian symbol of all the 'sleeping dead'. At the same time, British society yearned for a hero, a leader above all petty controversies of the time. This role was assigned to a renowned warrior, Earl Kitchener of Khartoum, who was drowned in 1916 when his ship struck a German mine. The field marshal was the perfect hero for the crisis-ridden mid-1920s. On the one hand, Kitchener seemed like a political and military superman: cool, competent, energetic and strong-willed. On the other hand, 'Like the death of every other mother's son during war', Joanna Bourke writes, 'his own was democratic: nobody was indispensable.'[101] Great deaths had already had a powerful impact on the public imagination in the late-Victorian and Edwardian periods. The funerals of the Duke of Clarence in 1892, William Gladstone in 1898, Queen Victoria in 1901 and Edward VII in 1910 had released painful memories of family bereavements. The lament for Kitchener continued the practice of identifying national losses with

hymn is cited in Edgar Rowan, 'The Abbey Service: Mothers and Wives at the Grave', *Daily Chronicle*, 18323, 12 November 1920, p. 7. Arkwright's hymn was also sung at the dedication of the Warriors' Chapel in Westminster Abbey in 1932. See 'In Memory of the Fallen: Warriors' Chapel in the Abbey', *The Times*, 46169, 25 June 1932, p. 9. On the label the 'Unknown Arthur', see Lloyd, *Battlefield Tourism*, p. 89.

99 WAML, Newspaper Cuttings, vol. 1, p. 19, 'What Shall We Say of Our Unknown? Suggested Epitaphs for the Abbey Tomb', *Evening News*, 12154, 3 November 1920, p. 5.

100 Philip Gibbs, 'A People's Homage to the Noble Dead: The Funeral in the Abbey', *Daily Chronicle*, 18323, 12 November 1920, p. 1, which is slightly misquoted from Sir Walter Scott's *Marmion*, first canto.

101 Bourke, *Dismembering the Male*, p. 244.

personal griefs.[102] Kitchener's body was never found, and rumours began to spread that he had been spirited away to some far-away island where he 'lay plunged, like King Arthur or Barbarossa, into an enchanted sleep from which he would presently awake'.[103]

There could be no burial of the great Field-Marshal, for the sea had taken his body. So far as men can know, the deep waters have kept their dead, and Lord Kitchener has no tomb that may be seen by this generation and those to come. It is fitting, therefore, that within the walls of St Paul's, where lie some of the most famous of those who fought for England, there was held yesterday another service associated with his name – a service which dedicated a Kitchener Memorial Chapel.[104]

Consecrated in December 1925 (but not completed until winter 1928–9), the Chapel of All Souls actually enshrines the memory of Kitchener 'And of all others who fell 1914–1918'. Untouched by the dominant trend towards the 'democratisation' of war remembrance, the managers of the Lord Kitchener National Memorial Fund (including Sir Aston Webb, the former president of the Royal Academy, and the sculptor Sir George Frampton RA) subsumed the memory of the ordinary citizen-soldiers into the celebration of a prominent death.[105] A white-marble figure of the 'water-cleansed' general, recumbent and in uniform, occupies the centre of the chapel; the sculpture is flanked by statues of St George and St Michael to accentuate 'the spirit of sacrifice', the key idea for the chapel (see figure 56). On the opposite side, the designer and academician William (later Sir William) Reid Dick placed a Pietà 'which represents the great Sacrifice once offered and the inscription over the Altar carries forward the story of Redemption'.[106]

[102] Wolffe, Great Deaths, p. 261.
[103] Philip Magnus, Kitchener: A Portrait of an Imperialist (London, John Murray, 1958), p. 379. See Keith Surridge, 'More than a Great Poster: Lord Kitchener and the Image of the Military Hero', Historical Research, 74 (2001), p. 313.
[104] 'Kitchener Memorial Chapel: Dedication Service in St. Paul's', The Times, 44142, 11 December 1925, p. 17.
[105] On the 'democratisation' of war remembrance generally, see Koselleck, 'Kriegerdenkmale als Identitätsstiftungen', pp. 259–60; Mosse, Fallen Soldiers, pp. 15–50.
[106] St Paul's Cathedral Library, London, 'Form of Service Used at the Dedication of the Kitchener Memorial Chapel', suppl., 10 December 1925. See 'The Kitchener Chapel', Manchester Guardian, 24744, 11 December 1925, p. 10; 'Kitchener Memorial Chapel: Work at St. Paul's Nearly Finished', The Times, 45071, 8 December 1928, p. 9. The inscription reads: 'Iesv. Hominvm. Salvator. Trivmphator. Mortis. Et / Rex. Aeternae. Gloriae. Exavdi. Precem. Nostram / Fac. Intrare. Servos. Tvos. In. Regnvm. Coeleste / Et. Lvx. Perpetva. Lvceat. Eis'. On the Pietà motif in war memorials, see Volker G. Probst, Bilder vom Tode: Eine Studie zum deutschen Kriegerdenkmal in der Weimarer Republik am Beispiel des Pietà-Motives und seiner profanisierten Varianten (Hamburg, Wayasbah, 1986), esp. pp. 7–11.

Figure 56. Lord Kitchener by William (later Sir William) Reid Dick. Kitchener Memorial Chapel, St Paul's Cathedral, London, 1925.

The design of the Kitchener memorial chapel is illustrative of the artistic standards laid down by the London art world. In summer 1919, the Victoria and Albert Museum, in collaboration with the Royal Academy War Memorials Committee, organised an exhibition of exemplary commemorative art. The retrospective section showed medieval tomb slabs to offer suggestions for treatment of pose; for instance, the figure of Henry III in Westminster Abbey which was praised as 'the high-water mark of English sepulchral sculpture'.[107] It is noteworthy that in both Britain and Germany, official arbiters of taste were instrumental in popularising recumbent effigies in the aftermath of the war. The respective artistic establishments arranged expositions in part to raise the aesthetic standards of proposed monuments at the local level. In phrasing their recommendations as inspirations rather than doctrines, the organisers avoided imposing their own criteria on the visitor. In Britain, the

---

[107] Victoria and Albert Museum, *Catalogue of the War Memorials Exhibition*, p. 13.

exhibition catalogue and the press broadcast the agenda of the Victoria and Albert Museum, and local memorial committees receptive to the authoritative viewpoint kept the booklet and press cuttings for reference. A lengthy review of the exhibition by Sir Claude Phillips, art critic and founder of the *Daily Telegraph*, has been filed away in a surviving volume of press clippings from Leeds. In this article, Phillips remarked of the exhibits that

There is no tomb of a youthful warrior triumphant in death so moving as that of Gaston de Foix, the hero of Ravenna, by Agostino Busti. He lies, fresh and faultless in beauty as a Greek god, but armoured as a Christian knight – his hands quietly folded across the magnificent cross-shaped sword which lies on his breast. A smile, childlike and happy, hovers around his lips – his duty done to God and man, he sleeps the long sleep, confident in the awakening. [. . .] The companion tomb in this exhibition – that of Guidarello Guidarelli, attributed to Giacomo Baldini – though a magnificently expressive piece of sculpture, is a perfect example of what a tomb should not be. The armoured knight is shown at the very moment when he is expiring, his noble face distorted by the final agony. Not this transient moment of physical struggle does it import to embody in the tomb of eternal marble and bronze, but the cloudless, the unending sleep – the sleep that Gaston, dead in the moment of victory, sleeps.[108]

The medieval pattern of tomb sculpture had already been revived for personal monuments in the nineteenth century, most famously by Henri de Triqueti for the cenotaph effigy of the Prince Consort and by Alfred Gilbert for the monument to the Duke of Clarence, both situated in the Prince Albert memorial chapel in Windsor Castle.[109] The Gothic revival tomb retained its social exclusivity after the First World War, commemorating primarily war heroes such as Lord Kitchener or T. E. Lawrence (see figure 57).[110] The organisers of the exhibition in the Victoria and Albert Museum had indeed realised that recumbent figures were most suitable to 'commemorate the individual rather than a group'.[111] Yet memorial designers faced the task of re-membering and re-presenting a large number of war dead instead of solitary individuals. Architect Sir Edwin Lutyens responded to this problem by placing a soldier's corpse high above the viewer on top of his memorials for Manchester, Rochdale and Southampton. A carved bier tops the Manchester memorial 'upon which is laid to rest the figure of a fighting man with equipment at his side and feet and a greatcoat thrown over the whole, conveying to those

[108] LCL, LQ 940.465 L 517, Claude Phillips, 'Victoria and Albert Museum: War Memorial Exhibition, 1919', *Daily Telegraph*, 20046, 15 July 1919, p. 9.
[109] Girouard, *Return to Camelot*, pp. 126–7.
[110] Knowles, 'Tale of an "Arabian Knight"', pp. 66–8.
[111] Victoria and Albert Museum, *Catalogue of the War Memorials Exhibition*, p. 13.

Figure 57. T. E. Lawrence's tomb by Eric Kennington. St Martin's church, Wareham, 1939.

who stand below no individual identity'.[112] Likewise, Charles Sargeant Jagger anonymised his recumbent effigy of a soldier for the Royal artillery memorial, unveiled in Hyde Park in 1925, by covering the face with a greatcoat.[113]

Commemorative sculpture in both Britain and Germany attempted to lift the thoughts of the spectators above physical death. Recumbent figures re-membered the soldier's body, dismembered on the battlefield. These monuments served as an indication of the refusal to perceive the dead as wholly dead. Death was conceived neither as a grim reaper nor as a divine providence but as a tranquil sleep. 'Sleep': the very term imaginatively configured the absent dead as ever present. Although a comforting idea, the notion of an enchanted sleep did not make it easier to acknowledge loss – in contrast to the Christian diction of redemption. The former concept enabled the bereaved to live with their losses, but the latter to leave them behind. Leaving the fallen soldiers behind: that the German far Right was anxious to prevent. Unwilling to concede a humiliating military defeat and to put up with its socio-political consequences, they consoled themselves with the dream of a triumphant return of the dead to save the Reich.

Germanic prophecies

'Death, which smote me, / gives me in my sleep / Heavenly serenity': thus sang Karl von Seeger, the compiler of an illustrated catalogue of Great War memorials, of the dead Siegfried, whose bust, lying on a black-marble plinth, commemorates the fallen students of the University of Vienna (see figure 58).[114] It was fitting that a university should choose a sculpture of Young Siegfried to represent the dead, for the hero was generally seen as the very embodiment of eternal youth, 'youth as symbolic of manhood, virility, and energy, and death as not death at all but sacrifice and resurrection'.[115] Under the motto 'Siegfried has awakened!', the Reich memorial committee of Haidmühle, Bavaria, strove to mobilise and unite the German adolescents living in the Reich, Austria, Bohemia and South Tyrol. The villagers' bold claim to the

---

[112] IWM, Eph. Mem., K 3764, 'Unveiling of the Manchester War Memorial: Programme of Arrangements', 1924, n.p. See also ibid., K 3861, 'Rochdale War Memorial Souvenir: Unveiling of the Rochdale War Memorial', 1922, p. 4; King, *Memorials of the Great War*, p. 150.

[113] Glaves-Smith, 'Realism and Propaganda', pp. 72–5.

[114] Seeger, *Denkmal des Weltkriegs*, p. 158: 'Tod, der mich traf, / Gibt mir im Schlaf / Himmlische Ruh'.

[115] Mosse, *Fallen Soldiers*, p. 73.

Figure 58. Siegfried by J. Müller. University of Vienna, 1922.

national war memorial derived from the area's sublime beauty. Allegedly, the landscape reminded the visitor of the 'invincible' Siegfried 'born out of a deep fairy-tale slumber [*Märchenschlummer*] in the midst of a primeval forest'.[116]

Siegfried's story was, of course, a tragic one. Betrayed by his friends (in revenge for his own unfaithfulness), Siegfried was killed from behind by the malevolent Hagen. 'As Siegfried could succumb only to betrayal', the Haidmühle committee contended, 'so the German army, unbeaten and standing firm on foreign soil, could fall victim to treachery'.[117] The overwhelming majority of agents of grass-roots commemorations, in contrast, dispensed with the politics of the *Dolchstoß*, the 'stab in the back'.[118] The legend of the victorious army remaining in the field until

[116] BArch, R 32/362, fos. 69–70, Denkmalausschuß Haidmühle to Reichskunstwart, 31 March 1927: 'Der Siegfried ist erwacht!', 'Aus tiefem Märchenschlummer wurde er uns aus Urwaldsmitte heraus geboren'.

[117] Ibid.: 'Wie Siegfried nur dem Verrat weichen musste, musste auch die deutsche Armee dem Verrat zum Opfer fallen, [. . .] unbesiegt und auf feindlichem Boden stehend.'

[118] On the *Dolchstoß* and Germanic mythology, see Münkler and Storch, *Siegfrieden*, esp. pp. 86–92; Wolfgang Schivelbusch, *The Culture of Defeat: On National Trauma, Mourning, and Recovery* (New York, Metropolitan, 2003). Generally, see Friedrich

the collapse of the home front in autumn 1918 amid agitation by paci-
fists, socialists, slackers and Jews did not strike a chord with commemorative congregations, at least not with civilian ones.[119] Although the
Dolchstoß myth might have assuaged some veterans' guilt complex
about the breakdown of military discipline in the summer and autumn
of 1918, in the context of communal remembrance the legend fell short
of yielding a form of emotional consolation to the bereaved. Yet the
political mobilisation of the *Song of the Nibelungen* in right-wing man-
oeuverings did not preclude Germanic mythology from informing commemorative narratives – that is, comforting rather than polarising
narratives which centred on two mythical prophecies: the Rhinegold
and Valhalla.

The Rhinegold

In July 1926, the mayor of Koblenz, Rhine Province, urged the Reich
Chancellor and his fellow Rhinelander, Wilhelm Marx of the Catholic
Centre Party, to establish the hotly disputed Reich memorial on the
River Rhine. Here it would have symbolic force, because the legendary
gold hoard of the Nibelungen, a blessing for the good but a curse for the
wicked, was lying at the bottom of the river:

Our ethos shall be like a new Nibelungen hoard of purest gold. When the
memorial rises on the River Rhine, we want to come to honour our dead.
A feeling of deep gratitude shall overcome us: gratitude for their loyalty, patriotism and devotion to the nation and state. It shall prompt us to emulate them.
The memorial shall be a substitute for the pilgrimage to the grave of the dead,
not only for their relatives, but for all their fellow countrymen [. . .]. 'Greater
love hath no man than this, that a man lay down his life for his fellow countrymen.'[120]

Hiller von Gaertringen, '"Dolchstoß"-Diskussion und "Dolchstoßlegende" im Wandel
von vier Jahrzehnten', in Waldemar Besson and Friedrich von Hiller Gaertringen
(eds.), *Geschichte und Gegenwartsbewußtsein: Historische Betrachtungen und Untersuchungen*
(Göttingen, Vandenhoeck & Rupprecht, 1963), pp. 122–60.

[119] Bernd Kasten, 'Das sogenannte "Dolchstoss-Denkmal" im Schweriner Schloßgarten',
Mecklenburgische Jahrbücher, 114 (1999), Beiheft, pp. 379–87, deals with a controversial *Dolchstoß* memorial established by veterans.

[120] BArch, R 43 I/714, folio 117, Oberbürgermeister Coblenz to Reichskanzler, 21 July
1926: 'Wie ein neuer Nibelungenhort von lauterstem Golde soll unsere Gesinnung
sein. Wenn sich das Denkmal am Rhein erhebt, wollen wir herantreten, um unsere
Toten zu ehren. Ein tiefes Dankgefühl soll uns beherrschen: der Dank für die Treue,
Vaterlandsliebe und Hingabe für Volk und Staat. Es soll uns anregen, ihnen nachzuei-
fern. Das Denkmal soll ein Ersatz sein für den Gang zum Grabe der Toten, nicht nur
für die Angehörigen, sondern für alle Volksgenossen, denen wir Dank schulden wie
unseren Eltern, niemanden auf dem Erdenrund. "Keine Liebe kann größer sein, als
wer sein Leben lässt für seine Volksgenossen."'

While the mayor and the chancellor were secretly conferring about the Rhineland's application, two members of the state college of art in Düsseldorf pressed ahead with a publicity campaign to designate one of the river islands as a sanctuary for Germany's war dead. Professors Richard Klapheck and Karl Wach issued a glossy brochure which stressed that 'In the Rhine lies the treasure of the Nibelungen, our promise.'[121] Full of mythological and historical references, the pamphlet had surprisingly little to say about the proposed design and the exact location of the 'Island of the Dead'. What might seem like an unfocused approach was in fact an exercise in commemorative *Realpolitik*. The campaign eschewed adding fuel to the flames of local rivalries which threatened to undermine the Rhineland's prospects. A number of locations were considered, namely the Eisenbolz, Grafenwerth, Hammersteiner Werth, Lorcher Werth, the Lorelei and Nonnenwerth.[122] Klapheck and Wach's strategy worked out in part; the vagueness of their scheme brought the professors the official endorsement of the district assembly of St Goar.[123]

---

[121] BArch, R 43 I/713, folio 200v, Richard Klapheck, *Das Reichsehrenmal für unsere Gefallenen: Die Toteninsel im Rhein* (Düsseldorf, Staatliche Kunstakademie, 1926), p. 2: 'Im Rheine liegt der Schatz der Nibelungen, unsere Verheißung.' See Bucher, 'Errichtung des Reichsehrenmals', p. 365. For a biting satire on the regenerative powers of Germanicism, see Jean Giraudoux, *My Friend from Limousin* (New York and London, Harper, 1923), pp. 98–9.

[122] StAMS, OP 5510, folio 161, Ausschuß für das Reichsehrenmal am Rhein, 'Das Reichsehrenmal am Rhein: Bericht über die Verhandlungen mit Vertretern von Organisationen der Frontkämpfer, der Kriegsbeschädigten, der Kriegshinterbliebenen und ehemaligen Kriegsgefangenen am 26. Juli 1926', August 1926, concerns various islands in the Rhine. On the Eisenbolz, see BArch, R 43 I/716, folio 45, Albert Maennchen, 'Wohin das Reichsehrenmal?', April 1930; BArch, R 43 I/715, fos. 224–7, Sybille Maennchen, 'Die Toten des Weltkrieges und das Reichsehrenmal – der Eisenbolz am Rhein: Entwurf von Professor Albert Maennchen', January 1928. On Grafenwerth, see BArch, R 43 I/714, fos. 305–28, 'Das Reichsehrenmal auf Grafenwerth: Werbelieder von Walther Stoltzing für Grafenwerth!', [c. 1926]. On Lorcher Werth, see BArch, R 32/494, 'Vorschlag Rheininsel bei Lorch: Presseausschnitte', 1926–7, and, for a critical note, GStAPK, 1. HA Rep. 77, Tit. 1215 Nr. 3c Beiheft 'Pressestimmen', Willy Lange, 'Um das Reichsehrenmal', *Tägliche Rundschau*, 188, 13 August 1926. On Hammersteiner Werth, see BArch, R 43 I/714, folio 330, 'Die Toteninsel im Rhein: Auszug aus einem Gutachten von Gartenarchitekt Wiepking-Jürgensmann an den Reichskunstwart Dr. Redslob', [c. 1926]; ibid., fos. 332–43, Hammerstein-Ausschuß, *Das Reichsehrenmal auf der Insel Hammerstein im Rhein* (Neuwied, Stründer, 1926); GStAPK, I. HA Rep. 77, Tit. 1215 Nr. 3c Bd. 1, fos. 148–9, C. Burger, 'Das Reichsehrenmal auf der Insel Hammerstein im Rhein', n.d. Generally, see Ziemann, 'Deutsche Nation', pp. 76–81.

[123] GStAPK, I. HA Rep. 77, Tit. 1215 Nr. 3c Bd. 1, folio 119, Resolution passed by Kreistag St. Goar, [c. 1926]. For a critique of the proposal, see BArch, R 32/361a, fos. 13–5, 'Rheinland: Gegen das Wachsche Projekt', n.d.

The Great War and Medieval Memory

The Lorelei, a precipitous rock on the River Rhine not far from St Goar, ranked as one of the most promising candidates. Folk myth maintained that the inexhaustible Nibelungen hoard, giving its owner omnipotence, lay hidden inside the rock. Dangerous to boatmen but celebrated for its echo, the Lorelei held a peculiar fascination for nineteenth-century German poets such as Clemens Brentano and Heinrich Heine. Brentano, a protagonist of the later phase of German Romanticism, which emphasised folklore and history, was most influential in reinventing the Lorelei. In the early nineteenth century he composed the famous ballad of the deceitful sorceress, a siren-like figure, luring sailors to their death. A prophecy both gloomy and uplifting, the tale of the Lorelei, popularised by Heinrich Heine, found popular resonance after 1914–18 in a society which had just lived through a military armageddon. 'A mysterious, fairy-tale magic [. . .] extends over the entire, beautiful area, cleaving to everything surrounding it, shimmering in the gold of the eternally victorious morning sun, which plays softeningly against the sinister Lorelei rock', wrote two people who offered a design.[124] A Berlin civil servant envisaged a sixty-metre-tall monument opposite the Lorelei rock; and one Frau Dr Roth, in writing to the editor of the left-liberal *Vossische Zeitung*, put forward an almost identical proposal.[125] To be sure, the Lorelei cult also excited ridicule. In 1928, anti-Semites painted the opening line of Heine's 'Lorelei' of 1824, 'I do not know what it means', and the star of David on a contentious war memorial by the Jewish artist Jupp Rübsam in Düsseldorf.[126]

Like the Lorelei, the island of Nonnenwerth, a few miles upstream from Bad Godesberg, was embedded in nineteenth-century Romanticism. In spring 1926, the national-liberal *Kölnische Zeitung* unearthed plans for a memorial on Nonnenwerth dating back to the age of the Wars

---

[124] BArch, R 43 I/715, folio 221v, Albert and Sibylle Maennchen, *Das Reichsehrenmal: Der Eisenbolz am Rhein*, ed. Gemeinden Boppard, Bad Salzig and Camp am Rhein (Camp am Rhein, Breuer, 1927): 'Ein geheimnisvoller, märchenhafter Zauber [. . .] bereitet sich über die ganze, wunderschöne Gegend aus, haftet allem das sie umgiebt, flimmert im Gold der ewig-sieghaften Morgensonne, das den finster dräunenden Lureleyfelsen [*sic*] mildernd umspielt.'

[125] BArch, R 43 I/713, folio 15v, 'Pressestimmen zu dem Gedanken der Errichtung eines Nationaldenkmals für die Gefallenen im Weltkrieg', p. 6; ibid., folio 114v, 'Zusammenstellung der dem Reichsministerium des Innern bekannt gewordenen Vorschläge zur Errichtung eines Nationaldenkmals für die Gefallenen im Weltkriege', p. 4; Frau Roth, 'Das Ehrenmal am Rhein' [letter to the editor], *Vossische Zeitung*, 402, 24 August 1924; GStAPK, I. HA Rep. 77, Tit. 1215 Nr. 3c Beiheft 'Pressestimmen', Friedrich Hussong, 'Die Toteninsel', *Berliner Lokal-Anzeiger*, 351, 26 July 1926.

[126] Kristine Pollack, 'Das 39er Denkmal in Düsseldorf', in *Skulptur und Macht: Figurative Plastik im Deutschland der 30er und 40er Jahre* (Berlin, Fröhlich & Kaufmann, 1983), p. 155. See also Thamer, 'Von der Monumentalisierung zur Verdrängung', p. 114.

of Liberation.[127] Around the same time, the newspaper's Catholic rival, the *Kölnische Volkszeitung*, presented a blueprint for turning Nonnenwerth into an 'Island of the Dead' comprising a heroes' grove and a monumental rotunda. Adorned with images from the *Song of the Nibelungen*, the rotunda was intended to house the mortal remains of fallen soldiers of all 'German tribes' as well as of confederate nations. Richly decorated coffins were to be arranged around a basin. At the rim of the basin, a statue featuring a Valkyrie presaging death to Siegfried was to be erected. Yet on the surface of the water, the visitor would discern a reflection of the ceiling fresco showing 'the resurrection of Germany'.[128] In short, the rotunda represented Valhalla, the hall of the slain built by Wotan (Odin) for the warriors who died bravely in battle.

Valhalla

The fact that a newspaper of the Catholic milieu invoked the mythological creed of Germanicism testifies to its cross-cultural prevalence in early twentieth-century Germany. Equally illuminating is the naming of the art gallery of Hagen, Westphalia, after Folkwang (Fólkvangar), the residence of Freya, the goddess of love and beauty, and her chosen dead in Valhalla. The Museum Folkwang founded by Karl Ernst Osthaus in 1902 (relocated to Essen in 1922) established itself quickly as a leading forum for avant-garde art in Imperial Germany. Osthaus's museum put the Ruhr region, hitherto associated with heavy industry, noise and pollution, on the map of high culture. 'So cities of work grew up, despised and avoided for their ugliness by strangers, hated by their inhabitants, feared and envied by the world as an expression of enormous, brutal power. Men appeared who issued a warning about this trend', recalled a brochure proposing a rather obscure national 'memorial house' in the Ruhr region dedicated to the war dead. 'You, Karl Ernst Osthaus, you were the greatest, the most far-sighted of them! With your idea of Folkwang, you prophetically showed the future goal. You called for an anthropogenesis [*Menschwerdung*], you sowed the seed which is now beginning to shoot up.'[129] Emulating the example of Osthaus's

---

[127] GStAPK, I. HA Rep. 77, Tit. 1215 Nr. 3c Beiheft 'Pressestimmen', 'Ein Plan aus der Zeit der Befreiungskriege', *Kölnische Zeitung*, 339, 9 May 1926.

[128] Ibid., E. Hölscher, 'Eine Toteninsel im Rhein', *Kölnische Volkszeitung*, 282, 18 Apr. 1926.

[129] GStAPK, I. HA Rep. 77, Tit. 1215 Nr. 3c Bd. 1, folio 274, Pamphlet by Hermann Kätelhön, n.d., p. 2: 'So wuchsen die Städte der Arbeit herauf, von den Fremden verachtet und gemieden ob ihrer Häßlichkeit, von ihren Bewohnern gehaßt, als ein

Museum Folkwang, the proposed project combined the bourgeois ideal of *Bildung*, education, with a penchant for things Germanic.

Although workers, too, conjured up images of men ascending into Valhalla in songs commemorating their comrades killed in the war, Germanic mythology was principally the intellectual property of the educated middle classes.[130] As one might expect, the war memorials of educational institutions offered effective media for imparting the Germanic heritage to the younger generation. In 1933, the *Oberrealschule* (a type of grammar school with an emphasis on modern languages and sciences) in Kaiserslautern, Bavarian Palatinate, inaugurated its war memorial, a relief representing a Valkyrie with a slain hero destined for Valhalla on the saddle of her horse (see figure 59). 'The dead stone tells more than words can say', a liberal commentator noted.[131] By contrast, the Nazi press gave a very explicit interpretation of the school's memorial as a 'symbol of the resurrection of the German spirit from the night of spiritual and political captivity'.[132]

Germanic notation built bridges between educated Germans and the political parvenus of the Nazi party. In accord with the commemorative discourse of the Weimar era, the Nazis continued to draw on Germanic mythology, but insisted on interpreting the arrival of the Third Reich – Hitler's 'Thousand-Year Reich' – as the ultimate fulfilment of Germanic prophecies. In 1936, on the occasion of the opening of the *Totenburg* rising above Bitola, Yugoslavia, 'timeless and eternal, like a Valhalla', a member of the German war-graves association remarked of the architecture that 'It is a symbol of German resurrection and rebirth. Already today, the people of Bitola and Macedonia

---

Ausdruck ungeheurer brutaler Kraft von der Welt geneidet und gefürchtet. Männer kamen herauf, die in dieses Beginnen ein Mahnen riefen. Du, Karl Ernst Osthaus, Du warst der Größte, der Weitschauendste unter ihnen! In Deinem Folkwanggedanken wiesest Du seherisch das künftige Ziel. Zur Menschwerdung riefest Du auf, Du sätest die Saat, die jetzt zu grünen beginnt.' See Herta Hesse-Frielinghaus, 'Folkwang 1. Teil', in Herta Hesse-Frielinghaus *et al.*, *Karl Ernst Osthaus: Leben und Werk* (Recklinghausen, Aurel Bongers, 1971), p. 130.

[130] On the working classes, see Dietmar Klenke, Peter Lilje and Franz Walter, *Arbeitersänger und Volksbühnen in der Weimarer Republik*, Solidargemeinschaft und Milieu, vol. III (Bonn, J. H. W. Dietz Nachf., 1992), pp. 85–6; Bernd Buchner, *Um nationale und republikanische Identität: Die deutsche Sozialdemokratie und der Kampf um die politischen Symbole in der Weimarer Republik* (Bonn, J. H. W. Dietz Nachf., 2001), p. 206.

[131] Schmidt, *Kriegerdenkmale in der Pfalz*, p. 97: 'Mehr als Worte zu sagen vermögen, spricht der tote Stein'. On visual representations of Valkyries, see Holsten, *Allegorische Darstellungen des Krieges*, pp. 44–6.

[132] As cited in Lurz, *Kriegerdenkmale*, vol. V, p. 218: 'Symbol für das Wiederauferstehen deutschen Geistes aus der Nacht geistiger und politischer Gefangenschaft'.

Figure 59. Valkyrie with a steel-helmeted soldier by Adolf Bernd. Oberrealschule Kaiserslautern, 1933.

are calling our memorial the Hitler castle. So past and present are interlinked, the dead of the world war have entered the New Reich.'[133]

The first modern Valhalla had been built under the Bavarian King, Ludwig I, between 1830 and 1842 on a promontory above the Danube near Regensburg Within this neo-classical temple, statuary and tablets commemorate great 'Germans' and illustrate the history and mythology of the 'German' nation – an indefinite entity, a circumstance which led to the inclusion of aliens such as Egbert, King of Wessex. Ludwig's *Walhalla* served as a point of reference in the discussion of war commemoration in the aftermath of the First World War. In the 1920s, the Reich Art Custodian received proposals to make a replica of Ludwig's folly, to create another 'German Valhalla similar to the ancient Greek temples', adorned with Christian imagery.[134] Interestingly, the *Walhalla* at Regensburg did not fail to impress (or disgust) British observers of the German art scene. In 1916, the *Architectural Review* dismissed the monument – alongside the Hall of Liberation at Kelheim and the Hall of Fame in Munich, all works by Leo von Klenze for Ludwig I – as a 'form of memorial which especially appeals to the Germans' and as 'specifically Teutonic'. The 'total absence of any definite architectural tradition in his country', the reviewer expounded, drove Ludwig I to blend the Parthenon of the Athenians with 'Scandinavian mythology'.[135]

In other words, for the architectural critic, the usage of the Valhalla motif, contaminated by German *Kultur*, was out of the question in Britain. Nevertheless, in practice many Britons relished the aesthetics of Nordic paganism. One of the city fathers of Leeds recommended 'a small temple or Walhalla [*sic*], neither large nor costly, somewhat on the lines of the small but beautiful temple of Vesta at Rome'.[136] Earlier, a Leeds newspaper had been impressed with plans for a 'Temple of Fame' at Manchester: 'the central portion of the new buildings should be set apart as a local Pantheon or Valhalla in which East Lancashire's part in

---

[133] Franz Hallbaum, 'Die Totenburg deutscher Helden in Bitola, Jugoslawien', *Kriegsgrä-berfürsorge*, 16,1 (1936), p. 9: 'Symbol ist es der deutschen Auferstehung und Wiedergeburt. Heute schon wird unser Mal im Volke Bitoljs und Mazedoniens die Hitlerburg genannt. So sind Vergangenheit und Gegenwart verknüpft, die Toten des Weltkrieges sind eingegangen in das Neue Reich', and p. 13: 'Zeitlos-ewig, wie ein Walhall'.

[134] BArch, R 32/355, folio 38, Reichskunstwart to Reichsminister des Innern, 4 June 1926: 'Eine deutsche Walhalla, ähnlich den alten griechischen Tempeln'. See also BArch, R 32/362, fos. 100–3, Anonymous to Reichskunstwart, 2 June 1927; Herre, *Deutsche Walhall*, p. 3. On the memorial temple near Regensburg, see Kerssen, *Interesse am Mittelalter*, pp. 136–53.

[135] 'Memorials of War: – VIII. German', *Architectural Review*, 40 (1916), pp. 101–2.

[136] WYASL, LC/TC/R 17, 'Suggestions Received subsequent to the Meeting of the Sub-Committee on the 29 January', n.d.

the war should be commemorated by means of flags, frescoes, and trophies'.[137] The Valhalla was far from being a commemorative oddity of the English north. Frequently, journalists compared Westminster Abbey, the final resting place of the Unknown Warrior, to Odin's hall of the slain: for example, the liberal *Daily Chronicle* ('the Valhalla of our race'), the conservative *Daily Express* ('the Valhalla of the heroic dead'), or the veterans' *British Legion Journal* ('the national Valhalla').[138] Ian Hay's guide to the Scottish National War Memorial, published in 1931, also dwelt on the lure of a heaven reserved for warriors. The ruling idea behind the wealth of regimental memorials inside the Edinburgh monument, he wrote, 'has been that in this, a nation's Valhalla, no service, however slight or humble, shall be overlooked'.[139]

How did the notion of Valhalla originate? Ludwig I had pioneered the Valhalla motif in architecture in the first half of the nineteenth century. Equally, if not more important, was the taste in music which his grandson, Ludwig II, developed. The operas of his protégé, Richard Wagner, enjoyed huge popularity not only with the German bourgeoisie but also with the British upper classes before the war. At the Proms in London's Royal Albert Hall, Mondays were reserved for productions of Wagner's works.[140] National mobilisation in 1914, however, brought about the fragmentation of European elite culture into national units. The British war effort rendered performances of Wagner's tetralogy, *Der Ring des Nibelungen*, composed between 1848 and 1878, politically impossible. But in Germany, the *Ring* cycle, which held the rank of a national opus, set the tone of signifying practices, particularly in academic circles. Wagner's music heightened the dramatic effect of the war memorial of Göttingen University, a monument of eight nude Herculean figures carrying a fallen comrade on their shoulders. At the request of the sculptor, Josef Kemmerich, the army orchestra played the music from the prelude to the second act of *Die Walküre*, which introduces the Valhalla theme, at the unveiling ceremony in November 1924. The

---

[137] LCL, LQ 940.465 L 517, 'A Temple of Fame', *Yorkshire Evening Post*, 4 November 1918.

[138] P. O'Donovan, 'Mothers and Wives: Queens in Tears', *Daily Express*, 6423, 12 November 1920, p. 7; 'In the Tomb of Triumph: Homage to All Who Fell in Service and Fellowship', *Daily Chronicle*, 18322, 11 November 1920, p. 1; Herbert Jeans, 'In Death's Cathedral Palace: The Story of the Unknown Warrior', *British Legion Journal*, 9 November 1929, p. 118. For a characterisation of these newspapers, see Reimann, *Krieg der Sprachen*, p. 21; Gregory, *Silence of Memory*, p. 75.

[139] Hay, *Their Name Liveth*, p. 48.

[140] Hynes, *War Imagined*, p. 74; Ferguson, *Pity of War*, p. 24. On the wartime mobilisation of music, see Glenn Watkins, *Proof Through the Night: Music and the Great War* (Berkeley, Los Angeles and London, University of California Press, 2003).

rector of the university, taking his cue from Wagner, called the dead students and lecturers 'a proud band of Einherjar', in other words the resurrected warriors living in Valhalla, who 'have entered Valhalla after brave battles'.[141]

At the University of Munich, an instrumental motif from Wagner's *Siegfried* rounded off a memorial service for the lost generation. In Berlin, student fraternities participated prominently in a commemoration of the dead of Flanders featuring the funeral march from *Götterdämmerung*. The same piece was played in remembrance of doctors from the capital fallen in the war.[142] Such events had an air of tragedy and sadness, but with an undertone of redemption. The use of Wagner's music in the context of war commemoration was absolutely in tune with new interpretations advanced by the Bayreuth circle during the 1920s. Denying Wagner's political and social criticism, hard-core Wagnerians viewed their idol as the prophet of the Great War and the *Ring* as a parable of Germany's military defeat and future rise.[143] In harmony with the tendencies towards political actualisation, Wagner's heirs granted the Volksbund Deutsche Kriegsgräberfürsorge permission to hold a commemoration ceremony in the festival theatre of Bayreuth, Bavaria, in 1921.[144]

The Valhalla of war remembrance stood not merely for a warrior's heaven but also for a military camp. The throng of resurrected Einherjar was destined to live until the Germanic doomsday, the Ragnarök, when they would march out of Odin's palace to fight on the gods' side against the giants. Evocations of Valhalla often resonated with revisionist or revanchist overtones in Germany, particularly in right-wing circles. British agents of memory, by contrast, did not grasp the political implications of the Valhalla motif. For them, Valhalla represented a kind of paradise which, apart from being exclusive to fallen soldiers, did not differ fundamentally from the Christian heaven.

[141] *Dem Andenken ihrer im Weltkriege Gefallenen*, p. 21: 'die [. . .] als eine stolze Schar von Einheriern nach mutigem Kampfe in Walhall eingezogen sind'. See Saathoff, *Göttinger Kriegsgedenkbuch*, p. 211; Carola Gottschalk, 'Götterdämmerung: Das Denkmal für die Gefallenen der Universität', in Carola Gottschalk (ed.), *Verewigt und Vergessen: Kriegerdenkmäler, Mahnmale und Gedenksteine in Göttingen* (Göttingen, Volker Schmerse, 1992), p. 29.
[142] BArch, R 8034 II/7691, folio 107, 'Gefallenen-Gedächtnisfeier der Universität', *Bayerische Staatszeitung*, 14, 18 January 1922; ibid., folio 93, 'Yser-Helden-Gedächtnisfeier', *Deutsche Tageszeitung*, 486, 17 October 1921; ibid., folio 40, 'Gedenkfeier für die Gefallenen Groß-Berliner Aerzte [*sic*]', *Tägliche Rundschau*, 627, 15 December 1919.
[143] Udo Bermbach, 'Richard Wagner as Prophet of the World War: On the Interpretation of the *Ring* in *Bayreuther Blätter* between 1878 and 1938', *Wagner*, 21 (2000), pp. 100–9.
[144] Schellack, *Nationalfeiertage in Deutschland*, p. 192.

Hope is a central theme in war remembrance, both religious and secular. Medievalist commemorations turned thoughts of destruction into the hope of regeneration and salvation; the dead would rise again and even inspire the living. Spiritual medievalism, whether religiously or mythologically inspired, originated in the popular need to give transcendental meaning to the enormous war losses. It colonised the domain of the sacred, mediating between the living and the (living) dead. Christian-medieval diction promised everlasting life in return for the supreme sacrifice; sleep metaphors speculated on the triumphant return of the glorious dead; finally, Germanic prophecies warranted a continued quest (for the omnipotent Rhinegold) and also spoke of a martial afterlife (in Valhalla). The three modes of thought explored in this chapter share a 'tendency to slide from metaphors about remembering those who have died to the metaphysics of life after death'.[145]

At the same time, the three modes disclose a conflict between a transcendent *Jenseitshoffnung*, a hope for the hereafter, on the one hand, and an earthly *Zukunftshoffnung*, a trust in a brighter future, on the other.[146] Characteristically, the aspect of *Zukunftshoffnung*, of future regeneration, was more pronounced in inter-war Germany than in Britain. German agents of memory venturing into the grey space between the personal and the political linked the salvation of the war dead to the re-awakening of the medieval Reich or the re-discovery of the Nibelungen hoard – symbolic reminders of German omnipotence and splendour. A growing number of Germans, haunted by the unbearable memories of death and defeat, found consolation in visions of national regeneration, visions which sometimes turned into cries for military revenge.

---

[145] Winter, *Sites of Memory*, p. 76.
[146] See Reinhart Koselleck, 'Einleitung', in Reinhart Koselleck and Michael Jeismann (eds.), *Der politische Totenkult: Kriegerdenkmäler in der Moderne* (Munich, Wilhelm Fink, 1994), p. 14.

Conclusion

The survivors of the Great War in both Britain and Germany strove to find ways of expressing their anguish as well as their pride. Their spokesmen, both formal and informal, operating in the borderland between civil society, the family and the state, embarked on creative efforts to give meaning to this shocking and unexpected experience. In order to make sense of the carnage of the First World War, they drew on their understanding of a remote yet meaningful past to help people to restore and regain control over their lives; medievalism, that eclectic amalgam of temporal notions, flourished. Instead of saying 'good-bye to all that' and starting afresh, the memorial makers gazed backwards to misty medieval times. Older lines of continuity were reasserted in an effort to turn history into a coherent narrative that overshadowed the rupture of 1914–18. Medievalism in war remembrance, recovering the fallen and the missing soldiers of the First World War and relocating them in the grammar of medieval history, entwined intimate responses with cultural ones. It was the search for images and themes which provided historical precedents for an unprecedented human catastrophe. Here was hope of redemption through tradition.

This study has shown the overlaps, imbrications and connections between personal loss, its public acknowledgment and political activism. Post 1914–18 *lieux de mémoire* reveal the dual force of private grief and political expediency. They occupied precisely the intermediate space between Jay Winter's 'sites of mourning' and George L. Mosse's 'sites of mobilisation'. The claim that war commemorations were exclusively about the management of bereavement is inadequate; but to reduce their meaning to political manipulation is cynical. Arising out of the shock of bereavement felt by the individual, war remembrance was, however, a socially framed signifying practice that could not be politically neutral. The matrix of interwoven memories underlying collective action materialised principally in war memorials. These artefacts of collective remembrance functioned as substitutes for the graves of the absent dead as well as carriers of ideological messages. In short, the politics of memory had to engage with the psychology of mourning and vice versa. One of the purposes of this study has been to venture beyond the deleterious divide between the grief school of thought and its functionalist counterpart in contemporary historical studies. Languages of historical continuity constituted both a set of meditations on the passing of the dead and a potent source of political imagery and ideas. As a discourse that bridged the gap between the personal and the political, the individual and the community, medievalism in the commemoration of the Great War may yet render older historiographical polarisations obsolete.

Scholars of the Great War interested in the origins of modernity have highlighted the pervasive sense of historical dislocation and the loss of coherence that underlay cultural patterns of language and perception emerging in the wake of war. Based on an archival exploration of social acts of commemoration, this book has demonstrated that established interpretations of the First World War as a cultural turning-point in modern history cannot be sustained with regard to the culture of public remembrance. *Pace* the seminal works of Paul Fussell on the rise of ironic 'modern memory', Samuel Hynes on the birth of a resentful 'myth of the war', and Modris Eksteins on the emergence of misanthropic 'rites of spring', I have argued that medievalist assertions of continuity rather than modernist revolutions against tradition provided the backbone of commemoration.

At the same time, I have avoided setting up a false dichotomy between modernism and medievalism, abstraction and ornament, realism and romanticism, anxiety and nostalgia. It is one of the most puzzling features of the cultural legacy of the Great War that medievalist sentiments could well find expression in modernist solutions to memorial art, particularly in Germany. The divide between modernist and traditionalist vocabularies of commemoration was a fluid, non-linear one. Moreover, the discursive field of medievalism – far from being identical with anti-modernism and cultural pessimism – proved capable of accommodating the very modernity of the machine war, namely the monstrosity of the battle of *matériel*. Enveloped in medievalist idioms, the glamour of technical innovations (which characterised, for instance, aerial warfare) appeared solidly grounded on historical foundations in the eyes of observers. Medievalism after 1914–18 was not primarily a nostalgic yearning for a different time, an accounting of loss, but an affirmation of continuity with a meaningful past in the shadow of a human catastrophe.

Medievalism in the remembrance of the Great War had two constituents: first, resonances of historically remote incidents, and secondly repercussions of recent events. Historical romance (grounded on the nation's collective memory) and human trauma (ingrained in the existential memory of the wartime sacrifice) formed a narrative symbiosis in medievalist commemoration in the inter-war period. Existential memory as a third category between impromptu communicative memory and sophisticated cultural memory combined features of both concepts: it originated in direct – in this case, traumatic – experience but relied on complex memory aids; it occurred immediately but endured in the institutions which it generated; it emanated from individual biographies but permeated the communal sphere. The process of joining the existential memory of death in industrialised war and the cultural memory of the distant past together in public was intended to vindicate memory down the ages. The dialectic of lamenting the human catastrophe and insisting on historical continuity was at the core of medievalist diction in war remembrance in Britain and Germany alike.

Furthermore, the comparative approach discloses significant overlaps between the composition of national medievalisms. Not only did British and German agents of remembrance employ the same mnemonic strategy and techniques, they also tended to rekindle or recast parallel, pre-existing frames of reference. The neo-medieval movements and fashions of nineteenth-century Europe had furnished a repertoire of cultural forms and idioms that could be drawn on in the aftermath of the First World War. What had essentially been a discourse of identity in the era of industrialisation was transformed into a discourse of mourning in an age of industrialised slaughter. Yet the war had brought about the fragmentation of this pan-European cultural memory into national units. Richard Wagner or Sir Walter Scott, to cite but two examples, had made their mark abroad almost as strongly as in their respective homelands; but after 1914, political chauvinism forbade acknowledging the shared inheritance of nineteenth-century medievalism. Nonetheless, the historian should not underestimate the significance of intersecting memories after 1914–18 stemming from mutual observation and inter-cultural transfer. Notably, large-scale, medievalist memorial projects (such as the Unknown Warrior or the Tannenberg monument) and war heroes (such as air aces) did not escape the attention of the former enemy, who invoked them either as anti-models or as a source of inspiration and imitation.

To stress the commonality of medievalism is not, however, to reject the view that the war also engendered culture-specific responses. On the contrary, one has to distinguish carefully between regional, religious, class-cultural, milieu-specific and national variants of the medievalist discourse. The vitality of localism and the plurality of agency promoted many different medievalist representations. Significantly, the diversities within the national communities were as pronounced as the divergences between the nations. On the one hand, Scots and East Friesians (proud of their respective freedom and riven by iconophobia), Anglo-Catholics and German Roman Catholics (both open to religious spiritualism and ornamentalism), or British public-school boys and German *Gymnasium* pupils (equally imbued with classical and chivalrous feats), shared, in a sense, more with each other than with their fellow countrymen. The idea of a collective narrative about the war is a generalisation which cannot hold. National memory is not homogenous but plural, and acts of remembrance underscored existing cleavages in society. On the other hand, the weight of national patterns in the commemoration of the Great War is indisputable. British representations of the First World War differed in a host of ways from German encodings.

New crusade versus national defence

From the earliest days of the war, people attached great importance to the nature of the conflict, for it legitimised military action and sanctified bloodshed. Initially, declared 'war enthusiasts' in both countries imagined the war as a holy war against evil. In the event, this trope was superseded by more profane and wistful concepts that mirrored the respective fortunes of war and also suited the mood of soldiers as their numbers shifted from life towards death. Spurred by the capture of Jerusalem, British memory-shaping activists reconfigured the Great War as a modern crusade in pursuit of justice and freedom. In Germany, messianic zeal gave way to renewed feelings of encirclement. This reorientation was triggered by the experience of the Russian invasion and Anglo-French counter-attacks. While notations of national defence (of freedom and/or territorial integrity) proliferated in mainstream German narratives about 'the war' in general, sub-narratives centring on one particular theatre of operation, namely Tannenberg, departed from the overall pattern. The rhetoric of spreading 'culture' and securing 'living-space' in the east belonged to the mental furniture of the radical Right. In this socio-political milieu, war remembrance faded into remobilisation.

Gentlemanly knights and civic values versus iron warriors and military virtues

The industrialised *Materialschlacht* (on the Western Front) revolutionised the connotations of destruction and endurance; the 'storm of steel' put an immense and often intolerable strain on the combatants. Many

Germans, socialised into a 'nation-at-arms', empathised with or, in reactionary circles, eulogised the soldier's ordeal of battle: his iron endurance in the midst of a frenzy of destruction. In fact, the 'eyewitnesses' themselves assumed an active role in shaping the course of commemoration. Tommy's *Kriegserlebnis*, by contrast, met with silence at home (though translations of German war literature sold well in Britain). British discourses, predominantly conducted by civilians, dwelt on the soldiers' conduct in war rather than their experience of war. In Britain, agents of remembrance propagated the ideal of the chivalrous gentleman rather than the iron warrior, and civic values rather than military virtues. Chivalric diction, firmly anchored in pre-war public life, translated the act of killing into a language that was comprehensible to the British, a nation without strong military traditions.

Hope for the hereafter versus trust in the future

The sacred did not vanish, although few sought it in organised religion. The medievalist tradition provided a template of associations, resonances and motifs (both religious and mythological in origin), rich in their signifying powers. The present lacked regenerative potential, but the past retained vitality. Medievalist war remembrance established a spiritual domain linking notions of personal salvation and national regeneration. Yet there remained a tension in medievalist commemorations between a transcendent hope for the hereafter, and an earthly trust in the future. Characteristically, the latter aspect was less accentuated in Britain than in Germany. Tormented by the twin horrors of personal loss and political humiliation, Germans, above all from the nationalist stratum of society, drew hope from visions of medieval greatness regained. The unacknowledged experience of defeat deprived some survivors of a sense of closure; it left a symbolic vacuum that right-wing millennialists attempted to fill. Nevertheless, one should not overestimate the significance of overt displays of 'revanchism': they were spectacular but not prevalent in Weimar Germany.

Such were the national variations of the medievalist theme. On the whole, however, the similarities outweigh the differences. Medievalism as a mode of commemoration linking an idealised past with the impact of industrialised warfare transcended national and cultural boundaries and simplistic distinctions between normal and special nations (the *Sonderweg* orthodoxy), conservative and dynamic interlopers in the war (Modris Eksteins), or victors and losers   (George L. Mosse). The

historiography of the First World War abounds with grand interpretations but distinctly lacks systematic cross-national comparisons. Further
comparative work, however, is necessary to discriminate between European convergences, national peculiarities, and sectional diversities in
cultural notation.

Is it possible that the preoccupation with the distant past (imagined or
real) represented principally an Anglo-German peculiarity? A cursory
inspection of the secondary literature does not support this view.[1] However, I have consciously avoided this kind of ad hoc comparison with
nations such as France and Italy, a method that has an initial heuristic
value but cannot withstand full scrutiny. Instead, by concentrating on
two cases, I have demonstrated the methodological potential of a fully
comparative study based on original research in two countries. In this
book, we have seen that medievalism represented an overarching, albeit
multi-faceted, phenomenon that made the catastrophe of war more
accessible and enduring. Britons and Germans followed very similar
commemorative paths in order to recover their dead, or rather to ascribe
historical meaning to the collective slaughter of 1914–18.

Medievalism after 1945

Ultimately, it was the Second World War which severed the link between
cultural and existential memory. In the aftermath of the second great
post-war transition of the twentieth century, it became infinitely more
difficult to locate the traumatic present within a coherent temporal
order. The very notion of historical meaning appeared problematic after
the horrors of genocidal war, the mass bombing of civilians and the
uprooting of millions of refugees. No significant upsurge of medievalism
in commemorative culture took place after 1945. To be sure, numerous
medievalist memorials dating from the 1920s and 1930s survived the
war intact (many of which were re-dedicated to include the dead of
the Second World War); also new ones sprang up in the 1950s. Nonetheless, the survival or revival of medievalist icons contrasted sharply
with the absence of medievalist diction. This time, agents of remembrance

---

[1] On the significance of Joan of Arc in France, see Krumeich, *Jeanne d'Arc in der Geschichte*.
On the Vercingetorix cult before the Great War, see Tacke, *Denkmal im sozialen Raum*,
and on Rheims Cathedral as a site of memory, see Lambourne, 'Moral Cathedrals'. See
also the images reproduced in Annette Becker, *Les monuments aux morts: Patrimoine
et mémoire de la Grande Guerre* (Paris, Errance, [1989]), esp. pp. 15, 36, 52, 69, and
some examples given in Sherman, *Construction of Memory*, pp. 44, 96–7.

did not consistently pick up the threads of narratives of historical continuity.

Consider the memorial window to 'the few', the airmen of the Battle of Britain who had inflicted the first military defeat on the Third Reich. Installed in Henry VII's chapel in 'that historic building',[2] Westminster Abbey (despite the fact that St Paul's Cathedral had a far stronger association with the events of 1940), the project had the potential to become another medievalist demonstration. The Battle of Britain memorial window takes the place of an ancient window shattered by the bomb which hit the House of Commons. A tiny hole through the stonework just under the new window has been allowed to remain, filled in with plain glass. Crafted in stained glass, the memorial window restates impressively the notion of redemptive sacrifice in a synthesis between Christian and patriotic themes. Dominating the background is the rose-tree badge of Henry VII; carved figures of St George and King Arthur in full armour adorn the altar below the window. Press accounts paid much attention to these design details but did not proffer an interpretation;[3] and although the unveiling programme cited a 1940 speech by Churchill in which the prime minister had compared the pilots to the Knights of the Round Table, this theme was not pursued any further.[4] The evocative design and setting of the memorial contrasted with the taciturnity of its commentators in 1947.

Semiotic contrasts between the iconography and vocabulary of the two periods of post-war commemoration were also much in evidence in West Germany. The medievalist context which had linked objects to words after 1914 evaporated after 1945. At commemorative events, speakers were hesitant and could not even be prompted by what used to be evocative memorial designs like erratic boulders and soldier saints. In an effort to break the awkward silence, it became customary to issue unspecific appeals for peace directed at nobody in particular.[5] In doing so, memorial makers soothed the victors' fear that defeat might once more spur feelings of revenge among Germans. Initially, the Allies had

---

[2] 'Victors of the Air', *The Times*, 50809, 10 July 1947, p. 5.

[3] 'Memorial in Westminster Abbey to the Battle of Britain', *Builder*, 173 (1947), pp. 31–3; 'Battle of Britain Memorial: Dedication Service in Westminster Abbey', *The Times*, 50810, 11 July 1947, p. 7; 'King Unveils Memorial to "the Few": Abbey Service', *Daily Telegraph*, 28720, 11 July 1947, p. 5. See also Adrian Gregory, 'The Commemoration of the Battle of Britain', in Paul Addison and Jeremy A. Crang (eds.), *The Burning Blue: A New History of the Battle of Britain* (London, Pimlico, 2000), pp. 220–1.

[4] WAML, Newspaper Cuttings, vol. 20, pp. 45–6, 'Battle of Britain Memorial Westminster Abbey: Unveiled by His Majesty King George VI on 10th July, 1947', 1947, p. 10.

[5] Meinhold Lurz, *Kriegerdenkmäler in Deutschland*, vol. VI, *Bundesrepublik* (Heidelberg, Esprint, 1987), pp. 143, 172–3, 398.

been determined to eradicate militarism. A directive of the Allied Control Council in May 1946 ordered the demolition of all monuments that glorified military tradition. In practice, the order was not uniformly enforced, at least not in the western zones of occupation.[6]

Ironically, it was the American military administration which choreographed the most significant restatement of the medievalist theme: the interment of Hindenburg's body in the St Elizabeth Church at Marburg in August 1946. With the Red Army hard on their heels, the Wehrmacht had blown up the Tannenberg memorial in January 1945, but not before removing from the vault the coffins of Hindenburg and his wife for safe keeping. An odyssey had begun which finally ended in a church originally built by the Teutonic Order – much to the annoyance of the Social-Democratic interim government of Hesse, which warned the occupation authorities of a potential revival of the Hindenburg myth. Needless to say, the Americans had their way. However, in the course of time, the grave of the last of the Teutonic Knights, surrounded by the heraldic arms of his historic predecessors, sank into obscurity.[7]

The collapse of the Reich in May 1945 marked not a single turning-point, but the beginning of a period of transition in commemorative culture. Medievalism was not yet dead, but certainly fading away. German war cemeteries, above all those in North Africa, proved a last, albeit crumbling, bastion of medievalism in war commemoration after 1945.[8] Significantly, war cemeteries abroad remained under the auspices of the Volksbund Deutsche Kriegsgräberfürsorge. Like so many old elites tainted by Nazism, the leaders of the German war graves association, too, reinvented themselves as pillars of the new republic. Robert Tischler, chief architect since 1926, not only kept his position until his death in 1959 but also continued to design *Totenburgen* during the 1950s. The official rhetoric, however, had changed. Peace, not defiance, was the order of the day, and *Volksbund* representatives were holding out the hand of friendship.[9]

[6] Ibid., pp. 123–7, 231; Thamer, 'Von der Monumentalisierung zur Verdrängung', pp. 127–31.

[7] Ingrid Krüger-Bulcke, 'Der Hohenzollern-Hindenburg-Zwischenfall in Marburg 1947: Wiederaufleben nationalistischer Strömungen oder Sturm im Wasserglas?', *Hessisches Jahrbuch für Landesgeschichte*, 39 (1989), pp. 311–52; Fischer, 'Tannenberg-Denkmal', pp. 46–7.

[8] See, for example, Fritz Debus, 'Vertretertag 1957 in der alten Kaiserstadt Speyer: Gegenwartsaufgaben des Volksbundes werden auf historischem Boden beraten', *Kriegsgräberfürsorge*, 33 (1957), p. 5.

[9] Mosse, *Fallen Soldiers*, pp. 214–16; Lurz, *Kriegerdenkmäler*, vol. VI, pp. 145–61. On Nazi elites in the post-war period generally, see Norbert Frei, *Adenauer's Germany and the Nazi*

The first post-war 'fortress of the dead' was completed at Tobruk, Libya, in November 1955. Dedicated jointly to the war dead and their field marshal, Erwin Rommel, this created ample opportunity to exalt peace and comradeship among former enemies: after all, had the fallen on both sides not been bound together by the code of chivalry? The main speaker, a vice-president of the lower house of parliament, recalled 'how chivalrously the men around Rommel fought in this age of unchivalrous weapons'.[10] Moreover, all participants in the event were anxious to pay their respects to the 'chivalrous opponents', that is former opponents who were now, of course, NATO Allies.[11] The language of chivalry, marginal in Germany during the 1920s and 1930s, came to the fore in the mid-1950s. Compatible with the new rhetoric of peace and reconciliation (with the western Allies), chivalric diction salvaged the Wehrmacht's reputation at a time of West German rearmament and western integration. To be sure, even in the restorative political climate of the Federal Republic, such blatant effort to exonerate the 'fair and chivalrous' German soldier from Hitler's war did not go unchallenged. In a scathing front-page commentary on the unveiling ceremony at Tobruk, the liberal weekly Die Zeit exposed this kind of language to ridicule.[12]

As Richard Bessel and Dirk Schumann have noted, monuments to the Second World War, especially Soviet ones, 'impress us with their enormity (and thus the enormity of what they commemorate), not with their profundity'.[13] The same is true of the post-war Totenburg. Ostensibly, the Volksbund adhered to the monumental scheme dating from the early 1930s for reasons of cost-effective upkeep and maintenance. The massive walls would protect the mass grave of the dead from the harsh

Past: The Politics of Amnesty and Integration (New York, Columbia University Press, 2002).

[10] 'Die Ehrenstätte bei Tobruk eingeweiht: Ehemalige Mitkämpfer und Angehörige der Gefallenen bei der Gedenkfeier', Frankfurter Allgemeine Zeitung, 270, 21 November 1955, p. 1: 'wie ritterlich die Männer um Rommel in diesem Zeitalter unritterlicher Waffen gekämpft haben'. See also Günter Seefried, 'Die Ehrenstätte Tobruk', Kriegsgräberfürsorge, 31 (1955), p. 188.

[11] Herwig Weber, 'Eine Reise der Besinnung: Deutsche besuchen die Gefallenen des Afrikakorps in Tunesien und Libyen', Frankfurter Allgemeine Zeitung, 270, 21 November 1955, p. 8: 'ritterlichen Gegener'. Note that the author is a veteran of the German Afrika Korps. See also [Fritz] Debus, 'Cyrenaika – Marmarika – Tobruk: Pilgerfahrt in eine fremde Welt', Kriegsgräberfürsorge, 32 (1956), p. 12.

[12] 'Tobruk', Die Zeit, 47, 24 November 1955, p. 1.

[13] Richard Bessel and Dirk Schumann, 'Introduction: Violence, Normality, and the Construction of Postwar Europe', in Richard Bessel and Dirk Schumann (eds.), Life after Death: Approaches to a Cultural and Social History of Europe during the 1940s and 1950s (Cambridge, Cambridge University Press, 2003), p. 2.

climate of the desert and acts of vandalism.[14] Such flimsy excuses merely
reveal the semiotic void created by the disappearance of older languages
of remembrance that had emphasised historical continuity. Still, there
was space for ambivalence in the early post-war period. The octagonal
fortress at El Alamein, built between 1956 and 1959 in the Egyptian
desert, invited occasional comparisons with the thirteenth-century
Castel del Monte in Apulia, southern Italy, that 'symbol of great planning, splendid deeds and eventual failure'.[15] Yet, in the long term,
attempts to reconnect the Second World War with the medieval past
were doomed to fall flat because the wider discursive current that had
given medievalism coherence and meaning after 1918 was fast drying up
after 1945.

This post-war transition is most noticeable on the former home front.
The Second World War was a different kind of war. It blurred the
boundaries between home and front and transformed towns and cities
into battlefields. The new totality of warfare meant that there was no
precedent for remembering civilian victims of war on a grand scale in
Germany. Neither was there a will to develop new comprehensive public
forms of commemoration in the immediate post-war period. Hannah
Arendt observed five years after the unconditional surrender that
'Amid the ruins, Germans mail each other picture postcards still showing the cathedrals and market places [. . .] that no longer exist. And the
indifference with which they walk through the rubble has its exact
counterpart in the absence of mourning for the dead.'[16] Germans like
other Europeans turned their back on death and sought 'to rebuild, in
a strangely anaesthetised state, "normal" life'.[17] Notably in West
Germany, socio-economic reconstruction and cultural amnesia, W. G.
Sebald has suggested, were two sides of the same coin. Politically stable

[14] 'Nach Tobruk nun El Alamein: 4200 gefallene deutsche Soldaten werden in sieben
Gruftkammern zur letzten Ruhe gebettet', *Kriegsgräberfürsorge*, 32 (1956), p. 56;
'Tobruk: Letzte Heimat für 6000 deutsche Afrika-Soldaten', *Kriegsgräberfürsorge*, 30
(1954), pp. 172–3.
[15] *Kriegsgräberstätten in Afrika: Aufgabe und Dienst* (Kassel, Volksbund Deutsche Kriegsgräberfürsorge, 1961), p. 8: 'Sinnbild großen Planens, glänzender Taten und
schließlichen Scheiterns'. See also Richard Wagner, 'El Alamein: Bericht einer unver-
geßlichen Reise', *Kriegsgräberfürsorge*, 35 (1959), p. 117.
[16] Hannah Arendt, 'The Aftermath of Nazi Rule: Report from Germany', *Commentary*
[American Jewish Committee], 10,4 (1950), p. 342. See also Gavriel D. Rosenfeld,
Munich and Memory: Architecture, Monuments, and the Legacy of the Third Reich (Berkeley, Los Angeles and London, University of California Press, 2000), ch. 1.
[17] Bessel and Schumann, 'Introduction', p. 3. See also Koshar, *From Monuments to Traces*,
pp. 153–7.

and economically successful, this was, however, a society populated by a new breed of citizen, the a-historical man.[18]

Collective remembrance of war takes place where individuals and groups come together 'because they have to speak out'.[19] After 1945, those Germans who tried to remember amid the ruins were at a loss for 'big words'. What Arendt identified as 'indifference' and 'lack of emotion' might be better described as a kind of speechlessness; the demise of medievalism had left a semiotic vacuum. Yet, while sincere mourning (for *all* the victims) was absent, self-pity prevailed. Ruined buildings of historical significance offered symbolic foci that filled the gap between post-war speechlessness and self-pity. In 1953, the magazine of the Volksbund Deutsche Kriegsgräberfürsorge featured an illuminating article on an unspecified (hence representative) medieval church in a German town destroyed in the war. After a night-time air raid, the battered spire was the only part of St Ägidien left standing the following morning. The parish church which for almost six hundred years had formed a bond between eighteen generations had gone up in smoke. In the aftermath of the bombing, the wrecked church became an informal site of pilgrimage and private remembrance and 'a symbol as it were of the destruction of man and beast, house and work which had swept over Germany in those years'.[20] Although the title of the article suggested that 'St Ägidien guards our heritage', it was manifest that the historical chain had been broken.

War ruins, notably scarred churches in larger cities, became the quintessential incarnation of the *Mahnmal*, a new type of memorial literally meaning 'monument of admonition'.[21] Monuments reduced in part to debris were left standing as tokens of warning against the madness of war that had not only killed innocent civilians but also destroyed the architectural heritage. War was, by implication, an anonymous fate for which no one could be held responsible. The preservation of war ruins enabled Germans to reflect on both personal suffering and cultural impoverishment without recrimination. Paradoxically, battered monuments proved a very convenient legacy of the war, for ruins-turned-memorials allowed the survivors to circumvent a key dilemma of the post-war era: how to

[18] W.G. Sebald, *Luftkrieg und Literatur: Mit einem Essay zu Alfred Andersch* (Munich and Vienna, Carl Hanser, 1999), pp. 13–20.
[19] Winter and Sivan, 'Setting the Framework', p. 9.
[20] Jürgen Bachmann, 'Das Kreuz in der Ruine: St. Ägidien hütet das Erbe', *Kriegsgräberfürsorge*, 29 (1953), p. 87: 'Gleichsam ein Sinnbild der Vernichtung von Mensch und Tier, Haus und Werk, die über Deutschland in diesen Jahren hinweggerast'.
[21] Schneider, '. . . nicht umsonst gefallen?', pp. 258, 305–10.

actively create commemorative forms and to assign some kind of historical meaning to what had happened.

The Kaiser Wilhelm-Gedächtniskirche on the Kurfürstendamm in Berlin illustrates the inherent ambiguity of war ruins. Built in neo-Romanesque style and richly adorned with mosaics, the church's architecture had aroused controversy in Imperial Germany. Thanks to Bomber Command, the medievalist kitsch of the 1890s became an 'unintentional monument' and was raised to the level of high art. In the eyes of the architect Wassili Luckhardt, the scars of the war enhanced the architectural value of the church, and the artist Alexander Calder went so far as to call the ruin one the finest abstract sculptures in the world.[22] This was a memorial of a frozen apocalypse, but it was aesthetically appealing (if not beautiful) all the same. The Berliners, too, grew fond of their ruin, which for them carried multiple meanings ranging from wartime suffering to eventual survival. By 'popular demand' (expressed by a local newspaper), the tower was left standing as a symbol in spite of the reservations of the architect of the new Gedächtniskirche, Egon Eiermann.[23] When the new foundation stone was laid in 1959, the conservative *Frankfurter Allgemeine Zeitung* characterised the tower as a '*Mahnmal* of transitoriness'.[24] The medievalist past had become a foreign country. The ruined neo-Romanesque tower vis-à-vis Eiermann's modernist structure pointed to a historical rupture.

In 1957, at a time when the future of the Gedächtniskirche was still hanging in the balance, a British war ruin captured the public imagination in Berlin. The British pavilion at the International Building Exhibition featured prominently a model of the new Coventry Cathedral that was being built adjacent to the one destroyed in the war: 'In the first minutes after the opening of the exhibition a great number of questions were asked about the Cathedral [. . .] One of the reasons for the attention being given to the model is that the Berliners have a similar problem in the ruined Kaiser Wilhelm Church', a British delegate

---

[22] 'Das Schicksal der Gedächtniskirche', *Tagesspiegel*, 3511, 24 March 1957, p. 6. See Vera Frowein-Ziroff, *Die Kaiser Wilhelm-Gedächtniskirche: Entstehung und Bedeutung* (Berlin, Mann, 1982), pp. 336–40. On the concept of 'unintentional monument', see Alois Riegl, 'The Modern Cult of Monument: Its Character and its Origins', *Oppositions*, 25 (1982), pp. 20–51.

[23] '90 Prozent für den Turm: Erstes Zwischenergebnis', *Tagesspiegel*, 3512, 26 March 1957, p. 10; 'Das Schicksal der Gedächtniskirche', *Tagesspiegel*, 3510, 23 March 1957, p. 7.

[24] Sabina Lietzmann, 'Dibelius legt den Grundstein für die Gedächtniskirche: Drei Neubauten sollen neben der Turmruine entstehen', *Frankfurter Allgemeine Zeitung*, 107, 11 May 1959, p. 5: 'Mahnmal der Vergänglichkeit'.

noted.[25] Unlike Eiermann and the Berlin clergy, Coventry Cathedral and its architects never seriously contemplated demolishing the remains of the Gothic cathedral church, because the ruins 'have been exceedingly impressive and have spoken to tens of thousands with a message that is beyond words'.[26] Yet a wordless token would not suffice. The wartime and post-war Provosts and Bishops of Coventry were determined to fill the semantic void with new meaning.

It was a wrong and 'debilitating sentiment', they argued in 1945, to want to perpetuate a ruin which in future would be 'only a beautiful shell'. What was needed instead was a positive and energising statement, 'a symbol of triumph over evil' that incorporated the ruins of the past.[27] In announcing their intention to rebuild next to the ruins, the cathedral authorities made a forceful intervention in the ongoing discussion about the commemorative and aesthetic possibilities of war-torn churches. A group of public figures (Kenneth Clark, T. S. Eliot and John Maynard Keynes among others) suggested in a letter to *The Times* in August 1944 that the condition of total war rendered traditional war memorials inadequate. 'Could there be a more appropriate memorial to the nation's crisis than the preservation of fragments of its battleground?' they wondered.[28] While the group's historical consciousness was rooted in the idea of violent dislocation, other participants in the debate unabashedly advocated 'garden ruins', invoking the timeless beauty of Tintern Abbey, Fountains Abbey or Raglan Castle.[29] In practice, few bombed churches were redesigned as garden ruins, and neo-romantic assertions of historical continuity abated in the 1950s.

The Blitz had fully disclosed the catastrophic potential of modernity, and yet, in Britain, the legacy of destruction did not bring about a radically disenchanted age. While medievalism became a commemorative mode without purchase, a post-national language of the sacred which acknowledged discontinuity emerged from the ruins of Coventry Cathedral. In the words of Provost H. C. N. Williams, the cathedral matured into 'a laboratory of experiment in Christian renewal' beyond

[25] CAC, R 26, Central Office of Information to Reconstruction Committee, 9 July 1957.
[26] CAC, R 23, The Provost, 'Coventry Cathedral Commission: Memorandum', February 1947.
[27] CAC, R 20, 'New Coventry Cathedral Plan and Scheme: Questions Asked and Answered', [1945].
[28] Marjory Allen of Hurtwood *et al.*, 'Ruined City Churches: Preservation as Memorials', *The Times*, 49935, 15 August 1944, p. 5; *Bombed Churches as War Memorials* (Cheam, Architectural Press, 1945), p. 4.
[29] *Bombed Churches*, pp. 17–19. See also Nicola Lambourne, *War Damage in Western Europe: The Destruction of Historic Monuments during the Second World War* (Edinburgh, Edinburgh University Press, 2001), pp. 180–3.

Figure 60. The new Coventry Cathedral by Basil (later Sir Basil) Spence adjacent to the ruins of the fifteenth century church. Coventry, 1962.

national boundaries.[30] The Cross of Nails, a relic of the ancient church, became a spark of life in the cathedral's international mission of peace and reconciliation. Fashioned in November 1940 from three wrought nails that had held the beams of St Michael's together for almost five hundred years, the cross evolved into the emblem of a worldwide pacifist network of Cross of Nails centres. The original cross was placed in the sanctuary behind the altar of rubble in the ruins. Carved on wall were Christ's words as he was nailed to the Cross: 'FATHER FORGIVE'. A guidebook of 1967 written for young people explains: 'As you stand before the altar, and read these words, you are in the presence of life and hope and healing.'[31]

The new cathedral, consecrated in 1962, should 'grow out of the old Cathedral and be incomplete without it', according to its architect, Basil (later Sir Basil) Spence.[32] Spence's predecessor, by contrast, had originally envisaged a new building that was meant to 'blend with the old mediæval remains'.[33] Sir Giles Gilbert Scott, commissioned during the war to build the new cathedral, submitted a neo-Gothic design which, however, clashed with the bishop's modernist taste. In the event, Scott stepped down. His resignation paved the way for an architectural competition from which Spence emerged as the winner. Faced with scathing attacks on his modernist solution ('looks like a factory'), Spence declared himself a traditionalist. If there had been no modern movement throughout the ages, he reasoned, architects would still be building in Norman style; there would have been no chapel at King's College, Cambridge, and no cathedrals at Ely, Gloucester or Peterborough.[34] The contrast between Spence's modernist architecture and his traditionalist commentary is most striking in the case of the Chapel of Unity. Set up jointly by the Church of England and the Free Churches, 'The Chapel's shape represents Christian Unity; in elevation it is shaped like a Crusader's tent, as Christian Unity is a modern Crusade, and an attempt has been made to use dynamic crystalline forms which are contemporary, yet have their roots deep in the past.'[35]

---

[30] H[arold] C. N. Williams, *A Guide to Coventry Cathedral* (Derby, English Life, 1979), p. 16.

[31] A[lfred] H. Dammers, *Guide to Coventry Cathedral for Young People* (London, Pitkin Pictorals, [1967]), p. 4.

[32] CAC, R 21, 'Report by Assessors to the Coventry Cathedral Reconstruction Committee', 14 August 1951.

[33] 'The New Coventry Cathedral: Sir Giles Scott Resigns', *Builder*, 172 (1947), p. 73.

[34] 'Coventry Cathedral', *Builder*, 181 (1951), p. 659; 'Progress at Coventry', *Builder*, 184 (1953), p. 331.

[35] CAC, R 23, Competitor No. 91 [Basil Spence], 'Report: Coventry Cathedral Competition', [1951]; 'The Winner's Report', *Builder*, 181 (1951), p. 239. For a critique of the

At Coventry, the word 'crusade' was reinvented to mean overcoming the consequences of military conflict and Christian disunity, and there was a strong desire to make this crusade as international as possible. In effect, post-1945 Coventry saw the reconfiguration (or rather demobilisation) of medievalism in war remembrance. Stripped of patriotic and military connotations, medievalist icons and rhetoric were put in the service of Christian pacifism and reconciliation. Benjamin Britten's *War Requiem*, composed for the opening of the new cathedral, is a case in point. In juxtaposing the ancient liturgical text of the Latin requiem mass with the Great War poetry of Wilfred Owen, Britten suggested a communion between the victims of the Coventry Blitz, the contemporaries of Owen and the dead across the ages remembered in the timeless formula of the requiem mass. The *War Requiem* rested on the composer's faith in human nature and offered hope to those willing to remember and forgive. Britten, a former conscientious objector, produced a masterwork with overt pacifist meaning. Here 'the meaning as well as the meaninglessness of the Great War', one musicologist writes, 'had found a new and resonant echo'.[36]

From the ruins of Coventry emerged a new mode of war commemoration, a mode which focused on the future rather than the past, a mode which invested the act of remembrance (that is reconciliation) rather than death on the battlefield with meaning. A local narrative with international appeal, it represented the antipodes of the semiotic voids created by the disappearance or fragmentation of medievalism in postwar Europe. The message of Christian pacifism and international reconciliation left no room for ambiguities or self-pity. The cathedral's agents of memory (above all, the clergy, the architect and artists) reconfigured the inter-war grammar of remembrance without blurring over the historical rupture of 1940–5. By contrast, inter-war medievalism had historicised the war dead, justified military action, glamorised acts of violence and ennobled soldiers' sacrifices. The romanticism intrinsic to languages of remembrance after the First World War appeared inappropriate after the Second World War. In 1945, the medievalist repository of images of noble warfare lay in ruins – alongside the rubble of Europe's bombed cities.

crusading diction, see R. Furneaux Jordan, 'Cathedral Church of St. Michael, Coventry', *Architectural Review*, 132 (1962), p. 33. On the architectural history of the cathedral, see Louise Campbell, *Coventry Cathedral: Art and Architecture in Post-War Britain* (Oxford, Clarendon, 1996).
[36] Watkins, *Proof through the Night*, p. 429. See also Eric Cross, 'Death in War: Britten and the *War Requiem*', in Jon Davies (ed.), *Ritual and Remembrance: Responses to Death in Human Societies* (Sheffield, Sheffield Academic Press, 1994), pp. 124–51.

Bibliography

ARCHIVAL SOURCES

BRITAIN

National archives and special collections
Public Record Office, The National Archives, Kew
> Cabinet Papers 27/99, Report, Proceedings and Memoranda of Cabinet Committee on Memorial Service (November 11th), 1920.

British Library, London
> India Office Records, Curzon Collection, MSS Eur F 112/318, Correspondence and Papers of the Cabinet Committee to Make Arrangements for the Unveiling of the Cenotaph and the Burial of the Unknown Warrior, 1920

Imperial War Museum, London
> Department of Art
> > Postcard Collection
> > Poster Collection
> Department of Printed Books
> > Ephemera Collection Memorials
> Photograph Archive
> > War Memorials Series
> National Inventory of War Memorials

Commonwealth War Graves Commission, Records Section, Maidenhead
> Add 8/1/4, Jerusalem Memorial and Ramleh War Cemetery, 1927
> F 604, Allenby Memorial: Jerusalem, 1922–8
> SDC 21, Cross and Stone, 1919–20
> SDC 30, Proposal for a Cruciform Headstone, 1919
> SDC 61, Transactions of Sir F. Kenyon, 1918–26
> WG 18, Adornment of Cemeteries, 1917–9
> WG 358, War Crosses: General File, 1921–9
> WG 1759, Memorial Chapel Notre Dame de Lorette, 1928–37

Regional archives

County Record Office, Cambridge
>P 38, St Peter and St Paul Parish Records, Chatteris
>P 150, St Mary's Parish Records, Swaffham Prior
>P 174, Great Wilbraham Parish Records

Essex Record Office, Colchester
>Acc. C 3, Borough Newspaper Cuttings
>Acc. C 4, Minutes of Colchester Borough War Memorial Committees and Sub-Committees, 1919–25

Cathedral Archives, Coventry
>R 20, Reconstruction, 1945–62
>R 21, Reconstruction Committee, 1945–58
>R 23, Reconstruction: Competition, 1947–62
>R 26, Reconstruction, 1946–64

Herefordshire Record Office, Hereford
>BH 45/20, Hereford County and City War Memorial, 1922

Suffolk Record Office, Ipswich
>FB 74, Higham St Mary Parish Records
>FB 132, Redgrave with Boesdale Parish Records
>FB 136, Burgate Parish Records

West Yorkshire Archive Service, Leeds
>LC/TC/R 17–8, R 26, and R 38, Leeds War Memorial, 1918–37

Norfolk Record Office, Norwich
>Dean and Chapter Records Norwich 106, The Cathedral: War Memorial Chapel, 1915–32

Local and institutional archives

Bedford Central Library
>Local Studies Collection, Pamphlets

Cambridge University Library
>Ely Dean and Chapter Archives 2/1/10, Order Book, 1915–32
>Ely Diocesan Records, D 3/4c and D 3/5, Faculties, 1917–27

King's College Modern Archives Centre, Cambridge
>College Papers
>Eric Milner-White Papers

Stewartry Museum, Dumfries and Galloway Museums Service, Kirkcudbright
>Acc. 7216, Newspaper Cuttings, 3 vols.

Leeds Central Library
>Local Studies Library, LQ 940.465 L 517, Leeds War Memorial: Press Cuttings, 1918–22

Guildhall Library, London
    Ms 24.468, Correspondence of Canon Sidney Arthur Alexander,
    1909–48

St Paul's Cathedral Library, London
    Orders of Service

Westminster Abbey Muniment Room and Library, London
    58667–61889, Unknown Warrior: Correspondence, 1920–56
    Newspaper Cuttings, vol. 1, Unknown Warrior, 1920–97
    Newspaper Cuttings, vol. 1a, Field of Remembrance, 1928–89
    Newspaper Cuttings, vol. 2, Warriors' Chapel, 1926–36
    Newspaper Cuttings, vol. 20, L. E. Tanner Collection, 1945–9
    Newspaper Cuttings, vol. 21, T. V. Pearce Collection, 1941–8

Christ Church Archive, Oxford
    GB xv.c.3, Governing Body Papers: Great War Memorial, 1919–27

Keble College Archives, Oxford
    Building Plans/OFF/S/01-03, Drawings of a War Memorial Cross by
    John Ninian Comper, 1919

St Helens Local History and Archives Library
    C/LH/1.6, Lowe House Memorial Chapel, 1918–23

Eton College Archives, Windsor
    COLL/P6/12, Visible Memorial: Correspondence and Papers,
    1917–23
    COLL/P6/17, St George Tapestry in Lower Chapel: Correspondence
    and Papers, 1921–3
    ED 53/2, Memorial Tower: Thomas Carter's Scrapbook, [c. 1918]

York Minster Library and Archives
    Pamphlets

GERMANY

National archives and special collections
Bundesarchiv, Berlin
    R 32 [Reichskunstwart]
        R 32/14–17, Friedhofskunst, Denkmalpflege und Heimatschutz,
        1920–30
        R 32/221, Gestaltung staatlicher Feiern und Gedenktage, 1922–4
        R 32/281, Gestaltung von Gedenktagen, Festen und Feierlichkeiten,
        1930–1
        R 32/347–350, Kriegerehrungen: Sammlung von Material für das
        geplante Sammelwerk, 1925–33
        R 32/353–462, Planung eines Reichsehrenmals, 1924–33
        R 32/372, Kriegerehrungen, vor allem Zusammenarbeit mit
        Verbänden sowie Vorbereitungen zur Herstellung eines
        Sammelwerkes, 1925–33

R 32/373–373b, Kriegerehrungen: Sammlung von Material für eine Ausstellung, 1925–33
R 32/377, Denkmalpflege sowie Heimat- und Naturschutz, 1930–2

R 36 [Deutscher Gemeindetag]
R 36/1216, Deutsche Kriegergräberfürsorge Berlin, 1926–36
R 36/1218, Ehrung der Gefallenen, Ehrenmale, Denkmäler, Wohlfahrtsanlagen, 1924–41
R 36/1219, Nationaldenkmal für die Gefallenen im Kriege, 1925–32
R 36/2099, Ehrenfriedhöfe für Krieger, Luftschutzdienstpflichtige, Opfer des Luftterrors, 1919–40

R 43 [Reichskanzlei]
R 43 I/710–712, Friedhöfe, Denkmäler und Gedenkfeiern für die im Kriege Gefallenen, 1919–32
R 43 I/713–716, Reichsehrenmal für die im Weltkriege Gefallenen, 1924–32
R 43 I/834, Denkmäler und Denkmalschutz, 1926–32

R 72 [Stahlhelm, Bund der Frontsoldaten]
R 72/1165, Pläne zur Errichtung eines Reichsehrenmals, 1925–33

R 80 [Zentralnachweiseamt für Kriegsverluste und Kriegergräber]
R 80/12–15, Bilder von Kriegerdenkmälern und Kriegergräbern mit Berichten, [c. 1928].

R 601 [Präsidialkanzlei/Büro des Reichspräsidenten]
R 601/1100–1103, Hindenburg-Spende: Allgemeines, 1927–36

R 1501 [Reichsministerium des Innern]
R 1501/108997, Gründung eines auf die Geschichte des Weltkrieges bezüglichen Museums und eines Kriegswirtschaftsmuseums, 1918–20
R 1501/113066, Ehrungen für Krieger, 1915–19

R 1601 [Reichsministerium für die besetzten Gebiete]
R 1601/1603, Bestrebungen auf Absonderung vom Reich, 1927–30

R 8034 II [Reichslandbund-Pressearchiv]
R 8034 II/7690–7692, Gefallenen-Ehrungen, 1915–33

Geheimes Staatsarchiv Preußischer Kulturbesitz, Berlin
I. HA Rep. 76 [Kultusministerium]
Va Sekt. 2 Tit. X Nr. 27 Bd. 6 (M), Universitätsgarten und Bepflanzung vor dem Bibliotheks-Gebäude zu Berlin, 1918–30

I. HA Rep. 77 [Ministerium des Innern]
Tit. 151 Nr. 15 Bd. 19 (M), Die Denkmäler in den preußischen Staaten, 1926–31

Tit. 151 Nr. 15 Fasz. 48 (M), Sühnekapelle Schlachtfeld
Tannenberg: Ankauf Gut Grünfelde, 1908–9
Tit. 1215 Nr. 3c Bd. 1–2 mit 2 Beiheften (M), Errichtung eines
Reichsehrenmals für die im Weltkriege Gefallenen, 1924–33
Tit. 1215 Nr. 3d Bd. 1–2 mit Beiakten (M), Ehrung unserer im
Weltkriege 1914/18 gefallenen Krieger, 1915–25

I. HA Rep. 89 [Geheimes Zivilkabinett]
Nr. 20862 (M), Errichtung von Denkmälern auf Schlachtfeldern,
1914–18
Nr. 20866 (M), Errichtung von Denkmälern für Gefallene,
1908–17
Nr. 20868 (M), Ruhmes- und Gedenkhallen zur Erinnerung an
den Krieg 1914 (außer Berlin), 1918

I. HA Rep. 90 [Staatsministerium]
Nr. 2548, Anlagenheft zum Antrag Goslars betr. Reichsehrenmal,
1925

I. HA Rep. 191 [Ministerium für Volkswohlfahrt]
Nr. 4368 (M), Ehrenmal für die im Weltkriege Gefallenen, 1924–6

Warburg-Haus, Forschungsstelle Politische Ikonographie, Hamburg
Bildindex zur politischen Ikonographie
Postkartensammlung

Bibliothek für Zeitgeschichte, Stuttgart
Dokumentesammlung 1914–1918
Feldpostsammlung Schüling
Fotografiensammlung
Plakatsammlung Erster Weltkrieg
Postkarten-Alben
Postkartensammlung
Postkartensammlung Knoch/Glogge/Wall

Regional archives
Staatsarchiv Aurich
Dep. 60/213, Errichtung eines Kreis-Kriegerdenkmals auf dem alten
Friedhof, 1918–26
Dep. 60, Acc. 1993/13, Kriegerdenkmal Memorial in Ludgeri-Kirche
Norden, 2 vols. [*c*. 1931–71]
Rep. 36/867, Errichtung eines Kriegerdenkmals auf dem alten Friedhof
in Norden, 1920–2

Landesarchiv Berlin
Gesch 921, Weihe des Ehrenmals für die gefallenen Kameraden der
Deutschen Eisenbahntruppen in Berlin Schöneberg, 1929

Staatsarchiv Bremen

3–B. 13. Nr. 92, Errichtung eines Ehrenmals für die im Kriege gefallenen Angehörigen des Infanterie-Regiments Bremen (1. Hans.) No. 75 in der Liebfrauenkirche, 1918–35

3–B. 13. Nr. 126, Gefallenenehrenmal auf der Altmannshöhe, 1915–57

3–M. 2. h. 2. Nr. 29 (59), Aufstellung eines hölzernen Roland-Standbilde, 1915–18

4,14/1–Kr. A. 20. b, Wohlfahrtspflege während des Krieges. Rotes Kreuz, 1914–24

7,60/2–9. b. 1, Eiserner Roland, 1915–20

10–B–Al–875, Eiserner Roland, 1915

10–B–1916-03, Eiserner Roland, 1915

13–G. 7. Nr. 140 (16), Aufbewahrung Gedenkbuch zu Ehren der gefallenen Angehörigen des früheren Infanterie-Regiments Bremen im Gobelinzimmer des Rathauses, 1925–6

Ab–53a, Gedenkbuch Inf. Rgt. Bremen (I. Hanseat.) No. 75, 2 vols., 1925

Ab–56, Infanterie-Regiments Bremen (1. Hanseat.) Nr. 75: Ehrenmal- und Fahnenweihe, 1924

Ag–9993–11, Ehrentafeln Gemeinde Unser Lieben Frauen in der Gedächtniskapelle, 1924

Staatsarchiv Münster

OP [Oberpräsidium]

    5510, Errichtung eines Reichsdenkmals für die Gefallenen des 1. Weltkriegs, 1924–33

    5540, Errichtung eines Bismarckdenkmals auf der Elisenhöhe bei Bingerbrück, 1908–16 and 1927–8

    5556, Kriegsgräberehrungen, 1920–36

    5603, Errichtung von Denkmälern, 1913–36

Staatsarchiv Munich

Pol.-Dir. [Polizeidirektion München]

    5568, Kösener Senioren Convent, 1924–35

    6889, Reichsbanner Schwarz-Rot-Gold: Politische Bewegung, 1924–32

Landbauamt, Photodokumentation 29, Kriegerdenkmal vor dem Armeemuseum, Hofgarten in München, [c. 1924]

Hauptstaatsarchiv Stuttgart

M 400/2, Heeresarchiv Stuttgart: Abteilung Zentralnachweiseamt, 1905–37

M 660/38, Militärischer Nachlaß Franz Ludwig von Soden, 1873–1945

M 746, Denkmäler und Ehrentafeln für die Gefallenen des Ersten Weltkrieges, 1923–31

M 746a, Württembergische Ehrentafeln, [c. 1918–39]

Local and institutional archives
Technische Universität Berlin, Hochschularchiv
Nachlaß Hermann Hosaeus

Stadtarchiv Dortmund
3–1352, Gedenkzeichen und Pflege der Erinnerung an den 1.
Weltkrieg, 1917–18
3–2026, Schaffung eines Heldenhains für die Gefallenen in Dortmund,
1916–17
3–2031, Ehrungen für den Generalfeldmarschall von Hindenburg,
1917–22
3–2036, Drucke zu Gefallenenehrungen, Sammlungen und Feiern
während des 1. Weltkrieges, 1915–16
3–2150, Unterstützung beim Aufbau eines Deutschen
Kriegswirtschaftsmuseums in Leipzig, 1918–19
3–3085, Schmuckplatz am Westfalendamm mit Weddigenlinde,
1915–16
3–3086, Projekt zur Errichtung einer Reinoldus-Säule auf dem
Marktplatz: Zeichnungen von dem Bildhauer Friedrich Bagdons
entworfenen Säule, 1913–26
11–740, Errichtung eines Kaiser-Wilhelm-Denkmals in der Provinz
Westfalen, 1889–1902
161–7, Errichtung eines Ehrenmals für die Gefallenen in
Bövinghausen, 1928–34
204/02–120, Kriegswahrzeichen 'Kohle und Schwert', 1917
501, Zeitungsausschnittssammlung
502, Postkarten- und Photosammlung
Ep 39, Kriegsausstellung Dortmund 1917 im Fredenbaum, 1917

Stadtarchiv Düsseldorf
III 1509, Wettbewerb zu einem Gedenkblatt für gefallene Krieger,
1914–15
XII 1374, Kriegschronik der Gemeinde Benrath, 1918
XVI 1669, Kriegerfriedhöfe, Gedenkblatt für Kaiserswerth, 1914–17
XVI 1670, Kaiserswerther Kriegerdenkmal und Ehrenfriedhof,
1920–6
XX 118–122, Ausschuß für Errichtung eines
Kriegergedächtniszeichens in Benrath, 1925–9
XXIV 996, Denkmäler, 1927–8
XXIV 1178–1179, Denkmäler, 1901–36 and 1932–7
XXIV 1691, Denkmäler, 1918–39

Stadtarchiv Essen
Rep. 102, Abt. I, Nr. 1012, Der Schmied von Essen: Abbildungen der
Bildertafeln, n.d.
Rep. 103, Abt. E I, Nr. 22, Protokollbuch über die Sitzungen des
Vaterländischen Bürgerausschusses Schmied von Essen, 1915–18
Bildsammlung D3/6–10, photos and postcards, 1915

Stadtarchiv Hagen
809/0, Denkmale: Der Eiserne Schmied, 1915–19
809/1, Denkmale: Der Eiserne Schmied, 1915–83
4102, Sammlung 'Eiserner Schmied' für bedürftige Familien von Kriegsteilnehmern, 1920–3
6605, Eiserner Schmied: Kriegswahrzeichen der Stadt Hagen, 1915
6328, Aufstellung von Denkmälern, 1900–15

Stadtarchiv Leer
1631, Errichtung eines Ehrenmals für die Gefallenen, 1919–42

Stadtarchiv Munich
BuR [Bürgermeister und Rat]
   551, Kriegerdenkmal vor dem Armeemuseum für die Gefallenen von 1914/18, 1920–39
   1424/2, Bürgermeister Hans Küfner: Reden, Presseerklärungen, Glückwünsche, Schriftwechsel, 1917–34
ZA Denkmäler, Kriegerdenkmäler und Bismarckdenkmal, 1920–82

Stadtarchiv Stuttgart
Postkartensammlung

Stadtarchiv Ulm
E 603, Ausschuß für das Münsterdenkmal, 1922–34
G 6/X 17.3, Albrecht Rieber, Die Kriegerdenkmäler in der Stadt Ulm, 1947

PUBLISHED PRIMARY SOURCES

NEWSPAPERS AND JOURNALS

Anhalter Anzeiger
Architectural Review
Bauwelt
Bayerischer Heimatschutz
Bedfordshire Times and Independent
Berliner Illustrierte Zeitung
Berliner Lokal-Anzeiger
Berliner Tageblatt
Bremer Nachrichten
British Legion Journal
Builder
Cavalry Journal
Cambridge Chronicle and University Journal
Cambridge Independent Press
Cambridgeshire Times and March Gazette
Daily Chronicle
Daily Express
Daily Herald

Daily Sketch
Daily Telegraph
Der 39er: Nachrichtenblatt des Verbandes ehem. 39er von Rheinland und Westfalen
Deutsche Bauzeitung
Dortmunder Zeitung
Draconian [Dragon School, Oxford]
East Anglian Daily Times
Eastern Daily Press
Essener Volks-Zeitung
Essex County Telegraph
Eton College Chronicle
Frankfurter Allgemeine Zeitung
General-Anzeiger für Dortmund und die Provinz Westfalen
Göppinger Zeitung
Herts and Cambs Reporter and Royston Crow
Guardian
Halberstädter Zeitung und Intelligenzblatt
Hannoverscher Kurier
Insurance Gem
Journal of Mental Science
Kriegsgräberfürsorge
Leeds Mercury and *Leeds and Yorkshire Mercury*
Leerer Anzeigeblatt
Leys Fortnightly [Leys School, Cambridge]
Life and Letters
Manchester Guardian
Münchner Neueste Nachrichten
Münstersche Zeitung
Neue Preußische Zeitung [*Kreuz-Zeitung*]
New York Times
Niedersachsen
Norfolk Chronicle
Northampton Independent
Nottingham Guardian
Ostfriesischer Kurier
Ostfreesland
Ousel [Bedford School]
Oxford Magazine
Paisley and Renfrewshire Gazette
Pall Mall Gazette
Pembrokeshire Telegraph
Das Plakat
Punch
Rheinisch-Westfälischer Anzeiger
Schwäbische Tagwacht
Scotsman
Stuttgarter Neues Tagblatt

Suffolk Chronicle and Mercury
Tablet
Tagesspiegel
Teutoburger Wald und Weserbergland
The Times
The Times Educational Supplement
Tremonia
Victorian [Victoria College, Jersey]
Vorwärts
Volksbote: Wochenblatt für Ostfriesland und Papenburg
Volks-Zeitung
Vossische Zeitung
Westfälisches Tageblatt
Wykehamist [Winchester College]
Yorkshire Post
Zeiten und Völker

Books and articles

Adcock, A. St John, *For Remembrance: Soldier Poets Who Have Fallen in the War* (London, New York and Toronto, Hodder and Stoughton, 1918).

Alckens, August, *Die Denkmäler und Denksteine der Stadt München*, ed. Kulturamt der Stadt München (Munich, Georg D. W. Callwey, 1936).

Dem Andenken ihrer im Weltkriege Gefallenen: Gewidment zum 1. März 1925 von der Georg-August-Universität Göttingen (Munich, C. Wolf, 1925).

Arkwright, John S., *The Supreme Sacrifice and Other Poems in Time of War* (London, Skeffington, 2nd edn 1919).

Beeching, H[enry] C., *Armageddon: A Sermon Upon the War Preached in Norwich Cathedral* (London and Brighton, SPCK, 1914).

Begbie, Harold, *On the Side of the Angels: A Reply to Arthur Machen* (London, New York and Toronto, Hodder and Stoughton, 3rd edn 1915).

Bethge, Ernst Heinrich (ed.), *Der heilige Krieg: Kriegsabende und Gedächtnisfeiern*, vol. I, *Kriegruf – Schwertweihe – Ausmarsch* (Leipzig, Arwed Strauch, [1915]).

Beumelburg, Werner, *Ypern 1914* (Oldenburg and Berlin, Gerhard Stalling, 2nd edn 1926).

Bombed Churches as War Memorials (Cheam, Architectural Press, 1945).

Bourchier, B[asil] G., *'For All We Have and Are': Being Ten Addresses during the Year 1915* (London, Skeffington, [1915]).

Briscoe, Walter A. and H. Russell Stannard, *Captain Ball V.C.: The Career of Flight-Commander Ball, V.C., D.S.O.* (London, Herbert Jenkins, 1918).

Buchheit, Gert, *Das Reichsehrenmal Tannenberg: Seine Entstehung, seine endgültige Gestaltung und seine Einzelkunstwerke* (Munich, Knorr & Hirth, 1936).

Buchwald, R[einhard] [ed.], *Der Heilige Krieg: Gedichte aus dem Beginn des Kampfes* (Jena, Eugen Diederichs, 1914).

Burns, J[ames], *Order of Memorial Service for those Fallen in the War* (London, James Clarke, [1917]).

Chesterton, G[ilbert] K., *Autobiography* (London, Hutchinson, 1936).

Cooper Willis, Irene, *England's Holy War: A Study of English Liberal Idealism during the Great War* (New York, Alfred A. Knopf, 1928).

Dammers, A[lfred] H., *Guide to Coventry Cathedral for Young People* (London, Pitkin Pictorals, [1967]).

Darracott, Joseph (ed.), *The First World War in Posters: From the Imperial War Museum, London* (New York, Dover, 1974).

Deas, F. W., *The Scottish National War Memorial: Official Guide* (Edinburgh, David Macdonald, [1928]).

The Decoration by General Pershing of the Grave of the Unknown British Warrior in Westminster Abbey and the Award of the Victoria Cross to the American Unknown: London October 17, 1921 (New York, Bankers Trust, 1921).

Delvos, Hubert, *Geschichte der Düsseldorfer Denkmäler, Gedenktafeln und Brunnen* (Düsseldorf, L. Schwann, 1938).

Deutscher Bund Heimatschutz (ed.), *Kriegergräber und Denkmäler: Unsere Wünsche und Pflichten* (Munich, Georg D. W. Callwey, [1918]).

Deutscher Ehrenhain für die Helden von 1914/18, intro. Ernst Bergmann (Leipzig, Dehain, 1931).

Deutsches Historisches Museum (ed.), *Plakate des Ersten Weltkrieges 1914–1918*, CD-ROM (Munich, K. G. Saur, 1996).

Der Eiserne Schmied von Hagen: Das Erste Jahr seiner Geschichte (Hagen, Verlag des Eisernen Schmiedes, 1916).

Festschrift zur Einweihung des Tannenberg-Denkmals am 18. September 1927 (Königsberg, Gräfe und Unzer, [1927]).

Fischer, Paul, *Bei Tannenberg 1914 und 1410: Die Schlacht bei Tannenberg-Grünfelde am 15. Juli 1410 und die Schlachten bei Gilgenburg-Hohenstein-Ortelsburg (Schlacht bei Tannenberg) 27., 28., 29. August 1914* (Lissa, Oskar Eulitz, 1915).

Fitzke, Benno and Paul Matzdorf, *Eiserne Kreuz-Nagelungen zum Besten der Kriegshilfe und zur Schaffung von Kriegswahrzeichen: Gebrauchsfertiges Material für vaterländische Volksunterhaltung durch Feiern in Schulen, Jugend-vereinigungen und Vereinen* (Leipzig, Arwed Strauch, 1916).

Galli, Gottfried, *Dschihad: Der Heilige Krieg des Islams und seine Bedeutung im Weltkrieg unter besonderer Berücksichtigung der Interessen Deutschlands: Vortrag gehalten in Freiburg i.B. und Cassel* (Freiburg, Br., C. Troemer, 1915).

Gedenkschrift zur Weihe des Krieger-Ehrenmals für die Gefallenen der Stadt Adorf: 20. September 1925 (Adorf, August Geilsdorf, 1925).

Gibbons, Floyd, *The Red Knight of Germany: Baron von Richthofen* (London, Cassell, 1930).

Gilbert, Vivian, *The Romance of the Last Crusade: With Allenby to Jerusalem* (New York, William B. Feakins, 1923).

Gildea, James, *For Remembrance and in Honour of Those Who Lost Their Lives in the South African War 1899–1902* (London, Eyre and Spottiswoode, 1911).

Gill, Eric, *Autobiography* (London, Jonathan Cape, 1940).

Giraudoux, Jean, *My Friend from Limousin* (New York and London, Harper, 1923).

Goldsmith, Margaret and Frederick Voigt, *Hindenburg: The Man and the Legend* (London, Faber & Faber, [1930]).

Grant, Reginald, *S.O.S. Stand To!* (New York and London, D. Appleton, 1918).

Graves, Robert, *Good-Bye to All That: An Autobiography* (London, Jonathan Cape, 1929).

Grosse, Walther, 'Tannenberg 1914', in Kuratorium für das Reichsehrenmal Tannenberg (ed.), *Tannenberg: Deutsches Schicksal – Deutsche Aufgabe* (Oldenburg and Berlin, Gerhard Stalling, [1939]), pp. 11–163.

Gstettner, Hans, *Deutsche Soldatenmale: Erbaut vom Volksbund Deutsche Kriegsgräberfürsorge e.V.* (Berlin, Volksbund Deutsche Kriegsgräberfürsorge, [1940]).

Haken, W., *Die Rabenklippen bei Höxter a/Weser und das Reichsehrenmal* (Paderborn, Junfermann, 1931).

Harcourt Smith, Cecil [ed.], *Inscriptions Suggested For War Memorials* (London, HMSO, 1919).

Hay, Ian, *Their Name Liveth: The Book of the Scottish National War Memorial* (London, Bodley Head, 1931).

Hayter Chubb, George, *The Memorial Chapel of the Leys School Cambridge: Its Structure, Windows, Carvings and Memorials* (London, Herbert Jenkins, 1925).

Herre, Paul, *Deutsche Walhall: Eine Auseinandersetzung und ein Programm zu einem Ehrenmal des Deutschen Volkes* (Potsdam, Athenaion, [1930]).

Heubes, Max (ed.), *Ehrenbuch der Feldeisenbahner* (Berlin, Wilhelm Kolk, 1931).

Hilpert, Fritz, *Das Reichsehrenmal und die Frontkämpfer: Nach authentischem Material der Frontkämpferverbände Reichskriegerbund Kyffhäuser, Reichsbanner, Stahlhelm und Reichsbund jüdischer Frontsoldaten* (Berlin, Deutsche Verlagsgesellschaft für Politik und Geschichte, 1927).

Hindenburg, [Paul] von, *Out of My Life* (London, Cassell, 1920).

Hundert Entwürfe aus dem Wettbewerb für das Bismarck-National-Denkmal auf der Elisenhöhe bei Bingerbrück-Bingen (Düsseldorf, Düsseldorfer Verlags-Anstalt, 1911).

Hunt, Edgar A. (ed.), *The Colchester Memorial Souvenir* (Colchester, Essex Telegraph, 1923).

Hurst, Sidney C., *The Silent Cities: An Illustrated Guide to the War Cemeteries and Memorials to the 'Missing' in France and Flanders: 1914–1918* (London, Methuen, 1929).

Institut für Zeitungsforschung, *Plakatsammlung des Instituts für Zeitungsforschung der Stadt Dortmund*, ed. Barbara Posthoff, microfiches (Munich, K. G. Saur, 1992).

Jessen, Peter *et al.*, *Kriegergräber im Felde und daheim*, ed. im Einvernehmen mit der Heeresverwaltung (Munich, F. Bruckmann, 1917).

Jones, David, *In Parenthesis: Seinnyessit e gledyf ym penn mameu* (London, Faber & Faber, [1937]).

Jünger, Ernst, *The Storm of Steel: From the Diary of a German Storm-Troop Officer on the Western Front*, intro. R[alph] H. Mottram (London, Chatto & Windus, 1929).

In Stahlgewittern: Ein Kriegstagebuch (Berlin, E. S. Mittler, 20th edn 1940).

Kaiser, Albrecht, *Das Denkmal der Gefallenen Lehrer und Schüler des Klosters Unserer Lieben Frauen zu Magdeburg* (Magdeburg, Haenel, 1920).

Kahns, Hans, *Das Reichsehrenmal Tannenberg* (Königsberg, Gräfe und Unzer, [1937]).

Kenyon, Frederic, *War Graves: How the Cemeteries Abroad will be Designed* (London, HMSO, 1918).

Kernot, C[harles] F., *British Public Schools War Memorials* (London, Roberts & Newton, 1927).

The King's Pilgrimage (London, Hodder and Stoughton, 1922).

K. K. Gewerbeförderungs-Amt (ed.), *Soldatengräber und Kriegsdenkmale* (Vienna, Anton Schroll, 1915).

Klemperer, Victor, *Leben sammeln, nicht fragen wozu und warum: Tagebücher 1918–1932*, ed. Walter Nowojski, 2 vols. (Berlin, Aufbau, 1996).

Koenigswald, Harald von, *Das verwandelte Antlitz* (Berlin, Kommodore, 1938).

Kohler, Josef, *Der heilige Krieg: Rede am 19. Februar 1915* (Berlin, Carl Heymann, 1915).

Kreß von Kreßenstein, [Otto], 'Eine Schlacht im Heiligen Lande', in [Ernst] von Eisenhart Rothe (ed.), *Ehrendenkmal der deutschen Armee und Marine* (Berlin and Munich, Deutscher National-Verlag, 4th edn [1928]), pp. 522–33.

Kriegerdenkmal und Soldatengräber: Ratschläge der Badischen Beratungsstelle für Kriegerehrungen (Karlsruhe, Braun, 1916).

Die Krieger-Gedächtniskapelle (Tresekammer) in Unser Lieben Frauen-Kirche zu Bremen (Bremen, G. A. Dörrbecker, n.d).

Kriegsgräberfürsorge 1915–1930 (Berlin, Volksbund Deutsche Kriegsgräberfürsorge, 3rd edn 1930).

Kriegsgräberstätten in Afrika: Aufgabe und Dienst (Kassel, Volksbund Deutsche Kriegsgräberfürsorge, 1961).

Kriegergrabmal und Kriegerdenkmal: Führer durch die 20. Ausstellung des Freien Bundes: Städt. Kunsthalle Mannheim 2. Januar–6. Februar 1916 (Mannheim, Haas, 1916).

'Kriegsnagelungen', in *Illustrierte Geschichte des Weltkrieges 1914/16*, vol. IV (Stuttgart, Union Deutsche Verlagsgesellschaft, [1916]), pp. 334–6.

Kriegs-Wahrzeichen zum Benageln: 69 Entwürfe aus dem Preiswettbewerb des Deutschen Werkbundes (Munich, F. Bruckmann, 1915).

Krüger, Walter and Johannes Krüger, 'Bauliche Gedanken um das Reichsehrenmal Tannenberg und seine Einfügung in die Landschaft', in Kuratorium für das Reichsehrenmal Tannenberg (ed.), *Tannenberg: Deutsches Schicksal – Deutsche Aufgabe* (Oldenburg and Berlin, Gerhard Stalling, [1939]), pp. 225–44.

Kuratorium für das Reichsehrenmal Tannenberg (ed.), *Tannenberg: Deutsches Schicksal – Deutsche Aufgabe* (Oldenburg and Berlin, Gerhard Stalling, [1939]).

Lange, Willy (ed.), *Deutsche Heldenhaine*, ed. im Auftrage der Arbeitsgemeinschaft für Deutschlands Heldenhaine (Leipzig, J. J. Weber, 1915).

Lasius, Julius, 'Kriegswahrzeichen in rheinisch-westfälischen Industriestädten', *Stahl und Eisen*, 36,6 (1916), pp. 133–7.

Lewis, Cecil, *Sagittarius Rising* (London, Peter Davies, 1936).

Lindenberg, Paul, 'Beim Armee-Oberkommando Hindenburgs während der Schlacht bei Tannenberg', in Paul Lindenberg (ed.), *Hindenburg-Denkmal für das deutsche Volk: Eine Ehrengabe zum 75. Geburtstage des Generalfeldmarschalls* (Berlin, C. U. Weller, 1922), pp. 117–26.

Lloyd George, David, *Through Terror to Triumph: Speeches and Pronouncements of the Right Hon. David Lloyd George, M. P., since the Beginning of the War*, ed. F[rances] L. Stevenson (London, New York and Toronto, Hodder and Stoughton, 1915).

The Great Crusade: Extracts from Speeches Delivered during the War, ed. F[rances] L. Stevenson (London, New York and Toronto, Hodder and Stoughton, 1918).

Loth, P[eter] (ed.), *Das Kriegswahrzeichen der Stadt Zweibrücken: Unserem tapferen Heere gewidmet: Eine Erinnerungsschrift* (Zweibrücken, Friedrich Lehmann, 1916).

Ludendorff, [Erich], *My War Memories 1914–1918*, 2 vols. (London, Hutchinson, [1919]).

Lynn, Escott, *Knights of the Air* (London, W. & R. Chambers, 1918).

Machen, Arthur, *The Angel of Mons: The Bowmen and Other Legends of the War* (London, Simpkin, Marshall, Hamilton Kent, 2nd edn 1915).

Magdalene College War Memorial: Dedication by the Bishop of Ely: November 11th 1923 (Cambridge, Magdalene College, 1923).

Maschke, Erich, 'Deutsche Wacht im Osten durch die Jahrhunderte', in Kuratorium für das Reichsehrenmal Tannenberg (ed.), *Tannenberg: Deutsches Schicksal – Deutsche Aufgabe* (Oldenburg and Berlin, Gerhard Stalling, [1939]), pp. 165–95.

Masefield, John, *St. George and the Dragon* (London, William Heinemann, 1919).

Gallipoli (London, William Heinemann, [2nd edn] 1923).

A Memorial Record of Men of Greenock Who Fell in the Great War, 1914–1918 (Greenock, Greenock Telegraph, 1924),

Müller-Loebnitz, Wilhelm (ed.), *Das Ehrenbuch der Westfalen: Die Westfalen im Weltkrieg* (Stuttgart, Oskar Hinderer, [1931]).

Molter, Bennett A., *Knights of the Air* (New York and London, D. Appelton, 1918).

Montague, C[harles] E., *Disenchantment* (London, Chatto & Windus, 1922).

Moult, Thomas (ed.), *Cenotaph: A Book of Remembrance in Poetry and Prose for November the Eleventh* (London, Jonathan Cape, 1923).

Newbolt, Henry, *The Book of the Happy Warrior* (London, Longmans and Green, 1917).

The Old Cheltonian South African War Memorials: Memorial Cross, Reredos in College Chapel, Kneeling Desk (Cheltenham, Norman Sawyer, 1904).

Oncken, Hermann, 'Gedächtnisrede auf die Gefallenen des großen Krieges: Heidelberg 1919', in Hermann Oncken, *Nation und Geschichte: Reden und Aufsätze 1919–1935* (Berlin, G. Grote, 1935), pp. 3–14.

Osborn, E[dward] B. (ed.), *The Muse in Arms: A Collection of War Poems for the Most Part Written in the Field of Action, by Seamen, Soldiers, and Flying Men Who Are Serving, or Have Served, in the Great War* (London, John Murray, 1917).

Owen, Wilfred, *Collected Letters*, ed. Harold Owen and John Bell (London and Oxford, Oxford University Press, 1967).

Provinzialberatungsstelle für Kriegerehrungen in Ostpreußen [ed.], *Kriegergrabmale und Heldenhaine* (Munich, Georg D. W. Callwey, [1917]).

Pulteney, William and Beatrix Brice, *The Immortal Salient: An Historical Record and Complete Guide for Pilgrims to Ypres* (London, John Murray, 4th edn 1926).

Rapsilber, Maximilian, *Der Eiserne Hindenburg von Berlin: Ein Gedenkblatt* (Berlin, Hermann Bartdorff, 1918).

Reed, J. Gurr, *Sir Galahad's Quest: Addresses on the War Memorial Window, Richmond Hill Congregational Church, Bournemouth* (London, Congregational Union of England & Wales, [1925]).

Reichsehrenmal Tannenberg: [Seine Geschichte. Der Weg durch das Ehrenmal] (Hohenstein, Verkehrsverein, [1936]).

Remarque, Erich Maria, *All Quiet on the Western Front* (London, G. P. Putnam, 1929).

Rendtorff, F[ranz], *Bittgottesdienst am Völkerschlachtdenkmal in Leipzig am 26. August 1914* (Leipzig, Krüger, 1914).

Rheinische Beratungsstelle für Kriegerehrungen, *Anregungen für Kriegsgedenkzeichen*, vol. IV (Moers, Aug. Steiger, 1921).

Richthofen, Manfred von, *Der rote Kampfflieger* (Berlin and Vienna, Ullstein, 1917).

Royal Academy of Arts, *Annual Report 1918* (London, Royal Academy of Arts, 1918).

War Memorials Exhibition 1919 (London, Royal Academy of Arts, 1919).

Saathoff, Albrecht (ed.), *Göttinger Kriegsgedenkbuch 1914–1918* (Göttingen, Vandenhoeck & Ruprecht, 1935).

Sassoon, Siegfried, *The War Poems*, ed. Rupert Hart-Davies (London, Faber and Faber, 1983).

Scharfe, Siegfried (ed.), *Deutschland über alles: Ehrenmale des Weltkrieges* (Königstein and Leipzig, Karl Robert Langewiesche, 1938).

Schindhelm, E[mil], *Reichsehrenmal im heiligen Hain bei Bad Berka-Weimar* (Weimar, Fritz Fink, [1933]).

Schmidt, G., *Kriegerdenkmale in der Pfalz: In Treue zur Heimat: 1914–1918* (Ludwigshafen, Waldkirch, 1934).

Schulte, Eduard, *Kriegschronik der Stadt Münster 1914/18* (Münster, Aschendorff, 1930).

Seeger, Karl von, *Das Denkmal des Weltkriegs* (Stuttgart, Hugo Matthaes, [1930]).

Sombart, Werner, *Händler und Helden: Patriotische Besinnungen* (Munich and Leipzig, Duncker & Humblot, 1915).

Strecker, Karl (ed.), *Das Deutsch Ordens-Infanterie-Regiment Nr. 152 im Weltkriege* (Berlin, Bernhard & Graefe, 1933).

Strobel, Hans (ed.), *Dortmund: Ein Blick in eine deutsche Industriestadt* (Dortmund, C. L. Krüger, 1922).

Thompson, Henry L., *Christ Church* (London, F. E. Robinson, 1900).

Ulrich, Bernd and Benjamin Ziemann (eds.), *Krieg im Frieden: Die umkämpfte Erinnerung an den Ersten Weltkrieg: Quellen und Dokumente* (Frankfurt am Main, Fischer, 1997).

Vereinigung ehemaliger Offiziere des Regiments (ed.), *Das 1. Masurische Infanterie-Regiment Nr. 146 1897–1919* (Berlin, Wilhelm Kolk, 1929).

Victoria and Albert Museum, *Catalogue of the War Memorials Exhibition 1919* (London, HMSO, 1919).

'Vigilant' [Claud W. Sykes], *Richthofen: The Red Knight of the Air* (London, John Hamilton, [1934]).

War Graves of the Empire: Reprinted from the Special Number of The Times *November 10, 1928* (London, The Times, [1928]).

Warr, C[harles] L., *The Unseen Host: Stories of the Great War* (Edinburgh, Robert Grant, repr. 1928).

Wayside Cross Society, *Wayside Crosses* (London, Chiswick, 2nd edn 1917).

Weaver, Lawrence, *Memorials & Monuments: Old and New: Two Hundred Subjects Chosen from Seven Centuries* (London, Country Life, 1915).

Weaver, Lawrence, *The Scottish National War Memorial: The Castle, Edinburgh* (London, Country Life, [1927]).

Der Weltkrieg im Bild: Originalaufnahmen des Kriegs-Bild- und Filmamtes aus der modernen Materialschlacht, [ed.] George Soldan (Berlin and Oldenburg, National Archiv, 1930).

Weltzien, O[tto], 'Kriegsnagelungen in Niederdeutschland', *Niedersachsen*, 22,3 (1916), pp. 39–43.

Werner, Johannes, *Boelcke der Mensch, der Flieger, der Führer der deutschen Jagdfliegerei* (Leipzig, von Hase & Koehler, [1932]).

Knight of Germany: Oswald Boelcke: German Ace (London, John Hamilton, 1933).

Werner, Johannes (ed.), *Briefe eines deutschen Kampffliegers an ein junges Mädchen* (Leipzig and Berlin, Hase & Koehler, 1930).

Wheeler-Bennett, John W., *Hindenburg: The Wooden Titan* (London, Macmillan, 1936).

Wiedenhöfer, Joseph, *Die Kriegergedächtnisstätte der Stadt Dorsten: Zum Weihetag 4. Oktober 1925* (Dorsten, Hermann Majert, 1925).

Williams, H[arold] C. N., *A Guide to Coventry Cathedral* (Derby, English Life, 1979).

Willson, Beckles, *Ypres: The Holy Ground of British Arms* (Bruges, C. Beyaert, 1920).

Winnington-Ingram, Arthur F., *The Potter and the Clay* (London, Wells Gardner and Darton, 1917).

Woods, Edward S., *Knights in Armour* (London, Robert Scott, 1916).

Die Zerstörung der Kathedrale von St. Quentin: Im amtlichen Auftrage zusammengestellt (Berlin, Karl Curtius, 1917).

SECONDARY LITERATURE

Ackermann, Volker, *Nationale Totenfeiern in Deutschland: Von Wilhelm I. bis Franz Josef Strauß: Eine Studie zur politischen Semiotik* (Stuttgart, Klett-Cotta, 1990).

'La vision allemande du soldat inconnu: débats politiques, réflexion philoso-phique et artistique', in Jean-Jacques Becker *et al.* (eds.), *Guerres et cultures, 1914–1918: Vers une histoire comparée de la Grande Guerre* (Paris, Armand Colin, 1994), pp. 385–96.

Adam, Hubertus, 'Hindenburgring und Grabmal Hohmeyer: Zwei Projekte Berhard Hoetgers für Hannover aus den Jahren des 1. Weltkriegs', *Hanno-versche Geschichtsblätter*, new ser., 43 (1989), pp. 57–84.

Adams, Michael C. C., *The Great Adventure: Male Desire and the Coming of World War I* (Bloomington and Indianapolis, Indiana University Press, 1990).

Adamski, Peter (ed.), *'Glücklich die Stadt, die keine Helden hat': Über Denkmäler in Kassel: Das 'Ehrenmal' in der Karlsaue* (Kassel, Friedrichsgymnasium, [1993]).

Ahrendts, Johannes, 'Wenn ein Denkmal rissig wird: Geschichte und Bedeu-tungswandel des Albachtener Kriegerdenkmals', in Heinrich Avenwedde and Heinz-Ulrich Eggert (eds.), *Denkmäler in Münster: Auf Entdeckungsreise in die Vergangenheit* (Münster, Schriftproben, 1996), pp. 171–246.

Alexander-Seitz-Geschichtswerkstatt (ed.), *'Furchtlos und Treu': Die Geschichte des Marbacher Kriegerdenkmals* (Marbach, Alexander-Seitz-Geschichtswerkstatt, 3rd edn 1994).

Alfred and Winifred Turner: The Sculpture of Alfred Turner and his Daughter Winifred Turner (Oxford, Ashmolean Museum, 1988).

Alings, Reinhard, *Monument und Nation: Das Bild vom Nationalstaat im Medium Denkmal – zum Verhältnis von Nation und Staat im Deutschen Kaiserreich 1871–1918* (Berlin and New York, Walter de Gruyter, 1996).

Allen, M[alcolm] D., *The Medievalism of Lawrence of Arabia* (University Park, Pennsylvania State University Press, 1991).

Althoff, Gerd, 'Die Beurteilung der mittelalterlichen Ostpolitik als Paradigma für zeitgebundene Geschichtsbewertung', in Gerd Althoff (ed.), *Die Deutschen und ihr Mittelalter: Themen und Funktionen moderner Geschichtsbilder vom Mittelalter* (Darmstadt, Wissenschaftliche Buchgesellschaft, 1992), pp. 145–64.

(ed.), *Die Deutschen und ihr Mittelalter: Themen und Funktionen moderner Geschichtsbilder vom Mittelalter* (Darmstadt, Wissenschaftliche Buchge-sellschaft, 1992).

Anderson, Olive, 'The Growth of Christian Militarism in Mid-Victorian Britain', *English Historical Review*, 86 (1971), pp. 46–72.

Applegate, Ceilia, *A Nation of Provincials: The German Idea of Heimat* (Berkeley, Los Angeles and Oxford, University of California Press, 1990).

Arendt, Hannah, 'The Aftermath of Nazi Rule: Report from Germany', *Com-mentary* [American Jewish Committee], 10,4 (1950), pp. 342–53.

Armstrong, Tim, *Modernism, Technology, and the Body: A Cultural Study* (Cam-bridge, Cambridge University Press, 1998).

Arndt, Monika, 'Das Kyffhäuser-Denkmal – Ein Beitrag zur politischen Ikono-graphie des Zweiten Kaiserreiches', *Wallraf-Richartz-Jahrbuch*, 40 (1978), pp. 75–127.

Ashplant, T[imothy] G., Graham Dawson and Michael Roper, 'The Politics of War Memory and Commemoration: Contexts, Structures and Dynamics', in T[imothy] G. Ashplant, Graham Dawson and Michael Roper (eds.), *The Politics of War Memory and Commemoration* (London and New York, Routledge, 2000), pp. 3–85.

Assmann, Aleida, *Arbeit am nationalen Gedächtnis: Eine kurze Geschichte der deutschen Bildungsidee* (Frankfurt am Main and New York, Campus, 1993).

Erinnerungsräume: Formen und Wandlungen des kulturellen Gedächtnisses (Munich, C. H. Beck, 1999).

Assmann, Jan, 'Collective Memory and Cultural Identity', *New German Critique*, 65 (1995), pp. 125–33.

Das kulturelle Gedächtnis: Schrift, Erinnerung und politische Identität in frühen Hochkulturen (Munich, C. H. Beck, 2nd edn 1997).

'Einführung: Was ist das "kulturelle Gedächtnis"?', in Jan Assmann, *Religion und kulturelles Gedächtnis: Zehn Studien* (Munich, C. H. Beck, 2000), pp. 11–44.

Audoin-Rouzeau, Stéphane and Annette Becker, *1914–1918: Understanding the Great War* (London, Profile, 2002).

Bach, Martin, *Studien zur Geschichte des deutschen Kriegerdenkmals in Westfalen und Lippe* (Frankfurt am Main, Peter Lang, 1985).

Baird, Jay W., *To Die for Germany: Heroes in the Nazi Pantheon* (Bloomington and Indianapolis, Indiana University Press, 1990).

Banbury, P. A. J., 'The Sledemere Cross', *Yorkshire Archaelogical Journal*, 72 (2000), pp. 193–216.

Banham, Joanna and Jennifer Harris (eds.), *William Morris and the Middle Ages* (Manchester and Dover, N.H., Manchester University Press, 1984).

Barczewski, Stephanie L., *Myth and National Identity in Nineteenth-Century Britain: The Legends of King Arthur and Robin Hood* (Oxford, Oxford University Press, 2000).

Baridon, Laurent and Nathalie Pinthus, *Le Château du Haut-Kœnigsbourg: A la recherche du Moyen Age* (Paris, CNRS Editions, 1998).

Barr, N[iall], 'The British Legion after the Great War: Its Identity and Character', in Bertrand Taithe and Tim Thornton (eds.), *War: Identities in Conflict 1300–2000* (Stroud, Sutton, 1998), pp. 213–33.

Bartlett, J. and K. M. Ellis, 'Remembering the Dead in Northop: First World War Memorials in a Welsh Parish', *Journal of Contemporary History*, 34 (1999), pp. 231–42.

Bartov, Omer, 'Trauma and Absence: France and Germany, 1914–1945', in Paul Addison and Angus Calder (eds.), *Time to Kill: The Soldier's Experience of War in the West 1939–1945* (London, Pimlico, 1997), pp. 347–58.

Bar-Yosef, Eitan, 'The Last Crusade? British Propaganda and the Palestine Campaign, 1917–18', *Journal of Contemporary History*, 36 (2001), pp. 87–109.

Baumeister, Martin, *Kriegstheater: Großstadt, Front und Massenkultur* (Essen, Klartext, 2005).

Becker, Annette, *Les monuments aux morts: Patrimoine et mémoire de la Grande Guerre* (Paris, Errance, [1989]).

War and Faith: The Religious Imagination in France, 1914–1930, intro. K[en] S. Inglis (Oxford and New York, Berg, 1998).

Becker, Frank, *Amerikanismus in Weimar: Sportsymbole und politische Kultur 1918–1933* (Wiesbaden, Deutscher Universitäts Verlag, 1993).

Bilder von Krieg und Nation: Die Einigungskriege in der bürgerlichen Öffentlichkeit Deutschlands 1864–1913 (Munich, R. Oldenbourg, 2001).

Behrenbeck, Sabine, *Der Kult um die toten Helden: Nationalsozialistische Mythen, Rituale und Symbole 1923–1945* (Vierow, SH, 1996).

'Zwischen Trauer und Heroisierung: Vom Umgang mit Kriegstod und Niederlage nach 1918', in Jörg Duppler and Gerhard P. Groß (eds.), *Kriegsende 1918: Ereignis, Wirkung, Nachwirkung* (Munich, R. Oldenbourg, 1999), pp. 315–39.

Bell, Gilbert Torrance, 'Monuments to the Fallen: Scottish War Memorials of the Great War', Ph.D. dissertation, University of Strathclyde, 1994.

Ben-Amos, Avner, *Funerals, Politics, and Memory in Modern France, 1789–1996* (Oxford, Oxford University Press, 2000).

Bendick, Rainer, 'Zur Wirkung und Verarbeitung nationaler Kriegskulturen: Die Darstellung des Ersten Weltkriegs in deutschen und französischen Schulbüchern', in Gerhard Hirschfeld *et al.* (eds.), *Kriegserfahrungen: Studien zur Sozial- und Mentalitätsgeschichte des Ersten Weltkriegs* (Essen, Klartext, 1997), pp. 403–23.

Benner, Thomas, *Die Strahlen der Krone: Die religiöse Dimension des Kaisertums unter Wilhelm II. vor dem Hintergrund der Orientreise 1898* (Marburg, Tectum, 2001).

Berg, Stefanie Barbara, *Heldenbilder und Gegensätze: Friedrich Barbarossa und Heinrich der Löwe im Urteil des 19. und 20. Jahrhunderts* (Münster and Hamburg, Lit, 1994).

Berger, Ursel, '"Immer war die Plastik die Kunst nach dem Kriege": Zur Rolle der Bildhauerei bei der Kriegerdenkmalproduktion in der Zeit der Weimarer Republik', in Rainer Rother (ed.), *Die letzten Tage der Menschheit: Bilder des Ersten Weltkrieges* (Berlin, Deutsches Historisches Museum, 1994), pp. 423–34.

Berghahn, Volker R., *Der Stahlhelm: Bund der Frontsoldaten 1918–1935* (Düsseldorf, Droste, 1966).

Bermbach, Udo, 'Richard Wagner as Prophet of the World War: On the Interpretation of the *Ring* in *Bayreuther Blätter* between 1878 and 1938', *Wagner*, 21 (2000), pp. 87–109.

Bessel, Richard, *Germany after the First World War* (Oxford, Clarendon, 1993).

'The "Front Generation" and the Politics of Weimar Germany', in Mark Roseman (ed.), *Generations in Conflict: Youth Revolt and Generation Formation in Germany 1770–1968* (Cambridge, Cambridge University Press, 1995), pp. 121–36.

Bessel, Richard and Dirk Schumann, 'Introduction: Violence, Normality, and the Construction of Postwar Europe', in Richard Bessel and Dirk Schumann (eds.), *Life after Death: Approaches to a Cultural and Social History of Europe during the 1940s and 1950s* (Cambridge, Cambridge University Press, 2003), pp. 1–13.

Bet-El, Ilana R., 'A Soldier's Pilgrimage: Jerusalem 1918', *Mediterranean Historical Review*, 8 (1993), pp. 218–35.

Biro, Matthew, 'The New Man as Cyborg: Figures of Technology in Weimar Visual Culture', *New German Critique*, 62 (1994), pp. 71–110.

Black, Jonathan, '"Neither Beasts, Nor Gods, But Men": Constructions of Masculinity and the Image of the Ordinary British Soldier or "Tommy" in the First World War Art of: C. R. W. Nevinson (1889–1946), Eric Henri Kennington (1888–1960) and Charles Sargeant Jagger (1885–1934)', Ph.D. dissertation, University of London, 2003.

Blackbourn, David, *Marpingen: Apparitions of the Virgin Mary in Bismarckian Germany* (Oxford, Clarendon Press, 1993).

Blackbourn, David and Geoff Eley, *The Peculiarities of German History: Bourgeois Society and Politics in Nineteenth-Century Germany* (Oxford, Oxford University Press, 1984).

Board, Marilynn Lincoln, 'Art's Moral Mission: Reading G. F. Watt's *Sir Galahad*', in Debra N. Mancoff (ed.), *The Arthurian Revival: Essays on Form, Tradition, Transformation* (New York and London, Garland, 1992), pp. 132–54.

Bogacz, Ted, '"A Tyranny of Words": Language, Poetry, and Antimodernism in England in the First World War', *Journal of Modern History*, 58 (1986), pp. 643–68.

Bontrager, Shannon Ty, 'The Imagined Crusade: The Church of England and the Mythology of Nationalism and Christianity during the Great War', *Church History*, 71 (2002), pp. 774–98.

Boockmann, Hartmut, *Die Marienburg im 19. Jahrhundert* (Frankfurt am Main, Berlin and Vienna, Ullstein-Propyläen, 1982).

Boorman, Derek, *At the Going Down of the Sun: British First World War Memorials* (York, Ebor, 1988).

For Your Tomorrow: British Second World War Memorials (York, Boorman, 1995).

Boos, Florence S. (ed.), *History and Community: Essays in Victorian Medievalism* (New York and London, Garland, 1992).

Booth, Allyson, *Postcards from the Trenches: Negotiating the Space between Modernism and the First World War* (New York and Oxford, Oxford University Press, 1996).

Borg, Alan, *War Memorials: From Antiquity to the Present* (London, Leo Cooper, 1991).

Borst, Arno, 'Barbarossas Erwachen – Zur Geschichte der deutschen Identität', in Odo Marquard and Karlheinz Stierle (eds.), *Identität* (Munich, Wilhelm Fink, 1979), pp. 17–60.

Bourdieu, Pierre, 'Die Besonderheiten der Nationalgeschichten: Vergleichende Geschichte relevanter Unterschiede zwischen den Nationen', in Pierre Bourdieu, *Schwierige Interdisziplinarität: Zum Verhältnis von Soziologie und Geschichtswissenschaft*, ed. Elke Ohnacker and Franz Schultheis (Münster, Westfälisches Dampfboot, 2004), pp. 152–70.

Bourke, Joanna, *Dismembering the Male: Men's Bodies, Britain and the Great War* (London, Reaktion, 1996).

An Intimate History of Killing: Face-to-Face Killing in Twentieth-Century Warfare (London, Granta, 1999).

Boyd, Ian, 'Chesterton's Medievalism', *Studies in Medievalism*, 3 (1991), pp. 243–55.

Bracco, Rosa Maria, *Merchants of Hope: British Middlebrow Writers and the First World War, 1919–1939* (Providence and Oxford, Berg, 1993).

Brandt, Susanne, 'Kriegssammlungen im Ersten Weltkrieg: Denkmäler oder Laboratoires d'histoire?', in Gerhard Hirschfeld, Gerd Krumeich and Irina Renz (eds.), *'Keiner fühlt sich hier mehr als Mensch. . .': Erlebnis und Wirkung des Ersten Weltkriegs* (Frankfurt am Main, Fischer, 1996), pp. 283–302.

'Bilder von der Zerstörung an der Westfront und die doppelte Verdrängung der Niederlage', in Gerhard Hirschfeld *et al.* (eds.), *Kriegserfahrungen: Studien zur Sozial- und Mentalitätsgeschichte des Ersten Weltkriegs* (Essen, Klartext, 1997), pp. 439–54.

Vom Kriegsschauplatz zum Gedächtnisraum: Die Westfront 1914–1940 (Baden-Baden, Nomos, 2000).

'Trauer und fortgesetzter Krieg: Totengedenken zwischen Trauer und Kriegsverherrlichung in Düsseldorf nach dem Ersten Weltkrieg', in Jost Dülffer and Gerd Krumeich (eds.), *Der verlorene Frieden: Politik und Kriegskultur nach 1918* (Essen, Klartext, 2002), pp. 243–60.

Braunfels-Esche, Sigrid, *Sankt Georg: Legende, Verehrung, Symbol* (Munich, Georg D. W. Callwey, 1976).

Breuilly, John, 'Introduction: Making Comparisons in History', in John Breuilly, *Labour and Liberalism in Nineteenth-Century Europe: Essays in Comparative History* (Manchester and New York, Manchester University Press, 1992), pp. 1–25.

Briggs, Asa, 'Saxons, Normans and Victorians', in *The Collected Essays of Asa Briggs*, vol. II, *Images, Problems, Standpoints, Forecasts* (Brighton, Harvester, 1985), pp. 215–35.

Brown, Stewart J., ' "A Solemn Purification by Fire": Responses to the Great War in Scottish Presbyterian Churches, 1914–19', *Journal of Ecclesiastical History*, 45 (1994), pp. 82–104.

Bruendel, Steffen, *Volksgemeinschaft oder Volksstaat: 'Die Ideen von 1914' und die Neuordnung Deutschlands im Ersten Weltkrieg* (Berlin, Akademie, 2003).

Brumme, Ilona, 'Das Kriegerdenkmal des Infanterie-Regiments Herzog Friedrich Wilhelm von Braunschweig (Ostfr.) Nr. 78 und seiner Töchterregimenter am Bocksturms', in Jutta Held (ed.), *Symbole des Friedens und des Krieges im öffentlichen Raum: Osnabrück, die 'Stadt des Westfälischen Friedens'* (Weimar, VDG, 1998), pp. 145–71.

Brune, Thomas, *Staufertraditionalismus im Spiegel einer Göppinger Zeitung seit 1863*, ed. Dieter Kauß (Göppingen, Stadt Göppingen, 1977).

Bucher, Peter, 'Die Errichtung des Reichsehrenmals nach dem ersten [sic] Weltkrieg', *Jahrbuch für westdeutsche Landesgeschichte*, 7 (1981), pp. 359–86.

Buchner, Bernd, *Um nationale und republikanische Identität: Die deutsche Sozialdemokratie und der Kampf um die politischen Symbole in der Weimarer Republik* (Bonn, J. H. W. Dietz Nachf., 2001).

Buitenhuis, Peter, *The Great War of Words: Literature as Propaganda 1914–18 and After* (London, B. T. Batsford, 1989).

Bushart, Magdalena, *Der Geist der Gotik und die expressionistische Kunst: Kunstgeschichte und Kunsttheorie 1911–1925* (Munich, Silke Schreiber, 1990).

Bushaway, Bob, 'Name upon Name: The Great War and Remembrance', in Roy
    Porter (ed.), *Myths of the English* (Cambridge, Polity, 1992), pp. 136–67.
'The Obligation of Remembrance or the Remembrance of Obligation: Society
    and Memory of World War', in Peter Liddle, John Bourne and Ian White-
    head (eds.), *The Great World War 1914–45*, vol. II, *The Peoples' Experience*
    (London, HarperCollins, 2001), pp. 489–508.
Campbell, Louise, *Coventry Cathedral: Art and Architecture in Post-War Britain*
    (Oxford, Clarendon, 1996).
Cannadine, David, 'War and Death, Grief and Mourning in Modern Britain', in
    Joachim Whaley (ed.), *Mirrors of Mortality: Studies in the Social History of
    Death* (London, Europa, 1981), pp. 187–242.
'Lord Curzon as Ceremonial Impressario', in David Cannadine, *Aspects of
    Aristocracy: Grandeur and Decline in Modern Britain* (New Haven and
    London, Yale University Press, 1994), pp. 77–108.
Cantor, Norman F., *Inventing the Middle Ages: The Lives, Works and Ideas of the
    Great Medievalists of the Twentieth Century* (New York, William Morrow,
    1991).
Carden-Coyne, Ana, 'Gendering Death and Renewal: Classical Monuments of
    the First World War', *Humanities Research*, 10,2 (2003), pp. 40–50.
Causey, Andrew, 'Wyndham Lewis and History Painting in the Later 1930s', in
    David Peters Corbett (ed.), *Wyndham Lewis and the Art of Modern War*
    (Cambridge, Cambridge University Press, 1998), pp. 154–80.
Chapman, Raymond, 'Last Enchantments: Medievalism and the Early Anglo-
    Catholic Movement', *Studies in Medievalism*, 4 (1992), pp. 170–86.
Charle, Christophe, *La crise des sociétés imperiales: Allemagne, France, Grande-
    Bretagne (1900–1940): Essai d'histoire sociale comparée* (Paris, Seuil, 2001).
Chartier, Roger, 'Intellectual History or Sociocultural History? The French
    Trajectories', in Dominick LaCapra and Steven L. Kaplan (eds.), *Modern
    European Intellectual History: Reappraisals and New Perspectives* (Ithaca and
    London, Cornell University Press, 1982), pp. 13–46.
Chickering, Roger, 'Total War: The Use and Abuse of a Concept', in Manfred F.
    Boemeke, Roger Chickering and Stig Förster (eds.), *Anticipating Total War:
    The German and American Experiences, 1871–1914* (Cambridge, Cambridge
    University Press, 1999), pp. 13–28.
Cieslik, Karin, 'Der Mythos vom Außenseiter: Klaus Störtebeker, Pirat und
    Volksheld des Nordens', in Ulrich Müller and Werner Wunderlich (eds.),
    Mittelaltermythen, vol. I, *Herrscher, Helden, Heilige* (St Gallen, UVK, 1996),
    pp. 451–66.
Clarke, David, 'Rumours of Angels: A Legend of the First World War', *Folklore*,
    113 (2002), pp. 151–73.
Cohen, Deborah, 'Comparative History: Buyer Beware', *Bulletin of the German
    Historical Institute, Washington, D.C.*, 29 (2001), pp. 23–33.
*The War Come Home: Disabled Veterans in Great Britain and Germany,
    1914–1939* (Berkeley, Los Angeles and London, University of California
    Press, 2001).
Cohen, Deborah and Maura O'Connor, 'Introduction: Comparative History,
    Cross-National History, Transnational History – Definitions', in Deborah

Cohen and Maura O'Connor (eds.), *Comparison and History: Europe in Cross-National Perspective* (New York and London, Routledge, 2004), pp. ix–xxiv.

Collini, Stefan, *Public Moralists: Political Thought and Intellectual Life in Britain 1850–1930* (Oxford, Clarendon, 1991).

Collins, Judith, *Eric Gill: The Sculpture: A Catalogue Raisonné* (London, Herbert, 1998).

Collins, Marcus, 'The Fall of the English Gentleman: The National Character in Decline, *c.* 1918–1970', *Historical Research*, 75 (2002), pp. 90–111.

Confino, Alon, *The Nation as a Local Metaphor: Württemberg, Imperial Germany, and National Memory, 1871–1918* (Chapel Hill and London, University of North Carolina Press, 1997).

Confino, Alon and Peter Fritzsche, 'Introduction: Noises of the Past', in Alon Confino and Peter Fritzsche (eds.), *The Work of Memory: New Directions in the Study of German Society and Culture* (Urbana and Chicago, University of Illinois Press, 2002), pp. 1–21.

Connelly, Mark, *Christmas: A Social History* (London and New York, I. B.Tauris, 1999).

The Great War, Memory and Ritual: Commemoration in the City and East London, 1916–1939 (Woodbridge and Rochester, NY, Boydell, 2002).

Cross, Eric, 'Death in War: Britten and the *War Requiem*', in Jon Davies (ed.), *Ritual and Remembrance: Responses to Death in Human Societies* (Sheffield, Sheffield Academic Press, 1994), pp. 124–51.

Curtis, Penelope, 'The Whitehall Cenotaph: An Accidental Monument', *Imperial War Museum Review*, 9 (1994), pp. 31–41.

Damousi, Joy, *The Labour of Loss: Mourning, Memory and Wartime Bereavement in Australia* (Cambridge, Cambridge University Press, 1999).

Davies, Jon, 'The Martial Uses of the Mass: War Remembrance as an Elementary Form of Religious Life', in Jon Davies (ed.), *Ritual and Remembrance: Responses to Death in Human Societies* (Sheffield, Sheffield Academic Press, 1994), pp. 152–64.

'Reconstructing Enmities: War and War Memorials, the Boundary Markers of the West', *History of European Ideas*, 19 (1994), pp. 47–52.

Dawson, Graham, *Soldier Heroes: British Adventure, Empire and the Imagining of Masculinities* (London and New York, Routledge, 1994).

DeGroot, Gerard J., *Blighty: British Society in the Era of the Great War* (London and New York, Longman, 1996).

Deininger, Friedrich, 'Goslars Bemühungen um den Reichsehrenhain', *Niedersächsisches Jahrbuch für Landesgeschichte*, 55 (1983), pp. 311–69.

Dellheim, Charles, *The Face of the Past: The Preservation of the Medieval Inheritance in Victorian England* (Cambridge, Cambridge University Press, 1982).

'Interpreting Victorian Medievalism', in Florence S. Boos (ed.), *History and Community: Essays in Victorian Medievalism* (New York and London, Garland, 1992), pp. 39–58.

Derez, Mark, 'The Flames of Louvain: The War Experience of an Academic Community', in Hugh Cecil and Peter H. Liddle (eds.), *Facing Armageddon: The First World War Experienced* (London, Leo Cooper, 1996), pp. 617–29.

Dickmänken, Holger *et al.*, 'Das Langemarck-Denkmal des Gymnasiums Dionysianum in Rheine', in Verein Alter Dionysianer (ed.), *Langemarck und ein Denkmal: Nachdenken über unsere Geschichte* (Berlin, News & Media, 1994), pp. 37–100.

Diers, Michael, 'Ernst Ludwig Kirchner und Friedrich Bagdons: Der Hagener Wettbewerb um den "Eisernen Schmied" – eine "Kunst im Krieg"-Episode des Jahres 1915', in Uwe Fleckner and Jürgen Zänker (eds.), *Friedrich Bagdons (1878–1937): Eine Bildhauerkarriere vom Kaiserreich zum Nationalsozialismus* (Stuttgart, Gerd Hatje, 1993), pp. 21–31.

'Nagelmänner: Propaganda mit ephemeren Denkmälern im Ersten Weltkrieg', in Michael Diers, *Schlagbilder: Zur politischen Ikonographie der Gegenwart* (Frankfurt am Main, Fischer, 1997), pp. 78–100.

Diehl, James M., *Paramilitary Politics in Weimar Germany* (Bloomington and London, Indiana University Press, 1977).

Dörner, Andreas, *Politischer Mythos und symbolische Politik: Sinnstiftung durch symbolische Formen am Beispiel des Hermannsmythos* (Opladen, Westdeutscher Verlag, 1995).

Dolan, Anne, *Commemorating the Irish Civil War: History and Memory, 1923–2000* (Cambridge, Cambridge University Press, 2003).

Donaldson, Peter McIntosh, 'The Memorialisation of the Great War in Folkestone, Canterbury and Dover, 1918–24', Ph.D. dissertation, University of Kent, 2005.

Douglas, Fiona Carol, 'Ritual and Remembrance: The Church of Scotland and National Services of Thanksgiving and Remembrance after Four Wars in the Twentieth Century', Ph.D. dissertation, University of Edinburgh, 1996.

Doyle, Barry M., 'Religion, Politics and Remembrance: A Free Church Community and its Great War Dead', in Martin Evans and Ken Lunn (eds.), *War and Memory in the Twentieth Century* (Oxford and New York, Berg, 1997), pp. 223–38.

Duhme, Thomas *et al.*, '*Unseren tapferen Helden. . .*': *Kriegs- und Kriegerdenkmäler und politische Ehrenmale: Dortmunder Beispiele*, ed. Fachbereich Design der Fachhochschule Dortmund (Essen, Klartext, 1987).

Dupront, Alphonse, *Le mythe de croisade*, vol. II (Paris, Gallimard, 1997).

Eisenberg, Christiane, '*English sports' und deutsche Bürger: Eine Gesellschaftsgeschichte 1800–1939* (Paderborn, Ferdinand Schöningh, 1999).

Ekdahl, Sven, 'Die Grunwald-Denkmäler in Polen: Politischer Kontext und nationale Funktion', *Nordost-Archiv*, new ser., 6 (1997), pp. 75–107.

'Tannenberg – Grunwald – Žalgiris: Eine mittelalterliche Schlacht im Spiegel deutscher, polnischer und litauischer Denkmäler', *Zeitschrift für Geschichtswissenschaft*, 50 (2002), pp. 103–18.

Eksteins, Modris, *Rites of Spring: The Great War and the Birth of the Modern Age* (London, Bantam, 1989).

Elliot, C. J., 'The Kriegervereine and the Weimar Republic', *Journal of Contemporary History*, 10 (1975), pp. 109–29.

Elze, Reinhard and Pierangelo Schiera (eds.), *Italia e Germania: Immagini, modelli, miti fra due popoli nell'Ottocento: il Medioevo* (Berlin and Bologna, Duncker & Humblot, 1988).

Espagne, Michel, 'Sur les limites du comparatisme en histoire culturelle', *Genèses*, 17 (1994), pp. 112–21.

Evans, Richard J., *Rethinking German History: Nineteenth-Century Germany and the Origins of the Third Reich* (London, Unwin Hyman, 1987).

The Coming of the Third Reich (London, Allen Lane, 2003).

Ferguson, Niall, *The Pity of War* (London, Allen Lane, 1998).

Fischer, Heike, 'Tannenberg-Denkmal und Hindenburgkult: Hintergründe eines Mythos', in Michael Hütt *et al.* (eds.), *Unglücklich das Land, das Helden nötig hat: Leiden und Sterben in den Kriegsdenkmälern des Ersten und Zweiten Weltkrieges* (Marburg, Jonas, 1990), pp. 28–49.

Fleckner, Uwe and Jürgen Zänker (eds.), *Friedrich Bagdons (1878–1937): Eine Bildhauerkarriere vom Kaiserreich zum Nationalsozialismus* (Stuttgart, Gerd Hatje, 1993).

Förster, Stig, 'Das Zeitalter des totalen Kriegs, 1861–1945: Konzeptionelle Überlegungen für einen historischen Strukturvergleich', *Mittelweg 36*, 8,6 (1999), pp. 12–29.

Frevert, Ute, *Men of Honour: A Social and Cultural History of the Duel* (Cambridge, Polity, 1995).

François, Etienne and Hagen Schulze (eds.), *Deutsche Erinnerungsorte*, 3 vols. (Munich, C. H. Beck, 2001).

Frantzen, Allen J., *Bloody Good: Chivalry, Sacrifice, and the Great War* (Chicago and London, University of Chicago Press, 2004).

Frei, Norbert, *Adenauer's Germany and the Nazi Past: The Politics of Amnesty and Integration* (New York, Columbia University Press, 2002).

Frenzel, Andreas, '"Daß das Reichsehrenmal eine würdige Stätte finde bei Höxter": Die Bewerbung um das geplante Reichsehrenmal (1924–1935)', *Westfälische Zeitschrift*, 150 (2000), pp. 367–89.

Fried, Johannes, 'Der Löwe als Objekt: Was Literaten, Historiker und Politiker aus Heinrich dem Löwen machten', *Historische Zeitschrift*, 262 (1996), pp. 673–93.

Fries, Helmut, *Die große Katharsis: Der Erste Weltkrieg in der Sicht deutscher Dichter und Gelehrter*, 2 vols. (Constance, Hockgraben, 1994–5).

Fritzsche, Peter, *A Nation of Fliers: German Aviation and the Popular Imagination* (Cambridge, MA and London, Harvard University Press, 1992).

'The Case of Modern Memory', *Journal of Modern History*, 73 (2001), pp. 87–117.

Frowein-Ziroff, Vera, *Die Kaiser Wilhelm-Gedächtniskirche: Entstehung und Bedeutung* (Berlin, Mann, 1982).

Fuchs, Ron and Gilbert Herbert, 'Representing Mandatory Palestine: Auden St Barbe Harrison and the Representational Buildings of the British Mandate in Palestine, 1922–37', *Architectural History*, 43 (2000), pp. 281–333.

Fuhrmeister, Christian, *Beton, Klinker, Granit: Material, Macht, Politik: Eine Materialikonographie* (Berlin, Bauwesen, 2001).

'Die "unsterbliche Landschaft", der Raum des Reiches und die Toten der Nation: Die Totenburgen Bitoli (1936) und Quero (1939) als strategische Nationalarchitektur', *kritische berichte*, 29,2 (2001), pp. 56–70.

Fulda, Bernhard, 'Press and Politics in Berlin, 1924–1930', Ph.D. dissertation, University of Cambridge, 2003.

Fuller, J[ohn] G., *Troop Morale and Popular Culture in the British and Dominion Armies 1914–1918* (Oxford, Clarendon, 1990).

Fussell, Paul, *The Great War and Modern Memory* (London and Oxford, Oxford University Press, 1975).

Wartime: Understanding and Behavior in the Second World War (New York and Oxford, Oxford University Press, 1989).

'The Fate of Chivalry and the Assault upon Mother', in Paul Fussell, *Killing, in Verse and Prose and Other Essays* (London, Bellew, 1990), pp. 217–44.

Gaffney, Angela, *Aftermath: Remembering the Great War in Wales* (Cardiff, University of Wales Press, 1998).

Gambarrotto, Laurent, 'Guerre sainte et juste paix', *14–18: Aujourd'hui – Today – Heute*, 1 (1998), pp. 27–38.

Gaskill, Malcolm, *Hellish Nell: Last of Britain's Witches* (London, Fourth Estate, 2001).

Gavaghan, Michael, *The Story of the Unknown Warrior: 11 November 1920* (Preston, M and L, 1995).

Geyer, Martin H., *Verkehrte Welt: Revolution, Inflation und Moderne, München 1914–1924* (Göttingen, Vandenhoeck & Ruprecht, 1998).

Giller, Joachim, Hubert Mader and Christina Seidl, *Wo sind sie geblieben..? Kriegerdenkmäler und Gefallenenehrung in Österreich* (Vienna, Österreichischer Bundesverlag, 1992).

Girouard, Mark, *The Return to Camelot: Chivalry and the English Gentleman* (New Haven and London, Yale University Press, 1981).

Glaves-Smith, John, 'Realism and Propaganda in the Work of Charles Sergeant Jagger and their Relationship to Artistic Tradition', in Ann Compton (ed.), *Charles Sargeant Jagger: War and Peace Sculpture* (London, Imperial War Museum, 1985), pp. 51–79.

Goebel, Stefan, 'Intersecting Memories: War and Remembrance in Twentieth-Century Europe', *Historical Journal*, 44 (2001), pp. 853–8.

'"Kohle und Schwert": Zur Konstruktion der Heimatfront in Kriegswahrzeichen des Ruhrgebietes im Ersten Weltkrieg', *Westfälische Forschungen*, 51 (2001), pp. 257–81.

'Forging the Industrial Home Front: Iron-Nail Memorials in the Ruhr', in Jenny Macleod and Pierre Purseigle (eds.), *Uncovered Fields: Perspectives in First World War Studies* (Leiden and Boston, Brill, 2004), pp. 159–78.

'Re-membered and Re-mobilized: The "Sleeping Dead" in Interwar Germany and Britain', *Journal of Contemporary History*, 39 (2004), pp. 487–501.

'Chivalrous Knights *versus* Iron Warriors: Representations of the Battle of Matériel and the Slaughter in Britain and Germany, 1914–1940', in Pearl James (ed.), *Picture This! Reading World War I Posters* (Lincoln, NE, University of Nebraska Press, forthcoming).

Goebel, Stefan, Kevin Repp and Jay Winter, 'Exhibitions', in Jay Winter, Jean-Louis Robert *et al.*, *Capital Cities at War: Paris, London, Berlin 1914–1919*, vol. II (Cambridge, Cambridge University Press, forthcoming).

Goldstein, Laurence, *The Flying Machine and Modern Literature* (Basingstoke and London, Macmillan, 1986).

Gollwitzer, Heinz, 'Deutsche Palästinafahrten des 19. Jahrhunderts als Glaubens- und Bildungserlebnis', in Wolfgang Stammler (ed.), *Lebenskräfte in der abendländischen Geistesgeschichte* (Marburg, Simons, 1948), pp. 286–324.

Gottschalk, Carola, 'Götterdämmerung: Das Denkmal für die Gefallenen der Universität', in Carola Gottschalk (ed.), *Verewigt und Vergessen: Kriegerdenkmäler, Mahnmale und Gedenksteine in Göttingen* (Göttingen, Volker Schmerse, 1992), pp. 26–33.

Grayzel, Susan R., *Women's Identities at War: Gender, Motherhood, and Politics in Britain and France during the First World War* (Chapel Hill and London, University of North Carolina Press, 1999).

Greenberg, Allan, 'Lutyens's Cenotaph', *Journal of the Society of Architectural Historians*, 48 (1989), pp. 5–23.

Gregory, Adrian, *The Silence of Memory: Armistice Day 1919–1946* (Oxford and Providence, Berg, 1994).

'Lost Generations: The Impact of Military Casualties on Paris, London, and Berlin', in Jay Winter, Jean-Louis Robert [*et al.*], *Capital Cities at War: Paris, London, Berlin 1914–1919* (Cambridge, Cambridge University Press, 1997), pp. 57–103.

'The Commemoration of the Battle of Britain', in Paul Addison and Jeremy A. Crang (eds.), *The Burning Blue: A New History of the Battle of Britain* (London, Pimlico, 2000), pp. 217–28.

'Demobilizing the Nation: Remobilizing the Dead: The Persistent Mythologies of British Commemoration', paper presented at the conference on 'Demobilizing the Mind: Culture, Politics and the Legacy of the Great War, 1919–1933', Trinity College, Dublin, 26 August–8 September 2001.

'Peculiarities of the British? War, Violence and Politics: 1900–1939', *Journal of Modern European History*, 1 (2003), pp. 44–59.

Grieves, Keith, 'C. E. Montague and the Making of *Disenchantment*, 1914–1921', *War in History*, 4 (1997), pp. 35–59.

'Common Meeting Places and the Brightening of Rural Life: Local Debates on Village Halls in Sussex after the First World War', *Rural History*, 10 (1999), pp. 171–92.

'Investigating Local War Memorial Committees: Demobilised Soldiers, the Bereaved and Expressions of Local Pride in Sussex Villages, 1918–1921', *Local Historian*, 30 (2000), pp. 39–58.

Grote, Bernd, *Der deutsche Michel: Ein Beitrag zur publizistischen Bedeutung der Nationalfiguren* (Dortmund, Ruhfus, 1967).

Gullace, Nicoletta F., 'Sexual Violence and Family Honor: British Propaganda and International Law during the First World War', *American Historical Review*, 102 (1997), pp. 714–47.

'The Blood of Our Sons': Men, Women, and the Renegotiation of British Citizenship during the Great War (New York and Basingstoke, Palgrave, 2002).

Haas, Stefan, 'Die neue Welt der Bilder: Werbung und visuelle Kultur der Moderne', in Peter Borscheid and Clemens Wischermann (eds.), *Bilderwelt des Alltags: Werbung in der Konsumgesellschaft des 19. und 20. Jahrhunderts* (Stuttgart, Franz Steiner, 1995), pp. 64–77.

'Philosophie der Erinnerung: Kategoriale Voraussetzungen einer mnemistischen Geschichtsbetrachtung', in Clemens Wischermann (ed.), *Die Legitimität der Erinnerung und die Geschichtswissenschaft* (Stuttgart, Franz Steiner, 1996), pp. 31–54.

Halbwachs, Maurice, *The Collective Memory* (New York, Harper & Row, 1980).

Haupt, Heinz-Gerhard and Jürgen Kocka, 'Historischer Vergleich: Methoden, Aufgaben, Probleme: Eine Einleitung', in Heinz-Gerhard Haupt and Jürgen Kocka (eds.), *Geschichte und Vergleich: Ansätze und Ergebnisse international vergleichender Geschichtsschreibung* (Frankfurt am Main and New York, Campus, 1996), pp. 9–45.

Harris, José, *Private Lives, Public Spirit: Britain 1870–1914* (Oxford, Oxford University Press, 1993).

'Introduction: Civil Society in British History: Paradigm or Peculiarity', in José Harris (ed.), *Civil Society in British History: Ideas, Identities, Institutions* (Oxford, Oxford University Press, 2003), pp. 1–12.

Harrison, Martin, 'Church Decoration and Stained Glass', in Linda Parry (ed.), *William Morris* (London, Victoria & Albert Museum, 1996), pp. 106–35.

Hazelgrove, Jenny, *Spiritualism and British Society between the Wars* (Manchester and New York, Manchester University Press, 2000).

Heffen, Annegret, *Der Reichskunstwart – Kunstpolitik in den Jahren 1920–1933: Zu den Bemühungen um eine offizielle Reichskunstpolitik in der Weimarer Republik* (Essen, Blaue Eule, 1986).

Heffernan, Michael, 'For Ever England: The Western Front and the Politics of Remembrance in Britain', *Ecumene*, 2 (1995), pp. 293–323.

Heinemann, Ulrich, *Die verdrängte Niederlage: Politische Öffentlichkeit und Kriegsschuldfrage in der Weimarer Republik* (Göttingen, Vandenhoeck & Ruprecht, 1983).

Herf, Jeffrey, *Reactionary Modernism: Technology, Culture, and Politics in Weimar and the Third Reich* (Cambridge, Cambridge University Press, 1984).

Herwig, Holger H., 'Total Rhetoric, Limited War: Germany's U-Boat Campaign, 1917–1918', in Roger Chickering and Stig Förster (eds.), *Great War, Total War: Combat and Mobilization on the Western Front, 1914–1918* (Cambridge, Cambridge University Press, 2000), pp. 189–206.

Hesse-Frielinghaus, Herta, 'Folkwang 1. Teil', in Herta Hesse-Frielinghaus et al., *Karl Ernst Osthaus: Leben und Werk* (Recklinghausen, Aurel Bongers, 1971), pp. 119–241.

Higham, N. J., *King Arthur: Myth-Making and History* (London and New York, Routledge, 2002).

Hiller von Gaertringen, Friedrich, ' "Dolchstoß"-Diskussion und "Dolchstoßlegende" im Wandel von vier Jahrzehnten', in Waldemar Besson and Friedrich Hiller von Gaertringen (eds.), *Geschichte und Gegenwartsbewußtsein: Historische Betrachtungen und Untersuchungen* (Göttingen, Vandenhoeck & Ruprecht, 1963), pp. 122–60.

Hoffenberg, Peter H., 'Landscape, Memory and the Australian War Experience, 1915–18', *Journal of Contemporary History*, 36 (2001), pp. 111–31.

Hoffmann, Stefan-Ludwig, 'Sakraler Monumentalismus um 1900: Das Leipziger Völkerschlachtdenkmal', in Reinhart Koselleck and Michael Jeismann (eds.), *Der politische Totenkult: Kriegerdenkmäler in der Moderne* (Munich, Wilhelm Fink, 1994), pp. 249–80.

Hoffmann-Curtius, Kathrin, 'Das Kreuz als Nationaldenkmal: Deutschland 1814 und 1931', *Zeitschrift für Kunstgeschichte*, 48 (1985), pp. 77–100.

'Das Kriegerdenkmal der Berliner Friedrich-Wilhelms-Universität 1919–1926: Siegexegese der Niederlage', *Jahrbuch für Universitätsgeschichte*, 5 (2002), pp. 87–116.

Holsten, Siegmar, *Allegorische Darstellungen des Krieges 1870–1918: Ikonologische und ideologiekritische Studien* (Munich, Prestel, 1976).

Homberger, Eric, 'The Story of the Cenotaph', *The Times Literary Supplement*, 3896, 12 November 1976, pp. 1429–30.

Horne, John and Alan Kramer, *German Atrocities, 1914: A History of Denial* (New Haven and London, Yale University Press, 2001).

Hornung, Klaus, *Der Jungdeutsche Orden* (Düsseldorf, Droste, 1958).

Hüppauf, Bernd, 'Schlachtenmythen und die Konstruktion des "Neuen Menschen"', in Gerhard Hirschfeld, Gerd Krumeich and Irina Renz (eds.), *'Keiner fühlt sich hier mehr als Mensch. . .': Erlebnis und Wirkung des Ersten Weltkriegs* (Frankfurt am Main, Fischer, 1996), pp. 53–103.

'Introduction: Modernity and Violence: Observations Concerning a Contradictory Relationship', in Bernd Hüppauf (ed.), *War, Violence and the Modern Condition* (Berlin and New York, Walter de Gruyter, 1997), pp. 1–29.

'Das Schlachtfeld als Raum im Kopf: Mit einem Postscriptum nach dem 11. September 2001', in Steffen Martus, Marina Münkler and Werner Röcke (eds.), *Schlachtfelder: Codierung von Gewalt im medialen Wandel* (Berlin, Akademie, 2003), pp. 207–33.

Hutter, Peter, *'Die feinste Barbarei': Das Völkerschlachtdenkmal bei Leipzig* (Mainz, Philipp von Zabern, 1990).

Hynes, Samuel, *A War Imagined: The First World War and English Culture* (London, Bodley Head, 1990).

Ilg, Reinhard, 'Katholische Bildungsbürger und die bedrohte Nation: Das katholische Gymnasium Ehingen (Donau) im Kaiserreich und während des Ersten Weltkriegs', in Gerhard Hirschfeld et al. (eds.), *Kriegserfahrungen: Studien zur Sozial- und Mentalitätsgeschichte des Ersten Weltkriegs* (Essen, Klartext, 1997), pp. 341–70.

Inglis, K[en] S., 'The Homecoming: The War Memorial Movement in Cambridge, England', *Journal of Contemporary History*, 27 (1992), pp. 583–605.

'War Memorials: Ten Questions for Historians', *Guerres Mondiales et Conflits Contemporains*, 167 (1992), pp. 5–21.

'Entombing Unknown Soldiers: From London and Paris to Baghdad', *History and Memory*, 5,2 (1993), pp. 7–31.

Sacred Places: War Memorials in the Australian Landscape (Melbourne, Melbourne University Press, 1998).

Ingold, Felix Philipp, *Literatur und Aviatik: Europäische Flugdichtung 1907–1929* (Basle and Stuttgart, Birkhäuser, 1978).

Jahn, Hubertus F., *Patriotic Culture in Russia during World War I* (Ithaca and London, Cornell University Press, 1995).

Jalland, Pat, *Death in the Victorian Family* (Oxford, Oxford University Press, 1996).

Jamet-Bellier de la Duboisière, Catherine, 'Commemorating "the Lost Generation"': First World War Memorials in Cambridge, Oxford and Some English Public Schools', M.Litt. dissertation, University of Cambridge, 1995.

Janz, Oliver, 'Zwischen privater Trauer und öffentlichem Gedenken: Der bürgerliche Gefallenenkult in Italien während des Ersten Weltkriegs', *Geschichte und Gesellschaft*, 28 (2002), pp. 554–73.

Jeffery, Keith, *Ireland and the Great War* (Cambridge, Cambridge University Press, 2000).

Jeismann, Michael, *Das Vaterland der Feinde: Studien zum nationalen Feindbegriff und Selbstverständnis in Deutschland und Frankreich 1792–1918* (Stuttgart, Klett-Cotta, 1992).

Jeismann, Michael and Rolf Westheider, 'Wofür stirbt der Bürger? Nationaler Totenkult und Staatsbürgertum in Deutschland und Frankreich seit der Französischen Revolution', in Reinhart Koselleck and Michael Jeismann (eds.), *Der politische Totenkult: Kriegerdenkmäler in der Moderne* (Munich), Wilhelm Fink, 1994), pp. 23–50.

Jenkyns, Richard, *The Victorians and Ancient Greece* (Oxford, Blackwell, 1980).

Jones, Max, *The Last Great Quest: Captain Scott's Antarctic Sacrifice* (Oxford, Oxford University Press, 2003).

Kaelble, Hartmut, *Der historische Vergleich: Eine Einführung zum 19. und 20. Jahrhundert* (Frankfurt am Main and New York, Campus, 1999).

Kasten, Bernd, 'Das sogenannte "Dolchstoss-Denkmal" im Schweriner Schloßgarten', *Mecklenburgische Jahrbücher*, 114 (1999), Beiheft, pp. 379–87.

Kerssen, Ludger, *Das Interesse am Mittelalter im deutschen Nationaldenkmal* (Berlin and New York, Walter de Gruyter, 1975).

Ketelsen, Uwe-K., ' "Die Jugend von Langemarck": Ein poetisch-politisches Motiv der Zwischenkriegszeit', in Thomas Koebner, Rolf-Peter Janz and Frank Trommler (eds.), *'Mit uns zieht die neue Zeit': Der Mythos der Jugend* (Frankfurt am Main, Suhrkamp, 1985), pp. 68–96.

Kettenacker, Lothar, 'Der Mythos vom Reich', in Karl Heinz Bohrer (ed.), *Mythos und Moderne: Begriff und Bild einer Rekonstruktion* (Frankfurt am Main, Suhrkamp, 1983), pp. 261–89.

Kiefer, Klaus H., 'Die Beschießung der Kathedrale von Reims: Bilddokument und Legendenbildung – Eine Semiotik der Zerstörung', *Krieg und Literatur*, 3–4 (1997–8), pp. 115–52.

Kienitz, Sabine, 'Der Krieg der Invaliden: Helden-Bilder und Männlichkeitskonstruktionen nach dem Ersten Weltkrieg', *Militärgeschichtliche Zeitschrift*, 60 (2001), pp. 367–402.

Kimball, Charles, 'The Ex-Service Movement in England and Wales, 1916–1930', Ph.D. dissertation, Stanford University, 1990.

King, Alex, *Memorials of the Great War in Britain: The Symbolism and Politics of Remembrance* (Oxford and New York, Berg, 1998).

Kipper, Rainer, *Der Germanenmythos im Deutschen Kaiserreich: Formen und Funktionen historischer Selbstthematisierung* (Göttingen, Vandenhoeck & Ruprecht, 2002).

Klenke, Dietmar, Peter Lilje and Franz Walter, *Arbeitersänger und Volksbühnen in der Weimarer Republik*, Solidargemeinschaft und Milieu, vol. III (Bonn, J. H. W. Dietz Nachf., 1992).

Knauff, Michael, 'Das Schlageter-Nationaldenkmal auf der Golzheimer Heide in Düsseldorf', *Geschichte im Westen*, 10 (1995), pp. 168–91.

Knowles, Richard, 'Tale of an "Arabian Knight": The T. E. Lawrence Effigy', *Church Monuments*, 6 (1991), pp. 67–76.

Koselleck, Reinhart, 'Kriegerdenkmale als Identitätsstiftungen der Überlebenden', in Odo Marquard and Karlheinz Stierle (eds.), *Identität* (Munich, Wilhelm Fink, 1979), pp. 255–76.

'Einleitung', in Reinhart Koselleck and Michael Jeismann (eds.), *Der politische Totenkult: Kriegerdenkmäler in der Moderne* (Munich, Wilhelm Fink, 1994), pp. 9–20.

Zur politischen Ikonologie des gewaltsamen Todes: Ein deutsch–französischer Vergleich (Basle, Schwabe, 1998).

'Erinnerungsschleusen und Erfahrungsgeschichten: Der Einfluß der beiden Weltkriege auf das soziale Bewußtsein', in Reinhart Koselleck, *Zeitgeschichten: Studien zur Historik* (Frankfurt am Main, Suhrkamp, 2000), pp. 265–84.

Koselleck, Reinhart and Michael Jeismann (eds.), *Der politische Totenkult: Kriegerdenkmäler in der Moderne* (Munich, Wilhelm Fink, 1994).

Koshar, Rudy, *Germany's Transient Pasts: Preservation and National Memory in the Twentieth Century* (Chapel Hill and London, University of North Carolina Press, 1998).

From Monuments to Traces: Artifacts of German Memory, 1870–1990 (Berkeley, Los Angeles and London, University of California Press, 2000).

Kotowski, Mathias, '"Noch ist ja der Krieg gar nicht zu Ende": Weltkriegsgedenken der Universität Tübingen in der Weimarer Republik', in Gerhard Hirschfeld *et al.* (eds.), *Kriegserfahrungen: Studien zur Sozial- und Mentalitätsgeschichte des Ersten Weltkriegs* (Essen, Klartext, 1997), pp. 424–38.

Kramer, Alan, '"Greultaten": Zum Problem der deutschen Kriegsverbrechen in Belgien und Frankreich 1914', in Gerhard Hirschfeld, Gerd Krumeich and Irina Renz (eds.), *'Keiner fühlt sich hier mehr als Mensch. . .': Erlebnis und Wirkung des Ersten Weltkriegs* (Frankfurt am Main, Fischer, 1996), pp. 104–39.

Kreis, Georg, 'Gefallenendenkmäler in kriegsverschontem Land: Zum politischen Totenkult der Schweiz', in Reinhart Koselleck and Michael Jeismann (eds.), *Der politische Totenkult: Kriegerdenkmäler in der Moderne* (Munich, Wilhelm Fink, 1994), pp. 129–43.

Ein Krieg wird ausgestellt: Die Weltkriegssammlung des Historischen Museums (1914–1918) (Frankfurt am Main, Dezernat für Kultur und Freizeit, 1976).

Krüger, Jürgen, *Rom und Jerusalem: Kirchenbauvorstellungen der Hohenzollern im 19. Jahrhundert* (Berlin, Akademie, 1995).

Krüger-Bulcke, Ingrid, 'Der Hohenzollern-Hindenburg-Zwischenfall in Marburg 1947: Wiederaufleben nationalistischer Strömungen oder Sturm im Wasserglas?', *Hessisches Jahrbuch für Landesgeschichte*, 39 (1989), pp. 311–52.

Krumeich, Gerd, *Jeanne d'Arc in der Geschichte: Historiographie – Politik – Kultur* (Sigmaringen, Jan Thorbecke, 1989).

'Kriegsfotografie zwischen Erleben und Propaganda: Verdun und die Somme in deutschen und französischen Fotografien des Ersten Weltkriegs', in Ute Daniel and Wolfram Siemann (eds.), *Propaganda: Meinungskampf, Verführung und politische Sinnstiftung (1789–1989)* (Frankfurt am Main, Fischer, 1994), pp. 117–32.

Kruse, Wolfgang, *Krieg und nationale Integration: Eine Neuinterpretation des sozialdemokratischen Burgfriedensschlusses 1914/15* (Essen, Klartext, 1993).

Kuberek, Monika, 'Die Kriegsgräberstätten des Volksbundes Deutsche Kriegsgräberfürsorge', in Michel Hütt *et al.* (eds.), *Unglücklich das Land, das Helden nötig hat: Leiden und Sterben in den Kriegsdenkmälern des Ersten und Zweiten Weltkrieges* (Marburg, Jonas, 1990), pp. 75–98.

Lambourne, Nicola, '"Moral Cathedrals": War Damage and Franco-German Cultural Propaganda on the Western Front 1870–1938', Ph.D. dissertation, University of London, 1997.

War Damage in Western Europe: The Destruction of Historic Monuments during the Second World War (Edinburgh, Edinburgh University Press, 2001).

Langenscheid, Birgit and Viktoria von Schönfeldt, '"Märtyrer" des deutschen Imperialismus: Das Ketteler-Denkmal im Schloßgarten in Münster', in Heinrich Avenwedde and Heinz-Ulrich Eggert (eds.), *Denkmäler in Münster: Auf Entdeckungsreise in die Vergangenheit* (Münster, Schriftproben, 1996), pp. 247–314.

Laqueur, Thomas W., 'Memory and Naming in the Great War', in John R. Gillis (ed.), *Commemorations: The Politics of National Identity* (Princeton, Princeton University Press, 1994), pp. 150–67.

'Names, Bodies, and the Anxiety of Erasure', in Theodore R. Schatzki and Wolfgang Natter (eds.), *The Social and Political Body* (New York and London, Guilford, 1996), pp. 123–39.

'Cemeteries and the Decline of the Occult: From Ghosts to Memory in the Modern Age', *Österreichische Zeitschrift für Geschichtswissenschaften*, 14,4 (2003), pp. 37–52.

Laube, Stefan, *Fest, Religion und Erinnerung: Konfessionelles Gedächtnis in Bayern von 1804 bis 1917* (Munich, C. H. Beck, 1999).

Lawrence, Jon, 'Forging a Peaceable Kingdom: War, Violence, and Fear of Brutalization in Post-First World War Britain', *Journal of Modern History*, 75 (2003), pp. 557–89.

Leed, Eric J., *No Man's Land: Combat & Identity in World War I* (Cambridge, Cambridge University Press, 1979).

Leese, Peter, '"Why Are They Not Cured?" British Shellshock Treatment during the Great War', in Mark S. Micale and Paul Lerner (eds.), *Traumatic Pasts: History, Psychiatry, and Trauma in the Modern Age, 1870–1930* (Cambridge, Cambridge University Press, 2001), pp. 205–21.

Shell Shock: Traumatic Neurosis and the British Soldiers of the First World War (Basingstoke and New York, Palgrave, 2002).

Le Goff, Jacques, 'Reims, City of Coronation', in Pierre Nora (ed.), *Realms of Memory: The Construction of the French Past*, vol. III, *Symbols* (New York, Columbia University Press, 1998), pp. 193–251.

Lehnert, Detlef, 'Die geschichtlichen Schattenbilder von "Tannenberg": Vom Hindenburg-Mythos im Ersten Weltkrieg zum ersatzmonarchischen Identifikationssymbol in der Weimarer Republik', in Kurt Imhof and Peter Schulz (eds.), *Medien und Krieg – Krieg in den Medien* (Zürich, Seismo, 1995), pp. 37–71.

Lenger, Friedrich, *Werner Sombart 1863–1941: Eine Biographie* (Munich, C. H. Beck, 1994).

Lerner, Paul, 'Psychiatry and Casualties of War in Germany, 1914–18', *Journal of Contemporary History*, 35 (2000), pp. 13–28.

Hysterical Men: War, Psychiatry, and the Politics of Trauma in Germany, 1890–1930 (London and Ithaca, Cornell University Press, 2003).

Lerner, Paul and Mark S. Micale, 'Trauma, Psychiatry, and History: A Conceptual and Historiographical Introduction', in Mark S. Micale and Paul Lerner (eds.), *Traumatic Pasts: History, Psychiatry, and Trauma in the Modern Age, 1870–1930* (Cambridge, Cambridge University Press, 2001), pp. 1–27.

Linse, Ulrich, '"Saatfrüchte sollen nicht vermahlen werden!" Zur Resymbolisierung des Soldatentodes', in Klaus Vondung (ed.), *Kriegserlebnis: Der Erste Weltkrieg in der literarischen Gestaltung und symbolischen Deutung der Nationen* (Göttingen, Vandenhoeck & Ruprecht, 1980), pp. 262–74.

Liulevicius, Vejas Gabriel, *War Land on the Eastern Front: Culture, National Identity, and German Occupation in World War I* (Cambridge, Cambridge University Press, 2000).

Lloyd, David W., *Battlefield Tourism: Pilgrimage and the Commemoration of the Great War in Great Britain, Australia and Canada, 1919–1939* (Oxford and New York, Berg, 1998).

Longworth, Philip, *The Unending Vigil: A History of the Commonwealth War Graves Commission 1917–1984* (London, Leo Cooper, [2nd edn] 1985).

Lurz, Meinhold, *Kriegerdenkmäler in Deutschland*, 6 vols. (Heidelberg, Esprint, 1985–7).

Maas, Annette, 'Politische Ikonographie im deutsch-französischen Spannungsfeld: Die Kriegerdenkmäler von 1870/71 auf dem Schlachtfeld um Metz', in Reinhart Koselleck and Michael Jeismann (eds.), *Der politische Totenkult: Kriegerdenkmäler in der Moderne* (Munich, Wilhelm Fink, 1994), pp. 195–222.

Mackaman, Douglas and Michael Mays (eds.), *World War I and the Cultures of Modernity* (Jackson, University Press of Mississippi, 2000).

McKernan, Luke, '"The Supreme Moment of the War": "General Allenby's Entry into Jerusalem"', *Historical Journal of Film, Radio and Television*, 13 (1993), pp. 169–80.

Maclean, Chris and Jock Phillips, *The Sorrow and the Pride: New Zealand War Memorials* (Wellington, GP, 1990).

MacLeod, James Lachlan, '"Greater Love Hath No Man than This": Scotland's Conflicting Religious Responses to Death in the Great War', *Scottish Historical Review*, 81 (2002), pp. 70–96.

Macleod, Jenny, *Reconsidering Gallipoli* (Manchester and New York, Manchester University Press, 2004).

Magnus, Philip, *Kitchener: A Portrait of an Imperialist* (London, John Murray, 1958).

Malvern, Sue, *Modern Art, Britain, and the Great War: Witnessing, Testimony and Remembrance* (New Haven and London, Yale University Press, 2004).

Mancoff, Debra N., *The Arthurian Revival in Victorian Art* (New York and London, Garland, 1990).

(ed.), *The Arthurian Revival: Essays on Form, Tradition, Transformation* (New York and London, Garland, 1992).

Mangan, J[ames] A., *Athleticism in the Victorian and Edwardian Public School: The Emergence and Consolidation of an Educational Ideology* (Cambridge, Cambridge University Press, 1981).

Mansfield, Nick, 'Class Conflict and Village War Memorials, 1914–24', *Rural History*, 6 (1995), pp. 67–87.

Marrin, Albert, *The Last Crusade: The Church of England in the First World War* (Durham, NC, Duke University Press, 1974).

Marsland, Elizabeth A., *The Nation's Cause: French, German and English Poetry of the First World War* (London and New York, Routledge, 1991).

Marwick, Arthur, 'Painting and Music during and after the Great War: The Art of Total War', in Roger Chickering and Stig Förster (eds.), *Great War, Total War: Combat and Mobilization on the Western Front, 1914–1918* (Cambridge, Cambridge University Press, 2000), pp. 501–17.

Matzner, Florian, 'Der "schlafende" Krieger: Ikonographische Aspekte zum ideologischen Stellenwert von Leben und Tod', in Michael Hütt *et al.* (eds.), *Unglücklich das Land, das Helden nötig hat: Leiden und Sterben in den Kriegsdenkmälern des Ersten und Zweiten Weltkrieges* (Marburg, Jonas, 1990), pp. 57–74.

May, Otto, *Deutsch sein heißt treu sein: Ansichtskarten als Spiegel von Mentalität und Untertanenerziehung in der Wilhelminischen Ära (1888–1918)* (Hildesheim, Lax, 1998).

Mews, Stuart Paul, 'Religion and English Society in the First World War', Ph.D. dissertation, University of Cambridge, 1974.

Mick, Christoph, '"Den Vorvätern zum Ruhm – den Brüdern zur Ermutigung": Variationen zum Thema Grunwald/Tannenberg', *zeitenblicke*, 3,1 (2004), URL: <http://zeitenblicke.historicum.net/2004/01/mick/index.html>.

Midgley, David, *Writing Weimar: Critical Realism in German Literature 1918–1933* (Oxford, Oxford University Press, 2000).

Missalla, Heinrich, *'Gott mit Uns': Die deutsche katholische Kriegspredigt 1914– 1918* (Munich, Kösel, 1968).

Mittig, Hans-Ernst, 'Dauerhaftigkeit, einst Denkmalargument', in Michael Diers (ed.), *Mo(nu)mente: Formen und Funktionen ephemerer Denkmäler* (Berlin, Akademie, 1993), pp. 11–34.

Morgan, Prys, 'From a Death to a View: The Hunt for the Welsh Past in the Romantic Period', in Eric Hobsbawm and Terence Ranger (eds.), *The Invention of Tradition* (Cambridge, Cambridge University Press, 1983), pp. 43–100.

Moriarty, Catherine, 'Christian Iconography and First World War Memorials', *Imperial War Museum Review*, 6 (1991), pp. 63–75.

'The Absent Dead and Figurative First World War Memorials', *Transactions of the Ancient Monuments Society*, 39 (1995), pp. 7–40.

'Narrative and the Absent Body: Mechanisms of Meaning in First World War Memorials', D.Phil. dissertation, University of Sussex, 1995.

Morrow, John H., 'Knights of the Sky: The Rise of Military Aviation', in Frans Coetzee and Marily Shevin-Coetzee (eds.), *Authority, Identity and the Social History of the Great War* (Oxford and Providence, Berghahn, 1995), pp. 305–24.

Mosse, George L., 'Soldatenfriedhöfe und nationale Wiedergeburt: Der Gefallenenkult in Deutschland', in Klaus Vondung (ed.), *Kriegserlebnis: Der Erste Weltkrieg in der literarischen Gestaltung und symbolischen Deutung der Nationen* (Göttingen, Vandenhoeck & Ruprecht, 1980), pp. 241–61.

Fallen Soldiers: Reshaping the Memory of the World Wars (New York, Oxford University Press, 1990).

'The Knights of the Sky and the Myth of the War Experience', in Robert A. Hinde and Helen E. Watson (eds.), *War: A Cruel Necessity? The Bases of Institutional Violence* (London and New York, I. B. Tauris, 1995), pp. 132–42.

The Image of Man: The Creation of Modern Masculinity (New York, Oxford University Press, 1996).

Mück, Hans-Dieter, 'Popularisierung des Mittelalters auf Propaganda-Postkarten der Gründerzeit (1870–1918)', in Jürgen Kühnel *et al.* (eds.), *Mittelalter-Rezeption*, vol. III, *Gesammelte Vorträge des 3. Salzburger Symposions: 'Mittelalter, Massenmedien, Neue Mythen'* (Göppingen, Kümmerle, 1988), pp. 231–47.

Müller, Hans-Harald, '"Herr Jünger Thinks War a Lovely Business" (On the Reception of Ernst Jünger's *In Stahlgewittern* in Germany and Britain before 1933)', in Franz Karl Stanzel and Martin Löschnigg (eds.), *Intimate Enemies: English and German Literary Reactions to the Great War 1914–1918* (Heidelberg, C. Winter, 1993), pp. 327–40.

Müller, Herbert Landolin, *Islam, gihad ('Heiliger Krieg') und Deutsches Reich: Ein Nachspiel zur wilhelminischen Weltpolitik im Maghreb 1914–1918* (Frankfurt am Main, Peter Lang, 1991).

Müller, Sven Oliver, *Die Nation als Waffe und Vorstellung: Nationalismus in Deutschland und Großbritannien im Ersten Weltkrieg* (Göttingen, Vandenhoeck & Ruprecht, 2002).

Müller, Ulrich and Werner Wunderlich (eds.), *Mittelaltermythen*, vol. I, *Herrscher, Helden, Heilige* (St Gallen, UVK, 1996).

Münkler, Herfried and Wolfgang Storch, *Siegfrieden: Politik mit einem deutschen Mythos* (Berlin, Rotbuch, 1988).

Muhs, Rudolf, Johannes Paulmann and Willibald Steinmetz (eds.), *Aneignung und Abwehr: Interkultureller Transfer zwischen Deutschland und Großbritannien im 19. Jahrhundert* (Bodenheim, Philo, [1998).

Nabrings, Arie, '. . .eine immerfort währende Mahnung. . .': Denkmäler für die Gefallenen des 1. Weltkriegs im Kreis Viersen* (Viersen, Kreis Viersen, 1996).

Newell, Jonathan, 'Allenby and the Palestine Campaign', in Brian Bond (ed.), *The First World War and British Military History* (Oxford, Clarendon, 1991), pp. 189–226.

Nipperdey, Thomas, 'Nationalidee und Nationaldenkmal in Deutschland im 19. Jahrhundert', *Historische Zeitschrift*, 206 (1968), pp. 529–85.

'Der Kölner Dom als Nationaldenkmal', *Historische Zeitschrift*, 233 (1981), pp. 595–613.

Oergel, Maike, *The Return of King Arthur and the Nibelungen: National Myth in Nineteenth-Century English and German Literature* (Berlin and New York, Walter de Gruyter, 1998).

Oexle, Otto Gerhard, 'Das Mittelalter und das Unbehagen an der Moderne: Mittelalterbeschwörungen in der Weimarer Republik und danach', in Susanna Burghartz *et al.* (eds.), *Spannungen und Widersprüche* (Sigmaringen, Jan Thorbecke, 1992), pp. 125–53.

Otte, Wulf, 'Heinrich der Löwe – in Eisen', *Braunschweigisches Landesmuseum: Informationen und Berichte*, 3 (1987), pp. 34–8.

Pabst, Ingeborg, 'Das Österreichische Heldendenkmal im äußeren Burgtor in Wien', in Michel Hütt *et al.* (eds.), *Unglücklich das Land, das Helden nötig hat: Leiden und Sterben in den Kriegsdenkmälern des Ersten und Zweiten Weltkrieges* (Marburg, Jonas, 1990), pp. 11–27.

Papenheim, Martin, '"Trauer und Propaganda" – eine Fallstudie zu Aussagen und Funktionen von Kriegerdenkmälern', in Franz-Josef Jakobi (ed.), *Stadtgesellschaft im Wandel: Untersuchungen zur Sozialgeschichte Münsters* (Münster, Regensberg, 1995), pp. 421–81.

Paret, Peter, Beth Irwin Lewis and Paul Paret, *Persuasive Images: Posters of War and Revolution from the Hoover Institution Archives* (Princeton, Princeton University Press, 1992).

Paris, Michael, *From the Wright Brothers to Top Gun: Aviation, Nationalism and Popular Cinema* (Manchester and New York, Manchester University Press, 1995).

Warrior Nation: Images of War in British Popular Culture, 1850–2000 (London, Reaktion, 2000).

Pemble, John, *The Mediterranean Passion: Victorians and Edwardians in the South* (Oxford, Clarendon, 1987).

Pollack, Kristine, 'Das 39er Denkmal in Düsseldorf', in *Skulptur und Macht: Figurative Plastik im Deutschland der 30er und 40er Jahre* (Berlin, Fröhlich & Kaufmann, 1983), pp. 155–7.

Prange, Thorsten, *Das Marine-Ehrenmal in Laboe: Geschichte eines deutschen Nationalsymbols* (Wilhelmshaven, Deutscher Marinebund, [1996]).

Probst, Volker G., *Bilder vom Tode: Eine Studie zum deutschen Kriegerdenkmal in der Weimarer Republik am Beispiel des Pietà-Motives und seiner profanisierten Varianten* (Hamburg, Wayasbah, 1986).

Prochasson, Christophe, 'Sur les atrocités allemandes: la guerre comme représentation', *Annales*, 58 (2003), pp. 879–94.

Prost, Antoine, 'The Impact of War on French and German Political Cultures', *Historical Journal*, 37 (1994), pp. 209–17.

'Monuments to the Dead', in Pierre Nora (ed.), *Realms of Memory: The Construction of the French Past*, vol. II, *Traditions* (New York, Columbia University Press, 1997), pp. 307–30.

'Representations of War in the Cultural History of France, 1914–1939', in Antoine Prost, *Republican Identities in War and Peace: Representations of France in the Nineteenth and Twentieth Centuries* (Oxford and New York, Berg, 2002), pp. 93–105.

Purseigle, Pierre, 'Beyond and Below the Nations: Towards a Comparative History of Local Communities at War', in Jenny Macleod and Pierre Purseigle (eds.), *Uncovered Fields: Perspectives in First World War Studies* (Leiden and Boston, Brill, 2004), pp. 95–123.

Radkau, Joachim, *Das Zeitalter der Nervosität: Deutschland zwischen Bismarck und Hitler* (Munich and Vienna, Carl Hanser, 1998).

'Das Stahlbad der Nervenkur? Nervöse Ursprünge des Ersten Weltkrieges', *Newsletter des Arbeitskreises Militärgeschichte*, 10 (1999), pp. 6–8.

Rasche, Uta, 'Geschichtsbilder im katholischen Milieu des Kaiserreichs: Konkurrenz und Parallelen zum nationalen Gedächtnis', in Clemens Wischermann (ed.), *Vom kollektiven Gedächtnis zur Individualisierung der Erinnerung* (Stuttgart, Franz Steiner, 2002), pp. 25–52.

Readman, Paul, 'The Place of the Past in English Culture *c*.1890–1914', *Past and Present*, 186 (2005), pp. 147–99.

Reid, Brian Holden, 'T. E. Lawrence and his Biographers', in Brian Bond (ed.), *The First World War and British Military History* (Oxford, Clarendon, 1991), pp. 237–59.

Reimann, Aribert, 'Die heile Welt im Stahlgewitter: Deutsche und englische Feldpost aus dem Ersten Weltkrieg', in Gerhard Hirschfeld *et al.* (eds.), *Kriegserfahrungen: Studien zur Sozial- und Mentalitätsgeschichte des Ersten Weltkriegs* (Essen, Klartext, 1997), pp. 129–45.

'Popular Culture and the Reconstruction of British Identity', in Hartmut Berghoff and Robert von Friedeburg (eds.), *Change and Inertia: Britain under the Impact of the Great War* (Bodenheim, Philo, 1998), pp. 99–120.

Der große Krieg der Sprachen: Untersuchungen zur historischen Semantik in Deutschland und England zur Zeit des Ersten Weltkriegs (Essen, Klartext, 2000).

Reinermann, Lothar, *Der Kaiser in England: Wilhelm II. und sein Bild in der britischen Öffentlichkeit* (Paderborn, Ferdinand Schöningh, 2001).

Rieger, Bernhard, *Technology and the Culture of Modernity in Britain and Germany, 1890–1945* (Cambridge, Cambridge University Press, 2005).

Rieger, Bernhard and Martin Daunton, 'Introduction', in Martin Daunton and Bernhard Rieger (eds.), *Meanings of Modernity: Britain from the Late-Victorian Era to World War II* (Oxford and New York, Berg, 2001), pp. 1–21.

Riegl, Alois, 'The Modern Cult of Monument: Its Character and its Origins', *Oppositions*, 25 (1982), pp. 20–51.

Riley-Smith, Jonathan, 'The Order of St John in England, 1827–1858', in Malcolm Barber (ed.), *The Military Orders: Fighting for Faith and Caring for the Sick* (Aldershot and Brookfield, Ashgate, 1994), pp. 121–38.

Robb, George, *British Culture and the First World War* (Basingstoke and New York, Palgrave, 2002).

Robert, Jean-Louis and Jay Winter, 'Conclusions: Towards a Social History of Capital Cities at War', in Jay Winter, Jean-Louis Robert [*et al.*], *Capital Cities at War: Paris, London, Berlin 1914–1919*, vol. I (Cambridge, Cambridge University Press, 1997), pp. 527–54.

Rohkrämer, Thomas, *Der Militarismus der 'kleinen Leute': Die Kriegervereine im Deutschen Kaiserreich 1871–1914* (Munich, R. Oldenbourg, 1990).

Rosenfeld, Gavriel D., *Munich and Memory: Architecture, Monuments, and the Legacy of the Third Reich* (Berkeley, Los Angeles and London, University of California Press, 2000).

Roshwald, Aviel and Richard Stites, 'Conclusion', in Aviel Roshwald and Richard Stites (eds.), *European Culture in the Great War: The Arts, Entertainment, and Propaganda, 1914–1918* (Cambridge, Cambridge University Press, 1999), pp. 349–58.

Rudolph, Harriet, 'Männerikonographie: Dimensionen von Männlichkeit in der Wirtschaftswerbung während des Ersten Weltkrieges in Deutschland und England', *Archiv für Sozialgeschichte*, 36 (1996), pp. 257–78.

Rürup, Reinhard, 'Der "Geist von 1914" in Deutschland: Kriegsbegeisterung und Ideologisierung des Krieges im Ersten Weltkrieg', in Bernd Hüppauf (ed.), *Ansichten vom Krieg: Vergleichende Studien zum Ersten Weltkrieg in Literatur und Gesellschaft* (Königstein, Athenäum, 1984), pp. 1–30.

Russell, Mark A., 'The Building of Hamburg's Bismarck Memorial, 1898–1906', *Historical Journal*, 46 (2000), pp. 133–56.

Saehrendt, Christian, *Der Stellungskrieg der Denkmäler: Kriegerdenkmäler im Berlin der Zwischenkriegszeit (1919-1939)* (Bonn, J. H. W. Dietz Nachf., 2004).

Said, Edward W., *Orientalism* (Harmondsworth, Penguin, 1995).

Saler, Michael T., *The Avant-Garde in Interwar England: Medieval Modernism and the London Underground* (New York, Oxford University Press, 1999).

Samuel, Raphael (ed.), *Patriotism: The Making and Unmaking of British National Identity*, vol. I, *History and Politics* (London and New York, Routledge, 1989).

Schellack, Fritz, *Nationalfeiertage in Deutschland von 1871 bis 1945* (Frankfurt am Main, Peter Lang, 1990).

Schiefer, Lothar, 'Das Schlageter-Denkmal: Vom Soldatengrab zum Forum', in Michael Hütt et al. (eds.), *Unglücklich das Land, das Helden nötig hat: Leiden und Sterben in den Kriegsdenkmälern des Ersten und Zweiten Weltkrieges* (Marburg, Jonas, 1990), pp. 50–6.

Schilling, René, *'Kriegshelden': Deutungsmuster heroischer Männlichkeit in Deutschland 1813–1945* (Paderborn, Ferdinand Schöningh, 2002).

Schirmer, Gisela, 'Osnabrück im Jahr 1916: Die Hausfassade Kranstraße 53', in Jutta Held (ed.), *Symbole des Friedens und des Krieges im öffentlichen Raum: Osnabrück, die 'Stadt des Westfälischen Friedens'* (Weimar, VDG, 1998), pp. 123–44.

Schivelbusch, Wolfgang, *Die Bibliothek von Löwen: Eine Episode aus der Zeit der Weltkriege* (Munich and Vienna, Carl Hanser, 1988).

The Culture of Defeat: On National Trauma, Mourning, and Recovery (New York, Metropolitan, 2003).

Schmid-Kemmer, Bernd, '". . .leuchtest mir zum frühen Tod": Kriegsdenkmäler im Landkreis Ludwigsburg als Geschichtsquellen', *Ludwigsburger Geschichtsblätter*, 46 (1992), pp. 84–160.

Schmoll, Friedemann, *Verewigte Nation: Studien zur Erinnerungskultur von Reich und Einzelstaat im württembergischen Denkmalkult des 19. Jahrhunderts* (Stuttgart, Silberburg, 1995).

Schneider, Gerhard, '. . .nicht umsonst gefallen'? *Kriegerdenkmäler und Kriegstotenkult in Hannover* (Hanover, Hahn, 1991).

'Über hannoversche Nagelfiguren im Ersten Weltkrieg', *Hannoversche Geschichtsblätter*, new ser., 50 (1996), pp. 207–58.

'Kriegspostkarten des Ersten Weltkrieges als Geschichtsquellen', in Udo Arnold, Peter Meyers and Uta C. Schmidt (eds.), *Stationen einer Hochschullaufbahn* (Dortmund, Ebersbach, 1999).

Serbien muß sterbien! Kriegspropaganda auf Postkarten des Ersten Weltkriegs (Hanover, Landeshauptstadt Hannover, 1999).

'Zur Mobilisierung der "Heimatfront": Das Nageln sogenannter Kriegswahrzeichen im Ersten Weltkrieg', *Zeitschrift für Volkskunde*, 95 (1999), pp. 32–62.

'Heldenhaine als Visualisierung der Volksgemeinschaft im Ersten Weltkrieg', in Gerhard Schneider (ed.), *Die visuelle Dimension des Historischen* (Schwalbach, Wochenschau, 2002), pp. 49–71.

'Nageln in Niedersachsen im Ersten Weltkrieg', *Niedersächsisches Jahrbuch für Landesgeschichte*, 76 (2004), pp. 245–84.

Schneider, Uwe and Gert Gröning, 'Nature Mystification and the Example of the Heroes Groves', *Environments by Design*, 2 (1998), pp. 205–28.

Schubert, Dietrich, 'Hoetgers Waldersee-Denkmal von 1915 in Hannover', *Wallraf-Richartz-Jahrbuch*, 43 (1982), pp. 231–46.

'Die Wandlung eines expressionistischen Krieger-Denkmals: Berhard Hoetgers "Niedersachsenstein" 1915–1922', *Wallraf-Richartz-Jahrbuch*, 44 (1983), pp. 285–306.

Schumann, Dirk, 'Europa, der Erste Weltkrieg und die Nachkriegszeit: eine Kontinuität der Gewalt?', *Journal of Modern European History*, 1 (2003), pp. 24–43.

Schwahn, Britta-R., 'Otto I. von Wittelsbach – ein politisches Denkmal im Münchner Hofgarten', in Ekkehard Mai and Stephan Waetzoldt (eds.), *Kunstverwaltung, Bau- und Denkmal-Politik im Kaiserreich* (Berlin, Mann, 1981), pp. 191–214.

Schwanitz, Wolfgang G., 'Djihad "Made in Germany": Der Streit um den Heiligen Krieg 1914–1915', *Sozial.Geschichte*, 18,2 (2003), pp. 7–34.

Schwartz, Frederic J., *The Werkbund: Design Theory and Mass Culture before the First World War* (New Haven and London, Yale University Press, 1996).

Sebald, W. G., *Luftkrieg und Literatur: Mit einem Essay zu Alfred Andersch* (Munich and Vienna, Carl Hanser, 1999).

Senekowitsch, Martin, *Ein ungewöhnliches Kriegerdenkmal: Das jüdische Heldendenkmal auf dem Wiener Zentralfriedhof* (Vienna, Militärkommando Wien, 1994).

Shaw, David Gary (ed.), 'Agency after Postmodernism', theme issue of *History and Theory*, 40 (2001).

Sherman, Daniel J., *The Construction of Memory in Interwar France* (Chicago and London, University of Chicago Press, 1999).

Siberry, Elizabeth, *The New Crusaders: Images of the Crusades in the Nineteenth and Early Twentieth Centuries* (Aldershot, Ashgate, 2000).

Sim, Martin, 'A Memorable Memorial. . .', *Leopard*, 258, December 1999, pp. 34–5.

Simmons, Clare A., *Reversing the Conquest: History and Myth in Nineteenth-Century British Literature* (New Brunswick and London, Rutgers University Press, 1990).

Smith, Leonard V., 'Paul Fussell's *The Great War and Modern Memory*: Twenty-Five Years Later', *History and Theory*, 40 (2001), pp. 241–60.

Sösemann, Bernd, 'Die sog. Hunnenrede Wilhelms II.: Textkritische und interpretatorische Bemerkungen zur Ansprache des Kaisers vom 27. Juli 1900 in Bremerhaven', *Historische Zeitschrift*, 222 (1976), pp. 342–58.

Soika, Aya R., 'The Public Face of German Expressionism: A Study of the Brücke's Interior Designs', Ph.D. dissertation, University of Cambridge, 2001.

Sontheimer, Kurt, *Antidemokratisches Denken in der Weimarer Republik: Die politischen Ideen des deutschen Nationalismus zwischen 1918 und 1933* (Munich, dtv, 1978).

Speitkamp, Winfried, 'Die Hohkönigsburg und die Denkmalpflege im Kaiserreich', *Neue Museumskunde*, 34 (1991), pp. 121–30.

'"Erziehung zur Nation": Reichskunstwart, Kulturpolitik und Identitätsstiftung im Staat von Weimar', in Helmut Berding (ed.), *Nationales Bewußtsein und kollektive Identität: Studien zur Entwicklung des kollektiven Bewußtseins in der Neuzeit*, vol. II (Frankfurt am Main, Suhrkamp, 1994), pp. 541–80.

Die Verwaltung der Geschichte: Denkmalpflege und Staat in Deutschland 1871–1933 (Göttingen, Vandenhoeck & Ruprecht, 1996).

(ed.), *Denkmalsturz: Zur Konfliktgeschichte politischer Symbolik* (Göttingen, Vandenhoeck & Ruprecht, 1997).

Stansky, Peter, *Redesigning the World: William Morris, the 1880s, and the Arts and Crafts* (Princeton, Princeton University Press, 1985).

Stargardt, Nicholas, *The German Idea of Militarism: Radical and Socialist Critics, 1866–1914* (Cambridge, Cambridge University Press, 1994).

Stibbe, Matthew, *German Anglophobia and the Great War, 1914–1918* (Cambridge, Cambridge University Press, 2001).

Stieglitz, Ann, 'The Reproduction of Agony: Toward a Reception-History of Grünewald's Isenheim Altar after the First World War', *Oxford Art Journal*, 12,2 (1989), pp. 87–103.

Strachan, Hew, *The First World War*, vol. I, *To Arms* (Oxford, Oxford University Press, 2001).

Stryker, Laurinda S., 'Languages of Sacrifice and Suffering in England in the First World War', Ph.D. dissertation, University of Cambridge, 1992.

Summers, Anne, 'Militarism in Britain before the Great War', *History Workshop*, 2 (1976), pp. 104–24.

Surridge, Keith, 'More than a Great Poster: Lord Kitchener and the Image of the Military Hero', *Historical Research*, 74 (2001), pp. 298–313.

Tacke, Charlotte, *Denkmal im sozialen Raum: Nationale Symbole in Deutschland und Frankreich im 19. Jahrhundert* (Göttingen, Vandenhoeck & Ruprecht, 1995).

Thamer, Hans-Ulrich, 'Nationalsozialismus und Denkmalskult', in *Historische Denkmäler: Vergangenheit im Dienste der Gegenwart?* (Bergisch-Gladbach, Thomas-Morus-Akademie, 1994), pp. 9–35.

'Von der Monumentalisierung zur Verdrängung der Geschichte: Nationalsozialistische Denkmalpolitik und die Entnazifizierung von Denkmälern nach 1945', in Winfried Speitkamp (ed.), *Denkmalsturz: Zur Konfliktgeschichte politischer Symbolik* (Göttingen, Vandenhoeck & Rupprecht, 1997), pp. 109–36.

Theweleit, Klaus, *Male Fantasies*, 2 vols. (Cambridge, Polity, 1987–9).

Thier, Dietrich, 'Das Kriegswahrzeichen von Wetter (Ruhr): die Nagelspende, das Eiserne Schwert', in Hans-Friedrich Kniehase and Dietrich Thier (eds.), *Projekte: Landeskundliche Studien im Bereich des mittleren Ruhrtals*, vol. I (Wetter a.d. Ruhr, Dierk Hobein, 1994), pp. 212–27.

Tietz, Jürgen, '"Es soll ein Ort der Begegnung sein" – Zur Geschichte des Münchner Kriegerdenkmals', *Jahrbuch der Bayerischen Denkmalspflege*, 47–8 (1993–4), pp. 238–53.

Das Tannenberg-Nationaldenkmal: Architektur, Geschichte, Kontext (Berlin, Bauwesen, 1999).

Tippett, Maria, *Art at the Service of War: Canada, Art, and the Great War* (Toronto, Buffalo and London, University of Toronto Press, 1984).

Traba, Robert, 'Kriegssyndrom in Ostpreußen: Ein Beitrag zum kollektiven Bewußtsein der Weimarer Zeit', *Krieg und Literatur*, 3–4 (1997–8), pp. 399–412.

Trentmann, Frank, 'Introduction: Paradoxes of Civil Society', in Frank Trentmann (ed.), *Paradoxes of Civil Society: New Perspectives on Modern German and British History* (New York and Oxford, Berghahn, 2000), pp. 3–46.

Ulrich, Bernd, *Die Augenzeugen: Deutsche Feldpostbriefe in Kriegs- und Nachkriegszeit 1914–1933* (Essen, Klartext, 1997).

Unruh, Karl, *Langemarck: Legende und Wirklichkeit* (Koblenz, Bernard & Graefe, 1986).

Utechin, Patricia, *The Trumpets Sounded: Commemoration of the War Dead in the Parish Churches of Oxfordshire* (Oxford, Robert Dugdale, 1996).

Sons of This Place: Commemoration of the War Dead in Oxford's Colleges and Institutions (Oxford, Robert Dugdale, 1998).

Vance, Jonathan F., *Death So Noble: Memory, Meaning, and the First World War* (Vancouver, University of British Columbia Press, 1997).

Veitch, Colin, '"Play up! Play up! and Win the War!" Football, the Nation and the First World War 1914–15', *Journal of Contemporary History*, 20 (1985), pp. 363–78.

Verhey, Jeffrey, *The Spirit of 1914: Militarism, Myth, and Mobilization in Germany* (Cambridge, Cambridge University Press, 2000).

Vogel, Jakob, *Nationen im Gleichschritt: Der Kult der 'Nation in Waffen' in Deutschland und Frankreich, 1871–1914* (Göttingen, Vandenhoeck & Ruprecht, 1997).

'Zwischen protestantischem Herrscherideal und Mittelaltermystik: Wilhelm I. und die "Mythomotorik" des Deutschen Kaiserreichs', in Gerd Krumeich and Hartmut Lehmann (eds.), *'Gott mit uns': Nation, Religion und Gewalt im 19. und frühen 20. Jahrhundert* (Göttingen, Vandenhoeck & Ruprecht, 2000), pp. 213–30.

Vogt, Arnold, *Den Lebenden zur Mahnung: Denkmäler und Gedenktstätten: Zur Traditionspflege und historischen Identität vom 19. Jahrhundert bis zur Gegenwart* (Hanover, Lutherisches Verlagshaus, 1993).

Vondung, Klaus, 'Deutsche Apokalypse 1914', in Klaus Vondung (ed.), *Das Wilhelminische Bürgertum: Zur Sozialgeschichte seiner Ideen* (Göttingen, Vandenhoeck & Ruprecht, 1976), pp. 153–71.

'Geschichte als Weltgericht: Genesis und Degradation einer Symbolik', in Klaus Vondung (ed.), *Kriegserlebnis: Der Erste Weltkrieg in der literarischen Gestaltung und symbolischen Deutung der Nationen* (Göttingen, Vandenhoeck & Ruprecht, 1980), pp. 62–84.

Watkins, Glenn, *Proof Through the Night: Music and the Great War* (Berkeley, Los Angeles and London, University of California Press, 2003).

Watson, Janet S. K., *Fighting Different Wars: Experience, Memory, and the First World War in Britain* (Cambridge, Cambridge University Press, 2004).

Wawn, Andrew, *The Vikings and the Victorians: Inventing the Old North in Nineteenth-Century Britain* (Cambridge, D. S. Brewer, 2000).

Wein, Franziska, *Deutschlands Strom – Frankreichs Grenze: Geschichte und Propaganda am Rhein 1919–1930* (Essen, Klartext, 1992).

Weinland, Martina, *Kriegerdenkmäler in Berlin 1870–1930* (Frankfurt am Main, Peter Lang, 1990).

Welch, David, *Germany, Propaganda and Total War, 1914–1918: The Sins of Omission* (London, Athlone, 2000).

Werner, Michael and Bénédicte Zimmermann, 'Vergleich, Transfer, Verflechtung: Der Ansatz der *Histoire croisée* und die Herausforderung des Transnationalen', *Geschichte und Gesellschaft*, 28 (2002), pp. 607–36.

Whalen, Robert Weldon, *Bitter Wounds: German Victims of the Great War, 1914–1939* (Ithaca and London, Cornell University Press, 1984).

White, James F., *The Cambridge Movement: The Ecclesiologists and the Gothic Revival* (Cambridge, Cambridge University Press, 1962).

Wilkinson, Alan, *The Church of England and the First World War* (London, SCM, 2nd edn 1996).

Winkler, Heinrich August, *Der lange Weg nach Westen*, 2 vols. (Munich, C. H. Beck, 2000).

The Long Shadow of the Reich: Weighing up German History (London, German Historical Institute, 2002).

Winter, J[ay] M., *Socialism and the Challenge of War: Ideas and Politics in Britain 1912–18* (London and Boston, Routledge & Kegan Paul, 1974).

'Die Legende der "verlorenen Generation" in Großbritannien', in Klaus Vondung (ed.), *Kriegserlebnis: Der Erste Weltkrieg in der literarischen Gestaltung und symbolischen Deutung der Nationen* (Göttingen, Vandenhoeck & Ruprecht, 1980), pp. 115–45.

The Great War and the British People (Basingstoke and London, Macmillan, 1986).

The Experience of World War I (London and Basingstoke, Macmillan, 1988).

'Catastrophe and Culture: Recent Trends in the Historiography of the First Word War', *Journal of Modern History*, 64 (1992), pp. 525–32.

'Nationalism, the Visual Arts, and the Myth of War Enthusiasm in 1914', *History of European Ideas*, 15 (1992), pp. 357–62.

'Oxford and the First World War', in Brian Harrison (ed.), *The History of the University of Oxford*, vol. VIII, *The Twentieth Century* (Oxford, Clarendon, 1994), pp. 3–25.

Sites of Memory, Sites of Mourning: The Great War in European Cultural History (Cambridge, Cambridge University Press, 1995).

'British National Identity and the First World War', in S[imon] J. D. Green and R. C. Whiting (eds.), *The Boundaries of the State in Modern Britain* (Cambridge, Cambridge University Press, 1996), pp. 261–77.

'Forms of Kinship and Remembrance in the Aftermath of the Great War', in Jay Winter and Emmanuel Sivan (eds.), *War and Remembrance in the Twentieth Century* (Cambridge, Cambridge University Press, 1999), pp. 40–60.

'The Generation of Memory: Reflections on the "Memory Boom" in Contemporary Historical Studies', *Bulletin of the German Historical Institute, Washington, D.C.*, 27 (2000), pp. 69–92.

'Shell-Shock and the Cultural History of the Great War', *Journal of Contemporary History*, 35 (2000), pp. 7–11.

'Representations of War on the Western Front, 1914–18: Some Reflections on Cultural Ambivalence', in Joseph Canning, Hartmut Lehmann and Jay Winter (eds.), *Power, Violence and Mass Death in Pre-Modern and Modern Times* (Aldershot and Burlington, VT, Ashgate, 2004), pp. 205–16.

Winter, Jay and Blaine Baggett, *1914–18: The Great War and the Shaping of the 20th Century* (London, BBC Books, 1996).

Winter, Jay, Jean-Louis Robert [*et al.*], *Capital Cities at War: Paris, London, Berlin 1914–1919*, vol. I (Cambridge, Cambridge University Press, 1997).

Capital Cities at War: Paris, London, Berlin 1914–1919, vol. II, *A Cultural History* (Cambridge, Cambridge University Press, forthcoming).

Winter, Jay and Emmanuel Sivan, 'Setting the Framework', in Jay Winter and Emmanuel Sivan (eds.), *War and Remembrance in the Twentieth Century* (Cambridge, Cambridge University Press, 1999), pp. 6–39.

Wippermann, Wolfgang, *Der Ordensstaat als Ideologie: Das Bild des Deutschen Ordens in der deutschen Geschichtsschreibung und Publizistik* (Berlin, Colloquium, 1979).

'Die Geschichte des "Reichsehrenmals Tannenberg"': Ein historisches Lehrstück', *Niemandsland*, 1,2 (1987), pp. 58–69.

Wischermann, Clemens (ed.), *Die Legitimität der Erinnerung und die Geschichtswissenschaft* (Stuttgart, Franz Steiner, 1996).

Wisskirchen, Hans, 'Mittelalterrezeption um 1920: Ein Beitrag zur Wirklichkeitsbewältigung der bürgerlich-konservativen Intelligenz nach dem 1. Weltkrieg', in Rüdiger Krohn (ed.), *Forum: Materialien und Beiträge zur Mittelalter-Rezeption*, vol. I (Göppingen, Kümmerle, 1986), pp. 257–75.

Wohl, Robert, *A Passion for Wings: Aviation and the Western Imagination 1908–1918* (New Haven and London, Yale University Press, 1994).

Wolffe, John, *Great Deaths: Grieving, Religion, and Nationhood in Victorian and Edwardian Britain* (Oxford, Oxford University Press, 2000).

Wolfrum, Edgar, *Geschichte als Waffe: Vom Kaiserreich bis zur Wiedervereinigung* (Göttingen, Vandenhoeck & Ruprecht, 2001).

Workman, Leslie J., 'Preface', *Studies in Medievalism*, 8 (1996), pp. 1–2.

Wülfing, Wulf, Karin Bruns and Rolf Parr, *Historische Mythologie der Deutschen 1789–1918* (Munich, Wilhelm Fink, 1991).

Yarrington, Alison, *The Commemoration of the Hero 1800–1864: Monuments to the British Victors of the Napoleonic Wars* (New York and London, Garland, 1988).

Young, James E., *The Texture of Memory: Holocaust Memorials and Meaning* (New Haven and London, Yale University Press, 1993).

Zacher, Inge, *Ewald Mataré: Der 'Tote Krieger' in Kleve* (Kleve, Boss, 1985).

Ziemann, Benjamin, *Front und Heimat: Ländliche Kriegserfahrungen im südlichen Bayern 1914–1923* (Essen, Klartext, 1997).

'Die Erinnerung an den Ersten Weltkrieg in den Milieukulturen der Weimarer Republik', *Krieg und Literatur*, 3–4 (1997–8), pp. 249–70.

'"Macht der Maschine": Mythen des industriellen Krieges', in Rolf Spilker and Bernd Ulrich (eds.), *Der Tod als Maschinist: Der industrialisierte Krieg 1914–1918* (Bramsche, Rasch, 1998), pp. 177–89.

'Republikanische Kriegserinnerung in einer polarisierten Öffentlichkeit: Das Reichsbanner Schwarz-Rot-Gold als Veteranenverband der sozialistischen Arbeiterschaft', *Historische Zeitschrift*, 267 (1998), pp. 357–98.

'Die deutsche Nation und ihr zentraler Erinnerungsort: Das "Nationaldenkmal für die Gefallenen im Weltkriege" und die Idee des "Unbekannten Soldaten" 1914–1935', in Helmut Berding, Klaus Heller and Winfried Speitkamp (eds.), *Krieg und Erinnerung: Fallstudien zum 19. und 20. Jahrhundert* (Göttingen, Vandenhoeck & Ruprecht, 2000), pp. 67–91.

Zilien, Johann, 'Der "Volksbund Deutsche Kriegsgräberfürsorge e.V." in der Weimarer Republik: Ein Beitrag zum politischen Denkmalkult zwischen Kaiserreich und Nationalsozialismus', *Archiv für Kulturgeschichte*, 75 (1993), pp. 445–78.

Index

Studies in the Social and Cultural History
of Modern Warfare